An
Adventure
in
Human
Relations

Muriel Crosby: **An Adventure in Human Relations**

Follett Publishing Company **Chicago**

PROVIDENCE
COLLEGE
LIBRARY

LC
5132
D4
C7

© Copyright 1965 by Follett Publishing Company, Chicago

All rights reserved. No portion of this book may be reproduced
in any form without the written permission of the publisher.

Printed in the United States of America

Library of Congress Catalog Card Number 65-17319

Design: Herbert Pinzke Design Associates

76748

SEP 27 1967

AN ADVENTURE IN HUMAN RELATIONS
is dedicated to **The People of Wilmington** and to
The Staff of the City's Public Elementary Schools
who demonstrated in action a commitment to the children of the city

In large measure AN ADVENTURE IN HUMAN RELATIONS
is a living memorial to two men who made it possible
Elmer Paul Brock, a young man with a dream, who,
as Regional Director of The National Conference of
Christians and Jews, first conceived of the Adventure and
William E. Vickery, Curriculum Consultant,
The National Conference of Christians and Jews,
who moved the dream closer to reality

Contents

Preface

Nowhere are social changes in a city reflected so clearly as in the inner life of its schools. When these have been rapid and sharp as they were in Wilmington, Del., in the decade of the fifties, the school's task of educating the young may become so complex as to have a demoralizing effect on the entire school system. Four interacting social factors —in-migration of the poor, out-migration of the better off, desegregation, and teacher shortage—were leading to such an educational impasse in Wilmington when in the fall of 1959 the Three-Year Experimental Project on Schools in Changing Neighborhoods was set up to counteract it.

The Three-Year Experimental Project on Schools in Changing Neighborhoods was set up under the joint sponsorship of the Wilmington Board of Public Education and the National Conference of Christians and Jews. It had two main goals: (1) the improvement of the schools through the development of appropriate curriculum and inservice teacher education to meet the human relations needs of the children and to stimulate motivation for learning, and (2) the upgrading of family and community life through the development of indigenous leadership. Thus the Project design had two aspects: (1) the school-centered aspect, and (2) the community-centered aspect.

The school-centered aspect included a teacher education program designed to help teachers change their attitudes toward children, provide them with techniques for diagnosing the human relations needs of children and their families, and learn ways of developing curricula appropriate to these needs. Its design was based on the belief that if children saw use value in what they were taught, their motivation to learn would be increased and their academic achievement would be greater.

The teachers were taught the use of diagnostic instruments, including sociograms, diaries, time budgets, autobiographies, and open-end questions. The open-end questions became the favorite and most used instrument. For example, the children were asked: "What do you like about your neighborhood?" "What would you like to change?" "What is the best thing that could happen to your family?" "What is the best thing that has happened to you?" "What is the worst thing that has happened to you?" "What do you like about the grown-ups you know? "What would you like to change about the grown-ups?"

The School-centered aspect was initiated because the school authorities knew that the schools could not do the job alone; that cooperative action with other agencies and organizations serving people was an imperative if conditions conducive to learning were to prevail. Therefore the community aspect of the Project was initiated. An invitation to various groups to join the school staff in this effort secured a warm response from some sixty-five agencies and organizations, among which were churches, settlement houses, the youth aid division of the Police Department, the Welfare Council, the Girls' Club, Boy Scouts and Girl Scouts, the American Association of University Women, the National Association for the Advancement of Colored People, the state university, the local housing authority.

The structure for action was informal. No attempt was made to create another organization. Conferences were held in which each agency and organization attempted to find ways of helping people help themselves through its own program. No funds were available to secure a professional community organizer, but consultation was provided by the National Conference of Christians and Jews.

The educational problems of our inner city schools have certainly not been solved by this short-term, inadequately financed project. But a pebble has been dropped in the pool and its ripples are still extending outward. We have demonstrated that much can be achieved without money, by utilizing available resources in a variety of ways, and by emphasis on inservice teacher education. But we have also learned more fully how much remains to be done. As Walt Whitman has written,

". . . it is in the essence of things that from any fruition of success, no matter what, shall come forth something to make a greater struggle necessary."

Throughout the progress of The Three-Year Experimental Project on Schools in Changing Neighborhoods, participants have demonstrated their commitment to the belief that people of the city have the potentiality for creating a better life for themselves and their families through their own hopes and aspirations, their skills and energies. It has been recognized that change is part of the American heritage and that it is the role of professional leaders to help people affect the direction of change.

The deep and pervading motivation underlying the efforts of participants in this study has been one of commitment to a dream, a dream that can become a reality, a dream that envisions the development of a people in command of its own destiny. It is a motivation which recognizes that the American heritage is more than words; that people, through their own will and courage, can affect the direction and course of change, which is an inevitable facet of life in a city, and not become victims of it.

Only those who hold deep convictions regarding the dignity and brotherhood of man will find the courage and fortitude to embark on the kind of adventure described in this report. Such people believe wholeheartedly in the words of an ancient Chinese philosopher:

> One of the measures of a man is his ability
> to live in the wide house of the world.

It is with pride and appreciation that I have discovered during the progress of this study so many Wilmingtonians, both lay and professional, who care enough to work earnestly and diligently to help today's boys and girls become the adults of tomorrow who will be able to create a better world than they have known as children.

—Muriel Crosby, PROJECT ADMINISTRATOR

This preface is based on an article by Muriel Crosby, which appeared in *Children*, January-February 1964, U.S. Department of Health, Education, and Welfare Administration, Children's Bureau.

People of the City

"My name is Legion:
for we are many."
St. Mark—5:9,b

The Children Speak

WE ARE CHILDREN OF THE CITY.

Our roots are in the past.
From the Ukraine and Greece,
From China, Italy and Africa,
From Ireland and England,
From the islands to the south
Our forebears came.

WE ARE YOUNG AMERICANS.

America is our land.

For some of us our roots
Are deeply buried in American soil.
Our families were the first to settle the land.
Along the Brandywine and Christiana,
Beside the Delaware our fathers stopped.
They fashioned homes and founded families.
Great industries began and flourished.
Family traditions were established.

For some of us our roots are young and tender,
Our families are on the move.
The city is merely an inn
For the nights of our journey.
We are the displaced, the migrants.
We are children seeking shelter.

For some of us our roots are spreading,
Spreading like the wild strawberry.
Out of the stagnant slums,
Out of the path of the Thruway,
Away from the wreckers and bulldozers,
We spread to the west, north, south,
Seeking a new home, a place for ourselves.

WE HAVE FAMILIES.

> For some of us the good life is a reality.
> Our world is bounded by our parents' love.
> Our mothers send us off to school.
> Each morning, comfortable and happy,
> Secure and confident,
> We seek new adventures.
> Each evening we welcome home our fathers.
> Eager-eyed and breathless,
> We share the happenings of the day.
>
> For some of us the good life is unknown.
> We carry the burdens of maturity early.
> Mother, Granny or the woman who cares for us
> Has risen long before we wake
> And departed quietly
> To work in other homes.
> We have no fathers.
> Or, if we do, the empty bottles,
> The numbers man, the rough companions,
> Are part and parcel of their lives.

WE HAVE HOMES.

> For some of us home is a refuge.
> We live together, giving our love freely.
> Birth and death, tragedy and success
> Bind us together.
>
> For some of us home is a place to avoid.
> Hunger and cold,
> Drunkenness and lust,
> Anger and harshness are our companions.

WE GO TO SCHOOL.

We find our teachers friendly or unfriendly,
Friendly for the most part.

We accept ourselves as teachers accept us.
Worthy or unworthy,
Troublesome or happy,
Able or unable,
Conforming or creative,
We see ourselves as teachers see us.

We find many children in school.
Privileged or deprived,
Gay or moody,
Accepting or rejecting,
We see ourselves as other children see us.

We learn many things in school.
We learn that people are alike,
Yet different.
We learn to trust others,
Or to distrust them.
We learn that there is a world of the imagination
And a world of reality
And that both are good.
We learn that we are the sons of our fathers,
That the world they have created
May be cherished or changed.
We learn to like school
Or to hate it.

WE ARE THE FUTURE.

    When you look at us
    You see yourselves.

    When you look at us
    You see the heritage of many peoples,
    Molded and melded into a common heritage.

    When you look at us
    You see the future you have shaped.

    When you look at us
    You see all children,
    Everywhere.

The Parents Speak

WE ARE PARENTS OF THE CITY.

We helped transplant
    Old roots to a new land.
    Leaving old lands,
    We traveled with our fathers,
    Seeking new hopes, new opportunities
    To find ourselves.

We are newly arrived.
    Away from farms and villages,
    Places of lost hopes,
    We journeyed with our children
    To the city.
    We seek a new home,
    A place for ourselves.
    We are on the move.

We are country born and bred.
    Ours was a land of green hills
    And quiet valleys.
    We find noise and confusion,
    Unfriendly neighbors and strange ways.
    We long for what we had.

We, too, are country born and bred.
    The farms we left
    Meant flight from poverty and hunger.
    We did not know
    Until we reached the city
    We had exchanged
    Poverty for greater poverty,
    Hunger for greater hunger.

WE are from the bayou and the canebrake.
　　We are the dispossessed.
　　What we left is far behind us.
　　New ways, new opportunities are ours.
　　We find the city friendly.

WE are city born and bred.
　　We look upon the city
　　And find it good or bad.
　　Changes that come about
　　Challenge or disturb us.
　　We look upon new neighbors
　　And see ourselves
　　Or strangers.
　　What we see will shape the city.
　　With new neighbors we can create
　　A new way of life for our children
　　And our children's children.
　　We could destroy the city
　　And the future with it
　　By rejection and hate.

WE ARE AMERICANS.

Our fathers established a new nation.
    Following the Western Star,
    They sought new opportunities
    And found them.
    We are First Families
    And will always be.
    We are Americans.

Our fathers came to a land well founded.
    Italians, Greeks, Ukranians, Chinese,
    They came in numbers,
    Seeking new opportunities,
    And found them.
    We are artisans and tradesmen,
    Politicians and priests.
    We are what we want to be.
    We band together,
    Taking pride in our past.
    But we are Americans first,
    And will always be.

Our fathers found refuge long ago
    In the land of the Delaware.
    Out of the south they fled
    Seeking sanctuary with the Quakers,
    The Society of Friends.
    We are still seeking,
    Seeking the rights of free men.
    But we are Americans
    And will always be.

WE HAVE FAMILIES.

> The bonds of blood bind US together.
> > We see our fathers' fathers
> > Mirrored in the faces of our children.
> > Past, present, and future
> > Are combined in them.
>
> For US the bonds of blood are unknown.
> > Our children have many fathers
> > They do not know.
> > The past has no power
> > To build their future.
> > They live in the present.
>
> ALL of us are part of the city
> > And the city is a part of us.
>
> OUR fathers peeled willow twigs
> > On a summer evening
> > For the powder mills along the Brandywine.
>
> OUR fathers drove
> > The last powder wagons
> > Through the cobbled streets
> > To death and destruction.
>
> OUR fathers built textile mills
> > In a young land.
>
> OUR fathers "whipped the first Quaker
> > Bloodily through the streets."

Our fathers created a new nation,
    Conceived as a dream,
    Yet to be fulfilled.

Our fathers fled to the city
    And were beaten by it.
    They brought nothing with them
    And found nothing.

However we came to be
    The city is our home.
    Here are our families.
    Here is our future.

We look at our children
    And see ourselves in them.
    What we see
    Comes back to them.

We face grueling poverty
    And seek to protect them.
    Degradation and despair
    Are our lot.
    But for our children
    We seek something better.

We are weak
    And seek to make them strong.

We look to the future
    And know that they will build it.
    For they are builders
    Of a great city
    Of First Families in the making.

WE HAVE HOMES.

That garage is OUR home.
It shelters us by night.
By day, we follow the refuse trucks,
Salvaging the castoffs of others.
A few coins, exchanged with the junkman,
Buy us wine to forget.
They call us "weinsteins."
We do not care.

That house, standing in the midst of desolation
Created by the bulldozers,
Is OUR home.
It is sturdy and strong.
Yet we must leave it.
They tell us it blocks the future.
"Redevelopment" is what they call it.
We have searched,
But we cannot find
Another house as good.

That small house, neatly standing in a row,
    Is OUR home.
    Others like it line the street.

    Once we knew our neighbors—
    Exchanged news on a summer morning,
    Gave help in time of trouble.

    Now there are strangers
    On each side of us.
    Dark of skin, strange of speech,
    Their ways are different,
    Not our ways.
    Our neighborhood is going down.

That house behind the garden wall
    Is OUR home.
    On each side apartments rise
    To the sky.

    Many generations of our family
    Have made this house a home.
    Some still call it "Mansion House."

    Drawn shutters close out
    Rising giants of the city.

    When we go, the house will go.
    Our children have no need for it.
    They like the suburbs.

WE GO TO WORK.

    WE enter the family business.
        Our jobs are made for us
        By past generations.
        We become executives
        To shape the future
        Of great industries.

    WE learn trades,
        As our fathers did before us.
        We face a future
        Which has no use
        For the creation of our hands.
        Machines have taken over.

    WE drift from job to job.
        Down by the railroad tracks
        We gather every morning,
        Seeking a day's work.

    WE work on the assembly line.
        The work is good—
        When you can get it.
        Too often, we face lay-offs.
        Times are bad.

WE work on the wharves.
>   Longshoremen, heaving and lifting
>   The cargoes of mighty ships.
>   When the ships are in
>   We work.

WE leave home each morning
>   Before the children wake.
>   We work each day
>   In a different home,
>   Building for others
>   What we would like to create
>   For ourselves.

WE are the "numbers" men.
>   That corner store is a "front."
>   Lounging on the street,
>   We take bets,
>   Small sums from those
>   Who seek the easy buck.
>   Each evening, the winning number—
>   Part of a "special sale" sign—
>   Appears in the window.

WE are the people of the city.
>   We work steadily
>   Or sporadically.
>   Earning a living
>   Or living on others.

WE ARE THE FUTURE.

When you look at us
You see the present.

When you look at us
You see the past.
You see our fathers
And our fathers' fathers.
You see the lands
From whence they came.

When you look at us
You see the future.
You see our children
And our children's children.

When you look at us
You see past, present, future,
Melded into a common heritage.

When you look at us
You see all parents,
Everywhere.

The Teachers Speak

WE ARE THE TEACHERS OF THE CITY.

WE came to the city for adventure.
Seeking independence and a new life,
We left our parents' homes.
We found loneliness at first,
The loneliness of independence.
Some of us returned to our parents.
But many remained, finding new homes,
New friends in a new profession.
We like the city.
This is where we want to be.

WE are native born.
The city has always been our home.
We find the city changed.
It is no longer the place of our childhood.
A new skyline rises.
Beneath it, blocks of desolation,
Bulldozed into anonymity.
They tell us a new city
Will rise from the rubble of the old.
Strange children with strange ways,
Fill our classrooms,
Forerunners of the future.
We long for the past,
The city of our childhood.
But we accept our city
And its children.

WE are native born.
     The new city frightens us.
     The people of the city
     Repel us.
     Their children flood our classrooms.
     Dirty, uncouth, strange of speech,
     They take our measure,
     With doubt and scorn reflected
     In their eyes.
     We will leave the city
     And its schools, to seek
     Our own kind in the suburbs.

xxx   *An Adventure in Human Relations*

WE are teachers on the move.
Transferred to the city with our husbands,
We seek new experiences,
New opportunities to put our skills to work.
We find new children, new to us,
In speech, in color and in custom.
But they are all the children
We have ever known.
We find what we seek,
Children avid to learn,
But not knowing how to tell us.
Children desperate for affection,
But afraid of rejection.
Timid children putting out feelers
To life, and withdrawing in fear.
Aggressive children, tough and brassy,
But only on the outside.
Children already beaten,
Learning early in life
That they are worthless
And unwanted.
We will leave the city
When our husbands move again.
But we will leave the children
Stronger than we found them.
For we are teachers
Committed to a dream.

WE ARE AMERICANS.

Our fathers established a new nation
Rooted in the power of education
To forge a new people
In command of their own destiny.
The schoolhouse rose in every settlement
Across the continent
Almost as quickly as the sod houses and the cabins.
And laws established the right
Of every child to learn.

Our fathers left their homes
In other lands.
Seeking a better life for their children,
Education became the "open sesame"
To a life unknown to them.
In a young country,
They became the possessors of a dream
For their children and their children's children.

Our fathers came out of degradation and despair,
    Transplanted to a new land
    Against their will, they survived,
    And made certain that their children
    Would survive.
    To become a teacher was the
    Fulfillment of our fathers' dream
    For us.
    We find it hard to teach.
    The color of our skin becomes a barrier.
    But we are climbing.
    The fruition of the dream
    Will be fulfilled in our children.

We are Americans.
    Our roots are deeply planted
    In the ghettos of the city.
    In the village and the town,
    In the forest and the farm
    In a heritage which
    Binds us all together.
    We are transmitters of a dream,
    Of the American dream.

WE ARE PEOPLE.

> My father came from Poland
>> To work in the mines.
>> My childhood, pinched and poor,
>> Made me afraid.
>> I came to the city.
>> I cannot break my narrow world.
>> The city has no place for me.
>> I will return to the poverty
>> Of my childhood.

> My father came from the cotton fields.
>> He found uncertain refuge
>> In the slums of the city.
>> He peddled fish in summer,
>> And in the winter,
>> Muskrats from the swamps.
>> He scrimped and saved
>> To make a teacher of me.
>> I am learning with my children,
>> For the poverty I knew
>> Must not impoverish them.

> My father lived in the past,
>> His family no longer great and powerful.
>> A daughter must be prepared
>> To earn a living.
>> Teaching, so he thought,
>> Was "ladylike,"
>> A sheltered life.
>> And I became a teacher.
>> A frugal life I've led.
>> Tomorrow I retire,
>> To live more frugally on pension.
>> This will not be hard;
>> Each day for many years
>> I have gone to school,
>> Hating my work and the greedy ones
>> Who demand more than I have to give.

My father learned a trade.
   At sixteen he came to the city
   From the farm.
   He worked with his hands,
   Creating beauty for others.
   And for his own,
   He created the same beauty.
   Our bodies were nourished
   On simple fare.
   But our minds and imaginations
   Feasted.
   Books were budgeted
   Along with rent and groceries.
   My father was a teacher.
   I carry on his work.

My father came from a family of teachers.
   To release young minds,
   To explore the known and the unknown,
   To share the world of the imagination,
   To kindle hope and aspiration in others,
   To build leaders for future generations,
   To move the American dream
   More closely to fruition,
   Were his reasons for being.
   His gift to me was commitment.
   A commitment to children
   And the American dream.

WE LOOK AT CHILDREN.

The CHILDREN in our school
Are not the same.
They tolerate us
Or defy us.
They are wary of friendliness
And listen, distrusting,
When we speak.
The children we knew
Are in the suburbs.
Next year we will teach
Our own.

The CHILDREN in our school
Are strangers to us.
Migrants, working the fields from farm to farm,
They come to the city for the winter months.
We clean and clothe them,
Provide free food for empty stomachs,
Get them to the clinic,
In preparation for learning.
And then they leave.
They will not pass this way again.

THE CHILDREN in our school
        Have come from many places
        To make the city their home.
        City-bred, children on the move,
        They find each city like the last.
        They carry their roots with them,
        Putting them down
        To strengthen and flourish
        In a new soil.
        Curious, bright, perceptive,
        They make each new experience
        An exciting adventure for themselves
        And for us.
        These are city children,
        Destined to create new cities
        Of the future.

WE look at children
        And see ourselves.

        Hope for the future,
        Or despair.

        High expectations,
        Or resignation.

        Builders of the dream
        Or despoilers.

        Creators of a new city
        Or vandals,
        Seeking to destroy the old.

        We look at children
        And see ourselves.

WE ARE THE FUTURE.

> When you look at us
> You see yourselves.
>
> When you look at us
> You see the heritage of many peoples
> Molded into a common heritage.
>
> When you look at us
> You see the future you have shaped.
>
> When you look at us
> You see your children,
> And what they will become.
>
> When you look at us
> You see all teachers,
> Everywhere.

An
Adventure
in
Human
Relations

Prologue

Revolution In Our Times

Delaware is a border state adjacent to the Mason-Dixon Line. Although it fought on the side of the Union during the Civil War, its people were of mixed loyalties for their roots are deeply buried in Southern tradition. In May, 1954, when the Supreme Court of the United States announced its decision on the desegregation of public schools, the races in Delaware were segregated by the State Constitution.

Wilmington, the only city in the state over 100,000 in population, enjoyed the advantages of great wealth as the headquarters of giant corporations and industries. At that time, its population was described generally as of middle income, with pockets of deprivation largely confined to the East Side and, to a limited extent, to south Wilmington.

The East Side had become a ghetto where a small Negro community had grown to a full-blown area of deprivation following the influx of Negroes during World War II. A federal low-cost housing development had made possible a growing Negro community in south Wilmington, formerly dominated by Ukrainian Americans. There, New Castle Avenue had become a sharp line of demarcation between white and Negro communities.

Prior to 1954, a small group of Negroes had escaped the ghetto and had located on the upper west side, creating a community of residents largely of middle- and lower-middle income. In a city of approximately 112,000, 15 per cent of the population was Negro living apart from the white community.

Wilmington's public schools were segregated in 1954. In the elementary schools, from kindergarten through grade six, 20 per cent of the enrollment of some 7400 children were Negro. Prior to 1953, these youngsters and their teachers were housed in outmoded, old school buildings, churches, and store fronts. A building program to replace these structures was in process of development. It was completed in 1953, leaving only one small, old Negro school on the west side of the city, and one Negro school in south Wilmington.

While Wilmington's public schoolchildren and staff were segregated by law, a number of practices of an interracial nature had become firmly established. All professional non-teaching activities were interracial. Staff members of both races worked on the same committees for curriculum development and book selections. All city-wide in-service education activities and all professional staff meetings were interracial.

Children obtained some racially integrated experiences in all-city music activities, in athletic events in the secondary schools, and in a number of cooperative ventures carried out by white and Negro schools. For example, the principal of the large white school on the upper west side had made the facilities of her school available to the small, neighboring Negro school. Assembly programs were often shared and the Negro staff and children felt welcome in this school.

In another section of the city, two sixth grade classes, one from a neighboring Negro and one from a white school, carried out a yearlong curriculum project with frequent intervisitation and the sharing of lunch.

For many years, representatives of Parent-Teacher Associations of all schools had met together in the Home and School Council of the Wilmington Public Schools.

These experiences had strong influence in the early days of desegregation, because people already knew each other as individuals and strong, working relationships had been established between the two races.

School districting policies prior to 1954 encouraged the attendance of elementary school children in neighborhood schools. But, traditionally, policy had permitted parents who desired to send their children to a school out of their district to do so provided they furnished the transportation, and room was available in the out-of-district school. Few parents used this privilege, but more Negro than white parents took advantage of it. Frequently, a working Negro mother preferred that her child enroll in a Negro school close to her place of employment.

This policy, too, had positive effects following desegregation, for its long establishment prevented its being looked upon as a dodge to avoid desegregation. It helped ease the tension during the initiation of desegregation, and, though seldom used as a dodge, it eventually became less used following desegregation than it had been under segregation.

2   *An Adventure in Human Relations*

A City School System Desegregates

In May, 1954, with the announcement by the Supreme Court of its decision requiring the desegregation of public schools, immediate desegregation was initiated by the Wilmington public schools. The announcement of the decision had come as a surprise. The school-building-replacement program, coming to completion over a ten-year period, had been predicated upon segregation. Thus, for example, two small, new schools only one city block apart, one built for white and the other for Negro children, were occupied only one year on a racially segregated basis.

Immediate problems facing the school staff were:
1. To prepare parents to accept desegregation
2. To prepare staff members to accept desegregation
3. To reorganize staffs and classes on a desegregated basis

The preparation of the staff had already occurred to a large extent. The interracial organization of all school-connected activities outside the classroom paid off. Particularly advantageous were the close working relationships among elementary principals which made possible free discussion of all racial problems. The elementary principals carried the major responsibility in neighborhood schools, planning with faculties and parent groups. Few principals took a vacation during the summer of 1954. Door to door visits were made, listening to parents, winning acceptance and, in some cases, winning support for desegregation. The most dramatic illustration of change of attitude occurred when a P.T.A. president, who had declared in May that Negro children would enter his child's school over his dead body, by September personally invited Negro parents to the first P.T.A. meeting and met each one at the door with a personal welcome. He explained that, while he personally disapproved, the law should be upheld. Of some twenty-five white parents, who requested transfers to avoid Negro children and Negro teachers, only five could not be persuaded to withdraw their requests. Upon receiving such a request, the principal usually advised a delay of six weeks to make certain of the need. Most parents complied, and withdrew the requests after their children experienced high quality teaching by Negro teachers in desegregated classes.

Decisions affecting desegregation placed the following priorities on its accomplishment:

■ All elementary schools were to desegregate immediately. The uniracial nature of school neighborhoods maintained five uniracial schools during 1954-55. The elementary schools were closed in June, 1954, as segregated institutions and reopened in September, 1954, as desegregated schools.

- All 1954 summer programs, both elementary and secondary, were to be desegregated.
- Only one step was taken in the secondary schools. White and Negro vocational education students were to attend either of two schools for desired courses not offered in both.
- During the second year of desegregation, 1955-56, seventh grades in junior high schools were to be desegregated.
- During the third year, 1956-57, all secondary schools were to be desegregated, with much flexibility between school districts as long as room was available for students wishing to transfer out of district.

After ten years of desegregation, which rapidly became genuine integration within the public schools, parents generally prefer elementary-age children to remain in their neighborhood schools. The opposite practice in the secondary schools has created problems of overcrowding in formerly all-white schools and of depletion of students in formerly all-Negro schools.

Staffing Problems

In May, 1954, prior to the announcement of desegregation, most staff vacancies in the elementary schools had been filled for the coming year. Careful staff selection procedures, established over a long period, had resulted in few requests for transfers of teachers from the school of original assignment. As a result, desegregation of staff presented problems in a school system traditionally having few transfers between schools.

It had been decided to close the old Negro school on the west side and to transfer the children to the two large, formerly white, schools in their residential districts. The principal of the Negro school had retired in June, 1954. Eight Negro teachers became the first staff members to be reassigned. The assistant superintendent met with the group. She explained the location of all remaining openings and asked each teacher to select one. Three teachers chose assignments to each of the two formerly white, but now desegregated schools. One teacher chose to enter a small white school which was to enroll approximately 10 per cent Negro children in the fall. She became the first Negro teacher of an entirely white class. The eighth teacher chose assignment to a former Negro school which was to continue largely Negro because it was located in an almost all-Negro neighborhood.

The quality of the staff of the closed Negro school was of high caliber. This was a fortunate circumstance, for it later resulted in parent satisfaction with high quality teaching in a desegregated situation.

In the fall of 1954, four of fifteen elementary schools opened with no

Negro children and one former Negro school had no white children. Racial ratios during the first year of desegregation ranged from only one or two families of another race in one school to an almost complete turnover of population in another school. The latter, a small school, had all white children in June, 1954, and ended the school year 1954-55 with 90 per cent Negro children.

Several important attitudes toward desegregation were revealed during the early years:

1. Some white teachers, in schools enrolling a large number (30-90 per cent) of Negro children for the first time, left their positions at the end of the year through retirement, resignation, or transfer. The number was not large the first year, but it marked the beginning of a trend.

2. Although few requested transfers, established Negro teachers usually accepted reassignment in the former white schools as vacancies occurred.

3. Established white teachers, generally, could not be persuaded to transfer to former Negro schools

4. Local white candidates for teaching positions as beginning teachers seldom accepted assignments in former Negro schools or in schools having Negro children in any proportion

5. Out-of-state white candidates for teaching positions only occasionally accepted appointments in schools with high percentages of Negroes.

6. Parents experiencing a desegregated assignment for their children tended to place a higher value on quality of teaching than on race. There were relatively few complaints of racial prejudice. Most of these were made by Negro parents against white staff, but not exclusively so. In only one case did investigation reveal a justification for the complaint.

7. White student teachers tended to refuse student teaching assignments in desegregated schools. In several instances students sought assignments or accepted them, but their parents required their withdrawal.

8. As the number of white applicants for teaching positions declined, there was a great increase in the number of local, state, and out of state Negro applicants. Increasing numbers applied from southern states, particularly North Carolina and Maryland.

During the second year of desegregation, 1955-56, a deliberate effort was made successfully by the school administration to place Negro teachers in vacancies in former white schools. Each teacher was selected on the basis of demonstrated quality of teaching and personal stability. Experience proved that not race, but personal and professional qualities of a racially different teacher generally determined his acceptability by parents. In most cases, Negro principals were generous in releasing valued teachers to initiate desegregation in former white schools.

Attempts to secure willingness of white teachers to transfer to former

Negro schools failed. Accordingly, an attempt was made during 1956-57 to arrange a volunteer exchange program between white and Negro teachers. Only one pair of teachers tried this plan for a one-year period. Ten years after desegregation, this trend continues to be a problem. One of the great inhibitions to successful integration of staff is the unwillingness of local white teachers to accept assignments in former Negro schools. White parents, too, generally continue to reject entrance of their children into a former Negro school. However, white teachers and parents usually accept the entrance of Negro children in a former white school with goodwill. New schools, not formerly associated with segregation, have no problems. However, while the process is slow, ten years after desegregation all elementary schools are biracial in enrollment and all have experienced desegregation of staff. Only occasionally have Negro teachers in former Negro schools expressed dissatisfaction with the appointment of a white teacher. They feel that positions formerly held by Negroes should be filled by Negroes. Negro staff members have occasionally questioned the transfer of outstanding Negro teachers to former white schools, claiming great need for such teachers by children in Negro neighborhoods. Whenever transfers occurred, replacements of high quality were found. Transferred teachers are still serving Negro children in former white schools. No teacher is required to transfer, and a few have refused to do so. Most Negro teachers transferring to former white schools feel the satisfaction of serving a noble cause. Experience has proven that edict might be faster, but re-education, especially in the area of human feelings, is a slow process, and taking time to lay strong foundations in human relationships pays dividends in attitude building and morale. Persistent and continuous effort is paying off in Wilmington.

The Trauma of Change

At the time of the Supreme Court Decision on the Desegregation of Public Schools, the white community—with the exception of some professional social agencies and some political and religious leaders—was largely unaware of the problems besetting the Negro community. The white community's concerns were centered chiefly in the decline of business in the inner city. The growth of suburban shopping centers had been keenly felt. There was uneasiness, slightly relieved by hope in the establishment of the Greater Wilmington Development Council by business leaders who sought the regeneration of business in the city.

Urban redevelopment plans were under way to level and rebuild a section of the East Side. Poplar Street Project A was initiated with hope, a hope that turned to bitterness as an area of 21½ acres was torn down, only to lie prone for a ten-year period.

A battle over the location of a north-south thruway emerged and continued as plans to cut a great swath through the city developed. The bulldozing of homes in its path began and continues, resulting in the further displacement of people.

A state public accommodations bill was sought to open eating places to Negroes, an effort that came to fruition in the spring of 1964.

An immediate acceleration in the movement of white families to the suburbs began with the Supreme Court announcement. This movement rapidly assumed the characteristics of a flight. Negro families, displaced by demolition of homes, began to move into the peripheries of their former neighborhoods, and the long process of the breakdown of racially segregated neighborhoods throughout the city began, accompanied by an acceleration in the deterioration of housing.

Almost immediately, the in-migration of deprived persons from the South began. In-migrants were usually Negroes, but a sizeable influx of deprived white people to the city also occurred. In-migration brought not only a change in the racial ratio of the city population, but also marked changes in the economic level of the white population. In a relatively brief period, Wilmington started a process of drastic economic change. It changed from a community of largely middle-income families into a city of preponderantly deprived people without sense of community. Wilmington became an outpost of a worldwide social revolution more potent in its effects upon the lives of people than that of any previous revolution.

Each city has a distinct personality of its own. This personality is shaped by people living together, creating traditions, perpetuating customs, and shaping the aspirations of its children. Like a person, a city often undergoes changes in personality, changes critical enough to produce mental illness. In a relatively short time, the long-smoldering illness had erupted, and Wilmington was engaged in a struggle for survival.

Portrait of Blight[1]

The signs indicating the distress of a city are noted first by the school staff, for children bring to school all that they are experiencing. Teachers who have worked over a period of years with large numbers of disadvantaged children have little difficulty in identifying these signs. They readily recognize characteristics which, if not treated and redirected, foretell failure for the school in making education count in the lives of children and their families.

---

[1] Crosby, Muriel. "Portrait of Blight," *Educational Leadership,* February 1963. Washington, D. C., Journal of the Association for Supervision and Curriculum Development, NEA. Reprinted with permission.

The Disadvantaged

What does a teacher see when he looks at his disadvantaged children?

A Self-Image That Reflects Worthlessness. Thousands of boys and girls entering the elementary school as five- and six-year-olds have already learned that they are worth little. Life has taught them this in a short span of time. Many do not know who their parents are; they have been shunted around among other adults, living in many homes. Many have a one-parent home, and often live with their mothers, brothers, and sisters in fatherless homes. Children in the same family group sometimes have different fathers. These youngsters are accustomed to seeing a succession of men in the home, whose relations with the mother are transitory. *Such children lack the stability of normal family life which helps them feel important and wanted because it is centered in the welfare of the children.*

Poverty That Overwhelms. Disadvantaged children are basically economically deprived. Many of these children have never known what it means to go to sleep with full stomachs. Their only complete meal each day is obtained as "free lunch" at school. One girl who was having her first lunch at school was observed wrapping half of her sandwich carefully. On being questioned, she explained that her father was hungry; there had been no food in the house for three days.

Economically deprived children suffer because of poor and inadequate housing. Let the children describe how they live:

> *Franklin:* "My family would like to move to another house because when it is cold the owner will not give us much heat to keep us warm. My mother said she was going to move when she finds a good house. That's what would please us the best."
>
> *Earl:* "I wish that we had enough food, money, and clothes for everyone in our house. Sometimes we run out of food and money, and when we run out of money the bills pile up."
>
> *Ursula:* "The best thing that could happen to my family is to move. I would like to move from the place we are living because of the living conditions. It is very bad. It is also a very slum area. We have no back yard to play in nor front. My sisters and brothers don't go outside unless we take them. So I think that is the best thing that could happen to my family."
>
> *Samuel:* "If we had more money we could get the house over Riverside because the apartment is falling apart. The door is falling down. The ceiling is falling down and when it rains the rain comes in. We have roaches now but I hope we won't have them if we move over to Riverside."
>
> *Louis:* "I wish that we could have a new house because the old house leaks when it snows. It has no back yard to play in and we will meet new friends."

Among deprived children, physical survival blots out all other needs. In many families, mother is the sole breadwinner. With long working hours in unskilled employment, the mother is away from home during most of the child's waking hours. The demands upon the mother during her short time at home make it impossible for her to meet the needs of growing children. Family meals are unknown in many instances.

The oldest children in the family are forced to assume the burdens of maturity too early in life. They handle the family food budget, shopping while mother is at work. They prepare whatever food is available for younger children. They often assume full responsibility for younger brothers and sisters. One nine-year-old explained that he loved his neighbor because she took care of his little brothers and sisters so that he could play.

Among economically deprived children are many whose health has been crippled. Poor nutrition, insufficient food, inadequate clothing and housing, and lack of simple, routine medical care make deep inroads prior to school entrance. In one typical city, 65 per cent of all public school children have never known what it means to have a family doctor or any medical attention other than emergency clinic care. A preventive program of inoculations, vaccinations, annual physical examinations, and dental service must be provided by the school.

Many disadvantaged children are the victims of a poverty so crushing that early in life poor health not only drains the energy, but also blights the spirit.

Values That Block Personal Development and Social Consciousness. For many disadvantaged children moral and spiritual perversion is the result of deprivation. Cramped and crowded living space denying any form of privacy introduces the child to adult sexual behavior before he is mature enough to comprehend the significance of it. He is often victimized by adults living in his home. This is particularly true of girls, who often become mothers when they are still little more than children. Illegitimacy is an accepted pattern of life, and marriage is of little consequence in sexual relationships.

The source of family income frequently affects the values developed by the disadvantaged child. Many children are growing up in an environment in which, for several generations, the chief income is from public and private welfare agencies. A pattern is established wherein it is normal and acceptable to receive financial support without individual effort and initiative. This factor, together with an early awareness of the fact that racial discrimination often closes the door to opportunities for work, results in an attitude of defeatism and the acceptance of the status quo. It produces generations of children without hope and without the will to become individuals with a sense of dignity and worth.

Values bred in deprivation are in sharp conflict with the established "middle-class" values held by the school and the community. As a result, we find youngsters caught in the bind; rejected, but not knowing why.

Blocks to Education. The disadvantaged child suffers most after he starts school. His experience in living has ill-prepared him for the demands of the typical school. Shaped by an environment whose harshness has, in his own eyes, stamped him indelibly as a person of little worth, he now must be able to conform in a situation which places primary emphasis upon verbal skills. He finds that his natural vocabulary fails him in communicating; and the school's means of communication, informal standard English, is almost a foreign language to him. He often resolves this problem by remaining silent, and his teacher classifies him as lacking in language facility, unable to express himself, in spite of the fact that his natural language is often dynamic and that he is quite facile in its use.

Next, the disadvantaged child becomes the victim of the group intelligence test. Lacking the experiences and the language tools upon which the typical group intelligence tests are based, the child emerges from this measuring of experiences he has never known as a "slow learner," one whose potential is severely limited. And his teacher proceeds to build his curriculum upon a false diagnosis, thereby making certain that a low ceiling potential for achievement is permanently established. In many schools the matter is confounded by rigid segregation based on the findings of group intelligence and achievement tests, thereby blocking the deprived child from the stimulation of association with more fortunate children.

And, finally, the typical school adheres to common standards and a common curriculum, sometimes watered down for the deprived. *The disadvantaged child early discovers that there is little relationship between the problems in living and his living in school.* He early discovers that there is little "use value" in what he learns in school and leaves it behind upon leaving school at night. This is the child for whom, figuratively, "drop-out" is the first entry on his school registration card the day he enters kindergarten.

Which Road?

The situation of the disadvantaged child, the one for whom "failure" succinctly describes the school's prognosis, is not totally dismal. Increasing numbers of the disadvantaged, frequently but not exclusively found in urban areas, are finding hope in their schools.

The tremendous acceleration of change, chiefly caused by social forces of mobility, racial desegregation, industrial mechanization, and world political tensions, is being met by changing concepts of education. Never before have educators been confronted with such difficult choices in selecting the road to take and the directions to follow.

Part of the difficulty is centered in the *bind* in which we find ourselves —a situation, wherein man's rapid conquest of the universe has left far behind his achievements in the social and spiritual aspects of his world. We find man standing at a crossroads. One road has a dual track balancing his material achievements with the needs of his spirit, each track lending support and strength in reaching his ultimate destination: a world in which men live in harmony with themselves, with others, and with the infinite world. The other is, like a monorail, deceptive in its speed, single-minded of purpose, and capable of delivering man to destruction of himself and his world. It is concerned alone with the material aspects of man's life.

Crossroads for teachers present two paths to the education of children—one fast-paced ignoring the developmental needs of children; the other, slow-paced, recognizing the fact that growth is slow and must be deeply rooted. Today, standing at a new crossroads, the direction teachers take depend upon—

- their ability to recognize their challenges;
- their ability to meet challenges;
- most of all, their commitment to children.

In Wilmington's recently completed formal study of schools in changing neighborhoods, it was found that—as could be expected—schools attained widely varying levels of achievement. In schools making the greatest gains, significant clues have been obtained, not only affecting *motivation,* which is the concern of schools for all children regardless of economic level, but also concerning *teaching processes* that are effective in helping deprived children in acquiring human relations skills, sensitivities, knowledge and information, and academic achievement.

Challenges and Clues

Some of the challenges and clues for meeting children's needs through education follow:

1. Lifting the ceiling on potential through—
   a. planning curriculum with high expectations, but realistic in nature;
   b. planning experiences able to change the self-image of the child.
2. Assuring economic survival of deprived children by improving their command of standard English.
3. Providing many experiences in seeing the relationship between cause

and effect. Making wise choices depends upon anticipating probable outcomes. In essence, this is the kind of thinking process which is notably lacking in the life experiences of deprived children.

4. Rooting the curriculum in the children's perception of their own needs through the use of diagnostic instruments designed to reveal children's perceptions, concepts, and needs; and leading teachers to change their attitudes toward children.

5. Planning curriculum that is rooted in "use value" for children.

Newer developments in teaching processes and instruments need to be examined critically. Examples of these are team teaching, programmed learning, teaching machines, and subject matter specialization for elementary teachers. These should be evaluated in the light of research in the field of human growth and development and in that of the learning process, if we believe that education to be effective *must* be an integrative experience.

1. The abilities and developmental needs of the learners differ in some respects from one educational level to another within the same school system. Therefore, practices which may be appropriate for one level, may be inappropriate for another. For example, team teaching in the secondary school may be just another way of organizing the staff for instruction within the departmental structure of the school. In the elementary school, team teaching, where it has been initiated, has usually resulted in a radical *change in organization* of the school, resulting in highly departmentalized teaching and learning in what have become miniature secondary schools. We need to ask ourselves, "What is the research basis which justifies this type of organization for elementary school students?"

2. The value of machine teaching and that of programmed learning for each level need to be assessed. Their value for elementary schools will probably be different from their value for secondary schools due to the difference in development characteristics of the youngsters. Questions such as these should be asked:

"What is gained and what is sacrificed in machine teaching?"— There are implications here for the quality and the cost of education, because certainly machine teaching and programmed learning are not inexpensive.

"How are machine teaching and programmed learning changing the role of the teacher and his impact upon children?" "Is teaching a 'tutor' role; and is this to be desired?"

3. The increasing number of armchair educators, often proficient and capable leaders in their own fields of specialization but completely unqualified to prescribe teaching methods, has panicked many professional

educators into regressive action which is unjustified by research and detrimental to children. We need to ask ourselves: "How can we develop the fortitude and courage to deal with pressures without bias and without fear?" "How can we develop the inner security to fight for deep convictions and to count upon a position which we are able to defend?" When educators know what they believe and are able to defend it, we will no longer deny children the things of the spirit.

In *The Fires of Spring*[2], James Michener has written:

> "For this is the journey that men make: to find themselves. If they fail in this, it doesn't matter much what else they find. Money, position, fame, many loves, revenge are all of little consequence, and when the tickets are collected at the end of the ride, they are tossed into a bin marked Failure. But if a man happens to find himself—if he knows what he can be depended upon to do, the limits of his courage, the position from which he will no longer retreat . . . the secret reservoirs of his determination, the extent of his dedication, the depth of his feeling for beauty, his honest and unpostured goals—then he has found a mansion which he can inhabit with dignity all the days of his life."

It is imperative that educators find this mansion which Michener describes. Whether or not it is found will depend upon the directions we take at "Crossroads Education." And our choice of direction will determine whether the disadvantaged child of today will become the father of a new generation of disadvantaged children or the creator of a new way of life for himself, his children, and his children's children.

The Need for Survival

In man's long journey to find himself, he has learned that the finite and infinite worlds of which he is a part encompass the "constants" which enable him to take his bearings, to fix his sights, and to select his directions.

The "constants" which have evolved in man's search for himself are universal, for all men of all times have been motivated by them.

- The quest for the reason for being
- The search for the power or force with which man can identify
- The need for man to find solace, support, challenge, and protection through association with others
- The desire to create an economic life which enables man to explore the endless potential of his intelligence and the mysteries of his spirit
- The need to assure through his children that his quest will continue

At any one time in an individual's life the immediate urgency of his basic needs may all but blot out the "constants" affecting him. Yet,

---

[2] Michener, James. *The Fires of Spring.* New York, Random House. Copyright 1949. Quoted with permission.

always they are present, pervading the innermost feelings and thoughts of each human being.

The strife and turmoil of the present are but reflections of man's needs. The current social revolution, spearheaded by minorities demanding equality of opportunity in every aspect of living, reflects the determination of all people to obtain that which is denied them. In an important sense, man is engaged in a blood bath of the spirit out of which must come the assuagement of his wounds if the human race is to grow economically, morally, and spiritually healthy.

The present agony of the city in its struggle for survival will not be assuaged by mere elimination of physical blight nor by accommodating to the flight of those who have and their replacement by the have-nots. It will require more than the creation of legal means for the prevention of injustice. All of these are necessary, but they are merely *symptoms* of a social revolution. The *causes* of social unrest must be treated if new cities are to rise out of the old.

An Adventure in Human Relations, the story of one school system's efforts in the renascence of one city is an attempt to deal with causes rather than symptoms. It is rooted in the conviction that education must become a powerful force behind the rebirth of the city. Small beginnings have been made in Wilmington, Delaware. This volume is the story of these beginnings.

Section

I

An Adventure is Launched

Section I describes the launching of an adventure in human relations. It provides a picture of a city in rapid and traumatic change. In a very important sense it provides the setting in which the public elementary schools move into action to develop educational programs geared to changing times. Section I is a documentary record which sets the stage for a subsequent portrayal of educational change in urban schools.

The Beginning of
an Adventure in Human Relations

In August, 1959, the Wilmington Public Elementary Schools initiated
The Three-Year Experimental Project on Schools in Changing
Neighborhoods, sponsored by the Wilmington Board of Public Education
and The National Conference of Christians and Jews. The need for
this study was urgent. The 1950's had been a period of rapid change,
economically, socially, culturally, and educationally. A number of key
terms characterized this period of rapid change.

Mobility

Like other urban communities, Wilmington was experiencing great
shifts in population. The movement north of migrants from the South,
largely from rural, deprived areas; the immigration of a smaller number
of middle-income, technical and professional workers attracted by the
industrial and professional opportunities for advancement in this area;
the movement out of the city of large numbers of middle-income and
professional workers attracted to suburban life; and the influx of increasing numbers of Puerto Ricans—all contributed to a constant change
in the city population. These factors placed Wilmington in the context
of the prevailing national patterns of mobility.

In addition, mobility within the city gained impetus as a result of the
uprooting of people from their neighborhoods to make way for the
development of a thruway cutting across the heart of the city, the
relocation of families living in a redevelopment area, and the fanning
out from deprived areas of the city into former middle-income areas
of people seeking to improve their standards of living.

Flight

Economic and social factors were not the only ones stimulating the movement of people into and out of the city and from one neighborhood to another. The flight to the suburbs of many urban, middle-income families, begun in earnest at the close of World War II, gained impetus as a result of the Supreme Court Decision of 1954 requiring the desegregation of public schools. While migration began long before the Supreme Court Decision, there is no question that it gained momentum as a result of it. In consequence, a large number of children from middle-income families were removed from the public schools in the inner city, and the character of child population in these schools changed as a result of the influx of a large number of migrant children, frequently from culturally deprived areas. These population shifts radically changed the demands made upon public education within the city.

Desegregation

At the time of the Supreme Court's announcement of its decision on desegregation of the public schools, in May, 1954, the Wilmington Board of Education immediately directed its administrative staff to arrange for the desegregation of elementary schools at the opening of schools in September, 1954. In June, 1954, the school year closed with an enrollment of 7437 children from kindergarten through grade six, in four segregated Negro schools and ten segregated white schools, all with segregated staffs. In September, 1954, the new school year opened with thirteen schools in use, only five of which were segregated because of the residential patterns of their neighborhoods. Seven of the thirteen schools opened with desegregated staffs. At this time, approximately 20 per cent of the children were Negro.

Six years later, during the school year 1959-60, the first year of the Project, only one school remained uniracial (white). This school was replaced by a new building in 1961 with a desegregated student body and staff. Enrollment in the school year 1959-60 had increased by five hundred over 1954, with 54 per cent of the children Negro.

The racial composition of the staff of the Wilmington Public Elementary Schools had changed markedly in the same six-year period. In 1954 there were 252 white teachers; in 1959-60 this number remained approximately the same, 254. The Negro staff had increased from 75 in 1954 to 109 in 1959-60, an increase of over 33 per cent.

Teacher Shortage

The burgeoning birthrate and the failure of communities to create conditions which can attract and hold young people in the profession of education is a national problem. During the 1950's Wilmington moved from a favorable competitive position in recruiting and holding teachers to an unfavorable one. Two factors were largely responsible for this change.

1. The State of Delaware is small. New Castle, its northernmost county, is highly industrialized. Its vast chemical industry, particularly, is responsible for bringing into the area large numbers of professional and technical workers. Wilmington, the major city in the state, is the hub of an industrial area comprising New Castle County, southern Pennsylvania, and lower New Jersey. Most of the wealth of the state is centered in its northern county. The influx of workers in this area, many of whom established residences within the city or in neighboring suburbs, demanded quality education. In the early years of the 1950's there were few schools, particularly secondary schools, in the suburban areas surrounding Wilmington. It became the established practice to send suburban children to Wilmington's schools.

With the "flight to the suburbs", the development of good schools in suburban districts, and the support of suburban schools by local taxation in the late 1950's, there was a reversal of the position Wilmington had long maintained in attracting and holding teachers.

In addition to these factors, certain conditions affecting the financial support of public education in Wilmington began to have their effect. The demands of other school districts in the State for equalization of financial support for all school districts and the rising protests against increased taxation for the support of public education in Delaware resulted in the failure of the State Legislature to continue providing a budget commensurate with the rising cost of education in Wilmington. In effect, legislative action resulted in a statewide equalization program which threatened to lower the financial support and thereby the quality of education in Wilmington.

Added to the failure of the State to continue its adequate financial support of the Wilmington Public School System was a second drive within the city to block increases in local taxation for school purposes. By State Supreme Court Decision in 1946, the Wilmington Board of Education has had fiscal independence, with the legal right to set school taxes within a limit of 70 cents per $100 of assessed valuation of property. By 1959-60 the local property tax for school purposes had risen to approximately 54 cents, exclusive of bonded indebtedness. The concern of the City Council over its lack of control of the taxing power of the Board of Education, coupled with local pressure exerted by the community against increased taxation, resulted in an extremely cautious use of its taxing power by the Board of Education. By the late 1950's

Wilmington had lost its favorable competitive position, and it was possible for teachers to earn from $400 to $1000 more in favored suburban school districts. The movement of Wilmington teachers to the suburbs began.

2. In addition to the financial situation, other factors began to operate which weakened recruitment and holding power in the Wilmington Public School System. Mobility, flight, and the opposition of some white families to desegregation—all played a part in creating undesirable educational conditions within the city.

The residential areas of the city, vacated by suburban-home seekers, became the sought-after neighborhoods of low-income families seeking to better their living conditions. Being financially unable to support these new homes alone, many families converted one-family homes to multi-family dwellings, with the result of overcrowding and a continuous downgrading of properties and neighborhoods. In essence, new slums are being created in areas that were once stable, residential city neighborhoods.

The increase in the Negro population in the City of Wilmington, the desegregation of the public schools, and the decline of certain city neighborhoods, while not the only causes of migration to the suburbs, have accelerated this development. The disorganization of families, the disorientation of people, and the degeneration of neighborhoods are urban characteristics. These are cultural, not racial, matters. As there are more Negro than white deprived families, people tend to assume that negative factors are associated with race. This is not so. Any culturally deprived child, regardless of race, suffers from the same emotional, physical, and intellectual blocks to education. Such a child, whether white or Negro, lacks the cultural experiences which are essential to the attainment of the long-established educational objectives of schools in general.

As more and more culturally deprived children entered the elementary schools in the inner city, the values held by middle-income teachers clashed with those of such children and their families. Successful teachers, earnestly committed to making school desegregation work, experienced the trauma of failure in teaching children from deprived environments. Social service demands consumed more and more teaching time and effort. Relatively few of Wilmington's teachers fled from desegregation. But the increasing difficulties encountered in teaching a changing population, the failure of adequate financial support, and the relatively superior and pleasant conditions found in suburban schools made it increasingly difficult to staff the public elementary schools in Wilmington. In 1957, a low point was reached.

Take-off

In this brief portrayal of a city in the process of change, we find the roots of the problems faced by its schools. The situation was not one of hopelessness, however, but one of challenge. Time and again, as schools have absorbed increasing numbers of culturally deprived youngsters, the staff has been impressed with the will and ability of many low-income families, working under great handicaps, to care for their children adequately; to instill in them respect for themselves and others; and to make sacrifices so that their children may have greater opportunity than their parents. While family values and ways of developing them may differ within and among all economic classes, the percentage of parents at any economic level who fail to hold high expectations for their children is relatively low. This is as true of parents in low-income brackets as it is of those in more favored economic circumstances.

Fully aware of the significance of the problems, the members of the administrative staff of the Wilmington Public Elementary Schools, found a spur to action in the words of William Bradford, who in earlier times faced the demands of leadership in building a nation out of a wilderness:

> "They are too delicate and unfitte to beginne new Plantations and Collonies that cannot endure the biting of a muskeeto."

They knew that their adversary was no "muskeeto." But their challenge was certainly no greater than that presented to a handful of weary, often frightened, but always courageous people, embarked on the conquering of a continent. They accepted the responsibility of creating educational programs which would serve the whole community. They were seeking the way. They were ready for the beginning of an adventure in human relations which, they hoped, would bring a little closer to reality the aspirations for a better life which the citizens expect their schools to help them achieve.

The Schools Face the Problem

The elementary school staffs were becoming acutely aware of the cultural changes occurring in the community through the problems children brought to school with them.

For instance, a principal who had been working with a group of older girls on personal appearance had advised them on the care of their clothing. Having occasion to visit the home of one of the girls, the principal was dismayed over the advice she had given the girl. There were no facilities in the home for proper care of clothes—no running water, no heat, no equipment of the simplest kind. There began a school program which enabled the girls to keep their clothes clean and in good condition by using school facilities. One effect of substandard housing was felt and recognized.

As an administrative leadership group, the elementary principals studied housing in Wilmington. An administrator of the Wilmington Housing Authority was invited to speak to the group, sharing needed information and exchanging thoughts on the causes and cure of housing problems.

Neglected, malnourished children became a focal point of study. Representatives of the Child Welfare Department visited the group. They provided necessary information on the scope of services available to the schools.

Conflicts in values in family living became increasingly a problem for the school. A Delaware State Department of Education specialist in family living, whose experience lay in the field of working with deprived children, helped the group understand the problems of substandard homes and suggested practical school approaches to helping children.

A principal who had surveyed his neighborhood to determine the interests of families found a need for adult recreational and educational opportunities. With the aid of the Adult Education Department he planned an evening program for working mothers which included sewing, cooking, budget planning, and other homemaking skills.

A city-wide school building program, which replaced more than half of the outmoded elementary schools of the city during the 1950's, highlighted the changing needs of the public school population. Parent-staff planning committees for each school to be replaced explored the needs of each neighborhood and developed the kinds of educational programs the new schools should serve.

The national concern for gifted and talented children was reflected in the establishment in 1956 of a three-year experimental project for exceptional children. This effort focused on the need of the public elementary schools to provide a range of educational programs in each school which would challenge the vast range of abilities, interests, and needs of above average schoolchildren. It was recognized that children of exceptional potential could be found among the deprived and that the school must be ingenious enough to identify this potential and encourage it to develop.

As the change in the child population became pronounced, and while the elementary schools were becoming truly integrated, behavior problems grew; concern over the increasing social welfare needs of the children and their parents mounted; and sharp conflict between the values of home and school emerged. The staff had studied these problems for five years. The members were convinced that public education had to become more effective in meeting these problems. Their eagerness to be more effective could not be questioned. Their lack of know-how was the Achilles' heel in this situation.

And from out of the community came the spur to action and the help that was needed. The schools would not have to attempt the impossible task of doing the job alone.

In August of 1959, the Director of the Delaware Regional Office of The National Conference of Christians and Jews, Mr. Elmer Paul Brock, proposed to the Assistant Superintendent in Charge of Elementary Education of the Wilmington Public Schools the initiation of the Project. Financial support of the Project by The National Conference of Christians and Jews was promised in the form of provision for consultant service and of funds for postage and office materials. The school system would provide the Project Administrator who was to have complete authority and responsibility for leadership.

Preparing for Action

During September of 1959, the proposed Project was given thorough study by the elementary principals during numerous group conferences and individual conferences within the Division of Elementary Education. A conference with the Delaware Regional Director of the National Conference of Christians and Jews was then held. By October, six elementary schools in four school communities had agreed to engage in the Project. These schools are referred to as "Project schools" throughout the remainder of this report. Only one school participated on a total faculty basis. In all, sixty-five teachers in the six schools became participants.

In early October, Dr. William E. Vickery, Director, Commission on Educational Organizations, The National Conference of Christians and Jews, New York, visited Wilmington and conferred with school officials. He agreed to act as curriculum consultant for the Project. A conference with Dr. Vickery and the Superintendent's Cabinet, composed of twelve department and division heads, was arranged so that all would be informed. In addition, an initial planning conference was provided for Project school principals, who were to provide leadership in the development of the Project in each participating school.

School organization for action constituted one important aspect of the study. Two other aspects were of equal importance. The public schools could not hope to accomplish the job alone. Involving community leaders from the beginning would be an important step. Accordingly, a beginning was made by securing three outstanding leaders in community affairs to form a nucleus of community representatives in planning the initial steps of the Project.

Involving the state university became the third organizational step. The Dean of the School of Education of the University of Delaware agreed to sponsor the Project.

Thus, a three-pronged approach to the problems of schools in changing neighborhoods was achieved: (1) A public school system and its community; (2) a university; and (3) an agency of the community, the Delaware Region of The National Conference of Christians and Jews.

Summary of Procedures

By early October, the initial steps in preparing for The Three-Year Experimental Project on Schools in Changing Neighborhoods had been completed.

1. The Project had been approved.
2. Six schools had volunteered to participate.
3. Sixty-five teachers had volunteered to participate.
4. A nucleus of community representatives had accepted responsibility to participate on the Central Planning Committee.
5. University liaison had been established; and its functions in the study, treating research data and providing a summer workshop as an in-service education activity, had been identified.
6. A curriculum consultant had been secured.
7. Preliminary planning by all participants had resulted in (a) modification and acceptance of basic goals, (b) establishment of procedures for consultant service in each Project center, and (c) provision for a monthly general meeting of all school participants and the Central Planning Committee with the curriculum consultant.
8. Responsibilities and relationships among participants had been agreed upon and charted.

We were on the way.

Project Schools Look at Themselves

In planning an action program designed to meet the problems of schools in changing neighborhoods, it is essential to look at the school communities involved, assess their strengths, and identify their needs. In October, 1959, Project principals were asked to provide descriptive information about participating schools. It should be noted that:

1. The Drew and Pyle Schools, working together in the Project as a single school unit, represented a culturally deprived area characterized by family displacement caused by the clearance of land for a low-cost housing development.

2. Gray School represented a community in which approximately 65 per cent of the former residents had been replaced by families many of whom were of low economic status.

3. Williams School represented a highly industrialized and commercialized school community where housing was deteriorating and families were being displaced through land clearance for a projected thruway.

4. Shortlidge and Washington Schools, working together in the Project as a single unit, represented predominantly middle- and upper middle-income families. Shortlidge represented the upper economic range among the Project schools, and was the only city school still segregated because of the uniracial residential pattern of the neighborhood. Washington represented families in the middle- and low-income groups, with approximately 20 per cent of its enrollment Negro. Families from deprived areas were moving into the Washington school district, creating the beginning of serious school housing problems. (In 1961, a building program replaced the old Shortlidge and Washington Schools with a single school, thus bringing school desegregation to some children at the beginning of the second year of the Project.)

In summary, during the first year of the study Project schools represented (1) a deprived area with efforts underway which gave hope for the future (Drew-Pyle), (2) a deprived area lacking efforts for improvement (Williams), (3) an area in which housing developments were drawing low-income families as replacements for middle-income families in flight from the area (Gray), and (4) an economically more favored area whose families had to be encouraged to maintain prevailing standards in the face of possible changes in the immediate future (Shortlidge-Washington).

At the initiation of the Project, principals described their schools as follows:

Charles Richard Drew School

Location: Lombard Street between Sixth and Seventh

Enrollment as of October 15, 1959: 477

Staff: 15 classroom teachers

    5 part-time teachers in specialized areas (art, music, instrumental music, physical education, and library)

    1 full-time and 5 part-time service personnel (nurse, home visitor, social worker, psychologist, speech correctionist, and visual piano instructor)

General Description of the School Community: The economic level of this community is low, with income mainly derived from the Department of Public Welfare, domestic work for women, and longshoring for men. Frequently, men hanging out on the corners or outside confectionery stores are paid "lookouts" or "runners" for numbers banks.

The slum clearance program (Poplar Street Project A), and the expectations of an urban redevelopment program are having some effect on the school community.

There has been an increase in the number of fatherless homes and of juvenile pregnancies. We suspect homosexuality in the girl gangs and among teen-age boys.

Participation in School and Community Life. Services for children and/or families are provided by Peoples Settlement House, Christina Community Center, Salvation Army, Department of Public Welfare, Family Service Society, Children's Bureau, Legal Aid Society, Prisoners Aid Society, Union Relief Committee (Hod Carriers and Day Laborers), and the Catholic Welfare Guild.

Although our school is used nightly by the broad community, with the Industrial League and the Council of Churches the chief users, the people involved live without exception outside our school community.

Parent participation in the P.T.A. is good; parent participation in school activities is increasing; and more and more parents show up for parent-teacher conferences. Parent participation in community activities is poor. It is generally confined to school or church affairs. Most of the adult activities are unorganized—nightclub, poolroom, beer parlor type.

Factors Significant in the School Program. We conceive our responsibility to our children as one of knowing, loving, serving, and influencing children in a way that will provide them with the necessary skills for living and that will help unleash their full potential of talents and skills.

Our hopes for our children and their families are for better self-understanding; increased understanding of our physical and social world; and a happy, satisfying, and meaningful life.

Children in classes are grouped heterogeneously, with the exception of the Individual Progress Class* and the kindergarten. Individual Progress Class children are grouped according to mental age. The kindergarten children are generally grouped according to chronological age.

Our strength is at least fourfold: (1) General sensitivity to the problems of deprived children—problems that are social and emotional as well as academic; (2) We have an increasing number of activities in which a child might feel successful—Art Club, Glee Club, Children's Council, and others; (3) Our children seem to have more success in arithmetic than in other academic areas; (4) There is increased attention given to the children's communication problems—talking, discussing, creating, and dramatizing.

Our needs are at least threefold: (1) Need for moral and spiritual development—helping children develop lasting values; helping them perceive consequences of their behavior; and familiarizing them with broad, conventional values; (2) Need for better reading; (3) Need for extending the children's horizons of experience.

---

*The mentally retarded, educable children

Sarah W. Pyle School

Location: Fifth and Lombard Streets

Enrollment as of October 15, 1959: 300

Staff: 10 classroom teachers

7 part-time teachers in specialized areas (music, art, library, physical education, piano, instrumental music, speech)

5 service personnel (nurse, psychologist, social worker, speech correctionist, home visitor)

General Description of the School Community. The economic level is very low; many of the families are on public welfare. Women support families as domestics, men as day laborers. Wages are very low and during the winter months the men seldom can find work. While rents are very high, the homes are in deplorable condition.

With parents working, there is an overall lack of parental supervision. There is an increase in the number of low-ability and emotionally disturbed children, and an increase in the number of children who, coming from the South, have had very little schooling.

Participation in School and Community Life. Peoples Settlement House, Christina Community Center, and the YMCA provide services for children and their families. Our own school is not used by the local residents for after-school activities. Occasionally, political meetings are held in the school.

P.T.A. attendance is not what it should be and parents seldom come into school unless requested to do so. A few parents belong to a club in the Christina Community Center, a few belong to church organizations, and a former P.T.A. vice-president helped during the summer with YMCA activities.

Factors Significant in the School Program. The members of the staff believe they should meet the individual needs of the pupils and develop in them the values and standards necessary to make them good citizens. One teacher is interested in the girls' club at the YWCA and another teacher is interested in working at the Peoples Settlement. For some reason the latter has not gone to work yet.

The children in each class are grouped according to their ability in reading and arithmetic. In social studies they are grouped according to their ability to work together.

Studying the needs of the pupils* in reading, and working with them for improvement are areas of strength in the curriculum. Our need: Planning and carrying through experiences in social studies.

---

*The Drew and Pyle Schools are new schools, opened in 1954 as segregated schools for white and Negro children. Since desegregation, these schools have served all children in the same school district. Because these schools are located within a block of each other, they are administered by a single principal, with Drew School as a primary school and Pyle school as an intermediate school.

George Gray School

Location: 22nd and Locust Streets

Enrollment as of October 15, 1959: 1,175

Staff: 36½ classroom teachers

    5 full-time teachers in specialized areas (art, music, library, and two in physical education)

    3 part-time teachers in specialized areas (instrumental music, lip-reading, and speech correction)

    4 service personnel (nurse, psychologist, social worker, and cafeteria manager)

General Description of the School Community. Our community is essentially lower-income class. Some of our children come from low middle class families, but a large number comes from deprived areas east of Governor Printz Boulevard, in the southern section of the district, and from near the railroad. Added to this is the large number of children who come from the Eastlake Public Housing Project Extension. In their families, the breadwinners are usually truck drivers or manual laborers, with day labor, such as washing and housecleaning, for many of the women.

There is an increase in low-cost public housing. Two hundred units were opened four years ago; four hundred units are to be opened during this school year. With this has come an influx of new families comprising many low-income Negro and white families.

These changes have resulted in giving the area what seems to be a rather high incidence of norm-violating behavior by adults—many parents jailed, many unwed mothers having children by several different men. Still, the actual rate of juvenile delinquency among our elementary school children has been low. We hear of many more misdemeanors among secondary school adolescents.

We have found a great increase in aggressive behavior on the elementary level among both boys and girls—real fighting and some reporting of "razors," though these usually turn out to be small razor blades. From time to time, family quarrels are carried over into the school.

Two hundred forty-four of our children come from broken homes. As far as we know of, and there are probably more, one hundred sixty-nine children carry door keys.

There is a complete lack of drive, of desire to learn, of ambition to prepare for a job, of family values which would encourage a child to do well in school, and of seeing merit in the goals set by the school.

Participation in School and Community Life. The area is served by the Boys Club at 17th and Church Streets, where there is an auxiliary Mothers' Club. There is also the Kingswood Community Center at Claymont Street, with a new building near the new 400-unit public housing project. Parents and other adults participate in the activities of the Center; young men enjoy the gymnasium; a day nursery and a recreational program are available for children.

In addition, our own building is open two nights each week for community recreational activities, but we must admit that it is on a rather meager level. Most teenagers want to dance; younger children enjoy the gymnasium activities; table games and some handcraft work have drawn interest. Although much effort has been expended to create various types of extension classes—sewing, lampshade making, upholstery, etc.—we have found no interest among those for whom these classes were established.

Factors Significant in the School Program. The goals of our professional staff are quite realistically related to the needs of our children. Teachers recognize the lack of opportunity for rich and varied experiences in the home, and the absence of motivation for going to school. Therefore, they try to initiate classroom activities that motivate learning. Our teachers participate in school district affairs, but not in community activities.

An effort is made to develop our children to their highest ability in skills as well as understandings, attitudes, and acquisition of worthwhile factual knowledge. Also, our program is set up to carry on continuous learning with due consideration to the slow as well as the rapid learners. Chiefly, we endeavor to help our children to live better in their every-day world.

Our children are grouped on the basis of maturity and rate or pattern of learning; first on maturity rating, second on achievement. Five classes have been organized as primary units and two as junior intermediate units. As far as possible, a room is so organized that not more than three levels of reading are included.

Part of our strength is in the flexibility of the curriculum. It can serve the child in need of a rich, strong program; it can serve the child in need of a very simple and slow-moving program.

Part of our need is to improve the reading ability of our children; our greatest need is to increase our skills as we try to motivate our children to yearn for what is now outside their reach.

Mary C. I. Williams School

Location: Third and Monroe Streets
Enrollment as of October 15, 1959: 1,124
Staff: 38 classroom teachers
   5 full-time teachers in specialized areas
   3 part-time teachers in specialized areas
   2 service personnel

General Description of the School Community. The people are at a low socio-economic level, with many families supported by the Department of Public Welfare. Fathers are mostly laborers and mothers do day work. Many of our children are in foster homes; families move frequently to avoid paying rent; children are shifted to aunts, grandmothers, or friends when a crisis arises in the home.

The community is becoming preponderantly Negro. At the same time, property is running down (broken windows, litter on pavements and steps, etc.). Larger homes, once having two or three apartments, have become multiple family dwellings with six or seven families living in quarters meant for only three.

Younger children are now involved in the Family Court. They have a lower standard of living, no concept of morals, and a great awareness of sex. Children talk freely about "the man living with my mother," or "the rape man," or "my mother wasn't married before I was born," or most unconcernedly, "my mother was never married."

Few of our children live in a complete family group. There is a high degree of illegitimacy, with no recognition that this is immoral or, at least, not the customary thing to happen. Mothers sign their letters "Miss" and correct the teachers who call them "Mrs." This is true regardless of the number of children they have.

Many families are constantly on the move within the city, or back and forth to Tennessee or North Carolina.

Participation in School and Community Life. Services for children and families are provided by the Boys Club, Deaconess Home, Zion Lutheran Church, Girls Club, Park Board, Cub Scout Troop, Brownie Troop, Salvation Army, and our own school community center.

The CYO Brownies, Cub Scouts, Sacred Heart Athletic Group, Barbers' Association, Board of Health, Democratic Committee, and Bricklayers' Association use our facilities afternoons and evenings.

About 11 per cent of the parents participate in some organized activity. The ones who join the P.T.A. are also our most faithful as workers on the Fair, as Home Room Mothers, or as Brownie Leaders. We have had as many as four hundred members of the P.T.A., with twelve hundred children enrolled—these are maximum figures.

Participation in community affairs is limited for two reasons: (1) There are practically no service organizations in the area with the exception of the Salvation Army and church groups. (2) Many parents are employed and have no time to devote to community affairs. At the same time, there is no staff participation in school-community affairs and activities.

Factors Significant in the School Program. We hope that everything we do with children will improve their way of living. To achieve this, we must help them to understand the importance of family life; to get along with each other, with teachers, with their families; to have respect for other people's feelings; to recognize that there is such a thing as a code of morals; to understand the need for authority and to respect it; to accept responsibility for their own conduct; to create a respect for work and a desire to use their energies and abilities to do what is required of them as students, members of a family, and citizens of a community; and to have pride in their ability to be independent (i.e., as kindergarteners to remove their clothing, to come safely to school, to go on errands through the building; as adults to provide for themselves and their families).

We hope we will accomplish some of these goals by our methods of living and working with the children and by teaching all the subjects of the curriculum.

At present, all groups are heterogeneous, but we hope to do some regrouping to prevent I.Q.'s that range from 66 to 120 from being grouped together. We find it impossible to do justice to all children when the spread is that great; and we have found that candidates for individual progress classes are better adjusted in our slow-moving groups. Part of the problem: with our ever-changing school population, it is extremely difficult to maintain a consistency in our grouping. Children entering without reports or transfers are not always properly placed as we have only our judgments and impressions of their achievements to go by.

Teachers' efforts to adjust their teaching practices to the ability and achievement levels of the children have resulted in that we are doing surprisingly well in reading and arithmetic. Only a few teachers complain about children being mentally slow or below grade level. One of our strengths: teachers think and plan in terms of the adjustments necessary to meet the needs of children.

Better coordination of the efforts of classroom and special subject teachers would result in a better curriculum. Also, the science program leaves much to be desired, and we need more emphasis on leisure-time activities, such as hobbies. Finally, we fail to stimulate our children to do the creative work of which they are capable.

Evan G. Shortlidge School

Location: Concord Avenue and Baynard Boulevard

Enrollment as of October 15, 1960: 328

Staff: 11 classroom teachers

4 half-time teachers (art, physical education, music, library)

3 part-time teachers (instrumental music, stringed instruments, speech)

4 service personnel (half-time nurse, clerk, 2 custodians)

General Description of the School Community. The occupations of the people in this community are extremely varied: doctor, dentist, lawyer, social worker, teacher, store owner, manager, commercial artist, chemist, engineer, shoe clerk, taxi driver, unskilled laborer, and unemployed. This variation makes it possible that some of the people are able to donate to charity, to spend winter vacations in Florida, to have three cars in the family, or to buy fur coats for teen-agers while others must depend on public welfare. Homes range from large, well-cared for, air-conditioned houses with full-time servants to three-room apartments located on the third floor.

Zoning changes have resulted in more apartment houses, while some houses have been converted to offices, especially for doctors. Traffic is both a hazard and a nuisance. At times, conversation is impossible when a truck goes by. The section of the city near Salesianum High School has parking problems on nights when the school is used for group meetings; traffic hazards increase when the park play area is used.

All of our experienced teachers agree that the neighborhood has undergone great change. There are more low-income families. Parents tend to have less education, to expect less of their children, and to provide less academic stimulation for their children.

Nine mothers of our kindergarten children work. One sixth grade has nine "door-key" children and three children from broken homes.

Participation in School and Community Life. The area is served by many religious agencies, YMCA, YMHA, YWCA, scout troops, cub groups, summer camps, day camps, CYO, branch library, and parks. There is an active Little League, and there are many parties for children in the various homes. Many children have lessons in Hebrew, Greek, music, and dancing.

Although our playground is used constantly, the school building is used only for our own group activities.

The better educated and high-income group attends the P.T.A., with the women taking turns being den mothers, home room mothers, or Brownie leaders. These women are also highly active in community affairs—they work in civic organizations, collect for the Red Cross and the United Fund. The men are lay leaders of churches, serve on boards of religious organizations, and are active in raising funds for public buildings.

On the other hand, the low socio-economic group tends to complete nonparticipation in community groups, with many families traveling outside the community to shop or to find recreation.

Finally, few of the parents who are new to the community are as active as those who have lived in the area a long time.

Factors Significant in the School Program. We try to help each child to travel from where he is to as far as he can go on the best road of educational opportunity. We try to keep combination classes reasonable in size and fairly stable. We try to group children according to friendships and other needs of the child. There is some carry-over of our influence into the community as our staff members tend to serve quietly on minor committees in a number of capacities.

Our strengths in curriculum are—

(1) social living, habits, attitudes;

(2) skills;

(3) trips, visual aids, use of resource people, enrichment.

In curriculum our needs are to work on large problems and centers of interest in some of the classrooms and to try to lessen the departmentalization of special subjects such as music.

George Washington School

Location: Fourteenth and Washington Streets

Enrollment as of October 15, 1959: 328

Staff: 11 classroom teachers

4 half-time teachers in specialized areas (art, physical education, music, library)

2 part-time teachers in specialized areas (speech, instrumental music)

6 service personnel (half-time nurse; clerk; 2 custodians, 2 cafeteria workers)

General Description of the School Community. The difficulty of collecting P.T.A. dues or insurance premiums reveals a lack of money, and "waiting for payday" is common. Men are employed in the skilled trades—truck driving, painting, carpentering, selling; mothers often work in retail stores or factories.

Houses tend to be the small, row type; many children live in apartments, some of which are rented by the week at exorbitant prices; in some cases, several generations live together. Nearly all the families have television, refrigerators, and other appliances.

Vacation may consist of a visit to family members in another state or of a week at one of the seashore resorts.

A block of houses is being torn down for a new school, and an area is being cleared for the Adams-Jackson Thruway. Generally, homes in these areas are owner-occupied. Now buildings in the thruway section are largely rented. The people cannot sink roots into the community because this housing is temporary.

Additional change is reflected in the increase in the number of children from broken homes, of "door-key" children, of children who know no father figure at home, and of instances of families where parents work different shifts.

Participation in School and Community Life. The area is served by the Curative Workshop, YMCA, AA, Golden Age Club, Temple Zoo, Happy Valley Playground, Peregoy's, Rock-a-Bye Nurseries, Visiting Nurses, Fire Department No. 1, Hanover Church, Delaware Hospital, Trinity Church, St. Patrick's Church, St. John's Cathedral, Planned Parenthood, Welfare Department, and Aid to Dependent Children. There is no after-school use of school facilities except for the playground, which is in constant but unsupervised use.

The school has an active P.T.A. Executive Committee, and parents come to P.T.A. meetings if their children perform. Generally, attendance at meetings is low—about 16 per cent attending. The P.T.A. is not active in December, since many parents take extra jobs at this time.

There is little participation in community affairs and activities.

Since many children have no church connections, parents probably have loose ones or none. However, some parents go to the "Y"; a few help with scouting; a few work for political parties; some are members of church choirs or other church organizations; some take much interest in the Little League; many of the men belong to labor unions. Bowling seems to be a popular recreation; parties for children usually seem to be family or neighborhood affairs; women give commercially sponsored parties in which the hostess gets a prize.

Factors Significant in the School Program. We try to provide educational opportunities for all children, according to their abilities, through a program which recognizes and provides for individual differences. We try to provide educational opportunities which are based on the needs of the children in a changing world.

Teachers come to P.T.A. meetings, tend to belong to a religious organization, and some take much responsibility for work there. Our teachers have worked well on professional committees and in such organizations as ACEI. One teacher does a great deal of social work with other agencies.

No one on the staff lives in the immediate neighborhood and no one is closely involved in activities near the school.

Teachers meet in small groups to set up new classes and consider things such as existing friendships, ability, size of class, balance between boys and girls, and balance between children with problems. We have no grouping by ability.

Areas of strength in the curriculum are language arts and arithmetic, social learnings, and the use of the library. Achievements in art, physical education, and music have been commended by supervisors. Class size is good and differences in ability are usually accepted. The curriculum is adapted to ability.

In general, the program is good. The children have healthy attitudes toward work and study, like school, cooperate with their groups, show ability to be fair, sensitive, and loyal. They are self-controlled to an excellent degree and contribute to the group in a democratic fashion.

Still, there are needs—and children's needs are not always considered. Work is departmentalized, not only for art, music, and physical education, but also for reading, writing, arithmetic, social studies, and science. We need to lessen departmentalization in special subject areas by cooperative planning. We need to focus on large problems, centers of interest, and giving choices to children.

Getting Underway in the Schools

Although the general goals of The Three-Year Experimental Project on Schools in Changing Neighborhoods were firmly established in the thinking of the leadership group directing the Project, it was recognized that the defining of these goals, the development and acceptance of basic assumptions underlying the study, and the initiation and development of a plan of action cooperatively with participants were major problems confronting us during the first year of the study.

Major Goals

In planning and developing the Project, major goals became clearly defined during the first year of the study:

1. The development of curricula emphasizing human relations concepts, skills, sensitivities, and understandings designed to meet the needs of children and their families in changing neighborhoods

2. The development of cooperative community action programs designed to make it possible for adults, working with children and their families in whatever capacity, to coordinate their efforts in identifying and developing indigenous leadership, making it possible for the people of a community to help themselves in achieving a more satisfying life

3. The development of a research design to provide—

(a) an accurate assessment of the social and personal needs of children and their families living in Wilmington's changing neighborhoods;

(b) a clear description of the processes used by school and community agencies and an assessment of their effectiveness;

(c) an assessment of the Project's effectiveness in helping teachers, administrators, and community leaders to make it possible for children and their families to better meet their human relations needs.

Basic Assumptions

As participants in the Project worked together, the assumptions underlying the development of the study became of increasing significance for they would give direction to our efforts and suggest areas of need in planning the total Project design. They would serve, also, as a point of reference for focusing on "needs":

The needs of children which are the motivating force in curriculum building (Curriculum)

The needs of teachers which underlie the research emphasis in the Project (Research)

The needs of parents of the community which shape the community-action aspect of the Project (Community Action)

Basic assumptions motivating and directing the Project follow:

1. That the curriculum of the elementary school should be a force in helping children meet their human relations needs.

2. That within the present framework of curriculum design in the Wilmington Public Elementary Schools there is opportunity to help children develop human relations concepts, sensitivities, and skills.

3. That the teacher in his daily work with children occupies a key position in effective curriculum development.

4. That children need to develop human relations concepts, sensitivities, and skills which have "use value" in and out of school so that they are able to select behavior appropriate to the situation.

5. That all agencies of a community must coordinate their services for the benefit of the people of a community and, especially, for the welfare of children.

6. That the people of a community will upgrade family and community life as indigenous leadership is identified and encouraged to develop.

7. That school and community agencies working for the welfare of children need to hold their action goals in common so that they are mutually supportive.

Plan of Action

Defining and accepting of goals and assumptions became forces in shaping the plan of action for the Project.

Procedures to be followed throughout the three years of study were developed under the direction of the consultant. These embraced seven major steps:

1. **Diagnosis**—During the first year of the study of schools in changing neighborhoods, diagnosis of children's human relations needs was emphasized, consisting of a study of—

   (a) relationships in the family—child-child, parent-child, parent-parent (Indoctrination and the categories of relationships mentioned provide the dynamics of prejudice);

   (b) relationships in communities—neighbors, families-agencies, families-institutions, families-community workers;

   (c) relationships in play groups—child-child, group standards, conflicts between group standards and family standards;

   (d) relationships in the American scene—relationships between themselves and American society.

2. **Diagnostic Instruments**—A variety of instruments was used to secure from children their perceptions of themselves and the world about them:

   (a) open-ended questions, such as, "What do you like about your neighborhood?" "What would you like changed about your neighborhood?" to determine children's perceptions of their neighborhoods, homes, and families, friends, and others;

   (b) sociograms, revealing children's choices of other children in work and play activities;

   (c) time budgets, providing some indication of how children spend their out-of-school time and with whom;

(d) autobiographies, providing insight into children's understanding of important events in their lives.

Children in the intermediate level usually wrote their responses and primary children frequently drew pictures, supplemented by explanatory comments dictated to the teachers.

3. **Analysis of human relations needs**—Children's responses were analyzed by participants to detect possible clues to children's needs. It was recognized that such responses provided clues only, for obviously they could not stand alone. Their significance, however, was found in their stimulation of participants' use of other sources of information available —records, test scores, observation, conferences with parents and colleagues, and teacher judgment. Children's responses then served to strengthen the teachers' study of their groups and to increase their professional competency in making judgments more effectively.

4. **Relating findings to the curriculum**—Throughout the first year of diagnosis and analysis of children's perceptions of their needs, the activities related to the two functions were incorporated in curriculum planning.

5. **Constructing teaching plans and curriculum materials**—The major emphasis of the second year of study was on curriculum development, utilizing the findings obtained in the diagnostic and analytical steps of the first year and continuing to use the skills learned in diagnosis and analysis as a basis for curriculum building.

6. **Trying out the plans**—Throughout the third year of the study, curriculum materials developed by participants were tried out; evaluated; and duplicated for others to try out, modify, adapt, and evaluate.

7. **Evaluation**—While evaluation was a continuous process throughout the study, emphasis during the third year of study was upon evaluation and redevelopment of curricula on the basis of strengths and needs determined as the Project developed.

A Project Design for Meeting the Human Relations Needs of Children Through Teacher Education and Community Action

Three basic goals motivated the participants in The Three-Year Experimental Project on Schools in Changing Neighborhoods. These goals were the development of a curriculum, more effective in meeting the human relations needs of children and their families; the initiation of community action programs, based upon the identification and development of indigenous leadership; and the development of a research study concerned with human relations in school-oriented and community-oriented settings. Thus, Curriculum Development, Community Action, and Research became the major objectives of the study. While the first two goals were of immediate concern to participants in the Project, the implications for research were profound.

In developing a Project design, two key assumptions provided the direction of plans and procedures geared to more effective curriculum development and community action:

1. That the teacher in her daily work with children occupied a key position in effective curriculum development.

2. That the people of a community will upgrade family and community life as indigenous leadership is identified and encouraged to develop.

If it is accepted that the teacher occupies the crucial position in determining curriculum development and that only the people of a community can improve the quality of family and community life, it follows that the emphasis in the development of the Project must be upon teacher education (curriculum development) and upon the development of indigenous leadership (community action). In other words, if teacher education was to become an increasingly effective means of building curricula geared to the human relations needs of boys and girls, the efforts of teachers must be focused on children; if the people of a community were to become increasingly effective in building a better life for themselves, the efforts of professional leadership in all agencies of a community serving adults and children must be focused upon identifying and developing indigenous leadership.

Teacher Education

In the school-oriented setting of the Project, teacher education was identified as the major emphasis. To increase the sensitivity, insight, understanding, and teaching skill of teachers, the focal point became the needs of children. In attempting to meet the needs of children, the teacher studied them in their social setting. Because the human relations needs of children affect all learning, and because these needs are usually intangible and often subjective, means had to be devised to learn what perceptions the children had of themselves and others. Projective techniques, usually not quantitative in nature, became the instruments for obtaining clues and information, which—when utilized to interpret all other sources of information about children available to the teacher— assumed important significance as research data of a descriptive and subjective nature. The fact that these data could not be quantitatively measured at this stage of development did not lessen their significance.

A basic premise underlying the study was that the term "teacher" embraced all professional staff members participating in the Project who had a role in the education of children. It was assumed that participants, whether they were teachers, administrators, specialists, or supervisors, had a primary concern with their own professional growth.

A second basic premise underlying the study was that teachers, that is all professional participants, themselves shaped their professional education through cooperative action with the consultant and other resource people. Only as the consultant was able to demonstrate in his work with participants the teaching qualities essential in a human relations-oriented education would participants have the opportunities to genuinely deepen their insight, sensitivity, knowledge, and skill in teaching and learning.

In the first year of the study, teacher-education functions centered in learning and using projective techniques and in learning analytical techniques. These functions constituted the diagnostic aspect of curriculum development and were utilized continuously as a permanent part of the teachers' battery of skills.

Table 1, "A Project Design for Meeting the Human Relations Needs of Children Through Teacher Education," column 1, "Curriculum Development," depicts the projected aspects of the Project which center upon a study of children in their social setting and the development of appropriate curricula.

Column 2, "Research," depicts the projected aspects of the study which center upon "Teacher Education." It is in this aspect, when combined with "Curriculum Development," columns 1 and 2, that we find a blueprint for professional and in-service education which, if incorporated in the professional curricula of teacher-education institutions, would assure the entry into the teaching profession of teachers and administrators who are prepared to accept the responsibility for developing on the job the insights, sensitivities, understandings, and skills needed in providing a human relations-oriented education of children. *To the Project Administrator this constitutes the major responsibility of teacher-education institutions and calls for reorientation of the professional curriculum of teachers and administrators.*

In the community-action aspect of the Project, there were two distinct yet interrelated functions. One related to and made possible a rounded and balanced development of a sound teacher-education program and a school-oriented emphasis in community action programs. The other related to a distinct community organization emphasis which was not school-oriented.

Table 1, column 3, "Community Action," depicts the projected school-oriented aspect of the community-action phase of the study.

A study of Table 1 reveals the school-oriented scope of the Project. Columns 1, 2, and 3 should be studied vertically and horizontally. The vertical arrangement reveals the projected scope of development for each of the three aspects of the study. The horizontal arrangement reveals the interrelationship and the parallel development of the three aspects.

To the Project Administrator the degree of success to be attained in the Project depended upon the selection, creation, use, and evaluation of instruments which would make possible the learnings sought for children, teachers, and the people of a community. Herein lay the challenge to all participants.

Community Organization

Table 2, "A Project Design for Meeting the Human Relations Needs of Children and Their Families Through Community Action," reveals the dual approach to the second major goal of the Project, namely, the development of community action programs based upon the identification and development of indigenous leadership among the people of a community. The conception of development of this aspect of the Project, Table 2, column 1, recognizes the role of education in achieving the goal sought and thus becomes the third prong of a teacher-education program in human relations which appears first, as column 3, "Community Action," in Table 1.

Table 2, column 2, "Community Organization," depicts the projected scope of development of the community-oriented phase of the study. It depicts the coordination of professional leadership and its responsibility in fostering indigenous leadership to improve family and community life.

In this aspect of the study, as in the teacher-education aspect, *the challenge to professional community leadership was that of developing, selecting, creating, and evaluating instruments and ways of working that were to realize the goals sought.*

Setting Sights

One of the most significant achievements during the first year of the Project was the development of a Project design for meeting the human relations needs of children and their families through teacher education and community action depicted in Tables 1 and 2.

The goals encompassed in the Project design began many centuries ago as a dream which found expression in the Hebraic-Christian philosophy of the Brotherhood of Man. They could be achieved within the context of the Project only as those who felt a moral commitment to foster the development of children and their families through effective education and community action were able to marshal their faith, energy, effort, sensitivity, skill, and knowledge to the task of developing means for their achievement. This was the challenge that faced the sponsors, the participants, the consultants, and the Project Administrator.

Table 1 **A Project Design for Meeting the Human Relations Needs of Children through Teacher Education (In Three Areas)**

	Curriculum Development	Research
"Needs" Focus	Children	Teachers
Diagnostic Techniques (for discovering needs)	Projective Techniques Open-ended questions Time budgets Diaries Autobiographies Sociograms etc.	Analytical Techniques Treatment of children's responses Interpreting findings through: Use of supporting data (evidence) records—tests—observations—etc. judgments—hunches
Curriculum Development (for meeting needs)	Units of Work Oriented Toward Meeting Human Relations Needs Concepts Experiences Activities Content (Subject Matter) Skills Sensitivities Understandings	Development of Sensitivities, Insights and Teaching Skills Developing teaching plans and materials reflecting: Knowledge of how children grow, develop and learn Insights into social forces of neighborhood and expanding community, nation, world Study of children in their social setting Understanding of the conceptual approach to learning and teaching Increasing knowledge and use of a battery of teaching skills which make it possible for teachers to work toward multiple objectives
Evaluation (for determining success of efforts)	Ability to Meet Adequately Human Relations Needs Developing insights, sensitivities, understandings, concepts Growth in academic skills and knowledge and its use Growing command of skills in living and working with people Increasing knowledge and acceptance of self and others	Ability to Meet Adequately Human Relations Needs Deepening of teacher-child-family relationships Increasing teaching effectiveness Increasing adequacy in planning Increasing knowledge and acceptance of self, colleagues, children and their families

*In the community action aspect of the study two emphases are significant, one of which relates directly to the focus of research, namely Teacher Education, and is thus school-oriented, and the other which relates directly to Community Organization to foster indigenous leadership for the improvement of family and community life, and is thus, non-school

Community Action

Parents
(**Teacher Education** School Oriented Emphasis in the Community Action Aspect of the Study)★

Participation Techniques

Learning skills for participating in the identification of indigenous leadership in a neighborhood

Learning skills for identifying problems of concern to the people of a neighborhood

Learning skills for working with other professional leaders in a neighborhood so that efforts are mutually supportive

Becoming able to interpret the needs of the school and the needs of a neighborhood to each other

Identifying and determining which neighborhood problems **recognized** by the people of a community may be incorporated in the curriculum of the school so that children's in and out of school living is enriched through opportunities to learn the concepts, skills and sensitivities needed in the selection of behavior appropriate to different situations.

Development of Insights, Sensitivities and Teaching Skills

Developing teaching plans and materials reflecting:

Knowledge and insight regarding how adults and children express their human relations needs

Understanding of the social forces at work in the neighborhood and the expanding community

Understanding of the role of social forces in the curriculum of the school

Developing skills in planning and teaching so that the social forces at work in the lives of children and their families are incorporated in the curriculum of the school

Developing skills in selecting curriculum experiences which foster the goals of the school in the education of children in the context of life situations, which enable children to become motivated toward achieving these goals

Developing understanding, sensitivity and skills in rooting the curriculum in concept building

Developing knowledge and skill in selecting, creating and utilizing resources (experiences, activities, subject matter, organizations and agencies, institutions and people) which enable children to develop concepts.

Ability to Meet Adequately Human Relations Needs

Deepening of school-home-community relationships

Increasing skills in working together with other people and agencies toward mutually desired goals in family and community life

Increasing skills in making the school, through its function of educating children, an effective agency in fostering more effective and satisfying home and community life

Increasing awareness of responsibility for and skill in helping the school function as an agency with unique responsibilities (education) and supportive responsibilities (participating in community action programs) so that the up-grading of community life becomes a reality.

oriented. The Teacher Education aspect of the community action phase of the study is included in Table 1. For study of the two aspects of community action, consult Table 2.

Table 2	A Project Design for Meeting the Human Relations Needs of Children and Their Families Through Community Action*

"Needs" Focus	Parents
Diagnostic Techniques (for discovering needs)	**Teacher Education** (School Oriented Emphasis in the Community Action Aspect of the Study) **Participation Techniques** Learning skills for participating in the identification of indigenous leadership in a neighborhood Learning skills for identifying problems of concern to the people of a neighborhood Learning skills for working with other professional leaders in a neighborhood so that efforts are mutually supportive Becoming able to interpret the needs of the school and the needs of a neighborhood to each other Identifying and determining which neighborhood problems **recognized** by the people of a community may be incorporated in the curriculum of the school so that children's in-and-out-of-school living is enriched through opportunities to learn the concepts, skills and sensitivities needed in different situations.
Curriculum Development (for meeting needs)	**Development of Insights, Sensitivities and Teaching Skills** Developing teaching plans and materials reflecting: Knowledge and insight regarding how adults and children express their human relations needs Understanding of the social forces at work in the neighborhood Understanding of the role of social forces in the curriculum of the school Developing skills in planning and teaching so that the social forces at work in the lives of children and their families are incorporated in the curriculum of the school Developing skills in selecting curriculum experiences which foster the goals of the school in the education of children in the context of life situations, which enable children to become motivated toward achieving these goals Developing understanding, sensitivity and skills in rooting the curriculum in concept building Developing knowledge and skill in selecting, creating and utilizing resources (experiences, activities, subject matter, organizations and agencies, institutions and people) which enable children to develop concepts.
Evaluation (for determining success of efforts)	**Ability to Meet Adequately Human Relations Needs** Deepening of school-home-community relationships Increasing skills in working together with other people and agencies toward mutually desired goals in family and community life Increasing skills in making the school, through its function of educating children, an effective agency in fostering more effective and satisfying home and community life Increasing awareness of responsibility for and skill in helping the school function as an agency with unique responsibilities (education) and supportive responsibilities (participating in community action program) so that the up-grading of community life becomes a reality.

Community Organization (Non-School Oriented Emphasis in the Community Action Aspect of the Study)

Leadership Techniques, Skills and Processes

Developing techniques for and skills in identifying the felt needs of people in a neighborhood

Developing techniques and skills in stimulating people in a neighborhood to become aware of possibilities for meeting their felt needs

Developing techniques and skills in identifying potential indigenous leadership among the people of a community

Developing insights, sensitivities and skills in coordinating the efforts of professional leadership so that they are mutually supportive in identifying indigenous leadership and needs and in planning an action program.

Action Techniques and Processes (Corresponding in School Oriented Approach to Curriculum Development Phase of the Study)	**Developing Action Programs** (The Role of Professional Leadership) Stimulating the people of a neighborhood to define a need for which an action program can be initiated Encouraging indigenous leadership for action in meeting the need Supporting indigenous leadership through personal relationships and the marshalling of resources available in the community for achieving the goal of a solution to a problem of concern to people Coordinating the efforts of professional leadership so that they are mutually supportive in working toward the achievement of common goals.

Ability to Meet Adequately Human Relations Needs

Increasing awareness of and confidence in the belief that the needs of a people may be more adequately met through cooperative action

Increasing awareness of leadership potential among the people of a neighborhood

Increasing opportunities for indigenous leadership potential to develop through the efforts of professional leadership

Increasing evidence of motivation among people of a neighborhood to act in their own behalf and of desirable changes brought about in family and neighborhood life through cooperative efforts and indigenous leadership.

*In the community action aspect of the study two emphases are significant, one of which relates directly to the focus of research, namely Teacher Education, and is thus school-oriented, and the other which relates directly to Community Organization to foster indigenous leadership for the improvement of family and community life, and is thus, non-school oriented.

Helen Keller has said that "there are two worlds, one that we can measure with line and rule and one that we find in our heart and imagination." The Project was an attempt to make these two worlds one.

The first year of the Project offered convincing evidence (reported in Section II) of the opportunities inherent in the curriculum of the school for meeting the human relations needs of children.

In the dark days of the Civil War, Robert E. Lee wrote words of significance to those who are dedicated to the promotion of the concept of the Brotherhood of Man:

> "The march of Providence is so slow and our desires so impatient, the work of Providence is so immense and our means of aiding it so feeble, the life of humanity is so long and that of the individual so brief, that we often see only the advancing wave and are thus discouraged. It is history that teaches us to hope."

As we began the second year of study, the work of the first year of the Project was history. We were taking a long look ahead with courage.

chapter

2

Another Look at the City

The school year 1960-61 marked the completion of the second year of The Three-Year Experimental Project on Schools in Changing Neighborhoods sponsored by the Wilmington Board of Education and The National Conference of Christians and Jews in the public elementary schools of Wilmington.

In Chapter 1 are described four significant factors reflecting the rapid changes occurring in the life of the city, which had serious implications for the schools. These factors are identified as "Mobility," "Flight," "Desegregation," and "Teacher Shortage."

In reporting the progress of the second year of the Project, it was necessary to re-examine factors reflecting change in order to note their impact on the community and its schools.

People on the Move

People are motivated to move by many forces and combinations of forces. Among the more common reasons underlying the movement of people are opportunities for employment, better housing, better education for children, and the desire to seek a better life in terms of economic and social conditions.

During the second year of the Project, the local papers provided clues to changes in the city of Wilmington which were influencing intra-city movement as well as in-migration from other cities and rural areas.

The economic recession of 1960-61 seriously affected Wilmington. In fact, the unemployment report of the Secretary of Labor, Arthur J. Goldberg, listed Wilmington among twenty-six cities experiencing substantial unemployment, with more than 6 per cent of the local work force without jobs. Wilmington's unemployed work force reached 7.3 per cent on February 15, 1961 *(Wilmington Morning News,* March 25, 1961).

James M. Rosbrow, Secretary of the Delaware Unemployment Compensation Commission, reported the following employment conditions (Wilmington *Evening Journal,* March 26, 1961):

- Delaware is no longer a largely white collar and agricultural state.
- Delaware's economy is definitely in a recession trough.
- The situation in the less stable industries, notably automobile and construction, has caused most of the unemployment.

Because of the economic recession which reached a peak in the winter of 1960-61, a number of the established industrial plants in the Wilmington area closed down permanently. Among these were the Ford plant in Chester and a long-established floor covering plant in the city. There were frequent shut-downs in the automobile plants in the area.

Increasing unemployment throughout the period of winter storms threw many parents of Wilmington's elementary schoolchildren out of work. The schools made valiant efforts to provide emergency lunches, warm clothing, and shoes for children; and assisted in marshaling welfare agency aid for desperate families.

The effects of the economic recession and the severity of the winter are reflected in a report by the Director of the Department of Public Welfare which is quoted from the May 18, 1961 edition of the Wilmington *Evening Journal.*

> Public assistance caseloads showed a drop in April but were considerably higher than in the corresponding month of 1960, according to the monthly report of the Department of Public Welfare.
>
> Decreases from the March figures were noted by Edgar Hare, Jr., director, in the general assistance, aid to dependent children, and old age assistance categories, with an increase reported in aid to the disabled.
>
> A recap of the year to date by Hare describes the present fiscal year which ends June 30, as "without question the toughest year the department has ever experienced."
>
> Overall figures show 5,644 public assistance caseloads in April involving 14,625 persons. In March, the caseload figure was 5,830, with 15,372 persons reached. The caseload in April, 1960, was 5,216.
>
> Case closings were considerably higher than case openings in April, 542 compared with 356, a normal trend for this time of year, Hare said. In March there were 472 openings and 350 closings.
>
> General assistance figures, down by 166 cases from the March figure of 2,278, will probably continue on the down trend until October or November, the report notes, but because of the high degree of continued unemployment in industrial New Castle County, they may not decrease as much as in previous years.
>
> Aid to dependent children dropped 20 cases from 1,917 in March, and should also continue to decrease moderately for the next several months if "normal" conditions prevail.

Old age assistance dropped five cases from March's 1,239, and indicates no considerable change for the foreseeable future. In March all three of these categories had risen from the February figures.

Aid to the disabled, the only category to go up in April, showed an increase of five cases from the 396 March total.

Hare attributed the "toughest year" condition to "appropriations, known to be insufficient when they were made; the continuing burgeoning of the state's population; the slashing of employment by a business recession, and the sledgehammer blow of an impossible winter.

"Almost all the factors that increase the needs for welfare help were in the ascendancy, while the factors required to meet those needs were in confused retreat," Hare said.

"With needs rocketing at a velocity that would make Cape Canaveral envious, the department, rather than rising to the challenge, had to restrict its activities and cut its grants and services."

Housing continued to be a major problem of the city. The East Side's Poplar A Redevelopment Area was completely leveled. A scene of devastation was the daily fare of residents remaining on the East Side. A common experience of children of the Drew and Pyle Schools during the year was to find a substantial house, still sturdy in the morning sun, reduced to a mass of rubble by the noon hour.

What demolition of property means to people living in a neighborhood is a factor often lost sight of by those who are not personally affected. One illustration serves to focus on this problem. The Wilmington *Evening Journal* of May 18, 1961 carried the following report:

> Rats apparently are moving into homes vacated after sale to the State Highway Department along the Adams-Jackson Streets Thruway route.
>
> The buildings, not yet slated for demolition, are being examined by exterminators. Extermination, to prevent the rats from heading for inhabited areas, is necessary before demolition permits will be issued by the city building inspector's office.
>
> Highway Department officials say they are working on an extermination program but the problem has been complicated by the uncertain demolition schedule.
>
> An 1100 block North Adams Street mother said she is terrified "to let my boy out alone." She said the Highway Department had promised to check the vacant house next door where she had seen a rat enter.
>
> "The man I first talked to told me to get some hamburger and put ground glass in it and spread it around the house," the woman said. She refused because of danger to pets and children and added "it is up to them to take care of this."
>
> Ernest Hunter, sexton of Trinity Episcopal Church, told of seeing a big sewer rat crossing North Adams Street. "Some folks on their way to church had to stop and let it go by," he said.

Housing codes and code enforcement became acute problems that stimulated to action political groups, real estate interests, service organizations, and individual citizens. The proposed new housing code was being debated bitterly. Militant citizens' groups opposed what many considered to be the conversion of single-family homes to multi-family dwellings. Action was so forceful that the City Council ordered the redrafting of the new code.

The displacement of people living in the city, resulting from redevelopment plans and the closing of houses in the path of the thruway and the urge of many people to seek better housing in a restricted market were major factors in the movement of people within the city.

The schools reflected this movement in changing enrollments throughout the year:

▪ Lore School reflected a trend which indicated that there was a small but steady transfer of pupils from Drew, Pyle, and Williams schools. Drew School, which enrolled twenty-two white children in 1960-61 compared to two during 1959-60, noted a gradual increase in the number of white families moving into the East Side.

▪ Gray School, whose capacity is 1050 students, enrolled 1250 during 1960-61, and found it necessary to transfer two sections of kindergarten to North East School. Its anticipated enrollment for 1961-62 was 1350, which made it necessary to plan for redistricting of schools in the northeast and east side sections of the city.

These were but a few of the changes noted in the schools. In addition to the movement of people within the city, Wilmington continued to experience the effects of migration from other sections of the country, chiefly from the rural South and Puerto Rico.

The first definite information available on the increasing Puerto Rican population was revealed in an article by James Parks which appeared in *Dateline Delaware,* March-April 1961. While no official statistics were available, it was estimated that there were from 800 to 1000 Puerto Rican families living in the city. Most of these newcomers came from "tiny country villages nestled in the rugged Caribbean mountains." The bulk of the Puerto Rican population lived in the area bounded by Front and Ninth Streets and Tatnall and Adams Streets. One family living in Wilmington for six years had moved fourteen times. Rents were reported to be comparatively high and living conditions crowded. Households numbering from eight to ten persons were reported living in three rooms and sharing a bath with another family. For such living quarters, Puerto Ricans claimed they paid a monthly rent of from $75 to $85, often higher.

While Puerto Ricans newly arrived tended to seek shelter in the old, crowded sections of the city, they began to move west and north as they became adjusted. Language barriers, poverty, and lack of urban skills created hardships for a group of people that had the courage to seek something better than they had known before.

Signs of the Times

A number of significant national and local reports of population changes and their causes appeared during 1960-61.

Will Lissner, in *The New York Times,* May 7, 1961, reported factors influencing urban life in a national setting, having implications for Wilmington.

> Suburbs of the nation's twelve largest metropolitan areas have maintained a population 93 to 99 per cent white since 1930, population analysts were told here yesterday.
>
> Harry P. Sharp, director of the University of Michigan's Detroit area study, said that lack of money and mortgage credit had been an important factor in keeping non-whites, mostly Negroes, out of these suburbs.
>
> But the chief factor, he told the Population Association of America, is racial prejudice reflected in restrictive selling practices of all kinds.
>
> Working with the latest census data, he compared the white and non-white populations with those reported in previous censuses.
>
> The metropolitan areas studied were New York, Los Angeles-Long Beach, Chicago, Philadelphia, Detroit, San Francisco-Oakland, Boston, Pittsburgh, St. Louis, Washington, Cleveland, and Baltimore.
>
> Since 1930, the proportion of non-whites in the suburbs has risen very slightly, Mr. Sharp told the parley at the Barbizon-Plaza Hotel. Non-whites were 3 per cent of the total in 1930 and 5 per cent in 1960.
>
> In six of the twelve suburban areas, including New York, there has been almost no change in the ratio of the non-white population since 1930. In five—Philadelphia, Pittsburgh, Washington, Cleveland and Baltimore—the population of non-whites has declined. In one, San Francisco-Oakland, it has increased.
>
> This has happened despite what Henry S. Shyrock, Jr. of the Census Bureau called the "striking extent" to which Negroes are continuing to diffuse from the South to the North and West and from rural areas to big cities.
>
> As for the large cities themselves, Mr. Sharp said, eight of the twelve cities had considerably fewer whites than in 1930. The exceptions are New York, San Francisco and Washington, with about the same as in 1930, and Los Angeles, with more. But in all the central cities the proportion of whites has "declined drastically," Mr. Sharp said.

In an editorial, "What's Happening to Wilmington," the Wilmington *Evening Journal,* January 27, 1961, the following observations were made:

> Now that the Census Bureau is breaking down the population returns for Wilmington, the new figures for known trends are startling.
>
> Several months ago came the first surprise. Along with other old, rigidly-bounded cities, Wilmington population declined—from 110,-356 in 1950 to 95,827 in 1960. Now we learn what was happening within the total figures. During that 13 per cent decline the "non-white" part of the population has risen by nearly 46 per cent! It is now 26.2 per cent, up from 15.6.
>
> In the Wilmington public schools the percentage of Negroes is "just under 40 per cent." Why is this proportion so much higher than the proportion of Negroes in the total population? Largely because there are but few Negro boys and girls in the Catholic parochial schools.
>
> Let's go on with the youngsters. The percentage of residents under 18 has risen in the decade. In 1950, it was 25.5 per cent. In 1960 it was 30.4. Meanwhile the percentage of old people has gone up steeply—from the 8.8 per cent in 1950 to the 12.4 per cent in 1960.
>
> What does all this add up to? For one thing it puts in statistical perspective how very fast large Negro families have been coming in and how very fast the whites of child-rearing age have been moving out.
>
> What we have is a shrunken population that shows a steep increase in Negroes along with a plummeting drop in the whites who provide most of the residential property-tax revenue.

Census Bureau tabulations provided significant data for Wilmingtonians committed to fostering the ideal of equality of opportunity for all residents (Wilmington *Evening Journal,* May 24, 1961).

> Almost three of every ten Wilmington residents are non-whites, Census Bureau tabulations indicate.
>
> On the East Side, the Negro population is as high as 92.9 per cent in one census tract—No. 9 bordered by Walnut and Ninth Streets and Brandywine Creek, according to advance statistics released by the Welfare Council of Delaware.
>
> Others of the city's 25,075 non-white population are located in the near West Side, just beyond the central business district.
>
> The smallest concentration of non-whites in the city's total population of 95,827 are in Census Tracts 2, 3, 4, and 5.
>
> Tract 2, bounded by West Thirtieth Street, North Market and the city line, has a total of six non-white residents.
>
> Tract 3, west of Washington between Concord Avenue, West Thirtieth Street and the city line has one non-white resident.
>
> Tract 4, bounded by Brandywine Creek, Washington Street, Concord Avenue and the city line, has six Negro residents and

Tract 5, between the Brandywine and Thirtieth Street and North Market and Washington Streets—Baynard Boulevard, has 5.

The figures show that most of Wilmington's 36,419 non-whites live in areas where the highest concentrations of deteriorated dwellings exist.

Among them is Tract 8, north of the Brandywine between Northeast Boulevard and the Pennsylvania Railroad, where more than 50 per cent of the homes are rated as deteriorated.

This is true of the East Side where the percentage of deterioration ranges from 43.5 to 50.2.

The Census Bureau lists deteriorated housing as buildings which are dilapidated, with critical defects.

Welfare workers say Negroes live in the older areas of the city, where deterioration is most advanced, largely because they have nowhere else to go.

The figures also indicated that the rest of New Castle County, with a population of 211,619 has only 10,344 more Negro residents than the city of Wilmington—a total of 36,419, or only 5.4 per cent of the suburban population.

St. Georges Hundred with 1,267 Negroes in a total population of 5,218 has the highest percentage, whereas Brandywine Hundred, with a total population of 58,228, has only 324 Negro residents, or 0.6 per cent.

The movement of middle-income, white families to the suburbs; the racial restrictions on suburban living that affected a large segment of the population; and the migration of low-income white, colored, and Puerto Rican families to the city—all were factors presenting social and economic, as well as moral, implications.

On May 9, 1961, the Wilmington *Evening Journal* reported:

> The Kendree report on Wilmington's East Side singled out one of the greatest causes of urban blight—lack of enforcement of the city's health and zone codes.
>
> Three elements in the report prepared by Jack M. Kendree Planning Consultants, of Philadelphia, which called attention to poor code enforcement, were a surprisingly high number of residences in the area with inadequate sanitary facilities, overcrowding, and rubbish, debris and rubble scattered throughout the area.
>
> Prepared by the Philadelphia firm as a study of the area around the Poplar Street Project A redevelopment site, the report followed closely an appeal by the Health Department for more inspectors.
>
> In the center city and East Side, which the study divided according to census tracts, the survey found dwellings lacking facilities ranged from 2 per cent to 16 per cent.
>
> These three tracts, east of Walnut Street, between the Brandywine and Christina Rivers, all showed a high number of deteriorating dwellings, totalling more than 1,000 out of a total of 3,325. Rated as dilapidated, were 496 more.

The number of standard dwellings was only 1,588, yet the average rent per single room was just over $11.50 a week, the report showed.

That children pay the price for conditions over which they have no control is reflected in a report on delinquency by former State Senator James H. Snowden, chairman of the Delaware Youth Services Committee. (Wilmington *Evening Journal,* May, 1961)

> In September of 1957 there were 387 children on the rolls of the Youth Services Commission and "as of tonight there are 600," the speaker disclosed.
>
> "There are more than 126 boys at Ferris School now and it has a capacity of 90, and we have the same staff as if we had 50 to 70 boys.
>
> "The Youth Services Commission has 629 children in its custody, which is more than 11 other states, all with a larger population than Delaware."
>
> That delinquency is not a condition unique to deprived neighborhoods is revealed in further comments from Senator Snowden:
>
> "It is not necessary to live in a low social order, in broken homes, in poor financial condition, or to be of low intelligence to produce delinquents."
>
> Incidentally, the speaker said, Brandywine Hundred with all its advantages, compares poorly with Wilmington's East Side in the matter of delinquency . . .
>
> "If any of us thinks he is immune from the germ of delinquency, he is dead wrong. Our children are all exposed to it."

Living in School

Every teacher knows that a child brings to school with him each day all that he has experienced. In its Biennial Report, 1959-60, The Family Court of the State of Delaware in and for New Castle County, of which Wilmington is the major city, revealed information of great significance regarding children's living in as well as out of school. The Report cited an increase of 259 juvenile and 1379 adult cases of delinquency in the past year. Judge Francis A. Reardon commented as follows:

> Most devastating to the moral fibre of our community was the alarming breakdown of the family unit in New Castle County. The records of the Superior Court disclose that 553 divorces were granted in 1960. The impact that "broken homes" have upon children of the family is pathetically great. It is from this group that many children require the services of the Family Court and the associated agencies of our community. The apathy which the public has toward the increasing divorce rate and its consequences is nothing less than alarming. State legislatures are inclined to make divorce more easy and "Quickie Divorces" are fast approaching a

national scandal. Even churchmen are relaxing in their crusade against the "Crippler of the Home."

It is little wonder that the child of today, the youth of to-morrow, wonders *not where he is going but where he is coming from*. His home is broken, big business and some public officials offer nothing inspiring to him. Material things are the only things of value in the fast moving world that is swirling about him. It is no surprise that he finds himself so mixed up that he joins the large army of dependent and delinquent children.

Our Federal government is now cognizant of the fact that delinquency in our nation has reached such proportions that it is a national problem; that the individual states are unable to cope with the situation.

The government has declared a state of war against delinquency. Its aim is to defeat the enemy, not on the battlefield of the streets and corners, but in the home and the schools where the seed of delinquency is first discovered, long before it comes into contact with the law.

With help from the government; more assistance from the State; continued vigilance by the police and Courts, this tide of anti-social conduct can be turned back. However, if we are to win this war it will not be won by the Generals who are the Courts, police, social workers and all other child agencies who comprise the high command of this army. It will be won by the infantry—the parents of the juveniles. Parents must assume their responsibilities; their duty to raise their children to have respect for authority. The parents are the authority in the home. If the child has no respect for the authority of the home how can he be expected to respect the teacher, the police, the Court and the Rehabilitation Officers. This respect of reverence is not engendered by accident but it is the result of effort on the part of the parents. I have found that respect from children increases in direct proportion to the discipline they receive.

The responsibility of the parent to the child is one that cannot be delegated. There is no substitute for real parenthood, nor is it a part-time job. It is not the duty of the school to raise our children much less the juvenile baby-sitter. Our recreation centers are not for child guidance, they are our body builders and play makers. The Courts are not to play the role of foster parents. It is the parents' job to supervise their children.

Once this responsibility is assumed by the parents and the youth learns to understand that there is more love and affection in a parental "No" than there is in dignified acquiescence, our first skirmish is a victory.

A more encouraging picture is drawn in the annual report of the Youth Aid Division of the Bureau of Police in Wilmington, which—one year later—reflects a decrease in juvenile crimes within the city. (Wilmington *Evening Journal,* January 16, 1961)

Captain Hollahan said the success of the division in the working with juveniles during 1960 was due to an increase in the staff which allowed more thorough investigation of complaints, cooperation by the judges of Family Court, and cooperation of school authorities and parents who took time out to find out just what their sons and daughters were doing with their spare time.

Community Reflections in the Schools

Although parents have primary responsibility for their children, the schools know full well that many parents are unable to discharge this responsibility. Some parents, like some children, are frequently overwhelmed by the circumstances of their lives, because they, too, grew up in an environment of poverty, degradation, and deprivation. To expect competent and adequate parenthood from adults who, as children, have never experienced what it means to have good parents, is to deny all that we know of the influence environment has upon the growing child. For too long, well-meaning professionals, both in schools and in other community institutions, have used the "blame" technique in dealing with parents. It does not work. In the school- and community-oriented aspects of The Three-Year Experimental Project on Schools in Changing Neighborhoods, an attempt was made to assay our responsibility of providing coordinated services for children *and their families* in order to help them in solving the problems of living more adequately.

In the school-oriented aspect of the Project, diagnostic techniques and instruments were used to determine children's perceptions of their world. Finding out more about how children feel and what their recognized and unrecognized needs are serves two purposes. When the causes of children's behavior are revealed to teachers, they tend to develop an empathy with children which results in closer bonds of affection and concern. When teachers care more about children, they are more effective in helping them. These are primary purposes in the use of diagnostic techniques and instruments.

Of equal value in diagnosis of needs is the opportunity it provides for making sure that the curriculum is centered in the real needs of children. When children are motivated to learn because what they are learning in school has carry-over value for the solution of personal and family problems, their effort and achievement tend to be greater and of more lasting quality.

Section II, "Curriculum Building in Schools in Changing Neighborhoods," reports fully on ways and means used by Project participants to affect children's social and academic learning so that it may help them in building a better life for themselves.

Section III, "The Community Organizes for Action," relates the efforts made by agencies and organizations in Wilmington to coordinate their programs in an attempt to help people in becoming more able to help themselves.

Project schools have found that when teachers have a moral commitment to the premise that "all children are our children," matters of

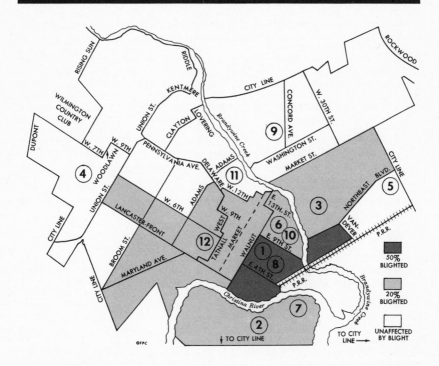

Creeping Blight—Wilmington, like many other cities, is threatened by creeping blight. The East Side (dark-shaded) is worst affected with over half of the homes in a state of dilapidation. From there the blight is creeping westward and has already affected one in five homes in the lightly shaded area. The letters on the map locate the schools participating in the Project:

1. Drew School
2. Elbert School
3. Gray School
4. Lore School
5. North East School
6. Opportunity School
7. Palmer School
8. Pyle School
9. Shortlidge School
10. Stubbs School
11. Washington School*
12. Williams School

* Washington School closed September 1961.–Map reproduced by permission of the Welfare Council of Delaware.

race, religion, and economic status are no longer blocks to teacher-child-family relationships.

The principal who responds to the question, "What proportion of your children are Negro?" with, "I don't know; I'm not aware of color when I live with the children," has moved beyond the color barrier. The white teacher who roundly protests the exclusion of her Negro boys from a youth organization shows her concern for children, not colored children or white children. The parents in a well-to-do neighborhood who request special permission for their children to go out of district for an integrated school experience have moved quite a distance from their earlier position that demanded redistricting to permit their children to attend a uniracial school. This change in position is a direct outgrowth of efforts by the school staff.

When administrative leadership accepts the responsibility for making it possible for teachers to learn new skills and new applications of old skills, there is less turnover in staff and greater power for recruiting a racially integrated staff. In the spring of 1961, for the first time, white applicants for teaching positions were sometimes asking for assignments in predominantly Negro schools. During 1960-61, there was less turnover in staff, and this trend continued while preparing for the staffing of schools for 1961-62.

While many hurdles remained, the second year of the Project highlighted a new morale based upon pride in what was being accomplished, a new satisfaction in the job of teaching, and a stabilization in school living in which incidents reflecting racial prejudice were becoming increasingly rare among staff, children, and parents.

Project Schools in Their Neighborhood Settings

Probably more than any other social institution, the public elementary school is becoming the "constant" factor in the life of a neighborhood. Neighborhoods change, new families replace old ones, churches follow their congregations to the suburbs, housing is torn down and replaced, single family homes become multi-family homes, business establishments replace residences, customs and ways of living change, but the public elementary school remains a changing institution in a changing setting in the same neighborhood. It is committed to the responsibility of accepting the children of the neighborhood and providing for them the kind of education that fosters the full flowering of their personalities, the fulfillment of their capacities, and the achievement of a good life.

To meet its responsibilities, the public elementary school must look at itself in its neighborhood setting. And what it finds provides the clues to the direction of its educational program in all of its aspects.

As the public elementary schools in Wilmington prepared for the second year of participation in the Project, it was found that the six original Project schools would continue their participation, and that an increased number of staff members would enter the Project. The neighborhood settings of these six schools in their first year of participation are described in Chapter One.

In addition, six more schools decided to enter the Project, so that a total of twelve out of fifteen[1] elementary schools in the city became participants. As a result, teacher participation increased from 65 the first year to 165 the second, or approximately 52 per cent of the teaching staff.

The neighborhood settings of the six schools entering the Project for the first time in the fall, 1960, are reported by their principals.

Charles B. Lore School

Location: Fourth Street and Woodlawn Avenue

Enrollment as of September 30, 1960: 1006

Staff: 35 classroom teachers (including 2 for blind, 2 for deaf, and 2 for educable retarded)

5 full-time teachers in specialized areas (2 for physical education, 1 for library, art, music)

2 part-time teachers in specialized areas (instrumental music, speech)

3 service personnel (nurse, full-time; psychologist and social worker, part-time)

Until recently, the economic status of the community could have been described as one of great variety with a good number of families in the upper middle-income class. This situation is changing rather rapidly. It is expected that the community will become a middle- to low-income neighborhood. There is a largely harmonious mixing of racial elements.

Participation in School and Community Life. Services for children and/or families are provided by various churches and the West End Neighborhood House.

There is increased mobility of population, with an influx of groups with a lower economic, educational, and cultural background than those they are replacing.

Traditionally the parents are very alert and active. But this

---

[1] A new school, North East, was opened in 1960-61.

interest is presently being maintained by a numerically decreasing group. There is an almost frantic desire on the part of some P.T.A. members to maintain past standards.

There is relatively light use of the school facilities for after-school activities. There are some school- and P.T.A.-sponsored play groups, Scout and Cub programs, and P.T.A. meetings.

Factors Significant in the School Program. There is an increase in the numbers of children from broken homes and of "door-key" children. These children are mainly from the lower economic-cultural levels. Teachers are confronted with a greater percentage of children of low ability while class sizes are on the increase.

Participation on the part of the staff in community affairs and activities seldom goes beyond P.T.A. meetings.

North East School (opened September 1, 1960)

Location: Claymont Street and Todds Lane
Enrollment as of September 30, 1960: 576
Staff: 18 classroom teachers
    1 full-time teacher in specialized area (physical education)
    3 part-time teachers in specialized areas (art, vocal music, library)
    1 nurse

General Description of the School Community. Low-rent housing project, many welfare cases, all incomes under $5,000.

Participation in School and Community Life. Services for children and/or families are provided by Kingswood Community Center, Presbyterian Church, and Roman Catholic Church.

The newness of the community, the homes, and the school demands an educational program that will weld forces together to build a good, strong community feeling.

We intend to ask parents to volunteer for work in the cafeteria, the library, preschool registration, and special projects. The P.T.A. will be organized as soon as possible.

The community at large will probably use the library, the cafeteria, the multipurpose room, and the gymnasium of the school.

Factors Significant in the School Program. Some parents are now intimately involved in Kingswood, P.T.A., and Community Center activities.

The principal is a member of the board of directors of the Kingswood Community Center. Some staff members will probably participate in this center's program. All will do much visiting in homes on a regular basis.

The goals of the school program will be determined by the staff. There are some inter-age groups—unit level grouping, some traditional grouping, and we have two individual progress classes.

Opportunity School
(for trainable, mentally retarded children)

Location: Twelfth and Poplar Streets (since this report was written the school has been relocated at Baynard Boulevard and Concord Avenue)

Enrollment as of January 1961 (date of entrance into Project): 65

Staff: 8 full-time classroom teachers
11 full-time service personnel (1 nurse, 2 teacher's aides, 4 bus attendants, 4 bus drivers)

General Description of the School Community. The children are of a heterogeneous background, ranging from the lowest to the highest socio-economic, intellectual, and educational levels.

All children depend on school bus transportation. They come from all sections of the city and a few come from suburban areas.

Participation in School and Community Life. Services for children and/or families are provided by:
Welfare Department
Delaware Association for Retarded Children
Boys Scouts
Girl Scouts
Neighborhood church groups
Neediest Families Fund
Christmas Stocking
The hospital clinics
Aid to Dependent Children
Delaware Society for Crippled Children and Adults
Kingswood Community Center

Children enrolled in Opportunity School come from many different neighborhoods. The percentage of children from the lower socio-economic areas is on the increase.

The parents from the better neighborhoods assume leadership in the P.T.A. Although they have made a tremendous effort, and even have provided transportation for them, these leaders find it difficult to get some of the other parents to participate.

All staff members belong to the Delaware Association for Retarded Children and all are active in community activities in their own neighborhoods. Since we do not have a defined school community, staff members do not have the opportunity to participate in school community affairs.

Factors Significant in the School Program. The children in Opportunity School will always need some supervision.

Our educational goals are to help these retarded children to acquire—
(1) greater self-sufficiency through self-help;
(2) social and emotional adjustment; and
(3) economic usefulness.

Children are grouped on the basis of:
1. Chronological age except in the two classes of older children. (The school tries not to have an age span of more than three years in any group.)
2. Level of intellectual, social, and emotional adjustment, and of self-sufficiency development.

Areas of need in the curriculum are—
(1) continued emphasis on interpersonal relationships;
(2) expanded opportunities for more children to have some home-making experiences; and
(3) a prevocational training program for the older children, who show readiness for transfer to Opportunity Center (a sheltered workshop).

Palmer and Elbert Schools

Location: Palmer—Claymont and Lobdell Streets
　　　　　Elbert—Townsend and C Streets

Enrollment as of September 30, 1906: Palmer—235
　　　　　　　　　　　　　　　　　　　Elbert—466

Staff: Palmer—9 classroom teachers
　　　8 part-time teachers in specialized areas (kindergarten, music, art, library, physical education, instrumental, piano, speech)
　　　Elbert—14 classroom teachers
　　　7 part-time teachers in specialized areas (music, art, library, physical education, piano, instrumental, speech)
　　　Elbert-Palmer combined—4 Professional Service Personnel (nurse, psychologist, social worker, home visitor)

General Description of the School Communities. A great change has taken place in the Palmer area. Formerly, Ukrainians lived here who usually owned their homes. They were very much interested in the care of the homes and community. These families have now moved to the suburbs. Most of the families who replaced them are colored. They have very low incomes, and many are dependent on welfare. Living conditions are poor.

In the Elbert School area, most families live in the Southbridge Extension, a Federally-sponsored low-income housing development. These families have low incomes and many are on welfare.

In both areas, parents take little interest in the appearance of homes or communities. Broken bottles and other debris litter the streets. Parents do not take the needed interest in their children's academic achievements.

There is an increase in the number of children with low ability, of emotionally disturbed children, and of children who do not get proper food and rest.

Participation in School and Community Life. Services for children and/or families are provided by the Mary Todd Gambrill Neighborhood House and the Southbridge Community Center. The latter has a clinic one day a week.

Parents in the Palmer School are reluctant to take any responsibility. They seldom participate in school activities. The attendance at P.T.A. is not what it should be.

Elbert School area parents do not attend P.T.A. as they should. A few parents volunteer their services to the school.

Palmer School is used for political meetings, Ukrainian social gatherings, and as a recreational center. Elbert School is used by church groups, Boy Scouts, political activities, and as a recreational center.

Factors Significant in the School Program. A number of parents are interested in their churches and church activities. A few parents are involved in the drum and bugle corps activities.

There is very little participation by staff members in community affairs. One teacher is very much interested in the recreational activities in the community. The members of the staff believe that they should meet the individual needs of the pupils and instill in them the values and standards of good citizenship.

In the Palmer School, the children are in heterogeneous groups. In the Elbert School, the children are grouped according to their reading ability and maturity levels. We are studying and developing skills necessary in the elementary school.

In both schools, there is a need for better understanding and for help in solving children's problems because of poor home and community environment.

Frederick D. Stubbs School

Location: Eleventh and Pine Streets

Enrollment as of September 30, 1960: 708

Staff: 23 classroom teachers
4 full-time teachers in specialized areas (art, music, library, physical education)
1 full-time service personnel (nurse)
8 part-time service personnel (psychologist, social worker, visiting teacher, speech teacher, lipreading teacher, dental hygienist, doctor, dentist)

General Description of the School Community. Compared to the city as a whole, the economic level may be described as average or lower than average. Compared to the East Side as a whole, it is considered above average.

The offices of five leading Negro physicians are located in this area, three of whom reside here. Two dentists and one chiropodist live and practice in the area.

Some parents are skilled or semi-skilled workers, but most of them are unskilled laborers or domestic servants.

Approximately one-fourth of the families receive assistance from the State Welfare Board. Applications for free dental work are numerous.

Housing ranges from excellent to horrible. About two-thirds of the families rent their homes. Many of these are overcrowded. Rents are exorbitant.

Participation in School and Community Life. Services for children and/or families are provided by:

Walnut Street Branch YMCA and YWCA
Peoples Settlement House
Christina Community Center
Family Court
Stubbs Community Center
City Park Association
One church center
The city and state social agencies

Changes occurring in the community which call for changes in the educational program are:

1. Exodus of middle and upper income families desiring to escape the unfortunate "East Side" or "slum area" label
2. The increasing number of mentally disturbed children—last year, six were committed to other institutions, a record for Stubbs School
3. The increase in the number of broken families replacing the stable families who are moving
4. The increase in the number of families who rent their homes

Changes occurring in pupil population which call for changes in the educational program are:

1. An increase in the number of families that move—more cases of frequent withdrawals and re-entries
2. The decline of economic status—more need for free lunches and clothing
3. An increase in the number of after-school fights
4. An increase in juvenile delinquency
5. The decrease of the median I. Q.

Parents are very active in all school activities, with this exception that it is becoming increasingly difficult to recruit P.T.A. officers from among them.

Girl Scout meetings, plays by church groups, banquets, and musical programs are typical of the uses made of the school.

There is an extended school program—two afternoons weekly for elementary children and two evenings weekly for teen-agers and adults. The evening program has failed to draw the adults as well as we had hoped. It is chiefly recreational with some educational offerings in the fields of music and art. A survey of the parents has revealed interest in cooking, sewing, and repairing—interests that can be met more adequately by the area's high school.

Factors Significant in the School Program. Some parents are active in agencies such as Peoples Settlement, YMCA, YWCA, and fraternal organizations. Two are Sunday school superintendents, several are choir members, several are active in the various association membership drives and annual programs. The art teacher is president and organizer of an East Side Arts Council, which aims to interest the community in aesthetic values.

The staff's philosophy centers in the belief that the creation of an efficient social personality is the goal of public education.

There is grade organization from kindergarten through grade six. Grade 1-6 children are divided into four groups according to their level of social and mental maturity—mostly by subjective standards. Then each grade teacher is given an equal number of each of the four divisions of pupils.

There was one sixth-grade section which, at the completion of the primary work, was grouped according to achievement based upon teacher judgment and test scores. This group was assigned to the same teacher who had taught it in grade 5. A similar class, which had the same teacher in their fourth and fifth years of experience, completed grade 6 in June 1960.

There is a genuine attempt to understand each child's health and home problems, and to set goals that he can meet. Excellent use is made of all specialized personnel. Curriculum and field trips are used wisely, and there is some use of parents as resource persons. There is a good follow-up of the testing program, many kinds of books and resource materials, and some unit teaching. Each member makes efforts to plan with children.

Kaleidoscope of the City

The constantly changing facets of life in the city make it difficult to categorize elementary school neighborhoods, but the economic status of the participating school communities may be identified loosely as economically deprived in the case of Drew, Pyle, Williams, Stubbs, Gray, North East, Palmer, Elbert, and Opportunity schools; and as middle or upper middle in the case of Shortlidge, Washington, and Lore schools.

While it is possible to thus categorize the participating schools, the following facts are of significance to the schools in planning appropriate educational programs for all the children:

1. Each participating school, regardless of the neighborhood's general economic status, enrolls children of families in all income brackets.

2. Each school's enrollment includes the children of families adhering to a vast range of values.

3. Each school's enrollment includes children representing the total range of human capacities, intellectual, emotional, and physical.

4. Each school's enrollment includes children who may be called the "advantaged," for the crippling influence of poverty upon children may

be avoided by parents whose love and care make it possible for a child to flourish in an environment of genuine emotional security. Project participants continually found ample evidence of this in what our economically deprived children said and did. When a child who looks at his degrading physical environment can say, "I like my neighborhood because my neighbor takes me in when I am cold;" when a child can write, "I want to be a plumber but first I must get my schooling. My mother never had schooling and she says that it is the most important thing a boy can have," then teachers know that values to live by are rooted in people, not in material possessions. This is the factor that makes a potent force of education focused on human relations skills, sensitivities, knowledge, and information.

Looking at a School Community in Rapid Change

How does it *feel* to face the fact that the house you struggled to buy is in the path of the bulldozers? How does it *feel* to reach retirement age and find that the house you prepared for your old age has been "overdeveloped" and the appraiser for the Public Housing Authority tells you that you must accept financial loss in the forced moving from your home? How does it *feel* to suffer the loss of a neighbor's care of your children while you are at work? How does it *feel* to lose the credit extended you by the neighborhood store in times of trouble? How does it *feel* to remain in a once friendly neighborhood and find each day new desolation, new rubble, and new loneliness created by the demolition of substandard homes?

The faculties of the Drew and Pyle Schools knew that feelings can be more important than facts, such as those connected with the redevelopment of deprived neighborhoods. Most of the teachers no longer lived in their school neighborhood. Most of them drove back to their homes in better neighborhoods at the close of the day. Each day, they lived with the children who brought their family and neighborhood experiences to school with them. But they realized that, no matter how well they knew the school neighborhood through the children, there still was much they did not know.

Accordingly, during Fall Workshop Week in September 1960, the staff members of Drew and Pyle schools set out on foot to discover for themselves what the neighborhood of their school district was like. Dividing into teams under a teacher leader thoroughly acquainted with the district, they covered every street that sent children to the two schools. The following reports reflect the sensitivity, insight, and understanding of teachers who seek to fulfill a commitment to children.

As the principal, Mrs. Kathryn Hazeur, related yesterday, there are many forces at work in the neighborhood which we serve. A quick glance at this community would indicate that by our standards these forces are all undesirable. However, a more thoughtful look reveals that there are positive as well as negative forces influencing the boys and girls whom we teach.

While most of you are familiar with many of the negative forces in the area, the team would like to bring to your attention that:

1. Many properties show little or no care. High grass borders the curbs. Battered sidewalks make walking precarious. The lack of paint and the need for obvious repairs make some houses appear unkept.

2. In spite of demolition, there is still a great number of taverns and liquor stores in the community.

3. There is evidence that a numbers bank is operating in a grocery store. Numbers are clearly displayed on cards in the window.

4. The smell of leather being processed in a tannery located in this residential area is quite penetrating. It makes being out of doors quite unpleasant.

5. Many buildings not included in the demolition project are vacant. This seems to indicate a tendency to flee from this uneasy neighborhood.

If it is true that good overcomes bad, then there is great hope for this community. Surprisingly, the positive factors which the team found outweighed the negative. These are:

1. Two very strong political organizations are working for the good of the community.

2. The Church of God, St. Mary's Church, Sisters of St. Francis, Bethel A.M.E. Church, Shiloh Baptist Church, and Christina Church represent religious influences touching many lives directly and indirectly.

3. Drew, Pyle, St. Mary's, St. Stanislaus, and Bancroft schools are in this community. These schools have opportunities for unlimited positive influence.

4. Lest we forget, this community can point with pride to such historical monuments as Old Swedes Church and the Hendrickson Museum.

5. The Christina Center helps boys and girls use leisure time wisely.

6. We saw many houses which were quite livable, and there is evidence of some care in their appearance. Many houses have recently been painted, especially on lower Sixth Street. Formstone has been added to the fronts of others. Flower boxes and small gardens were a noticeable touch of beauty.

7. The expected groups of loafers were absent. Those persons that were in the streets seemed to be engaged in something useful. Others were walking to and from somewhere.

8. The people were friendly and seemed willing to talk. They seemed especially well informed about the demolition project.

As I walked, there was one thing which made me pause. It was the feeling of uncertainty which seemed to permeate the air. Even though I am acquainted with the development of Project A, at times I am still startled by this part of the East Side's new look. Knowing how much the familiar helps to establish stability in our lives, I wonder what the children or even the adults think or feel when they look at all the shattered buildings and empty spaces around them. While this situation is only temporary and the buildings will be replaced, it still means that a way of life in this community is slipping away. While progress is good and change inevitable they are often the cause of many temporary problems.

I feel that for quite a while to come we will have to bear the brunt and deal with the children of this unsettled community. However, with thoughtful awareness, a little insight, and a great deal of patience, we will meet this challenge.

— Muriel Cooper

REPORT ON NEIGHBORHOOD 2

"Redevelopment" is an appalling word. It conveys a mental picture of mass destruction—destruction of homes once beloved by many families, of the corner store that seemed to be always open, of small, nondescript churches that saved many a wandering soul.

Although the homes were substandard—bursting at the seams with five or six too many people, they housed, in many instances, happy be it somewhat haphazard families. Many of these people were migrants from the Deep South and victims of high-rent landlords. This is the picture that flashed through my mind as I strolled from Eight and Walnut Streets toward Front Street.

Where have these families gone? Many went to nearby housing projects and some to west Wilmington—areas that were one step up for them. Surely, this shows forced advancement. Will they carry their old ways of living with them? This remains to be seen —the probability we know.

As we continued to walk the old, brick-type pavements, we could picture the new East Side—possibly modern apartment houses stretching skyward, semi-detached homes with trees in every block, and playground areas to keep children well occupied in their spare time. In this picture the corner store is absent. Instead, we see a conveniently located shopping center nearby.

One would say that this is a complete change from the past. Yes, a different higher-income group would enter, and a new spirit would permeate the entire area.

Yes, the word "redevelopment" sounds dismal, but the phrase, "Every cloud has a silver lining," dispels the gloom.

— Beily Byrd

REPORT ON NEIGHBORHOOD 3

One of the highlights of our fall workshop was a walking tour through the immediate vicinity of Drew and Pyle Schools. Teachers were divided into groups, and each group was assigned a given area.

The group to which I was assigned toured Seventh Street from Lombard and back up Eighth Street to Lombard.

On the tour we saw very few people. There was evidence of changes being made; many houses had been evacuated and others were boarded up prior to later demolition. Some houses, still inhabited, seemed in poor condition. In one particular block the houses were exceptionally well kept.

We were quite concerned with the condition of the sidewalks. Few were in good repair. Most of them were littered with broken bottles and in very poor condition.

A highlight of our tour was a visit to the beautiful and well-kept Christina Park. This park faces the water and is quiet and peaceful. From an educational point of view, Christina Park is a "gold mine." It is seething with historical, aesthetic, artistic, and recreational values. The park attendant told us that literature is being prepared concerning the history of the Park and may soon be ready for publication. — Sadie Peterson

One of the teachers taking the tour of this neighborhood recalled an earlier experience which she has reported below.

On the last Sunday in August each year, Mother A.U.M.P. Church, at Eighth and French Streets, holds its annual Founder's[1] Day Meeting called the "August Quarterly." This annual affair attracts people from far and near and from all walks of life.

This past August Quarterly, as I was walking toward Ninth and French Streets, I overheard a very striking conversation going on between two young girls. After having worked with the Project for a period of one year, I realized that these youngsters were indirectly giving me some very valuable information. I became so engrossed in their conversation that I actually stopped and listened until they changed the subject. The visiting girl said to her little friend as she looked all around, "Wilmington is a dumpy old town because you don't have no nice houses and stores. I don't like Wilmington. You live in a dumpy old town." Wilmington child: "You live in a dumpy town, too." Visitor: "Oh, no I don't. My town is pretty because we have nice houses and lots of pretty stores." Wilmington child: "My mother says we are gonna have some new ones." Visitor: "I don't care. I don't ever want to come to Wilmington again. It's too dumpy." — Rosa J. Peaco

The Status of Change in Project School Neighborhoods

As part of their annual progress report for the second year of participation, principals of Project schools were asked to report changes which seemed to be occurring in neighborhoods during the school year 1960-61. Their reports follow. They are significant because they reflect hopeful signs of prevention of deterioration in one neighborhood, and of rapid or subtle change in others.

---

[1] Peter Spencer.

Drew-Pyle Schools

1. Razing of the houses for the Poplar Street A Project is 95 per cent complete. The last buildings will be razed July 15, 1961.
2. Public concern for the area surrounding the Poplar A Project may mean further demolition or rehabilitation of substandard properties in the area.
3. Public concern for locating the Government Service Building at Seventh and French Streets, and the Post Office near Front and French Streets, may have great influence on the type of community developed around Drew and Pyle Schools.
4. There is a decrease in Puerto Rican population, and an increase in the Spanish and Greek populations. Thirteen of these children are in our schools. Five of them are between the ages of 11 and 13. These five are attending school for the first time.
5. Three white families that lived in this community several years ago have returned to the area. Unemployment forced their return to this low-rent neighborhood.
6. Expansion of the industrial park at the foot of Seventh Street has resulted in an increase of traffic around our schools.

Elbert-Palmer Schools

1. A greater number of our parents are depending on public welfare.
2. Although it is not permitted by regulations, a number of families secretly move in with relatives who have obtained apartments in the low-rent Federal housing project.

Gray School

1. The tremendous increase in Negro population in our school district resulting from changing property ownership during 1960-61 presents a very serious problem in adjusting curriculum and methods to meet needs of this student body. This trend continues with many houses constantly being put on the market by white owners. As shown in recent California Mental Maturity Test Charts, one-fourth of our children in the lower quantile score below 79, the Median I.Q. being about 90.
2. There is the likelihood of continued lowering of standards. For the present, a rezoning proposal which would permit houses to be broken up into small apartments has not been approved by the city council. However, this tendency has begun to menace the district. If the council does not approve the change in zoning, it may keep slum conditions from rapidly overtaking the district. Nevertheless, there is already an increase in conversion, in deterioration of property, and in the number of large families housed in many single-family dwellings. The lowering of the caliber of living is likely to affect the school greatly.
3. The new change in the Gray School district should relieve the school of overcrowding. If this should allow us to keep many of the classes slightly smaller, the kind of program we know is desirable could more easily be put into effect. Just the reduction in numbers would have a favorable effect on the children—and teachers.

Lore School

1. There appears to be an increase in conversion of homes in at least one area; though the increase is not at present great, it may be portentous.

Shortlidge-Washington Schools

A. Shortlidge Area:
1. Our big change came three years ago. Since then we have held our ground. Prices of homes have not continued to fall.
2. The conversion of single-family homes to multi-family dwellings has not continued. Houses are being well cared for.
3. Gardens are being cared for.
4. Junior high school zoning seems to be a concern.
B. Washington Area:
1. The thruway houses are being torn down.
2. Parking facilities have been improved.
3. Some improvement in stores has taken place.
4. Houses are in just as good condition as before, generally.
5. Prices are holding.
6. A few Puerto Ricans have moved into the neighborhood. They are not a problem.
7. Junior high school zoning seems to be a concern.

Stubbs School

1. As the medium-income families and established Wilmington families move to other areas, Negro families with less stable incomes replace them.
2. Some families, not in the Project A area, and who otherwise would be satisfied, resent the association of the entire East Side with the term "slum area," and are contemplating to move.
3. New horizons in employment for Negroes could possibly raise the status of many neighborhood families, providing the trend toward moving is stabilized.

Williams School

1. Demolition of property for the thruway has not meant a decrease of population—only more people living in the remaining cramped quarters. The change has meant even poorer housing.
2. Negroes from the East Side have flocked to the area around Jefferson Street. Homes are rapidly becoming substandard.
3. The appearance of the neighborhood has gone down. Beautifying or improving property seems an impossible task, and for the most part is not done by owner or renter.

Opportunity School

1. Since we have admitted new children only from the city and since most of the new children are from the low-income groups, there has been a marked change downward in the student and parent population. If the county children should be removed, this change will be even more marked than it is now.

2. Such a change would affect the P.T.A. unfavorably, because it is the parents from the higher socio-economic groups who run the P.T.A. and provide transportation for the others. It will be a real problem to get our working and less able parents to leave their home communities and provide leadership in Opportunity School P.T.A. Many of our parents are members of three or four P.T.A. groups. It is more convenient to participate in neighborhood school activities than to have to go across town at nighttime.

North East School

1. Our parents are young and are still having children (whether the father lives at home or not). For 1961-62 we will have only four intermediate classes. All others are grade three or below.

3

A City Touched by the Sun

During the third year of The Three-Year Experimental Project on Schools in Changing Neighborhoods, 1961-62, a reexamination of the impact made by the forces at work in the city was undertaken.

A House of Want

The ills of a city are the ills of its people. As with people, the ills of a city must be diagnosed before treatment can begin. Where ills are multiple, a city lies prostrate and its people are crippled physically and spiritually. Participants in the Project were determined that the city would not become a house of want. But the signs of illness were conspicuous. Its symptoms had led the citizens to seek out causes so that remedies could be devised.

City planners frequently use the term, "overgrown but underplanned." This term may well be descriptive not only of the present but also of the future situation unless professional city planning becomes an adjunct of the present.[1] Although the 1960 United States Census reveals that Wilmington suffered a population loss of 13 per cent since 1950, the tenth largest loss among 129 cities, the population analysis of Wilmington prepared by the Welfare Council of Delaware indicated that by 1970 a truly explosive population spurt could be expected. The *Kiplinger Washington Newsletter* of January 1962 is quoted:

> Delaware's population in 1975 will exceed the 1960 total by 366,000 or 82 per cent. In a special forecast of 15-year population increases for 19 states, Delaware stood fourth percentagewise behind Arizona, Nevada, and Florida.

It is unlikely that Wilmington's population will not be affected by increases predicted for the State. This is especially true in the light of increasing urbanization trends in the city.

---

[1] A city planner was appointed on July 3, 1962.

Factors related to the racial composition of the city's population provide ample evidence of a coming population boom. The Negro birth rate is much higher than the white birth rate. Wilmington has a declining white population (24 per cent) and an increasing Negro population (45 per cent). The 1960 birth rate for Negroes was twice that for whites. Currently, 42 per cent of the population under 20 years of age is Negro. In 1950, one of six people in the city was a Negro; in 1960, one of four was a Negro. While the white population is an aging one, the Negro population is young. The average age of Negro women is approximately 21 years, while that of white women is approximately 36. This means that among women of childbearing age, the number of Negro women greatly exceeds that of white women; and that a much larger percentage of Negroes may be expected by 1970.

"American cities are faced with a population explosion as acute as any in Asia and Africa," a University of Chicago sociologist, Dr. Donald J. Bogue said in a speech at the annual meeting of the Planned Parenthood Federation of America. He said that fertility rates among low-income and minority groups in the nation's cities are only a few points below the highest rates ever recorded in India and other overpopulated countries. (*Evening Journal,* October 24, 1961, Wilmington)

Within the city, the displacement of people continued to be reflected in population changes in all areas. The central business district suffered a loss of 42 per cent. The East Side lost 37 per cent. Areas of the city reflecting large increases in population were the northeast section, with a gain of 124 per cent, and the west side, with a 22 per cent gain.

Recreational opportunities become of increasing significance to people on the move. In 1961-62, eleven of the eighteen recreational agencies in the city were concentrated in an area that had only 22 per cent of the population under 18 years of age. Only one recreational agency was located in the section of the city having the greatest need.

A more detailed analysis of needs in specific aspects of community life is warranted if a true assessment of the ills of the city is to be attained.

Economic Trends

The *Evening Journal* of April 23, 1962, is quoted:

> The U.S. Department of Commerce reported per capita income in Delaware last year at $3,026. This was $13 higher than in 1960 and tops among the 50 states. The national average was $2,265, up from $2,223 in 1960.

Wilmington, the largest city in the state, is one of extremes of great wealth and great poverty. In 1961, one-fourth of Wilmington's families had a substandard income of less than $3000. When this startling fact is viewed in the context of general increases in family income for the state, the significance of the economic level of city dwellers assumes new importance. An editorial in the *Evening Journal,* February 19, 1962, is quoted:

> What jumps out is the fact that the median income of Delaware families in the decade has nearly doubled—from the $3,193 of 1950 to the $6,197 of 1960! Allowing for inflation, that is an amazing increase, and confirms Delaware in solid first place in per capita income.
>
> This general affluence can sensibly be viewed alongside some other striking facts of life today in Delaware. The number of families earning over $10,000 a year has risen tenfold, from 2,085 to a shade under 22,000!

In the midst of wealth, conditions in the city reflect the instability and insecurity of the economic status of many city families. It will be recalled that the winter of 1960-61 marked a period of acute unemployment. News stories and reports in the *Evening Journal* during the school year 1961-62 reveal the uncertainties faced by city families.

August 8, 1961:

> Foreclosures in homes in New Castle County are at an all-time record rate, Sheriff Frederick Klair reported today.
>
> The sheriff said that in this year's three terms of court, sheriff sales have been running more than 100 per term with 120 sales scheduled for the September term, compared to an average last year of 75 sales per term.
>
> Per terms of court, the sheriff's office is now listing four sales per day instead of three as in previous years. The average sales per day is running 25 to 27.

February 1, 1962:

> The number of unemployed in Delaware rose by 200 in December, but the total was 800 below the figure for the same month in 1960.
>
> With an estimated 8,500 out of work in mid-December, the unemployed represented 4.4 per cent of the state's total labor force of 193,500, compared with 4.8 per cent a year earlier, the Unemployment Compensation Commission reported yesterday.
>
> The number of people holding wage and salaried jobs—that excludes farm workers and the self-employed—showed no change from November to December. The total was 154,300.
>
> A loss of 400 jobs in manufacturing industries was offset by a gain of the same number in non-manufacturing.

March 24, 1962:

> Total employment rose by 900 jobs and unemployment by 1,200 between Jan. 15 and Feb. 15 in the Wilmington labor market.

At the end of the period, employment totaled 151,800. The total jobless stood at 10,600.

The total labor force, 162,400 on Feb. 15, was a gain of 2,100 over the previous month, 600 from mid-February 1961.

These facts were disclosed today by Joseph A. Bradshaw, chairman-executive director of the Employment Security Commission.

The Wilmington labor market area covers New Castle County and Salem County in New Jersey.

The Feb. 15 unemployment estimates represent 6.5 per cent of the total labor force.

Wilmington area manufacturing workers received $107.32 in earnings for the week ending Feb. 17, on the basis of a 39.6 hour workweek and average hourly earnings of $2.71. Average weekly earnings were $1.48 lower than comparable January figures but were $3.17 higher than in February 1961.

Unemployment of youth became an acute problem.

The Delaware Commission on Children and Youth has informed Delaware members of Congress that it considers passage of a federal youth employment opportunities program vital for Delaware youth.

There are more than 1,000 unemployed young people under 21 registered with the State Employment Service, 65 per cent of whom lack high school education, and many with no work experience at all.

A combination program of retraining and work experience is needed to prevent the development of a group of "hardcore unemployables" for the decade ahead, with its attendant problems of welfare, allowances, delinquency, and crime, according to a report on out-of-school, unemployed youth in Delaware today issued by the commission. (*Evening Journal*, Jan. 26, 1962)

Added to the usual instability of fluctuating unemployment trends is the threat of automation which already is a reality in some of the Wilmington area industries. A report from the *Evening Journal*, May 4, 1962, predicted the heavy toll to be expected in an economy in transition.

Machines will eliminate at least 200,000 jobs a year in the next decade, says a new report described as the first attempt to reduce automation job losses to actual figures.

The report, by Ewan Clague, U.S. Commissioner of Labor Statistics, and Leon Greenberg, Bureau of Labor Statistics, was prepared for the American Assembly conference here on technological changes.

The report, on "disemployment," says that the economy thus needs to create 200,000 jobs a year—one way or another—just to take care of those people whom technological change displaces.

Some of the people could go into producing and maintaining the machines, but increased consumption and new products and services would be needed to prevent mass additions to unemployment rolls, the report said.

The conference, drawing 70 leaders from industry, labor, colleges and Government, is studying how to reap the fruits of technological advance while minimizing its pains.

Housing

Adequate housing in the city continues to be a problem of top priority among the economically deprived. This is not exclusively a matter of inability to pay for housing. The current survey of the Welfare Council of Delaware reveals that in the neighborhoods with the most serious deterioration and dilapidation (64 per cent) the average monthly rental was $64. In the neighborhoods with practically no dilapidation the average monthly rental was $61. The former neighborhood was almost entirely Negro; the latter neighborhood was white. The exploitation of the disadvantaged is a grave moral problem which permeates the future of society. Out of a deprived home come problems of health, safety, morals, and education. One-fourth of the nonwhite population occupies one-half of the deteriorated and dilapidated housing. It is no wonder that the incidence of tuberculosis among non-whites has sharply increased nor that syphilis is more common among non-whites than among whites.

In his report on venereal disease (*Evening Journal,* Jan. 10, 1962), Dr. Strong, of the Board of Health, "released figures showing that, of the 59 syphilis cases reported by doctors and hospitals, 52 were non-white; 7 were white; 32 were male; 27 female."

Illegitimacy had increased. The *Evening Journal,* September 6, 1962, carried the following report:

> Twenty-two per cent of all births to Wilmington mothers in the first six months of the year were illegitimate.
> This was disclosed in a statistical report submitted to the Wilmington Board of Health by Dr. James C. Strong, health commissioner.
> The report shows a total of 3,744 births recorded in Wilmington between Jan. 1 and June 30. Of these 1,080 were to Wilmington mothers and 2,664 to nonresident mothers.
> A break-down of the Wilmington total shows 236 illegitimate births. Out of the non-resident total there were 72 illegitimate births or less than three per cent.
> Of the illegitimate births in Wilmington, 64 were white and 172 non-white. Of the white mothers, 17 had records of previous illegitimate births. In the non-white category 116 had previous illegitimate births.
> In the non-resident statistics 33 illegitimate babies were white and 39 non-white. Five white and 25 non-white mothers had previous illegitimate births.

It is important in interpreting illegitimacy statistics to remember that, unlike many other states, Delaware does not recognize common-law marriages, and the offspring of such marriages is considered illegitimate. In addition, abortion is less frequently practiced among non-whites than among whites. Of genuine concern is the striking rise of illegitimacy among white residents. The *Evening Journal,* October 5, 1961, quotes the Reverend Thomas J. Reese, director of the Catholic Welfare Guild, who said the most striking fact shown by the Department of Health statistics "is the rise in the rate of illegitimate births in the white, city-resident population. If only white births are counted, this year's rate for city and suburban residents would be 32 per 1,000, or less than 1957's rate of 47.4. Among white city residents, however, this year's rate is 101."

The demolition of homes on the East Side in Poplar A Redevelopment Area and of those in the path of the Adams-Jackson Thruway across the heart of the city revealed the need for a new housing code. An editorial, "This Is How the Slums Grow," *Evening Journal,* April 5, 1962, showed how blight may creep from a contaminated area into a pleasant, comfortable neighborhood of modest homes.

> Take an old house owned by someone who doesn't live in it any more. Rent it to someone else, who may or may not be interested in living there.
> Let him, in turn, sublet it to several others who need a roof over their heads and don't care too much how well it's kept up as long as it's dry.
> Slums breed when houses are neglected. There is too much neglect in Wilmington today. Too many codes go unenforced. We've torn down one slum. How many more will we allow to grow before we move effectively to halt the process?

How fare the children who call the city their home? Some come to school clean, well cared for, bright, and perceptive. We look at them and wonder how their parents can accomplish the impossible; how, with limited income, a continuing battle against the inroads of depravity around them, their parents can manage to provide so well for their children. It is from such families that the schools learn that values are in people and are not confined to certain economic levels; that the love and determination of parents which make them care for their children are not qualities reserved for the advantaged among our people.

But most of the children who are disadvantaged are not so fortunate. Their parents have been overwhelmed long ago by the forces of living in deprivation. These are the children blunted physically and emotionally long before they enter school. They are the victims of a society that demonstrates through these children man's inhumanity to man. It is in these children that the school finds its greatest challenge. It must take a child beaten by life by the time he is five and help him create an image of himself that gives him respect, hope, and aspiration. Because the home is the greatest influence in a child's life, the school is faced with a task of Herculean proportions. How well the Wilmington schools are meeting this challenge is discussed in Sections II and III.

A House of Hope

In an editorial in the Philadelphia Fellowship Commission's *Report to the Community,* May 1960, Judge Thomas D. McBride writes:

> No crash program will wipe out slums, inadequate education, low income, broken homes, poor motivation, prejudice, bigotry, delinquency and crime, discrimination and segregation, no matter how much money is poured into such a crash program.
>
> Unless we make up our minds as a community to attack such evils as a community, we will never reduce the problems to manageable size. Half the job is wanting to get it done; the rest is patience and never-failing faith in the power of religion and democracy to unite all men, if we work at it ceaselessly.
>
> The challenges and opportunities we face are to facilitate the research, the unity, the planning, the training and mobilization of resources to enable Greater Philadelphia to make the next decade one in which more and more of our energies can be devoted to Brotherly Living instead of talking about it or hoping for it.

During 1961-62, citizen action in Wilmington reflects a commitment to Judge McBride's convictions. A selection of progress reports reflects the wide range of attacks upon the problems of the city which justify the belief that a house of want can become a house of hope. An extract from the minutes of this meeting follows:

ESTABLISHING A COMMISSION ON HUMAN
RELATIONS IN WILMINGTON

> Approximately twenty-five leading citizens of the community, representing as many different organizations that have a concern for better human relations practices in Wilmington, met for a two-and-one-half hour conference to discuss the human relations needs and ways in which they might better be met in the community.
>
> Each of the representatives spoke of the depth and scope of the interest which their organization had in this field. In almost every case the sentiment expressed was that there should be a Human Relations Commission in Wilmington with legislative power to bring about equal opportunity in employment, housing, education, recreation, and public accommodation.
>
> The gathered assembly voted unanimously to constitute the present Steering Committee with full authority to direct all moves toward the creation of an effective Wilmington Commission on Human Relations.
>
> The Steering Committee was authorized to establish a citizens' organization. All interested civic, religious and community organi-

zations are to be invited to send an interested member to the citizens' group as a regular participant. Organizational and individual members are to be asked to help with the research, education, and action and to give financial support.

The Steering Committee was asked to outline the purpose of the citizens group, spell out its approach, and summarize its program. The next meeting of the large group is left in the hands of the Committee, but urgency was expressed about meeting soon.

The following extracts from editorials show that the community at large was aware of aspects of these problems.

FIRST POLICE-COMMUNITY RELATIONS SEMINAR HELD

The first of eight seminars on police-community relations, a part of the Wilmington police in-training school program, is being held today.

Leaders of The National Conference of Christians and Jews, in addition to local speakers, are participating.

Dr. Donald N. Lombardi, regional director of the national conference, is moderator. Lombardi said the aim of the seminars is to provide police with information and skills which will assist them in their community role.

He said three aspects will be stressed, including basic concepts of self-understanding and social relations, trends and developments within the law enforcement profession, and an understanding of sub-groups and social forces in a community.
(*Evening Journal,* May 5, 1962)

CITY WARNS EATING SPOTS OF DEADLINE ON SEGREGATION

Beginning Jan. 1 Wilmington restaurant owners will have to serve customers regardless of their race if they are to stay in business.

The City License Bureau is mailing to all restaurants, soda fountains and other eating places license applications for 1962. No license will be issued to any owner who refuses to swear he will not discriminate against any person because of race, color or religion.

Under provisions of a law passed by City Council in June, if he does discriminate he is liable to a fine of from $50 to $300.
(*Evening Journal,* December 13, 1961)

CITY RESTAURANT BIAS LAW FACES TEST

A court test loomed today for the Wilmington ordinance against discrimination in restaurants.

The possibility arose when two restaurants were denied city licenses to do business because their proprietors had failed to sign affidavits swearing not to discriminate against customers on the basis of race or religion.

Without a license from the City License Bureau they are legally barred from doing business after Jan. 31, the deadline for obtaining 1962 business licenses. (*Evening Journal,* January 4, 1962)

TALK CALLED TO MAP WAR ON BLIGHT

The Wilmington Board of Health will meet with public officials and a citizen group tomorrow to study the prospects of a new battle plan against blight.

Plans for the meeting were made yesterday after O. Francis Biondi, assistant city solicitor, made a field tour of the 16-block area where there had been a concentrated enforcement program.

This area is bounded by Washington, Adams, Fourth and Eighth Streets. It was included in a tour by Dr. Anthony F. Vitiello, board president, and others last week.

Biondi, after additional briefing from William T. Sweeney, executive secretary of the board, on the efforts of housing and health inspectors in the area, will take steps to prepare legal action against property owners who have failed to comply with warnings.

(*Evening Journal,* September 19, 1961)

PRESBYTERY MOVES TO WELD CITY, SUBURBAN STRATIFICATION

Presbyterian leaders have shouldered some of the blame for racial segregation here.

At its meeting this week, the New Castle Presbytery approved a resolution which affirmed as a fact that "the Church in its present life accentuates the brokenness of the city."

The resolution says, "This community is actually broken in that it is stratified into neighborhoods along racial, cultural and economic lines."

The resolution proposed that members do something about the stratification and consider Greater Wilmington as a single community.

One of the most significant items in the resolution calls on suburban churches to encourage their members to join downtown churches.

The city churches are asked to develop metropolitan congregations, each representing in its membership all strata of the population of the Greater Wilmington community.

Among the means suggested to reach this goal are that the city churches shall minister to their city neighborhood while urging members who move to suburbs to retain their membership and service downtown.

The resolution says the Church should perform the ministry of reconciliation among all kinds of people by witnessing to the community the healing power of love through the inclusive fellowship of congregational life.

In a related action, the Presbytery authorized its church and society committee to work with other groups to establish a Delaware Leadership Council to spearhead voter registration and other citizen action by the Negro people of Delaware.

(*Evening Journal,* April 6, 1962)

NEIGHBORHOOD GROUP FILES FREEWAY RECOMMENDATIONS

A resolution adopted last night by the West Center City Neighborhood Association cited "an old Russian proverb" to bolster the group's five recommendations on the proposed Adams-Jackson Streets Freeway.

"It is better to impose upon the poor," goes the proverb, "the rich won't stand for it."

"When one hears of the arguments that were used to urge the placing of the freeway here instead of in other nicer areas of town, one is reminded of that proverb," the resolution states.

The resolution, which carries recommendations from the planning through the construction phases of the proposed route, will be sent to Mayor John E. Babiarz, the president of City Council, and the Department of Public Works.

The association's members live in the area between Market Street and the proposed freeway route and between Front Street and Delaware Avenue. According to the resolution:

"There may be no area in the State of Delaware in which it is so difficult to live and to raise children."

Housing is deteriorating, rents are high, streets are heavily traveled and poorly cared for, there is little playground space or community facilities, and there is an excessive number of taverns, the resolution states.

The freeway will make living conditions even more difficult for the "people who have far more problems to cope with than most of the residents of the Wilmington area," it adds.

To avoid further deterioration of the community, the resolution asks the city officials to take these steps:

Give first consideration in planning to the needs and interests of the community's residents.

Support the community's attempts to improve living conditions.

Appoint a special committee to minimize hazards, inconvenience, and property destruction.

Influence the State Highway Department to use retaining walls in constructing sections of the freeway below ground level, to allow space for park areas.

(*Evening Journal,* September 29, 1961)

REVIVAL OF DISPUTE EXPECTED AS ZONE CODE HEARINGS OPEN

What city officials hope will be the final go-round in their 2½-year effort to modernize Wilmington's 37-year-old zoning code opens tonight in City Council Chambers.

When John Julian, chairman of the Zoning Commission, raps his gavel for order at 7 p.m. a series of public hearings on the 103-page draft of a new zoning ordinance will begin.

With the opening of hearings, much of the bitterness that over-flowed last spring's City Council hearings is expected to flow again, charge and countercharge focused on four specific points.

Three of the points are particular areas on the proposed zoning map accompanying the Zoning Commission's draft of a new code.

The fourth, if it materializes, is expected to center on what has been described as "status-quo zoning."

The three controversial areas are new, so-called R-4 conversion zones in the Ninth Ward, re-zoning in the Miller Road-Lea Boulevard area, and re-zoning in a residential strip astride Pennsylvania Avenue in the Seventh Ward.

The present draft, which is not materially changed from one drawn up the first of the year by Superior Court Judge Stewart Lynch, then city solicitor, is considered by some opponents only an up-dating of the legal framework for zoning.

Prepared with the assistance of Harold M. Lewis, New York consultant, opponents have said the proposed code does not take sufficient account of planning for the future, and will probably need piecemeal revision from the moment it is enacted.

Last night the Citizens Conference on Planning, Zoning and Housing adopted a series of resolutions on the proposed code.

One of the Conference's objectives is "refinements in the code at the earliest possible date" by a professional staff the city is pledged to engage once the ordinance is passed and the zoning and planning commissions have been merged.

The Citizens Conference also went on record as opposing the extensive R-4 conversion areas proposed for the Ninth Ward which the Price Run Community Council is bitterly contesting. The Citizens Conference wants this type of zoning—in which single family dwellings can be converted to multiple occupancy—revised and corrected before adoption.

However, the Wilmington Federation of Neighborhood Associations and Councils has gone even further and urged postponement and final action on the zoning code until after the projected merger of the zoning and planning commissions and wholesale revision of the new code by the combined commission's professional staff.
(*Evening Journal,* December 1, 1961)

"Workshop for Study of Community-wide Human Relations"

This is a three-session series planned for persons responsible for programs and community service projects in women's clubs, church organizations, etc. It covers in capsule form a study of the changing character of Wilmington and environs; the aims, accomplishments and limitations of our various social agencies; and gives specific suggestions for ways in which volunteers can give practical, needed help. This is open to all AAUW members.
(*Bulletin,* American Association of University Women, Wilmington, Delaware Branch, October 1961)

Fight Set to Keep People in City

Mayor John E. Babiarz said last night the city's redevelopment is moving from the era of massive demolition and reconstruction into a period of conservation.

The mayor pledged renewed efforts to combat the flight of residents to the suburbs in a talk before the Wilmington Federation of Neighborhood Associations and Councils in a meeting in the Riverside Development.

The new phase of the fight, he said, will stress work toward assimilation of new arrivals from rural Delaware and other states.

New housing, he said, will have to be offered on a racially integrated basis and competitive in price with suburban developments.

The mayor pledged strict city enforcement of the new housing code, but said he hoped most of the enforcement will come as a result of persuasive action.

The newly formed federation elected its first officers at last night's meeting.

(*Evening Journal,* May 24, 1962)

In September 1959, during the initial stages of the Project, an atmosphere of helplessness and despair, brought about by the flight to the suburbs by established lay leaders in the community characterized gatherings of professional leaders in schools and other service agencies. One of the most exciting developments in the city during the second year of the Project was the awakening of a sleeping giant, the power of the people to act in their own behalf, in which determination to overwhelm the forces of inertia was reflected by cooperative action on many fronts.

In *The Lonely Crowd,* David Reisman has written that "We are only beginning to understand the power of individuals to shape their own character by their selection among models and experiences." This statement applies equally to cities. And the citizens of Wilmington were demonstrating their determination to build a city from which "no man can be excommunicated . . . but by the death of goodness in his own breast." (William Ellery Channing)

Increasing concern over the problems of urbanization and their effect upon children and youth was manifested by lay and professional leaders in Wilmington. Increasing numbers of out-of-school youth without salable skills for a changing labor market have spotlighted the need for acceptance of a responsibility by the nation for its youth.

American society seems to be separating into two groups with a widening gap between them, a woman told the Massachusetts Conference on Social Welfare today.

Mrs. Thomas Herlihy, Jr., chairman of the National Committee for Children and Youth, told the meeting in Boston a growing number of citizens remain outside the mainstream of American life because of poverty, discrimination or cultural retardation.

While a large number has advanced in education, skill, and income level, a very large group has not, she said:

"Call them culturally deprived, underprivileged, disadvantaged, or what you will, these are the people who have fallen through the cracks in our society."

The growing numbers of unskilled youth in the city slums, many recruited from those driven from farms, especially in the South, are making an old problem worse, Mrs. Herlihy said.

Most of them are Negroes, she said, who face a 50-50 chance

of virtual unemployment even if they finish high school, and a worse chance if they drop out before graduation.

"We are actually in danger of creating two worlds," Mrs. Herlihy said, charging that middle-class society, including professional social workers, has little understanding of how the children of the slums and their parents think and behave.

She suggested an internship in the slums for social workers, and tours of slums and migrant labor camps for non-professionals.

The incident of a Peace Corps girl who admitted she was unprepared for the primitive squalor she found in Africa is a reflection of the ignorance of middle-class America and of its own downtrodden, she said:

"We do not help our children in understanding and knowledge by keeping them aloof from the facts of life. Primitive living conditions exist here in America, and we do our children a disservice if we do not acquaint them with this fact. . . .

"I do not mean to suggest we should undergo a great leveling program, but I would question the wisdom of keeping one group of children 'protected' from exposure to the other."

There is discontent on both sides, Mrs. Herlihy said. On one side are riots and open defiance of police, she said; on the other, growing criticism and repudiation of welfare programs and rebellion against their mounting costs, a la Newburg.

Mrs. Herlihy said it is the task of social workers to bridge the gap.

She told the meeting that, while the rising pace of industrial revolution is a major factor in the technological unemployment of such a large group of unskilled youngsters, the national committee was aware of the agricultural revolution's role and is planning a Conference on Opportunities for Rural Youth in a Changing Environment.

(*Evening Journal,* November 1, 1961)

That Delaware accepted its responsibilities for youth is reflected in the action reported in the *Evening Journal,* November 29, 1961:

A three-member panel will lead the discussion tomorrow in Dover at the conference of the Delaware Commission on Children and Youth considering the problems of unemployed school drop-outs.

The objectives of the conference are:

—To ascertain the extent of the present state of unemployment and school drop-outs among Delaware youth.

—To achieve a closer relationship than now exists among the schools, employers, and labor unions, as well as social agencies and employment offices.

—To plan constructive action toward meeting the unemployment needs of today's youth, as well as long range planning for the needs of those reaching maturity in the decade ahead.

More direct personal service was rendered by women's organizations to children in the public elementary schools. Members of the Junior League of Wilmington organized volunteer service for a library project at the Lore School. A well established service, rendered by the Wilmington Branch of the American Association of University Women, was reported in the *Evening Journal* of January 26, 1962:

> Volunteers under the sponsorship of the Wilmington Branch of the American Association of University Women have become "reading aides" on a part-time basis in two Wilmington public schools.
>
> The purpose of this service is to help children who are falling behind in reading achievement and are frustrated. The volunteers work with these children twice a week with appropriate materials and receive help from the two helping teachers as well as aid from Dr. Muriel Crosby, assistant superintendent in charge of elementary education in the Wilmington schools. Dr. Crosby is also a member of the association.
>
> A similar service is being organized to function in the kindergarten of the Lore School, where volunteers will assist teachers with the enlarged enrollment of children.
>
> Many of the aides received preliminary training in the annual workshop for substitute teachers, sponsored by the Wilmington Branch of the Association for the last six years.

The suburban First Unitarian Church summarized its services to the children of the city in its *Newsletter:*

> The Three-Year Experimental Project on Schools in Changing Neighborhoods, co-sponsored by the Wilmington Board of Education and The National Conference of Christians and Jews, has involved several of our church members, representing community agencies and organizations and our own committee—
>
> The first and second year reports, profound and insightful, by Dr. Muriel Crosby, may be borrowed through the Social Action Committee.
>
> Most of the problems being discussed at the Changing Neighborhoods Committee meetings are of wide scope and are being studied by the developing neighborhood associations as well as by welfare agencies, churches, etc. We found that by meeting some of the basic requirements of children in city public schools our church groups and individuals filled a gap in services available.
>
> We intend to keep posted on activities and needs revealed through the Changing Neighborhoods Project and will keep church members informed of the areas in which we can be helpful.

Youth study centers were established in a number of Wilmington's churches. For youngsters without a place to study, these centers were a potent force. A letter from the director of one of these centers, Susan Weber, of West Presbyterian Church, describes the initial stage in an effort which gives hope of becoming a flourishing enterprise. She writes:

> The Center is going beautifully. Our only complaint is that we are running out of space, and we find that three adults each evening are not enough. We have grown gradually each night, until our enrollment is up to 31, with about 18 young people coming any one night. Six teenagers have been present every single evening we have been open, and most of them have been there at least two nights a week since they have begun attending. The study helpers are finding that when the young people finish their homework they stay to look up magazines (*National Geographic* and *Du Pont*), and when they are done with that they stay longer to talk with the adults and relax. Indeed, I feel that some of them would not miss this for anything. It is interesting, productive, encouraging and relaxing. It gives meaning to their long evenings, and to their sometimes restless days in school.
>
> Our study helpers are beginning to know the teenagers now, and what kind of help they need. They constantly are kept busy from the moment they arrive, and the young people are not in the least hesitant about approaching them. We have acquired sufficient reference books for the present, so the young people don't have to run to the library for material. One study helper discovered on his first night that his training in mechanical drawing would be helpful. He returned the following night, on his own, with a drawing board and tools in hand, sat down and read the textbook of the boy who needed help, and then proceeded to teach him the basic principles which the boy did not understand. Another helper came one night, helped a boy with his math problem, and realized when he got home that he had helped incorrectly. The next night, on his own, he returned and made certain that his error, and the boy's understanding were corrected. Another helper has worked regularly, in half-hour intervals during his work night, tutoring individual youngsters who need help in math. Another has become so interested that she comes every night she is free to follow the progress of those with whom she has been working. It is amazing to me that these busy adults would muster this kind of concern—for each one of them makes sacrifices to come. Perhaps they did not start out with this concern. I am sure it has grown, as they have become interested and involved in the lives and work of the young people themselves.
>
> As for the teenagers—the community which is building among them is a classic example of the meaning of personal concern and individual attention. They are generally quiet and cooperative, welcome help and are eager to improve. We have become relatively well acquainted with the ones who have come, because our increased attendance has been gradual enough to allow this. Each one has been personally received, registered and helped to begin. Many of them have received extensive and regular tutoring. One boy, of whom I spoke at the principals' meeting, has given up football in order to spend two hours with us each evening, bring

up his grades and learn how to study. If he continues, there is every hope that he can go on to college. This boy, who has been sliding through his first three years with the intent of entering the service when he finished, came to me tonight and said he has become really interested in biology. His teacher has given him homework assignments to do ahead. He has moved ahead in his algebra as a result of his tutoring, and is planning to read extra books in English to gain extra credits. This boy missed forty-five days of school last year, and completely lacked motivation and initiative in his work. He has recently brought in three other teenagers. At his suggestion and encouragement, one of them has talked to me about the possibility of college for which he is undoubtedly capable if he applies himself this year. Still others who have come have discovered friends who need help in a particular subject. They go by the homes of these friends and bring them in personally, introducing them to us and explaining their needs. One Individual Progress student who is a senior at Howard has been referred to us for help in reading, and he is planning to come every night to work with us. He wants to improve, and is fundamentally encouraged in this possibility. A number of sixth graders, who have occasional homework assignments, come in to use our reference books or work their arithmetic problems. We even have one boy who dropped out of school two years ago, who comes to use our reference books for his Scout troop. The variety and range of this project is extensive, as you can see.

To me, as a part of the ministry of the church, this is the image of the Beloved Community—the Christian Fellowship at work in the deepest sense. As the adults have shown personal concern for the young people, valued their efforts and encouraged their persistence—so the young people have begun to relate in this manner to one another. The mutual sharing of this task of "school" has lifted up the value of education, of learning, and of persons—all in one. To see this in action, building up a little more each week, has been absolutely amazing to me. In my opinion, the possibility of this kind of help, beginning with children as early as 5th and 6th grade, could do wonders with this drop-out problem.

That the state of Delaware has far to go in discharging its responsibility to children is reflected in a "Letter to the Editor," *Evening Journal,* March 6, 1962, part of which is quoted:

> The September 1961 issue of *Changing Times Magazine* reports that in 1959 the per capita income of $2,946 ranked Delaware first in the United States. However, the per cent of personal income spent on schools of 2.8 per cent ranked this state an inglorious 47th. Apparently the feeling prevails that purchasing a second car or a second television set is considerably more worthwhile than paying larger school taxes for something so intangible as education.

In summary, increasing numbers of citizens in all walks of life were becoming aware of their house of want. Their efforts reflect the fact that

Wilmington was also a house of hope. Later sections of this report on progress by participants in The Three-Year Experimental Project on Schools in Changing Neighborhoods reaffirm the determination of the people of the city to create a dynamic, satisfying life for themselves and their children. Radhakrishnan, of India, has stated in another context the commitment Wilmington faces in creating a new interpretation of its heritage:

> The new world environment requires a tradition which is neither Eastern nor Western but universal and based on the conception of man, on the recognition of his uniqueness, the freedom and creativity of the individual person, the demand for personal dignity and autonomy.

Project Schools in Changing Neighborhoods

To the Project Administrator looking at schools in changing neighborhoods, "schools" are at once synonymous with "children" and "teachers." And the children stand out, first, with clarity and wonder. The poignancy of childhood is its vulnerability. This is particularly true in relation to the disadvantaged.

The participants in the Project saw and felt this wonder. Among the disadvantaged, however, they found more than wonder. They saw insecurity, fear, hope, and helplessness. Because of their deepening insights, their identification with children, their genuine acceptance of all children as their children, they began to see some other things that speak for the child, which told them that a disadvantaged youngster can feel: "I am worth something; I can become something. There are people who care enough to help me."

Aldous Huxley has written, "Children are remarkable for their intelligence and ardor, for their curiosity, their intolerance of shams, the clarity and ruthlessness of their vision." These characteristics of all children, and particularly of disadvantaged children, motivated participants to take a new look at the children as they began the third year, 1961-62, of the Project.

Racial Integration of the Schools

All of the Project schools were racially integrated. Enrollment of Negro children ranged from approximately 20 per cent in one school to approximately 98 per cent in three other schools. The most notable change occurred in one small school which was formerly a segregated white school and is now 98 per cent Negro. Two of the largest schools, with enrollments of 1000-1250, changed from 100 per cent white enrollment to approximately 85 per cent Negro. One of these schools, in the northeast section of the city, had rapidly accelerating Negro enrollment as evidenced by the fact that in 1960-61 its enrollment of Negro children was 65 per cent of its total; in 1961-62, it was 80 per cent.

Growth and Racial Distribution of Pupil   Table 3
Population in the Elementary Schools

	1953-54		1959-60		1960-61		1961-62	
	No.	%	No.	%	No.	%	No.	%
White	5950	80	3653	46	3584	45	3614	44
Negro	1487	20	4288	54	4457	55	4583	56
Total	7437	100	7941	100	8041	100	8197	100

Size and Racial Distribution of the Staff   Table 4
of the Elementary Schools

	1953-54		1959-60		1960-61		1961-62	
	No.	%	No.	%	No.	%	No.	%
White	212	74	214	69	200	64	196	61
Negro	75	26	102	31	114	36	124	39
Total	287	100	316	100	314	100	320	100

Table 3, "Growth and Racial Distribution of Pupil Population in the Elementary Schools," reveals significant population changes in the public schools of the city. At the close of the school year 1953-54, the last year of segregation, the percentage of Negro pupils was 20 per cent of the total; at the opening of the school year 1961-62, this had risen to 56 per cent.

With a declining total city population of 13 per cent between the 1950 and 1960 censuses, the public elementary school population rose steadily from 7437 in 1954 to 8197 in 1962.

In Table 4 it will be noted that the number and percentage of Negro staff members continue to increase, with a corresponding decline in the number and percentage of white staff members. The ratio of new teaching positions to increased enrollments reflected the gradual increase in class size at a time when increasing needs of children demanded more individual attention from teachers if teaching and learning were to be effective.

A notable advance in the integration of staff was achieved by the appointment of the first Negro to the Helping Teacher Service. Helping teachers functioned as general supervisors in the elementary division. Recommendation for appointment was made by a racially integrated staff selection committee. The Negro candidate received the unanimous recommendation as first choice of the committee, based on superior qualifications. Thus, the first Negro to enter a supervisory position in the city schools marked an important "first" in the system. It is significant that no racial distinction was made in assigning teachers to a helping teacher. The success of this helping teacher and her genuine acceptance by the staff was reflected in the large number of experienced teachers who voluntarily elected a short course she offered during 1961-62. The fact that not a single complaint or incident occurred throughout the first year of her service reflected the acceptance by white teachers of service and leadership from a Negro supervisor. For a border city with a strong Southern tradition of racial segregation, the elementary staff had truly come a long way in conquering prejudice in a few years.

The desegregation of staff in the public elementary schools presented one of the major problems of the late 1950's. At the close of the Project, six of the Project schools were well integrated, with well-balanced staffs of Negro and white teachers. Five of the Project schools had made beginnings in the desegregation of staffs. The three non-Project schools maintained white staffs. All of the city elementary schools had a desegregated pupil enrollment. To the Project Administrator, the fact that a school has relatively few Negro or white children enrolled is no justification for maintaining a segregated staff. Children living in a racially segregated residential community, with slight daily contact with members of another race, will—as adults—live in a world far different from the one they have known as children. Because prejudice is rooted in the childhood years and is largely the result of ignorance, it is important that all Negro and white children experience the satisfaction of living for one or more years with a quality teacher of another race. Wilmington may take pride in the progress made in the desegregation of staff, but we have "miles to go before we sleep."

Staffing the Schools

Recruiting and holding competent teachers is a national problem. In a school system faced with the problems of racial desegregation, staffing the schools can become an acute problem. How fared Wilmington in this respect?

Holding Power—In the early years of desegregation, there was a marked decline in the number of white teachers and a great increase in the number of Negro teachers. Desegregation was not the only factor responsible. Wilmington was also in an unfavorable competitive position with surrounding suburban school systems whose salary scale exceeded that of the city's. But desegregation and increasing numbers of disadvantaged children, both Negro and white, contributed to making suburban teaching more desirable to some teachers.

From July 1955 to August 1961, the Wilmington elementary schools lost twenty-seven teachers to the suburbs. While this number is not large, its significance lies in the trend implied. Encouraging was the fact that of the twenty-seven teachers leaving the system, only two had been Project participants. It seemed reasonable to feel that the Project had increased the holding power of the schools. In one large Project school of more than forty staff members, whose annual turnover of staff throughout the 1950's had been the greatest in the city with an average of fifteen vacancies each year, there were only five vacancies for the school year 1962-63.

Educational Qualifications—It is a generally accepted premise that the quality of preparation for teaching is directly related to the quality of teaching and learning. In this period of shortage of qualified teachers, the Wilmington public elementary schools were fortunate in the quality of preparation of their staffs.

In 1961-62, 108 out of the 320 elementary teachers had a master's degree or better, 164 had a bachelor's degree, and 48 had no degree. There were six teachers in special services, such as teaching the deaf, speech correction, and lipreading. Three held master's degrees and two, bachelor's degrees.

Extent of Staff Participation in the Project—In a human relations-focused project, it seemed to the Project Administrator highly important that participation be of a voluntary nature. This premise was based upon a deep conviction not only that staff members have the right to freedom of choice, but also that their quality of participation depends upon their motivation in meeting their responsibilities. For this reason, participation was voluntary, and entailed commitment for one year only. The holding power of the Project may be determined to some extent by the number of participants who entered and the number of years they participated.

Wilmington, like other cities, has its share of staff members who leave the system because of retirement, marriage, moving from the city, maternity, and leaves of absence for military and educational purposes. Such causes for separation from the school system may be classified as causes of "normal" turnover. These factors entered into the "holding power" of participants in the Project. Personnel data for the three-year period of the Project follow:

Number of Participants	Year
65	1959-60
165	1960-61
143	1961-62

Staff registration at the beginning of the third year of the Project is shown below in Table 5. Later, others entered the Project.

It should be noted that Table 5 relates only to the teaching staff. Other members of the staff participating in the Project, such as helping teachers, psychologists, social workers, and others are not included.

Of the sixty-five school participants who entered during the first year of the Project, thirty-seven remained throughout the three years. Eleven of the sixty-five left the school system at the end of their first year, and others left at the end of their second year in the Project. Relatively few teachers remaining in the school system failed to complete the Project.

At the end of the second year of the Project, 23 of the 165 left the school system. Of this group 106 completed the Project.

It is interesting to note that at the beginning of the third year of the Project, twenty-seven teachers entered for the first time. While many of these teachers were new to the school system, others had been on the staff and could have entered at an earlier date.

Number of Years of Participation in the Three-Year   Table 5
Experimental Project on Schools in Changing
Neighborhoods by Staff Members Participating During 1961-62

School	Total Participating	Year of Entry in the Project		
		1961-62	1960-61	1959-60
Drew	14	1	6	7
Pyle	10	5	1	4
Gray	39	6	19	14
Elbert	7	1	4	2
Palmer	5		2	3
Lore	5		5	
Opportunity	11	3	8	
North East	22	5	16	1
Shortlidge	2			2
Stubbs	12	4	8	
Williams	6	2		4
Total Number	133*	27	69	37
Percentage	100	20	52	28

Number of Participants Working for Professional Growth Credit........................ 129
Number of Participants Not Working for Credit 14
Total Number of Participants for Year 1961-62...................................... 143

* 10 late registrants for participation are not included in this column.

An interesting fact is that, although the above data refer only to participants formally registered in the Project, many other teachers in participating and nonparticipating schools became interested and tried out the processes and techniques employed by the participants. Generally, the Project greatly influenced a large percentage of the staff and its holding power was exceptionally good.

And What of the Children?

Changing urban populations, with their increase in the proportion of people in economically deprived circumstances, have given rise to fears for a decrease in the mental ability of the children in public schools. This situation requires a critical examination of the validity of group intelligence test scores. Group intelligence tests generally measure experience, not ability or potential. The tests are based upon a national sampling of children from all economic levels, geographic localities, and cultural backgrounds. An urban public school population such as Wilmington's does not reflect the national sampling, but is heavily weighted with disadvantaged children, handicapped not only in experiences generally needed for success in the traditional school goals, but crippled in command of language which plays such a vital role in standardized testing. Add to experience and language, handicaps of physical and social deprivation and the result can only be low mental maturity scores on most standardized group tests. Such tests do not reflect the potential of these disadvantaged children.

The value of group intelligence tests is that they reveal the problem faced by the school in a national sampling context. Great danger exists if the staff accepts the results of such tests as valid, and, accordingly, plans a curriculum which sets low expectations for the staff and the children. This, in effect, places a ceiling upon children's potential which prevents their achievement at a higher level. Test makers are aware of this danger and are rendering a vital service to children in urging teachers not to put a ceiling on learning by accepting as valid the scores obtained through group intelligence tests. Typical is the following quotation from the *Evening Journal* of May 23, 1962:

> A child's IQ may vary as much as 40 points—depending on circumstances and tests.
> Dr. S. Donald Melville, director of the Cooperative Test Division of the Education Testing Service of Princeton, N. J., told 140 educators in Dover yesterday IQ tests, therefore, may have lost their usefulness.
> Speaking at a conference on testing sponsored by the Delaware School Study Council, he said: "I'm not opposed to IQ tests. It's the IQ label that bothers me."
> He said parents and teachers may be misled by an early IQ score and base their guidance—wrongly—on that score for years.

Scores based on national norms and grade equivalents were also attacked by the tester. He said he favored a system of percentile rank. He advocated comparing tests with as many different norms as possible.

A second-grade teacher in a Project school describes conditions affecting her children which could be matched by many Wilmington teachers:

> The children in my second grade come, in general, from families of extremely meager means and experiences, as do many children in the changing neighborhoods of the city. Their recreational facilities are the streets in front of their homes, and their knowledge of the world is limited to their immediate neighborhood.
>
> Many of the children are undernourished resulting in a great prevalence of skin eruptions of various types. Many are not adequately dressed, and rainy or extremely cold days generally see an attendance drop due to lack of proper clothing. Clothes in many cases are soiled and torn, and are worn day after day without washing or mending.
>
> These children, coming from poor backgrounds and all too often from broken homes, cannot fail to have an entirely different set of values than children in better socio-economic situations. Their cultural deprivation is readily seen in their talk, play, and associations with their peers and elders. Low morality, high rate of illegitimacy, and the substandard mores and language of the family group make it difficult in every way for the children from these families to grow up to be good and useful citizens unless they receive a great deal of help. The burden falls to a great extent upon the school, which becomes for most of he children not only the seat of learning, but, more important to them, also the center of their happiest social moments.
>
> In line with all this is an absence of good health habits, cleanliness, and knowledge of the importance of the right foods. Their lack of proper diet is evident in the poor condition of their skin and teeth. In the school cafeteria, the children are suspicious of unfamiliar foods, and there is an incredible number of healthful foods which they have never seen. The trays go back empty, only when the menu consists of hot dogs, sauerkraut, or other foods which they are used to eating at home.

Within the framework of understanding of the values and hazards associated with group intelligence test results, Table 6, a study of the status of the mental maturity of all sixth graders. (1033) in 1961-62 in the public elementary schools is revealing.

In interpreting this table, it should be noted that the median score is that score at which 50 per cent of the children are above and 50 per cent below. For the sixth-grade population as a whole, it can be seen that the median (95) is a low average intelligence score. Schools A, D, and E did not participate in the Project. Of the Project schools, two are just average (98; 103), two are low average (91), five are below average (82-88). Two Project schools are not included; one is the school for trainable mentally retarded and the other is a primary school without sixth graders. In each of the Project schools, however, children range in intelligence from the highest to the lowest, thus necessitating a range in curriculum which challenges all.

Wilmington Public Schools Core Testing Program   Table 6
Median Intelligence Quotients
California Test of Mental Maturity 57 S Form
Administered 1961-62 - Sixth Grade

Median Intelligence Quotients	School												
	A	B	C	D	E	F	G	H	I	J	K	L	Total
Language	89	86	90	119	106	96	80	86	86	105	90	91	94
Non-Language	91	76	87	115	106	98	86	89	80	99	91	91	94
Total	90	82	88	117	107	98	84	86	86	103	91	91	95

That Project participants are convinced of the hazards of giving validity to group intelligence scores will be demonstrated in Section II of this report. We use these scores only as a challenge to provide experiences for children which will enable them to reach a potential far greater than the puny means at hand indicate.

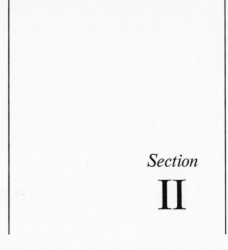

The Development of Curricula for Human Relations Education

Section II describes the efforts of school participants in The Three-Year Experimental Project on Schools in Changing Neighborhoods to develop educational programs for children of a changing city. Throughout the Project, the work of the staff was centered in an in-service education program geared to gaining information and developing more effective teaching skills and processes which affect children's motivation to learn.

4

Diagnosing Human Relations Needs

Teachers in a modern elementary school are accustomed to developing educational programs centered in the needs of children. They usually draw upon many sources of information to determine these needs. Among these are school records of progress, health records, intelligence and achievement tests, the observation of children at work and at play, and consultation with parents and staff members, including social workers, psychologists, psychiatrists, and medical personnel. One frequently neglected, but crucially important source of information is the perceptions the children have of themselves and their world. Children's perceptions are the base for the development of a human relations–focused education, for they provide vital clues to the human relations needs of the youngsters and their families. Diagnosis of the human relations needs of children became the first phase of curriculum study for Project participants.

In-Service Education

The Inter-Group Education Studies, sponsored by the American Council on Education during the late 1940's and early 1950's, resulted in the development of a number of reliable instruments for diagnosis of human relations needs. Such instruments as sociograms, autobiographies, time budgets, and open-ended questions have demonstrated their value and have become well established as part of the battery of instruments used in many schools. With modifications and adaptations these were to become an important part of the in-service education program for the Wilmington staff during the first year of the Project.

Dr. William E. Vickery, consultant for the Project, who had participated as a staff member of the Inter-Group Education Studies, met with participants monthly. He taught the use of specific diagnostic instruments and helped teachers analyze and use the information obtained from the children. At the close of the first year, he prepared a bulletin describing diagnostic instruments and their use. This became an important tool for participants throughout the years of the Project. This bulletin follows.

Diagnostic Instruments and Their Purposes
by Dr. William E. Vickery

Identifying the needs of children is the first important step in building a school program. When needs are accurately and adequately diagnosed, we can proceed with confidence to develop units of instruction, plan improvements in school clubs and organizations, and help community youth-serving organizations and schools in working together more effectively for the welfare of boys and girls.

As we undertake to diagnose the human relations needs of our pupils, we need instruments which tap a wide range of information about the children. Such instruments should be able to give us important data about the children's life experiences, their feelings, their out-of-school behavior, and the values and standards they apply in making choices. Such instruments also should reflect and keep intact the relationships that exist in real life among concepts, feelings, motivations, and behavior; rather than separating a total life experience into the categories of knowledge, attitudes, and skills as many tests do.

Because we want to tap simultaneously the many dimensions of our pupils' living experiences, we use "open" devices in the diagnoses of human relations needs, open in the sense that they cannot be scored as tests can. Among the instruments used for our diagnostic purposes are projective questions, time budgets or diaries, autobiographies, observations of children in free play and role-playing sessions, and many others. Sociometric questions and interviews are, among "open" diagnostic devices, the ones most adaptable to a standardized process of tabulation and diagramming. As our experimental work proceeds, we will develop increasingly our skill in using instruments to diagnose human relations needs, a skill which will prove valuable to us every year we teach.

Purposes of this Bulletin

This bulletin has two main purposes:
1. To suggest a variety of open diagnostic instruments, related to the curriculum themes of the elementary school and to the concepts for cur-

riculum planning. These instruments can be used to look at the social world through children's eyes and so to assess their human relations needs.

2. To provide ways of organizing, analyzing, and interpreting the data supplied by the children's responses to the diagnostic devices so that we can keep records which will be useful to us in planning units of instruction and programs for school clubs and organizations. Suggested charts for summarizing children's responses to the different types of diagnostic instruments are provided in Appendix A of this bulletin.

Diagnostic Instruments Related to the Curriculum Theme, "Home and Family Living"

Open-ended Questions. Three open questions were tested last year in the Project schools and found to be very useful in assessing the pupil's perceptions of home and family living. The questions asked invited completion of the following statements:

1. The time I had the most fun with my whole family was . . . (Used in primary grades only. The children drew pictures and individually told the teacher the "story" of the picture. The teacher wrote the story down on a card and attached it to the pictures.)

2. Things my parents ask me to do that I don't like to do are . . . (Primary grades only, using the same picture and story technique described above.)

3. The best thing that could happen to my family and why is . . . (Intermediate grades only, written essays or stories told privately to the teacher by children who wrote only with difficulty.)

In addition to these questions there are several others which we might try out to help us gain insight into the children's concepts regarding home and family.

1. How I help my mother (or whomever has the position of mother in the home)
2. How I help my father
3. How my mother helps me
4. How my father helps me
5. Rules my parents expect me to obey
6. What I do that makes my parents proud of me
7. My favorite relatives (not father, mother, brothers or sisters), and why I like them
8. Things I like to do with my brothers and sisters
9. Things my brothers and sisters do that bother me
10. A time my family moved: what we left behind that we miss, and what we left behind and were glad to leave there

The Time Budget or Diary. This was another valuable instrument tested in the Project schools last year. These time charts revealed a great deal about the pattern of the children's home life, their privileges and responsibilities; their relationships with parents, other adult relatives, and brothers and sisters; and the kinds of activities in which the whole family participated. Teachers who used the time budgets with their middle-grade children generally introduced their assignment in a manner similar to the following:

> All of us know fairly well what school is like to each of us, but any one of us is apt to know very little about what other children like to do when school is out. If you keep a time budget for just one day (or several days or even over the week-end) from the time school is out until school starts the next day, I will know more about the things you do and the things that are important to you. This will help me plan our activities in school. Perhaps, too, the school can be of help in assisting you to plan out-of-school activities.
>
> I will read your time budgets and report back to you the things that are important to all. All time budgets are confidential, and I will not talk to you as a class about what you will say—only about what many of you will say.
>
> Many boys might name the sports they do well, others might say where they went, and what they did when they were alone and what they did with a group of friends. It's easy to keep a time budget like this. Take lined paper. Mark along the left-hand margin half hour spaces . . .

Often the teacher demonstrated how to make a time budget on the board before letting the children undertake the task on their own. In the primary grades some teachers had children draw pictures in a sequence on the subject, "What I do from the time I get up until the time I get to school", and "What I do from the time I leave school until I go to bed." In young children, whose sense of time is not developed, the picture sequences are not as complete as the time budgets of older boys and girls, though the data they supply are extremely helpful in planning classroom activities.

Time budgets supply such a rich store of information that the teachers who use them are often tempted to overanalyze the data. In some circumstances it is good to analyze the time budget material completely. And other times the teacher who is concerned primarily with gaining insight into the children's home and family living legitimately selects from the time budgets only the data relevant to her purpose.

Home Visits and Parent Conferences. These are extremely useful in giving the teacher a clearer understanding of the home and family background of the children in her class. Observations during a home visit or the conversations with the parents can readily be summarized in the teacher's log book as soon after the visit or conference as possible. Important details tend to slip from the mind as time passes, so that the extra effort of recording them pays off in many ways.

For teachers who would like a flexible interview schedule geared specifically to tapping the parents' assessment of their children's social needs, *Diagnosing Human Relations Needs* [1] offers such a set of interview questions and suggests how to interpret responses.

Conversations and conferences with individual pupils are, of course, an integral part of the teacher's daily work. Often children's papers will indicate that a private conference is needed to clarify an idea or to provide counsel and guidance on a personal problem. Teachers who worked with the Project last year found that the topics on which the children wrote or about which they drew pictures stimulated many boys and girls to seek individual conferences with the teachers, conferences which helped to illuminate the teacher's understanding of their home and family living patterns.

Diagnostic Instruments Related to Community Studies

Open Questions. Four open questions were used in the first year of the Project to look at the neighborhood and wider community through the eyes of the children:
1. What do you like best in your neighborhood?
2. What would you like to see changed in your neighborhood?
3. What do grownups do (not family) that you like?
4. What do grownups do (not family) that you don't like?

Primary- and upper-grade children all responded to these questions. The picture and story technique was used with younger boys and girls and with those who had difficulty in writing; the older children wrote their answers.

Some teachers in primary grades also asked the boys and girls to take home a sheet of manila paper and sketch daddy's hand (or mother's or grandma's hand if daddy is not the family breadwinner) and to ask the person who works for the family what the hand does all day to earn a living or to take care of the home. Some teachers felt that this diagnostic device also served to extend the children's understanding of who was a "community helper" and to lay the groundwork for a better understanding of the idea that all jobs are interdependent.

To explore further the children's views of their neighborhoods and of the people among whom they live, these questions are suggested:

[1] Taba, H. & others—*Diagnosing Human Relations Needs.* Council on Education, 1951, Chapter 3, "Parent Interviews" pp. 31-47.

1. What do teen-agers in your neighborhood do that you like and why?
2. What do teen-agers in your neighborhood do that you don't like, and why?
3. Which downtown stores do you like to shop in, and why?
4. Which neighborhood in Wilmington makes you feel uncomfortable when you go there, and why do you feel that way?
5. Why would you like (or not like) to be a policeman when you grow up?
6. Who do you believe are the three most important people in Wilmington, and why?
7. What is the nicest home you ever visited—who lives there and why do you like it?
8. What things do people in your neighborhood do to help each other?
9. What helps people who have just moved into your neighborhood feel at home?
10. What makes it hard for newcomers to feel at home in your neighborhood?

Time Budgets. Time budgets provide valuable data concerning children's perceptions of community activities and of their participation in them. They supply information about children's work patterns outside the home; their travel range; their association with storekeepers, policemen, welfare workers, and other adults; their use of recreational facilities provided by the city and private youth-serving agencies; their relationships to their churches; and many other significant aspects of their daily lives.

Diagnostic Instruments Related to Understanding the American Heritage and to Developing National Loyalty

In the past, teachers were much more concerned with deciding what their pupils needed to know about the history and the traditions of the United States than with finding out how children, at different levels of their development, understood their relationship to their community, state, nation, and democratic values. Today, we are really breaking new ground in trying to assess the children's perceptions and feelings regarding the American heritage and democratic values.

One set of open questions suggested here serves to explore children's perceptions of their relationship to the nation as a whole, and to identify the basis of their feelings of patriotism. Some questions that can at least be tried are:
1. What does it mean to you to be an American?
2. What does the city (or state or nation) do for you and your family?
3. What can you and your family do for your city (state or nation)?

PROVIDENCE
COLLEGE
LIBRARY

4. Who is your favorite American hero, and why is he your favorite?
5. What national holiday do you like best, and why?
6. What song about America do you like best, and why?
7. Is there a soldier in your family who told you a story about his experiences? If so, what was the story?
8. Is there a story your grandfather or grandmother told you about an important national event that happened when he or she was a child your age, or one that he had a part in? If so, what was the story?
9. What did your father or mother tell you about the places their families used to live in before they came to Wilmington?

A diagnostic activity useful in the upper grades is to ask the children to explain in their own words what the pledge of allegiance means to them. For this purpose the pledge might be divided as follows, the children writing about each section separately:

First section: "I pledge allegiance to the flag of the United States of America and to the Republic for which it stands."

Second section: "One nation, under God, indivisible."

Third section: "With liberty and justice for all."

Another important diagnostic effort is centered on determining how children understand and accept democratic values.

Perhaps the most important of these values is to respect the dignity and worth of each individual human being. People act in accord with this value when they judge other people on their individual merits, rather than rejecting them arbitrarily on the basis of group prejudices, narrow social conventions, or restricted, provincial viewpoints. They also show respect for the dignity and worth of individuals when their actions take the welfare of others into consideration, even at the expense of some personal inconvenience. Self-respect and self-acceptance are prerequisites for being able to accept favors without servility and to bestow favors without condescension.

To discover how children perceive and act on this value the following open questions may prove useful:
1. What kind of person do you want as a member of your crowd (or club or gang)?
2. What kind of person do you not want as a member of your crowd (club or gang)?
3. What kind of person do you like to have as a neighbor?
4. What kind of person do you prefer not to have as a neighbor?
5. How do you feel about people who have more money than your family has?
6. How do you feel about people who have less money than your family has?

Another democratic value is equality of opportunity. In the context of school life this value is translated into action when the rules of the schools are applied without discrimination and when privileges or rewards are allocated on the basis of individual merit instead of favoritism, popularity, or social status.

Some open questions which may be used to tap student's feelings and knowledge about equal opportunity are:

1. Do you recall a time when you were treated unfairly—what happened and how did you feel?
2. What makes a boy or girl a leader in our school?
3. What teachers do you get along with best and why?
4. Who is the most popular boy in your class and why is he popular? Who is the most popular girl in your class and why is she popular?

Another democratic value important in adult society is sharing in the rights and duties of citizenship. In the experience of elementary school pupils this value is developed in the context of teacher-pupil planning, working for the general good of the class as well as the individual, voting for student council representatives, and taking part in the school's club program and recreational activities. Some open questions useful in seeing how pupils define the value of participation include:

1. What do other pupils do that makes it easy for our class to work together?
2. What do other pupils do that makes it hard to work together?
3. What do you do that helps the class do its work?
4. What do you do that makes it hard for the class to do its work?
5. What would you do if you were our class representative in the student council?
6. What does it take to become a student leader in our school?

The value of participating in making decisions has as a corollary the value of assuming responsibility for one's acts. In the school context it is important to see how pupils feel about school rules and customs, their responsibility to work and study, and their obligation to do their full share as school citizens. Among the open questions that can be used to determine how the pupils view responsibility are:

1. What school rules do you find easiest to obey?
2. What school rules do you find hardest to obey?
3. If you were the teacher (or principal), what would you do to pupils who disobeyed the rules?
4. What do you do when you are playing a game and someone doesn't obey the rules?
5. What do you do when two children get in a fight and there are no grown-ups around?

6. When is it all right to break a rule?
7. What would you do if you saw some kids breaking into the school at night?
8. What is the difference between helping someone with his work and cheating?

Some of the values in our society are humane and altruistic while others are materialistic and self-centered. This conflict occurs in children when they are called upon to make a choice between gratifying an immediate, personal desire and taking the feelings and welfare of others into account. Such choices are conditioned, of course, by the processes of physical and emotional maturation in the child. But all people, children and adults, are persons in culture, and the culture defines what choices should be made. When values conflict, as they do in our society, the task of teaching children to make ethical and rational choices is greatly complicated. In general, teachers stand—and are expected by society to stand—firmly on the side of the humane and altruistic values. At the same time schools are asked to help children learn to live in a materialistic and highly competitive world. To strike a balance between such conflicting demands requires much thought and skill. A good starting point is to learn from children how they see these conflicting values and on what basis they make choices between different courses of action.

Some open questions that are useful in learning about children's values are:

1. What would you wish for if you had three wishes?
2. What would you do if you had $100? (Also $500—also $1,000, for testing realism vs. fantasy.)
3. What things make you mad (angry)?
4. What things worry you?
5. What do you like about yourself?
6. What things would you like to change about yourself?
7. What was the hardest choice you ever had to make, and why was it hard?
8. If you were twenty-one, what kind of person would you like to be?
9. What do others say they like about you?
10. How do others criticize you?
11. What should happen to a person who "tells on" ("snitches on") a friend?
12. What person your own age would you like most to be, and why?
13. What would a person have to do so that you and your friends wouldn't play with him or even speak to him?
14. Who is the most successful person you know and why do you think he is successful?

Diagnostic Instruments Related to the Theme,
"How Groups Function"

The importance of children's relationships with each other can hardly be overestimated in developing a program of human relations education. Upon the quality of these relations will depend, in large measure, the self-concept each child develops, his attitudes toward others, the satisfaction he gets from working in groups, the social skills he acquires, and his capacity for self-control and self-direction. Peer relations are, therefore, of great concern to the teacher since they influence all aspects of classroom work including motivation for study and discipline.

Sociometric Questions. This instrument, which enables us to construct Sociograms, is the most thoroughly developed diagnostic instrument we have to assess the nature and quality of our pupils' relationships with each other. Sociometric questions used by teachers are generally of four kinds:

1. With whom would you like to sit in the classroom?
2. With whom would you like to work?
3. With whom would you like to work on a committee?
4. Whom would you like to have in the same club with you?

Other questions can, of course, be framed. Playground teams, field trip companions, and groups for assembly programs and classroom parties provide opportunities for choices, and therefore for sociometric diagnosis.

From the children's responses to sociometric questions we can construct sociograms, charts which reveal at a glance the pattern of social relations in the class. Directions for constructing and interpreting sociograms can be found in *Sociometry In Group Relations* [2] and *Diagnosing Human Relations Needs.*[3]

Responses to sociometric questions need to be followed up by individual interviews if we are to learn the reasons for choice and thereby the standards our pupils use in accepting and rejecting their classmates. "How did you happen to choose Jane?" is a better way of phrasing the interview question than "Why did you choose Jane?". The word "why" has so often been used in a punishing sense—*"Why* did you do *that?"*— that it blocks response from many children. And remember, sociometric interviews should be individual and private.

Open Questions. This instrument provides valuable insights into the quality of children's relationships with each other. Useful questions are:

1. What do you like in your best friend, and why?
2. How do you expect to be treated by your friends?
3. What people do you like best to play with, and why?

---

[2] Jennings, H. H. *Sociometry in Group Relations,* Revised Edition, Washington: American Council on Education, 1960.
[3] Taba, H. & others. *Op. cit.,* pp. 71-97.

4. What kind of people don't you like to play with, and why?

5. What do you expect of people who work with you on an assignment?

6. Was there a time you were left out of a (group, club, gang) you wanted to belong to? How did you feel and what did you do?

7. Was there a time you helped a person your age to do something he wanted to do? What did you do and how did you feel about it?

There are many other open questions suggested in other sections of this bulletin which provide insights into peer relationships. For example, the questions on democratic values are often phrased in terms of peer group relations. Questions on leadership, popularity, rules of the game, "snitching" or "telling on" other children—all are relevant in this area as they are in assessing values.

Some Guidelines for Using Diagnostic Instruments

Administration and Use. If we want the information we gain from children's drawings and stories to be accurate, our methods of administering and using the diagnostic instruments must be carefully thought through. Some suggestions that may be helpful to you are:

1. When you ask the children to write stories or draw pictures in response to an open-ended question, be sure that you do not prestructure their responses. Boys and girls often put down on their papers what they believe the teacher wants them to say. Or, if the class discusses the question in advance, students may merely echo in their papers an idea expressed by another student. Each teacher will, of course, prepare his pupils to answer open questions in the way that best fits his teaching style, and adapt his procedures to the boys and girls who are in his class.

2. We must be careful not to use too many open questions, or the children may lose the spontaneity in responses that makes the answers valuable. One sixth-grade boy in a class where the teacher used too many open questions said one day, "What do I think? What do I think? Phooey!"

3. Relating the diagnostic devices to the regular classroom work is an effective way of motivating children to respond honestly and with continuing interest. The honesty of their responses increases as they see that their papers are useful to both the teacher and themselves.

4. Not all open questions are suitable for all grade and ability levels. Selecting questions that suit your class and teaching purposes is a skill we all need to develop. And since in all classes there are pupils of different abilities, some may prefer to draw pictures and tell stories while others prefer to write their responses to the open questions. As long as a response is obtained from each pupil, it matters little whether the response is oral or written. However, for his own use and for the use

of the Project research director, the teacher needs to record oral responses in the child's own words.

5. Many open questions and other diagnostic devices provide a take-off point for follow-up discussions. Usually children are eager to discuss experiences that they have reported in their papers. The teacher must be careful, however, to keep the discussions centered on what *many* children do, rather than on the activities of one or two individual pupils.

In the heat of the discussion pupils may be stimulated to talk about experiences in an overly frank and revealing way which later may embarrass them. All elementary school teachers have had experience with some pupils who reveal too intimate details of their lives in class discussions. Through experience, we develop skills for dealing with such incidents. In follow-up discussions of open-ended questions, we need to be particularly alert to helping the pupils safeguard their personal integrity.

6. Responses to open-ended questions are confidential material between the teacher and each individual pupil. Such information must be handled professionally as information obtained from private counseling sessions and psychological tests.

Summarization, Analyzation, and Interpretation

While responses to open-ended questions, time budgets, parent interviews, and observations of role playing and free play activities cannot be scored as tests can, the children's responses can be summarized in ways that increase their usefulness for teachers. A systematic summary leads to a more complete analysis of the whole class' papers, and thus to an interpretation which provides a sound basis for program planning. Some ideas you may find helpful in summarizing, analyzing and interpreting the data obtained from children's papers are included in Appendix A.

Appendix A: Master List of Activities Written About in Time Budgets

Work Activities:

1. Paying jobs: include such activities as caring for babies and young children, distributing handbills, delivering newspapers, clerking at a soda fountain, making deliveries for a grocery store, housecleaning and window washing, mowing or raking lawns, and acting as messenger.

2. Home chores: include such activities as caring for young brothers, and sisters, cleaning the house, washing and ironing, setting and clearing the table, washing dishes, firing the furnace, running errands or shopping, mowing and raking the lawn, weeding the garden, preparing meals, taking care of one's own clothes, room, toys, pets, etc., washing or repairing

the automobile, and feeding cows, chickens, pigs, etc.

3. Out-of-school lessons (not including religious instruction) include: foreign language, music, singing, dancing, drawing, and painting.

Active Recreation

1. Hobbies and games: include such activities as playing cards, checkers, chess, and similar games; making collections of Army insignia, butterflies, match covers, minerals and rocks, stamps, phonograph records, movie star pictures; cooking, sewing, and other domestic arts; playing imaginative games such as "house," cowboys and Indians, cops, and robbers, soldiers, etc.; playing traditional games such as hide and seek, hopscotch, jacks, skipping rope, singing games, etc.; painting and drawing; taking photographs or moving pictures; developing and projecting them; making models of airplanes, ships, trains, etc.; modeling in clay, soap, or wax; playing a musical instrument; singing; dancing; working on puzzles; playing with pets; etc.

2. Sports: include such activities as archery, baseball, basketball, bowling, camping, canoeing, cycling, motorcycling, fishing, football, handball, hiking, hockey, horseback riding, hunting, soccer, ice- or roller-skating, skiing, swimming, tennis, volleyball, etc.

Passive Entertainment: In general terms, includes such activities as attending a concert or lecture, visiting a museum, watching other children play, listening to a phonograph or radio, watching a sports event, listening to stories, "window shopping."

1. Moving pictures
2. Reading: the teacher might wish to subdivide this category further to show what is read—books, comics, magazines, newspapers, etc.
3. Television

Social Activities: in general terms, include such activities as club meetings, youth centers, fraternity, and sorority affairs; Scout activities, YM and YWCA (and similar groups) activities; parties of various sorts, such as birthday and holiday celebrations, dances, dinners, games, theaters; and eating out.

1. Visiting: includes receiving visitors or going on a visit.
2. Social communication: includes such activities as arguing, asking advice, or telling one's troubles to somebody, fighting, giving advice, gossiping, talking (face to face), telephoning, trading possessions, writing letters and notes.

Loafing: include such activities as "fooling around", "hanging around", "playing around", "sitting around", "sitting by the drug store", "going out on the avenue with the fellows", etc.

Meals: include snacks

Routine Movements: include such activities as going to school, to church, to the park, going downtown, going home, etc.

Religious Activities: include such activities as practicing for or singing in the choir, preparing lessons for and attending church school, attending church services, going to young people's church organizations, saying prayers, etc.

Grooming and Health Care: include such activities as taking a bath or shower, caring for the hair, washing and pressing clothes, shining shoes, taking a nap, brushing one's teeth, "washing up," visiting the doctor or dentist, etc.

In your analysis, when you have a clear idea of the range of activities in which your pupils might participate, get a general impression of the activities in which they do participate. Read quickly through the whole set of time budgets. Scanning will supply information and give some hints as to the form of analysis likely to prove most useful. Certain children will stand out for their full or restricted round of activities, their personal freedom or lack of independence, their light or heavy load of home responsibilities. Jot down notes as you read. They'll remind you of the activities to examine carefully later and of pupils to check on in more detail.

Try to find a way of tabulating essential information. The Tabulation Form on the following page is only a sample. Do not take it as a fixed outline. Every teacher using the time budget as a diagnostic instrument will have purposes that are uniquely his. For example, the teachers who helped develop the above tabulation form wanted to know what place movies, television, and reading had in their pupils' activities. All of these activities could logically have been listed under the category Passive Entertainment and entered in this broad category. The purposes of the teacher, and not the form or content of the tabulation sheet, determined that these particular items were selected for emphasis. Generally, you will find it more profitable to start with an expanded rather than an abridged tabulation form. If you start with a detailed listing, you can always combine. Breaking up large groupings, however, requires retabulation. By selecting certain items for examination you can meet your special needs. But keep the main categories intact. Then you can compare your findings with those of other teachers who have used time budgets as a diagnostic instrument or with time budgets of your own successive groups.

Time Budget Tabulation Form

Categories			School			
			1. John A.	2. Mary B.	3. Donna C.	4. Etc.
I.	Work	Paying Jobs				
		Home Chores				
		School Homework				
		Out-of-School Lessons				
		Total Work				
II.	Active Recreation	Hobbies and Games				
		Sports				
		Total				
III.	Passive Entertainment	Moving Pictures				
		Television				
		Reading				
		Miscellany				
		Total				
IV.	Social Activity	Visiting				
		Dating				
		Social Communication				
		Miscellany				
		Total				
V.	Loafing	Loafing				
		Total				
VI.	Meals Snacks					
		Total				
VII.	Routine Movements					
		Total				
VIII.	Religious Activities					
		Total				
IX.	Grooming and Health Care					
		Total				
X.	Remarks					

See Appendix A, pp. 96–119, for suggestions on summarizing and analyzing time budgets.

Make a tabulation form based on the pattern suggested here but adapted to your own purposes.

Here are some hints to make it easier for you to set up your table and arrange your data:

1. Make a list of the headings for your table. Star activities you want to single out for special attention. Ask yourself, "What activities will show me what I want to know about my pupils?" Maybe all you want to know is the work your pupils do. In that case tabulate everything under the general heading, "Work." However, if you want to know more specifically about their work, then tabulate under the subheadings Paying Jobs, Home Chores, School Homework, and Out-of-School Lessons. Your purposes in assigning the time budgets will determine what subheadings to use, as you cannot set up categories except on this basis.

2. Beside each category and separate activity on the list, indicate the subheadings needed to show with whom the pupils engage in their activities.

These preliminary listings will tell exactly how many spaces you need to tabulate the activities you are studying. Divide the sheet of paper so that you make the most efficient use of the space. Then enter your headings in the larger margin of the tabulation sheet. Use pencil so that you can erase errors easily.

3. Enter the name of each pupil in the class in the margin of the shorter side of the paper. Enter the names in alphabetical order, not by subgroups. The alphabetical arrangement permits flexibility and economy in analysis.

Make your first categories descriptive, not interpretive; concrete, not abstract. Here are categories one school used for an open question on "What I Like and What I Would Like to Change About My Home." These teachers were interested not only in what the students said about their homes, but also which relationships the remarks covered, such as relationships of the writer to father, mother, siblings, or family as a whole.

1. General undifferentiated response of—
    a) satisfaction: "I would change nothing; I like everything."
    b) dissatisfaction: "I would change everything; I like nothing."
2. Response regarding the physical features of the—
    a) neighborhood's appearance, convenience, and comfort: "We have nice gardens and trees. We are close to school. We have good places to play. There's too much traffic and noise. The houses are ugly and there's a lot of dirt and smoke."
    b) community's appearance, convenience and comfort: "I like Jonesville. This town has good schools."

3. Response regarding the physical features of the—

a) house and yard—its appearance, comfort, arrangements: "My house is very nice. I'd like to have a whole new house. It would be nice to have more rooms (or bigger rooms). It's warm and cozy. It's a nice place to go when it's rainy and cold. It is painted a pretty color. It has a nice garden."

b) furniture, interior decoration, and conveniences: "I'd like to re-decorate my room. We should move the television set to the front room. We need new curtains. We need new kitchen equipment (or other household appliances)."

4. Response regarding the facilities for recreation—

a) space available: "I'd like to have a recreation room. We could use a bigger yard. There should be a place for hobbies."

b) equipment: "It would be nice to have a television set (or radio, phonograph, musical instrument, home movie equipment, football, skis, skates, bicycle, etc.)."

c) pets: "I've always wanted a dog."

5. Response regarding privacy—

a) for self: "I really need a room to myself. Everyone should have closet space of his own. I'd like to have a desk for my homework."

b) for another member of the family: "My younger brother needs a place to play. Dad likes to have a place for his workshop."

c) for the family as a whole: "I wish we owned our own home. It would be nice not to have to share our kitchen (or bath). I don't like living in an apartment building."

6. Response regarding chores and work—

a) home duties: "I like to work around the house. I wish I did not need to wash the dishes every day. I wish Mother would let me cook a whole meal."

b) jobs: "I like my job. I can help with family expenses. I wish Mother didn't have to work. I wish Dad had a better job."

7. Response regarding personal relations—

a) activities: "I like going on family trips. I go hunting with Dad. I enjoy playing with the kids in the block."

b) attitudes: "The landlord is crabby with me. The neighbors butt into my business."

c) characteristics and behavior of neighbors (not implying direct relationship): "The people around here are quiet. They are clean people. I wish there were no Negroes next door. The neighbors are too noisy."

The following illustration shows a tabulation sheet made for a thorough analysis of the types of relationships covered in remarks on personal relations.

**Sample Form of Tabulation Sheet for Analyses
Made from Answers to Open Questions**

Names of Students	Personal Relations	A. Self to							
		Father	Mother	Siblings	Family as a whole	Adult Relatives	Peer Neighbors	Adult Neighbors	Landlord
Frank N.	Like								
	Change								
Ann J.	Like								
	Change								
Class Totals	Like								
	Change								

The more papers you work on, the easier you will find it to set up headings. The classifications you first use will almost surely seem inadequate to you later on when your understanding of this device has deepened. You learn how to set up categories by setting up categories.

No amount of working with ready-made tabulation sheets or with somebody else's classification scheme will give you the insight into your pupils' feelings and sensitivities that you will gain by making your own study from the ground up.

After you have set up the first categories and have finished the first rough draft groupings of data, you are ready for detailed study. At this point remind yourself of the reasons why you asked your pupils to write on a particular open question. Will your purpose be served by tabulating only one or two categories? If so, you need not classify every remark in the papers. Suppose, for example, you have asked your students to write on "What I Like About Our School" and "How Our School Could be Improved." You want to find out what the youngsters think of the status system and the social relationships in school. You won't need to tabulate all the statements. Some may deal with the school building, with athletic facilities, or with the school bus. On the other hand, you may want to have as complete a picture as you can get of your pupils' ideas on school life. Then use categories that include all the data.

Discoveries and Rediscoveries

During the first year of The Three-Year Experimental Project on Schools in Changing Neighborhoods, the participants made some discoveries and rediscoveries. It was too early to point to any generalizations or even tentative conclusions which might ultimately be found in the materials collected from children and in the use of projective techniques by teachers. It was possible, however, to detect important clues and implications which would affect the work of the second year in curriculum building.

A sampling of findings obtained reflect some of the clues for curriculum emphasis which were later used during the second year of the study.

How do young children see their neighborhoods? The children speak of things they like and would like to change in their neighborhoods:

"My friend gave me popcorn, candy, and potato chips and that's what I call sharing."

"We have a doll doctor down the street."

"There are all races. The people are friendly too."

"I have a nice big park across the street which I take my troubles to."

"In the summertime when I walk near my house in my bare feet there are trees to shade me."

"I feel sorry for a man in my neighborhood. I don't think people understand him."

"I don't like my outside toilet. It is cold out there."

"We have a building called Kingswood where we can go to have all our fun."

"Some people are mad at all children."

"I like to live where I have nice neighbors and not bad neighbors."

"There is one lady that tried to kill Nellie." (a dog)

"The neighborhood is noisy because of a boardinghouse next door. The men get very noisy and I cannot go to sleep at night."

"On Saturdays a gang of men would stand in front of my doorway and start singing and talking."

"At night babies cry and cars crash. Men and women are drunk. Dogs bark and cats mew."

"I would like more places for men to go when they don't have any place to go."

"I don't like my house."

"Some of them look bad and the landlords are charging high rent."

"Some of them are not fit to live in."

"I don't like outside toilets."

"I want my house burned down so I can move to a new one."

"My house is dirty inside. The wallpaper is off."

"Tear down the houses they built on the baseball field."

"Own the house we live in so we won't have to move."

"Cops, I don't like cops."

"People who don't like children. They always tell you to get off something."

"People who do not speak to me, sometimes."

"We can't skate on their pavements."
"Rough boys and teenagers are awful."
"There is a fight every Friday."
"The factories here stink."
"There are not enough clubs."
"There is too much rape here."

Things that make children angry were revealing:

"I'd rather have a mouse than a girl."
"Girls blame you for everything they do."
"When I go to school they say things about me."
"I don't have any friends."
"When someone bites me I cry and I am mad."
"Big children take things from little children."
"My brother gets mad at my mother and takes it out on my sister and brother."
"They talk about my mother and father."
"You go to the store for people they do not give you money."
"Something is missing and they say we stole it."
"I don't like fussy people."

When children spoke about their families, new insights were gained. The responses occurring most frequently to the question, "What is the best thing that could happen to your family and why?" were:

"For our family to have a new home, because —
. . . our place is falling to pieces;
. . . all of us can't get into one room together;
. . . it would be nicer to live in a new house;
. . . new neighborhood;
. . . different school district.
"For us to be together again —
. . . brothers are in the army;
. . . parent is in the hospital;
. . . parents are divorced;
. . . uncles, aunts, cousins are absent.
"For us to have more money for —
. . . paying bills;
. . . buying more necessities of life;
. . . a vacation in Europe;
. . . an advanced education.
"For us to have a car so we could —
. . . see my aunts and cousins;
. . . visit our old home and grandparents."

Many children expressed a wish to have more brothers and sisters. There seemed to be much concern about family illness. In one school, approximately one out of every five children seemed concerned with health problems in the family.

In the lower grades in response to the question regarding what they "like to do" and "don't like to do," some children regarded things families did together as chores. Performing solitary chores such as washing dishes, running errands, and child care seemed to be the biggest burdens.

Two or three children were concerned with parents' fighting. Every set of papers showed that at least one child was in a tragic situation. Children with a story to tell and children from sharply contrasting family and neighborhood environments, highlighted the problems of growing up in an urban environment. Typical are the following responses received from children:

MY NEIGHBORHOOD

I like my neighborhood the most because the park is near and I can practice tacking and things like that for scouts. I'm glad I live near town because I like the movies especially comedies and horror movies. Also there is the 5 and 10's for models and repairs for them. About five blocks from me my scout troop meets. We have a lot of fun there. I like the paintings and sculptures in the art center and I see them often because I live just around the corner from it. I like my community because I live near my church. Our church has many social activities like bowling and basketball to name a few. I also like our minister.

Now don't get the idea my neighborhood is perfect because it isn't. There are a couple of neighbors who are pests and I'll tell you why. The couple on the left side are pretty old and crabby. They run the vacuum cleaner and wreck the television screen. They slam doors all day and all night and worst of all as soon as we start hammering and sawing they run over and ask us to stop. One day when we were working on our dining room they ran over and asked us what's going on! Can you beat that? But the neighbors on the other side are even worse. One day Jiggs and I were playing a game of catch and the only boy in a family of six girls and one boy came over and asked us if we would let him play. But we said no because he can't catch and you can't tell him how. He probably will never know how anyway. But he kept on stealing the ball from us so finally we hauled off and told him that if he didn't get away we'd get drastic. So he went home bawling and his bodyguard mother came out to give us a talk. So we told her what really happened but she didn't believe us. So the next day we played up at school so pesty wouldn't find us. Unfortunately, he did. Again he tried to play with us but we didn't want him to. So he went home bawling again. When he told his bodyguard mother again she began to get drastic. She barged into our house, and told my mother about her "poor defenseless darling." My mother and Mrs. G. were as mad as hornets. Well after a while we got it straightened out at the expense of a day in the house for Jiggs and me and a belting for "pesty."

— Joe, Sixth Grade

MY LIFE STORY

I was born in the Wil. Del hospital. When I was about four months old I started cutting two teeth. My mother said I used to cry for an hour. My father had to rock me to sleep when my mother was busy. All of a sudden I had all my teeth. Then I was one. I used to think I was four because my sister is three years older than me. So, when I was one she was four. When I was two I broke my father's watch. My father was fighting with everybody but me because I was hiding under my mother's bed so he could not find me. Then I was three. When I was three I went to my aunt's house for two weeks because my mother had a baby. I was so bad my aunt could not do anything with me. So one day she said that if I kept on being bad she was going to tell my mother on me. I started being good. One day I broke my aunt's dish by mistake. I did not mean it. But she thought I did mean it so she beat me and put me to bed. The next day my mother and father came after me. My aunt did not tell on me. So when I got ready to leave I said good by and slammed the door and broke my aunt's window. When I got home my mother beat me so hard I laughed. When I was four I fell on two soda bottles and had 8 stitches in my arm. When I was five I had to start school. I did not like it very much but I had to go. When I was six I use to fight everybody I could fight I had a lot of fun. But one day I started a fight with some boy and he beat me up after that I did not start a fight. When I was seven I used to throw stones at people and windows. One day I threw a stone at some big boy and hid and there was an nother boy next to him. He beat that boy up and said, "Why did you hit me with that stone?" The boy could not talk his mouth was full with blood. He went home crying. When they got out of sight I took off and ran all the way home. When I was eight I was in Mrs. B.'s room and I play hookey two times.

My girl friend wrote me a lettle and Mrs. B. could not tell the differens between her handwriting and my mother's. One day my mother kept me home. Mrs. B. ast her why. She send us a lettle and Mrs. B. could tell for the other lettle and she ast my mother about it. My mother was surprised and when she got me home she said "I will wait for your father to come home and he will waste you because I probably could not hit you as hard as I want to. So I waited until my father came home. I was more afraid than I am when I go to the dentist. My father beat me so hard he liked to kill me. After that I did not play hookey any more. When I was nine. I went in town and stayed for about five hours. It was dark. Diane the girl in Mrs. N. room was with me and I said "Diane lets ast the police to take us home because I did not feel like walking home. Diane said "Oh you ask." I said no you ask. Diane said, "It was your idea." I said "oh." I went up to the police and said, "Where is South bridge? The police said, Why do you want to know where South bridge is this time of night. I said, I live there. Well you keep straight until you come to it. We were asking all kinds of questions life we did not know. The police man said "You better let me take you home. We got in the car and we put our heads down so no one would see us. When we got home Diane's mother laughed as hard as she could. "The police asked "why are you laughing?" She could not talk as she said she was laughing so hard next thing you know he was gone when I was ten I spilt shoe polsh all over the floor but my mother did not know it. She soon found out and I had to buy her another box.

When I was 11 I moved to Pennsylvania. I lived next door to my Aunt's house. When I was twelve, I moved over here. My first girl friend was Judy. When I was thirteen I had a big party but I was not happy because I could not invite anybody.

— Shirley, Sixth Grade

Children of elementary school age are keenly sensitive to everything in their environment. They see with the discerning and disarming insight of childhood the world as it is. While degrading environment blunts the minds and emotions of some of the children, the ability to focus upon human values is still an attribute of the very young. Thus in a neighborhood where exposure to drunkenness and degeneration is the daily fare of a child, we find him declaring that in spite of these things, "My neighborhood is a friendly place; my neighbor takes me in when I am cold; my neighbor babysits for me so I can play." Where human values are prized there is hope for the future, a future in which the school plays a major role.

Rediscoveries

As teachers used projective techniques, they gained useful insights of value in their task of curriculum building. For instance:

1. Seeing children's neighborhoods through the eyes of children gave new direction to a study of family and community life.

2. Staff members felt that they gained new insights into the needs, interests, and abilities of children.

3. In many cases, children, rather than books, became the sources of inspiration for meaningful educational effort. This was particularly noted by principals working with beginning teachers.

4. Staff members became much more aware of their own needs as people and as professional teachers.

5. A deeper rapport developed among staff members and between some children and their families.

6. A new significance was found in being thoroughly informed about children and in utilizing all available records in making plans for the guidance of children.

A sampling of some of the achievements made possible by projective techniques follows:

A Kindergarten Teacher Reported:

On Time Budgets—"As a result of the time budget, it was found that a number of kindergarten children were coming to school without breakfast. During the morning, instead of the usual cookies and milk, a number of times the children received cereal and fruit. Money was donated by an organization to help needy children."

A Grade 1 Teacher Reported:

On Time Budgets—"During the study of the time budgets it was found that a small number of boys and girls beg on the streets for pennies and nickels to buy candy and trinkets. Stress was placed on the fact that we *earn* our money—we don't beg for it. A study followed on honest ways to earn a living."

A Grade 2 Teacher Reported:

On Time Budgets—"The time budgets revealed that most children do not relax or have fun with their families. Stress was put on the recreational facilities available for adults and children in the area that do not cost much money. Several children made remarks that their parents had not heard of these recreational areas, and were not sure they were permitted to use them."

An Individual Progress Class Teacher Reported:

On Time Budgets—"As a result of the time budgets, it was found that many children get into mischief after class dismissal and before the return of parents from work. A study of the recreational facilities in the neighborhood interested these children in swimming at the YMCA and in activities of the Christina Center, the Peoples Settlement, and the Salvation Army. A number of boys and girls took advantage of these facilities."

Getting under way in the curriculum building aspect of the Project, which, during the first year, was centered in learning to use projective techniques as a means of diagnosing and analyzing children's needs, had been a satisfying and productive experience. It had firmly established the Project and the identification of staff members with it, and it had made possible a broadening of the number of participants for the second year. Instead of six, there would be twelve schools involved in the study. Additional staff members in the original group of six participating schools had indicated their intention to continue.

Progress in the curriculum aspect of the Project seemed to be a result of several important factors:

1. The readiness of participants to engage in the study.

2. The quality of leadership among administrators and teachers, based upon recognition of the moral obligation of teaching.

3. The skills, insights, sensitivity, and personality of the consultant, which enabled him to establish rapport and confidence among the participants.

4. The administration of the Project, which was geared to establishing a working team and attuned to the need of developing effective means of communication among all concerned.

5

A Design for Building a Human Relations Curriculum

With primary emphasis upon curriculum development during the second year of The Three-Year Experimental Project on Schools in Changing Neighborhoods, it became essential that a thorough understanding of the relationship between the achievement of goals in education for human understanding and the attainments of the goals of academic achievement should underlie efforts in curriculum development. Project participants defined curriculum in human relations education as understanding oneself in relation to other people and to human institutions.

Some Bases for Curriculum Planning

Several important premises were established to guide efforts to assure the achievement of goals in human relations education and in academic learning:

1. The premise, *children learn better when they see a need to learn,* means that getting at children's felt needs through diagnostic techniques has use value for the teacher.

2. The premise, *the child's motivation to learn acutely affects the quality of his learning,* means that when a child sees purpose in his learning, his academic achievement can be expected to improve.

3. The premise, *a human relations focused curriculum is conducive to the development of human relations skills, sensitivities, knowledge, and appreciation,* means that we are concerned with helping children and their families to achieve a more satisfying social life.

4. The premise, *academic skills and human relations skills reinforce one another.* There is no dichotomy between the two. Mastering the traditional academic skills becomes of greater significance than ever, because competency in living demands the ability to read; to use arithmetic; a knowledge of science and the social sciences; an ability to

appreciate art and music, and the practice of good physical and mental health habits.

At the beginning of the second year of the Project, the Project Administrator prepared a bulletin[1] for participants which was to serve as a base for curriculum planning. The following is based on the text of that bulletin.

The second year of development of the Project emphasizes curriculum building which is geared to helping children meet their human relations needs more effectively. We will be building plans for experience units in which the concepts essential in a human relations oriented education are of paramount importance.

This bulletin is designed to stimulate thinking and provide some help in understanding the terms:

concept,	experience,
generalization,	activity.

It suggests guidelines for developing teaching plans which are found through analysis of the work of the first year of the Project, and illustrates how these guidelines may be interrelated in curriculum planning.

The learning process is basically subjective in character; that is, each child learns from his experiences that which has meaning for him. The teacher who understands the nature of the learning process recognizes the error of attempting to provide "common learnings" of subject matter and content for all. "Common learnings" for all children must be conceptual in nature. And even then, a concept which a teacher is striving to help all children to learn will vary in depth, dimension, scope, and meaning for each child in her group. For example, the concept "home" may mean a different thing to each child in a first-grade group. The associations each child in the group makes with this concept will depend upon his past experiences and his present need to enlarge his concept of "home." Experience and need are different for each individual child.

What is a Concept?

A concept is an abstraction. This is why a concept is difficult to teach and why it is even more difficult to evaluate the quality of learning

---

[1] An excellent reference which was consulted in preparing this bulletin and which further develops the concepts presented is: *Learning and Instruction*, National Society for the Study of Education, 49th Yearbook, 1950, Part 1, Chapter 1, "How Children Learn Concepts and Generalizations," Brownell, William A., and Gordon Henrickson.

A second reference will be helpful to educators who wish detailed information on curriculum planning for human understanding: Crosby, Muriel, *Curriculum Development for Elementary Schools in a Changing Society*, D. C. Heath, Boston, 1964.

associated with it. Particularly is this true for concepts identified with human relations. The concept, "star" is applied to a given object but it is not restricted to that object. It also applies to a group of objects which have certain characteristics in common. One may see a "star" and recognize it, although if a child's concept of "star" goes no further than this it is extremely limited, for the concept "star" may be associated with its effect on the way of life of a people, on commerce, or on a multitude of other objects.

The concept, "faith" is even more complex for it may relate to nothing directly related to sense. One does not see the concept, "faith" for it has an intangible quality. The child in the elementary school may recognize the *word,* "faith," but he will not have much of a *concept* of "faith" until he has lived a while.

In either case, as deeper meanings are derived by the child in his concept of "star" or "faith" concepts break their limits of narrow classification and systems of ideas and become a part of other systems of ideas. For example, even when a concept such as "star" takes on deeper meaning and greater dimensions than those associated with an object to which the *word* "star" can be attached, such as "star of attraction" to describe a quality of personality, the concept moves from the tangible to the intangible. The learning process thus becomes one of integration and synthesis.

Because concepts are the results of continuous changes brought about by experiences, it can be expected that, when the teacher is skillful in selecting school experiences needed by the child in concept building, the degree of meaningfulness for each child will be unique and progressive. Thus for one five-year-old, the concept, "family" may mean simply the people he lives with at home—his mother, father, brother and sister. When he is six, the concept, "family" may include another association, that of the role of each family member, e.g. father as the breadwinner, mother as the homemaker. At seven this same youngster may add another association to the concept, "family"—that of the dependence of the family on others who serve it, e.g. the postman, the milkman. Later this same youngster may associate the concept, "family," with "clan" as branches of his family come together, with "neighborhood" as composed of a group of families, and, ultimately, with "world" as the home of the family of man.

In his kindergarten group, this five-year-old may live with siblings to whom the concept, "family," is simply a word and with still others, who at five, already associate "family" with the meaningfulness of the concept typical of seven- or eight-year-olds.

The abstractions of concepts become meaningful to the child, in increasing degrees of complexity, as he is able to make generalizations through experiences which in turn develop through activities.

What is a Generalization?

When the learner is able to state the formulation of a relationship which may be applied broadly, he has made a generalization. Thus, if a child is able to verbalize with comprehension the generalization, "It takes money to run a home," he is demonstrating that he has some understanding of the concepts "money" and "home" and comprehends a relationship between the two.

A generalization always expresses some abstract relationship between two or more concepts. Generalizations are complex for they are based upon more than one concept and are therefore the ultimate achievement in conceptual learning.

Generalizations result from problem-solving (thinking). To solve a problem successfully, the individual must be aware that the problem exists. He must have a background of information, associations, concepts, and related generalizations which may be drawn upon to solve the problem, and he must have a method of working toward a solution. Only through problem solving (thinking) will generalizations be achieved. Thus the teaching of generalizations must be through guidance of children in problem-solving. The multitude of generalizations must enable the child to live successfully and satisfyingly, and the teacher must select with discernment and judgment those to be included in the curriculum. Selection should be based upon the quality of meaning implicit in the generalization and its use value in living.

What is an Experience?

Human beings learn only through experience. When an individual interacts with his environment, he is experiencing. All experiencing is learning, although all learning is not necessarily desirable or positive. When the school speaks of experiences, it is concerned with the kinds of experiences which will result in the kinds of learnings it seeks for its children. The school that organizes its curriculum around experience units accepts the premise that to stimulate functional learning, the unit of work must be centered in children's problems, which *they* recognize, and that the solutions to these problems are effected through the utilization of socially useful content, subject matter, skills and materials. The utilization of content, subject matter, skills and materials becomes the means to an end, that of problem solving and, ultimately, to concept formulation and the making of generalizations.

What is an Activity?

"Learning by doing" has become so thoroughly established as a basic principle of modern education that little controversy is associated with it today. When a teacher provides guided activities for children, she recognizes that human beings "learn what they do," that is, they are learning what they are doing; they are learning their responses. The mistake that is commonly made, however, is in interpreting "activity" to mean overt, observable action only. Frequently, "activity" does mean this. But it means more. It means that often a learning activity can be implicit, not overt. When a child is learning to read, for example, some of his responses are overt. He is engaging in an activity (reading) which is observable. At the same time, his activity embraces learning to like or hate reading, which may or may not reflect overt evidences of these responses. Again, the child who is quietly listening to music, may be experiencing deep emotional responses (activity) for which there is no overt activity discernible. Because attitudes, values and beliefs are frequently implicit learnings associated with activities, the teacher dedicated to human relations-oriented education is alert to detect implicit as well as overt manifestations of learning by doing.

Learning occurs through:
1. Deliberately selected experiences
2. Carefully planned activities
3. Building concepts
4. Seeing the relationships between concepts in the formulation of generalizations

Unless the relationships between all of these steps are comprehended and planned for by the teacher, the ultimate achievement of learning (thinking), that is, the ability to make generalizations, will remain on a low level. Incorporating these steps in plans for the process of learning, is the crucial factor in developing curricula for a human relations-oriented education of children. The teacher begins with the identification and selection of concepts and generalizations needed by the children and plans for experiences and activities which will most likely result in the kinds of learnings (concepts and generalizations) she feels are appropriate for her children. When the steps are reversed and when activities become the first step in the learning process, the concepts children develop and the quality of these concepts will often be unrelated to the educational goals of the school.

Thus the teacher concerned with a human relations-oriented curriculum is faced with three developmental steps in planning for curriculum building with her children:

1. The identification and selection of concepts and generalizations to be learned
2. The selection and organization of experiences which she will provide in school to foster concept and generalization building
3. The provision for problem-solving activities which will enable the child to make generalizations—generalizations which, in turn, are incorporated in the continuously expanding dimensions of the child's concepts.

Categories of Concepts Needed in Effective Human Relations

The Project Administrator's bulletin, "Some Bâses for Curriculum Planning," went on to point out that concepts, which must be defined and selected before they can be deliberately planned for, developed, and learned on increasing maturity levels as children move from childhood to adolescence and adulthood, may be categorized.

Within the expanding community organization of the typical elementary school curriculum—in which the child moves from "self" to the identification of "self" with family, neighborhood, city, state, region, nation, and world—the number and varieties of concepts are infinite. In the categories of concepts needed in human relations education, cited on page 157, examples given may be repeated and enlarged in each category. But for individual children, at any given moment in their development, the meaning associated with each concept will vary, depending on the experience of the child and his current need.

In fostering the human-relations education of each child within his social setting, the problems for the teacher become those of determining common needs of children in her group and selecting for teaching and learning those concepts which should receive emphasis. A frequent criticism of teaching is that we attempt too much and select too many concepts for development at any given time in a child's school life. This results in a watering down and a superficial treatment of concept development. What is called for is a careful and deliberate identification and selection of several concepts most needed by the children at their present stage of maturity and need. Concepts thus fully learned on one level of maturity become the base of subsequent teaching on increasing maturity levels as well as the foundation for a broadening out of the total scope of concepts selected by an elementary school faculty for its total human relations oriented curriculum.

Categories of concepts needed by children in the elementary school follow.
1. Concepts regarding self: self, me, mine, feelings, love, hate
2. Concepts regarding other children: friendship, love, hate

3. Concepts regarding the home and family: home, family, controls, authority, love, values, responsibility, money, hostility, fun

4. Concepts regarding other adults: adults, dependence, friendliness, hostility

5. Concepts regarding the neighborhood: neighborhood interdependence, beauty, responsibility, recreation, work

6. Concepts regarding the larger community (city): community, city, industry, religion, work

7. Concepts regarding the state and region: state, region, taxes, traditions, nationalities, cultures

8. Concepts regarding the nation and American heritage: nation, American heritage, classes, government, faith

9. Concepts regarding the world: world, brotherhood, conflict, order, resources, hope

Essential Characteristics of Planning for Concept Building

Some characteristics essential in teaching and learning concepts needed in effective human relations education follow:

a) Concepts in each of the categories enumerated must come to fruition through deliberately planned experiences on each level of maturity throughout the school life of a child. The beginning of planned concept building occurs at the moment of school entrance and utilizes all that has gone before in the life of the child prior to his school entrance.

This calls for a thorough study of a child's past and continuing development in the environment in which he lives.

b) Major emphasis upon concepts or categories of concepts may well be placed at specific levels of maturity, designated for convenience as placement in grades, age groups, or educational levels—but all categories will receive some emphasis in each stage of a child's development, for a child's experiences, and therefore, his needs, are unconfined and uncontrollable. They are certainly not limited to what a child's parents and teachers feel is appropriate to his maturity.

When to place emphasis upon a specific concept and how deeply it is to be developed, depends upon the child and his need and upon a faculty's total plan for concept development throughout the elementary school.

This calls for functional record keeping and utilization; for unified and continuous faculty action in developing skills; for understanding the processes in curriculum development; and for the individual teacher's increasing understanding, sensitivity, and skill, in building with children an appropriate curriculum.

c) Concept building for human relations must function within the framework of typical content areas of the curriculum. These are not distinct and separate, but interrelate with one another:
1. Arts
2. Health and Physical Education
3. Social Studies
4. Language Arts
5. Mathematics and Science

By emphasizing human relations needs, the child's purposes and motivation for learning information and for acquiring skills, knowledge, and attitudes bring into perspective the *use value* of subject matter and tools which are of prime importance in helping a child meet his needs. They become means rather than ends in education.

This calls for a new approach in teaching; one in which books and organized bodies of content and information contribute to the child's growth and development as resources in meeting his problems, and not as material to be memorized and reproduced out of the context of a life situation.

Guidelines for Curriculum Development

From the first year of study during The Three-Year Experimental Project on Schools in Changing Neighborhoods may be identified the guidelines for curriculum development during the second year. These guidelines make it possible for teachers to develop teaching plans which foster the growth and development of children in terms of effective human relations (skills, sensitivities, understandings, concept building) in the context of educational programs long established as the responsibility of the elementary school (emphasizing skills, content, information, knowledge, attitudes, appreciations and concept building).

Following are the guidelines suggested in the preliminary planning of a major experience unit of work for the children by the teacher.

Guideline 1: The Needs of Children
a) The need to belong
b) The need for affection and love
c) The need for at least a minimum of economic security
d) The need for recognition and respect
e) The need for achievement
f) The need for understanding the world around them
g) The need for freedom from excessive feelings of guilt
h) The need for freedom from excessive feelings of fear

Guideline 2: The Human Relations Needs of People in a Community

a) Relationships in the family—child-child, parent-child, parent-parent
b) Relationships in the community—child with neighbor; with older and younger boys and girls; with storekeeper, policeman; with teachers and others
c) Relationships in play and work groups—child-child, group standards, conflicts between group standards and family standards
d) Relationships in the American society—between individuals and groups, especially in the area of moral values and democratic ideals

Guideline 3: Broad Curriculum Themes of the Elementary School

a) Home and Family Living
b) How Groups Function
c) Neighborhood and Community Studies
d) Expanding Community Studies—state, region, nation, world

Guideline 4: Major Emphases in School Progression of Curriculum Themes

Age or Grade Groups	Themes
Beyond the elementary school	
11-12 (sixth grade)	America and the World
10-11 (fifth grade)	Our Nation
9-10 (fourth grade)	Delaware and Its Region
8-9 (third grade)	The City of Wilmington
7-8 (second grade)	Our Neighborhood
6-7 (first grade)	Home and Family Living
5-6 (kindergarten)	My Family and I
Birth—5 (the pre-school years)	Experiences in Living

Developing New Insights and Skills

Throughout the second and third years of The Three-Year Experimental Project on Schools in Changing Neighborhoods, the focus of teacher education continued to be the development of skills in curriculum building through planned experience units that would help children grow in human relations, sensitivities, skills, knowledge, and information.

Developing new insights and skills in curriculum planning presented difficulties during the second year. Effective curriculum planning demands from teachers knowledge of content, skill in selecting content which will contribute to the solutions of the human relations problems of

---

↑ * Once introduced at the appropriate level, concepts related to the theme are systematically, sequentially and continuously developed through school instruction.

children, and knowledge of the relationships between the needs children experience in their daily lives and the academic achievement they need for problem solving, now and in the future. The basic bulletin on curriculum planning prepared by the Project Administrator for use by participants at the beginning of the second year of the Project, provided the guidance necessary for learning new planning processes and techniques. But more was needed to help participants interpret the processes described in the first bulletin and to develop skill and security in using it.

Accordingly, Dr. Vickery, the curriculum consultant, prepared the following companion bulletin.

Building Resource Units in Human Relations Education

Resource units in human relations education are to the teacher what a painting is to an artist. Developing a unit, like painting a picture, is a creative act, calling for talent, inspiration, knowledge, technical skill, planning, discipline, and labor. And like a painting, a unit is a living, growing thing, with room to add fresh ideas to the basic design as the teacher works with his children in the continuous process of learning. But units end, and paintings are completed. And the teacher will never again teach the same unit in the same way, any more than an artist will go on making exact copies of a picture which pleases him. New inspiration, deeper knowledge and insights, and increased skill will certainly change the form and content of both the artist's and the teacher's work, although their distinctive styles will persist in every new situation because each has his unique talents and gifts.

The Characteristics of Unit Building

In The Three-Year Experimental Project on Schools in Changing Neighborhoods, we are building units of work centered on the human relations needs of children. What are the characteristics of such units? What is involved in planning and teaching them? Let us answer these basic questions in brief before we explore in more detail what each step in unit building involves.

Units are built with and for children. Kluckhohn and Murray have said that "Every man is in certain respects like all other men, like some other men, like no other man." The same generalization applies to the boys and girls who make up each class in our schools. In certain respects they are like all other groups of children their age, like some other groups, and like no other group. We build our units with and for our particular class, basing instruction on what they know and what they need to know.

Units relate school instruction to life needs and experiences. A distinctive feature of human relations education is its concentration on helping children understand themselves in relation to other people, to the social groups they and other people belong to, and to human institutions. So immediate and persistent are the needs of people in these vital areas that human relations education is a particularly effective way of relating school instruction to the children's daily lives and experiences. What is learned in school can be applied both immediately and in the future. As children see the "use value" of human relations education, the strong motivation for serious thought and careful study that such instruction carries with it helps to facilitate the mastery of such subjects as reading, writing, and arithmetic.

Units give focus, pattern, and wholeness to the learning process. By organizing knowledge, skills, and feelings around ideas, units enable children to explore and expand concepts, to form generalizations and to learn processes for solving problems. Unit teaching helps us to overcome the tendency to fragment instruction, to set children at many separate and often unrelated tasks which they find difficult to integrate into functional systems of thought and behavior.

Units provide for inductive learning. Unit teaching begins with providing activities and opportunities for experiences which help children to explore and test an idea, and to come to a conclusion which they can use to guide their behavior. The idea the children are asked to explore and test corresponds to a hypothesis set up by a scientist to guide and discipline his thinking. The activities and experiences the children have are like the data the scientist gathers to test his hypothesis. The conclusions the children come to, the concepts they develop, and the generalizations they form demand the same kind of rigorous thinking that the scientist uses as he accepts, rejects, or modifies the hypothesis which guided his explorations.

The process of testing a hypothesis, of solving a problem inductively, is a way of thinking valuable in many different kinds of situations—in human relationships as well as in scientific and technical fields.

Unit teaching makes it possible for children of different abilities to work together toward common goals in the same classroom. If we try to measure all the children in our class by the same yardstick—for instance by their capacity to master, retain, and repeat the same body of factual information—we are almost forced into some form of ability grouping. On the other hand, if we regard learning as a process of testing ideas and solving problems, children of differing abilities (within limits, of course) can work together on problems of common concern to them. Subject matter and materials will vary with the child's interest and ability, but the learning process will be the same for all, and the concepts and generalizations will be the same though they may be developed to different degrees by different pupils.

When teaching is so planned, children can help and learn from each other, the cultural handicaps of some boys and girls can be lessened, and each child can more easily undertake his most necessary and difficult task—the task of discovering what his individual capacities and limitations are in comparison with others, and of learning to use and accept them.

Units in a program of human relations education integrate knowledge, sensitivities, skills, and ways of thinking. We arrange our teaching objectives under the headings of knowledge, sensitivities, skills, and ways of thinking—the dimensions in which all learning takes place—to guide us in providing children with the activities and experiences they need.

A teacher in a Project school planned with her class a visit to the Opportunity Center. She wanted the children to see how people with severe handicaps, physical and mental, can become at least partially self-supporting. Her objectives included learning what jobs handicapped people did, how they prepared themselves for their jobs, and what they earned. She also wanted the boys and girls to feel how important jobs are to handicapped people; how a job helps to meet the needs everybody has for achievement, independence, and being a part of the big world.

The activity she selected to work toward both these objectives was interviews with the workers, and she began training her children for such interviews. Then it occurred to her, "What does stopping work in order to talk with children do to handicapped workers, paid as they are on a piecework basis?" Instead of proceeding with the interview training, she raised this question with her class. The children decided not to take the time of the workers, much as they wanted to find out first hand what their jobs meant to them, but to ask the director of the Center instead.

The sensitivities the children acquired and the skills in problem-solving they developed in the course of their discussion proved even better human relations education than the activity originally planned. The children learned to see that an action which would benefit them might not benefit the other people involved, and made their decision accordingly.

The wise teacher fully utilizes each activity to provide for learning in many dimensions, while making sure all categories of objectives have activities and experiences directly related to them.

Units in human relations education utilize fully existing curriculum themes, subject matter, and materials. There is no separation, much less conflict, between human relations education and the curricular themes, subject matter, and teaching materials already established in the Wilmington elementary schools. Rather, human relations education organizes subject matter in such a way that it helps children develop concepts and form generalizations concerning themselves in relation to other people in the contexts of family living, the community, the nation, and the world.

A focus on human relations motivates children to learn, helps them cover more subject matter and retain it better, and advances their mastery of academic skills.

Units in human relations education are so planned that learning throughout the school years is sequential and cumulative in its effect. The faculty of one Project school identified the concept "interdependence" as an important one to be developed from the time a child enters kindergarten until he leaves the sixth grade. Meeting together, the faculty planned a sequence of generalizations around which units of work could be built, beginning with interdependence in the family and culminating in interdependence among the nations of North and South America. Such planning makes possible a continuous growth in children's knowledge, in their feelings about themselves and the people with whom they associate, in their social skills, and in their capacity to think rationally and objectively. Most important of all, it helps them to develop values to live by, including a sense of personal responsibility based on an understanding of man's interdependence.

We should not be disturbed that the sequential learning in human relations cannot be as precisely defined, the steps in the process as neatly planned, and the results of instruction as objectively measured as sequential learning in mathematics and the natural sciences, for example. We can follow the established curriculum themes—home and family living, expanding community studies, the American Heritage, and learning to function in work and social groups—to give contexts for and continuity to the experiences we hope our children will have. Through unit building we provide a focus for the children's work within the curriculum themes, based on our diagnosis of their experiences, interests, capacities, and needs. We can improve our teaching skills so that the boys' and girls' school experiences will be of the highest quality. But our work in human relations education rests ultimately on our faith in the individual human being. We believe that the children themselves, with our help, can and will explore ideas, acquire knowledge, and wisely select principles to guide their lives—each child in his own unique way. We would not plan a learning sequence to condition children to accept our or any person's ideas uncritically, even if we could. To do so would be to lay the foundations for a totalitarian state.

Units in human relations education deal with significant ideas of lasting importance. Human relations education is not at the edge of the school's program; it is at its very center. It seeks to help children develop for themselves and apply in their daily living a system of ethics based on respect for themselves and a humane regard for other people—in short on the concept of the brotherhood of man. It seeks further to build a sense of responsibility to match their rights—as members of a family; as neighbors; and as participating citizens of the community, state, and nation. It endeavors to make them conscious of their heritage as Americans who are responsible for the nation's future. It emphasizes the interdependence of nations and each person's place in the whole family of man.

None of these objectives is new or strange to elementary education. All of us in the Project hope simply to come closer to attaining these goals by planning and organizing our teaching in a better way. Our aim is to provide quality education for all children.

The Relationship Between Diagnosing Human Relations Needs and Unit Building

Since units are built with and for children, the first step in the unit-building process is an identification of the children's human relations needs. And since each class is in some ways like no other group of children; and because boys and girls change as they grow, learn, and develop, diagnosis of needs is a continuous process. The more we use diagnostic devices; and the more we practice organizing, analyzing, and interpreting the data the devices yield—the more expert we become in accurately identifying the needs of children.

The instruments available for the diagnosis of children's needs are many. Open-ended questions, time budgets or diaries, sociometric questions, autobiographies, and parent interviews are particularly valuable because they yield data directly relevant to human relations education. But no one instrument provides an assessment of needs sufficient and accurate enough to serve as a basis for unit planning.

Our confidence in the validity of our data increases when:

1. Different instruments supply data supporting similar conclusions: A sociometric question may reveal that a class is composed of several mutually exclusive groups with many unchosen boys and girls. The "with whom" column in the class' time budget shows that the same cliques prevail in the children's out-of-school life, and that many of the unchosen ones have only limited social contacts. The clues to children's needs which the two instruments supply are much more convincing than those provided by either one alone.

2. Instruments used at different times indicate the same or similar needs: An analysis of children's comments on "The Best Thing That Could Happen to My Family and Why" reveals a deep concern of many children for their parents' economic needs—a better home, payment of bills, new furniture, hospital care. Their comments two weeks later on "If I Had $500," indicate the same concerns. Similar comments to similar topics at different times show that the need for economic security is persistent with these children, not a transient one based on an immediate crisis.

3. Our findings are consistent with the reports of other research studies: Children's time budgets and responses to open-ended questions indicate that many of them are "on their own" a great deal of the time, unsupervised by adults. At the same time many of these same children carry heavy loads of family responsibility, particularly in caring for younger brothers and sisters and in doing the family shopping.

Our confidence in the validity of these responses increases when we compare our findings with those of Allison Davis, Lloyd Warner, Robert Havighurst, and other authorities whose research shows that an early independence of adult authority and assumption of responsibility are indeed characteristic of children from comparable social and economic backgrounds.

We should, however, recognize that our data legitimately may call other research into question. For example, a widely held current theory is that migration often leads to psychological "rootlessness," with a consequent loss of aspirations and values. The data we have gathered in Wilmington suggest that even though children may be "rootless" they cling to their aspirations for the good things in life, and to such values as neighborliness and strong family feeling, despite their families' mobility, low economic level, and cultural handicaps.

Children's written responses are consistent with their responses in individual interviews. A teacher studying his children's time budgets found many reports of shopping for the family, principally buying food and sometimes shopping for their own clothes. He checked the written reports with private oral interviews to determine whether the children's shopping was a regular part of their families' way of life or only an occasional chore. When the children's oral responses coincided with their written reports which suggested that shopping was one of their regular responsibilities, the teacher proceeded with confidence in identifying their needs and planning his work to meet them.

Children's responses are consistent with the reports of other independent observers. When the children wrote their answers to the question, "What do you like best about your neighborhood" one of the most frequent responses was "The lady down the street who helps us." Specifically, they mention such items as "the neighbor who helps us keep warm until mother gets home from work, or the lady who brings us soup when mother is sick, who gives us a dime to go to the store for her, who takes care of my younger brothers and sisters so I can go out and play." When such responses are reinforced by what the parents say when the teacher makes a home visit, our confidence in our data increases. We can build with more assurance on the "neighborly experience" of the children as we develop our teaching plans.

Children's responses are consistent with our own and other people's observation of their day-by-day behavior. The children's papers on two subjects, "The Best Thing That Could Happen to My Family and Why" and "Things That Grown-Ups Do That I Don't Like" reveal a lack of stability in family life and inconsistency in parental and adult behavior that greatly disturb them. When grown-ups, particularly parents, cannot afford to buy the things they need, quarrel, stay out late leaving children on their own, show favoritism, or are inconsistent in discipline, the children are upset and angry.

In the daily classroom work, the teacher notes the children's need for set patterns of work and regular routine. A change in schedule or a variation in the daily pattern of work disturbs them inordinately. The children's need for security and consistency expressed in their papers, reinforced by the teacher's observations, clearly identifies a psychological need which the school can help to meet.

The Process of Diagnosis in Action

Diagnosis of needs is the first fundamental step in unit planning. For an adequate diagnosis we require carefully selected, appropriate instruments. Our choice of diagnostic instruments is guided by these principles:

1. *We select instruments related to the curriculum theme we are developing and the unit we are building.* A teacher in the primary grades is developing the theme of home and family living, through a unit on the ways different members of the family help each other. One of the topics in the unit deals with how families have fun together. To discover the children's experiences in this area of living, she asks them to draw pictures about "The Time I Had the Most Fun With My Whole Family." Each child brings his picture to the teacher and tells her the story that the picture shows.

Or again, a teacher is working to develop the theme of the American heritage, through a unit on the people who settled Delaware. So that she can relate the experiences of pioneer families with the children's own experiences, she asks them to write on the topic "A Time My Family Moved: What Made It Hard to Feel at Home in Our New Neighborhood." Children who had not had the experience of moving could write about a visit they had made to another city, what helped them to feel at home there, and what made it hard for them to feel at home. The unit points up the similarities and differences in the motivations and experiences of the pioneers and of families now "on the move," increasing the children's knowledge of, and identification, with the settlers of Delaware.

2. *We select instruments appropriate for human relations education.* Diagnostic questions for human relations education always ask children to express their thoughts, feelings, and experiences as they relate themselves to other people, to social groups, and to human institutions. The questions and devices suggested in the bulletin, "Diagnosing Human Relations Needs," illustrate how such instruments may be developed and used. Many teachers, using this bulletin as a guide, have invented questions appropriate for their children and to the unit which they were developing.

All of us are familiar with the pretest technique as it relates to subject matter. For example, if our subject matter sample covers the role of Delaware in the American Revolution, we might ask the children a number of preliminary questions to see if they have any factual knowledge of the persons, events, important ideas, and dates related to that period of history. Such a preliminary study is useful in planning our work.

Human relations education holds that it is equally important for the teacher to find out how the children feel about and relate themselves to historical figures and events. For this reason we formulate questions which tap, for example, the children's understanding of the motives and aspirations that led the founding fathers to establish their political independence. If we assume that among their motives was a desire to have a voice in making the laws under which they lived, we can then ask the children questions related to this motive, such as "The Rules in School That I Find Easiest to Obey, and Why;" "The Rules in School That I Find Hardest to Obey, and Why." When the children's experiences with rules can be compared with the founding fathers' feelings about the arbitrary laws imposed on the colonies by England, the psychological connections between present and past are more easily established.

3. *Supplementary instruments are used to fill in gaps in the data.* Many teachers in the Wilmington Project have used the open-ended questions,

"What do you like best about your neighborhood?" and "What would you like most to see changed in your neighborhood?" The responses to these questions often indicate that adults outside of the children's families strongly influence the children's feelings about the neighborhood they live in. To get clearer and more detailed information about the relationships between children and adults in the neighborhood, many teachers use the supplementary questions "What do grown-ups (not in your family) do that you like; What do grown-ups do that you don't like?" The supplementary questions supply data valuable in lesson planning which were not supplied by the first set of papers.

4. *We help children see the connections between the instruments we use and the work they are or will be doing.* Diagnostic techniques are a part of teacher-pupil planning. Children are motivated to respond to diagnostic questions when they see that what they write, draw, or say really makes a difference in their regular school program.

For example, we might begin our planning by saying to the children, "We are going to study the neighborhood we live in and learn how our neighborhood is an important part of the whole city of Wilmington. It will help me a great deal in making plans for our study if you will write a paragraph or two about our neighborhood as you see it. Let's begin by writing about 'The Thing I Like Best in My Neighborhood.' Think about the question for a while, and when you have made up your mind tell what you think by writing a paragraph or two. I'll be glad to help you with words and spelling but I want you to put down your ideas, not anyone else's. What you write will help make our neighborhood study more interesting to all of us."

The relationship between the regular classwork and what the children say in response to questions can also be established by referring to the group's responses in discussions. For example, if the children indicate that they have many responsibilities for taking care of younger brothers and sisters, the teacher might say, "When I read your papers I found that over half the boys and girls in this class take care of their younger brothers and sisters, before school and after school. Let's see how many different things we do for our brothers and sisters; let's find out how our 'babysitting' helps us, the younger children in our family, and our parents." Such a discussion, rooted in the reality of children's experiences, and helping them to solve some of the problems that the care of brothers and sisters entails, can establish closer relations between the teacher and his pupils. Such a discussion can also enable the children to see diagnostic instruments as a way of making their school work more interesting and meaningful to them.

5. *The children's responses are used professionally.* In using children's responses to open-ended questions and other semi-projective devices, it is imperative that we accept our responsibilities as teachers. The children's privacy is to be respected and their confidences treated confidentially. When we use the material as a basis for class discussion, the names of specific children are never linked with what they have said or written. Rather, we use such phrases as "several children reported that . . , " or "many boys and girls in the class said that . . . ." When we share our findings with our colleagues, as we must if we are to work together for the welfare of the children in our school, we treat the data as professional people, observing in our relationship with our children the self-imposed discipline that a doctor observes with his patients, a lawyer with his clients, or a clergyman with his parishioners.

Summary of the Steps in Building Resource Units for Human Relations Education

Unit building follows an orderly process and is based on an inductive, scientific approach. It begins with the diagnosis of children's human relations needs: what they need to know about themselves and other people; what feelings and sensitivities they need to develop; what social skills they need to master; what capacities to think rationally and to solve problems they need to acquire. From the identification of needs it moves to the formulation of teaching objectives. Teaching objectives are drawn together into generalizations, stated as ideas which the children can explore, test, and take into themselves to guide their actions. The generalizations or focusing ideas suggest subject matter—experiences and activities which serve as the means of exploring, testing, and internalizing an idea.

After a teaching unit is planned we have reached the point that an artist reaches when he has developed his design for a painting, made his sketches, and decided upon the approach to his subject. As he begins to paint, we begin to teach our children. The unit design guides and focuses our instruction, but our daily work with boys and girls constitutes the art of teaching, which calls upon all the creative imagination and technical skill we can bring to it.

The final evaluation of our children's work, the last step in unit planning, takes many forms. We can test objectively for the mastery and retention of specific information, for certain skills, and for the ability to draw conclusions from data or to reason logically from a given premise. Such tests are valuable and necessary. But how can we evaluate the children's growth in sensitivity to the feelings of other people? their capacity to relate well to many different people in different social situations? to choose the form of behavior most appropriate to the situation? to be inclusive and discriminating in their choice of associates and fellow workers rather than exclusive and stereotypic? Objective measures of sensitivity, values, and human relations skills are few, and many are of doubtful validity. Systematic observations of children's behavior, projective instruments such as open-ended questions, and the boys' and girls' own subjective estimates of what they have learned offer the best hopes for evaluating the "intangibles" in human relations education. Selecting appropriate methods of evaluation are as much a part of unit development as is any other step in the process.

Each of the steps in the unit-building process can be described and illustrated in as much detail as we have here devoted to clarifying the relationship between the planning of a unit and the diagnosis of human relations needs.

The Proof is in the Eating

An old proverb tells us that "the proof of the pudding is in the eating." An illustration of an experience unit of great value to a group of ten- to twelve-year-olds in North East School is reported by Dr. Agnes Snyder, volunteer curriculum consultant to the Project. This illustration is significant not only in its depiction of curriculum building, but also in its portrayal of the processes of in-service education engaged in by participants in The Three-Year Experimental Project on Schools in Changing Neighborhoods.

Pioneer Day: A Culminating Experience in the Development of a Study of The Westward Movement

I. On the Day

There was something different about the halls of North East School that snappy November morning. Those halls are always interesting and always friendly. Too young to claim a traditional atmosphere—the school is just in its second year—it already has something distinctive about it, something that is unmistakably human. The school is part of the Riverside Community of Wilmington, Delaware, a low-income housing development, one in which no racial barriers are reared.

Descendants of old Delawareans whose clear blondness proclaims their Dutch, English, or Swedish ancestry live side by side with Negro and Puerto Rican newcomers who in increasing numbers are arriving daily from the South. The school reflects the ethnic composition of its community with its 20-38 per cent white and 62-80 per cent Negro children, the ratio varying as families move in or out of the neighborhood. The faculty, while drawn from far and wide, is similarly heterogeneous ethnically. The school exemplifies to an exceptional degree the recognition of the common denominator in all people.

On this particular morning as I entered the building I was attracted to two groups of children, one standing before a bulletin board and the other before a glass display case. The children did not look the same as usual, not that they had changed but that their clothes had. Broad-brimmed black paper hats shadowed the boys' faces, while wide white collars covered much of their shirts. The girls wore white caps tied beneath their chins, white collars, and long, voluminous, bright-colored skirts gathered in at their small waists.

The bulletin board which had the attention of one group was labeled "Pioneer Day." On it were both silhouettes and three-dimensional figures of pioneers. In the display case attracting the other group were all manner of pioneer artifacts, pioneer dolls, and books about pioneer life.

As I approached the office I saw Mrs. LeVigne joining a group of children; not the Mrs. LeVigne in her usual professional character as efficient school nurse, but a demure Mrs. LeVigne in soft gray dress with long full skirt, broad quilted white collar, and white cap on her head. I walked into the office and there sat Mrs. Foreman, secretary, fingers flying over the typewriter as usual, but she, too, a different personality in a white cap.

The next person I saw was Miss Patterson, the helping teacher. Her transformation was the most complete of all. No full skirt for her. Instead, dark trousers pushed into high boots, a black cut-away coat, a white shirt, a flowing tie. For Miss Patterson was Mr. Brinkley, the school master of Pioneer Day.

Now Mrs. Wilson, the principal, came from her office, she, too, wearing a white cap. She took me to what is usually called the multipurpose room. But not today. For one day it was not that at all, but very much a single-purpose room, the pioneer cabin of the day's activities. Something of a cabin effect had been produced by the pictured logs on cardboard covering the lower parts of the walls. But the amazing thing to me was the great array of articles, relics of pioneer days, scattered about the room.

Mrs. Coker, teacher of the group of children responsible for Pioneer Day and coordinator of all the activities involved, came forward to greet me. She was lovely in a two-toned long-skirted dress protected by a bibbed apron and wearing, of course, the emblematic white cap.

I hardly knew where to begin to look. Naturally, the big things first caught my eye: A beautifully made patchwork quilt appliquéd in a colorful geometric design; the custodian helping a group of children set up a quilting frame near the wall on which the completed quilt was hanging; a spinning wheel; a child's crib; a wooden churn along with wooden milk pails; and a big, black iron pot.

On one of the walls were samples of the rugs children had been weaving of strips of rags on their own hand-made looms, and samples of their knitting, some done with their own hand-made knitting needles. On tables were smaller articles. A big iron key sent my mind wandering to massive gates locked against marauding tribes; a powder horn and a musket brought back the ever-present need for defense, the tramp of hoofs, the Indian war cries. The candle molds, the old knives and forks and wooden spoons, the fireplace crane spoke of the simple life that went on from day to day in those pioneer cabins, while the footwarmer set me shivering as I thought of the cold bedroom and the colder church this was meant to make less grim.

One table was given over to old textbooks. One that particularly impressed me was a copy of *National Arithmetic,* published, I was surprised to learn, no later than 1874. I copied one of the problems:

> If 24 men in $5\frac{1}{2}$ days of 11 hours each dig a trench of 7 degrees of hardness and $232\frac{1}{2}$ ft. long, $3\frac{2}{3}$ ft. wide, and $2\frac{1}{3}$ ft. deep, in how many days of 9 hrs. each will 24 men dig a trench of 4 degrees of hardness, and $357\frac{1}{2}$ ft. long, $5\frac{3}{5}$ ft. wide, and $3\frac{1}{2}$ ft. deep?

I wondered—is this what the critics of modern education would have us return to?

The readers were no less forbidding. No color, but quite a few black-and-white line drawings—the ruins of Pompeii, the combat of a man with a jaguar, a forest fire, an agonized face struggling to keep above flood waters. The stern realities which the pioneer daily faced were not escaped in a brighter world of books.

While I was wandering around the room living in the past, the children were intently examining what was there. No adults were with them. They were free to satisfy their natural curiosity.

I asked Mrs. Coker how the collection had been acquired, and if the children had had any share in it. She said that there was little of anything like this in the children's homes, and that these were the contributions of the teachers from their own homes and those of their friends. She said that the community had been most generous in lending what often could not be duplicated as, for example, the beautiful patchwork quilt.

I learned from my program, which a child had given me earlier, just what the design of the whole day was. The participants, children and teachers, all belonged to one or the other of two pioneer families, the

Weavers and the Daniels. Mrs. Coker was Mrs. Weaver and Mrs. Klug, Mrs. Daniels. The Daniels family would spend the day with the Weaver family, sharing in the work to be done, attending school, and joining in recreation.

Now the Weaver family was all assembled, and was busy making last minute preparations for the guests. Mrs. Weaver asked her "boys" to lay their bows and arrows, with which they were all armed, on the floor and go to their classroom and bring down extra chairs. This they did quietly and rapidly. A touch here and there by Mrs. Weaver and her "daughters," and the room was in readiness.

Mrs. Daniels entered the room with her "family" and was warmly greeted by Mrs. Weaver. Then both families seated themselves around a very long table. At the head of the table was "Mr. Weaver," on other days Howard Jones, the tallest boy in his class. Mrs. Weaver called on Mr. Weaver to offer a prayer. He had written this prayer some days before, promptly lost it, but assured Mrs. Coker he "had it in his head." All bowed their heads while Mr. Weaver gave the following:

> Father, we thank you for letting us wake up another morning with the blood running warm in our veins. We thank Thee for keeping our family from hurt or harm in the dark, dark night from the people and animals that will harm us. We thank Thee also for giving us strength to walk and talk and sing your songs. We thank Thee for clothing, food, and shelter. Most of all we thank Thee for letting us reach this rich land. We pray that you hear our prayer. Continue to shower us with Thy blessings.

After this children and adults scattered to the various tasks of the day. One group went to the quilting frame, and soon the material for the quilt was stretched on the frame. Another group sat on the floor with Mrs. Daniels, weaving on their looms and knitting. Others joined "Aunt Hattie" (Mrs. LeVigne) preparing vegetables for the huge pot of simmering soup stock, the savory odors of which soon permeated the room; a few took turns at churning; others made candles in the old molds; some made dyes of pokeberries, which they had previously gathered, and of onions. When "Mr. Brinkley" (Miss Patterson) rang the school bell, the younger children went to school. Both boys and girls participated in each of the activities apparently with no more consciousness of sex differences than of racial ones. Some of the children persisted in the same activity throughout the morning, while others shifted among the activities.

The school activity particularly intrigued me because of the way both teacher and children played their roles. Miss Patterson *was* Mr. Brinkley, and the children *were* pioneer children. The materials helped in this: the horn books which the children had made and from which they read and the birch rod in Mr. Brinkley's hand.

Slowly and laboriously, horn books in hands, the children read the alphabet, the combinations of the letters into syllables and, finally, into words. Mr. Brinkley wrote two maxims on the board:

A good character shines like a candle.
The only jewel which will not decay is knowledge.

Shades of the old copybook days when as a child I wrote such mottoes, ten to a page, twenty-four pages to a book, each line getting progressively worse on each page, and the same fate happening to successive pages!

Mr. Brinkley did not have the children copy the maxims but, instead, he tried to explain their meaning. The difficulty these children have in expressing themselves, coming as they do from homes in which conversation of any kind is often at a minimum, and that often in a foreign language or dialect, showed up here. The following illustrates:

Mr. B: "What is character?"
Child: "A good citizen."
Mr. B: "Could you have a bad character?"
Child: "Some good, some bad."
Child: "How you act."
Child: "How you think."
Mr. B: "Yes, and how you feel."

Whenever Mr. Brinkley called on a group to read, he had the children "toe the line." If one got out of line he tapped him with the birch rod and sent him to the end of the line. This amused the children, and they played up to "teacher" by becoming mildly naughty. At one point, "Big Sister Sally" (Miss Redding, physical and health education instructor) left the group and stood nearby, whereupon one of the children waved his hand and called out, "Look, teacher, that girl is standing up!"

Toward the end of the morning the final preparations for lunch had to be made. The table was to be set, no small task for twenty-nine children, six teachers, and five guests. Then the corn muffins, left to the last so they could be served hot, had to be mixed and baked. A group looked after each of these chores. The rest had a merry time dancing the old reels and square dances learned during the course of study. Big Sister Sally directed the dancing; Mrs. Rittenhouse, the music teacher at North East, thrummed her guitar; and Mr. Richardson, the music supervisor for the district, fiddled. Away they all went—girls, boys, teachers—in vigorous dance: *Virginia Reel, Music in the Barn, Birdie in the Barn,* and *Circle All Around.*

Tired from the strenuous exercise, they all sat on the floor at the feet of the "lovely lady," Mrs. Edgell, the school librarian. Unlike the rest she was not in work clothes, but wore an attractive long-skirted flowered dress and, instead of a cap tied under the chin, a filmy lacy handkerchief above "her bonny brown hair." Then she read to them "Whittling Johnny," from *Children of the Handcrafts* by Caroline Bailey.

All through the morning the churning had gone on. I suppose sooner or later everyone had had a turn at the churn. But all the turns put together had not made the butter "turn." Mrs. Weaver evidently had expected trouble and had provided "store" butter in case the children's failed. Those good hot corn muffins just had to be buttered by the old formula, "Take two and butter them while they're hot."

After lunch Mrs. Coker's mother and some friends arrived from "downstate" and with the hands of experience soon had butter, and the children had the pleasure of seeing a big pat of golden butter which they had not quite made, but had had a share in making. The candles, however, never would leave their molds. I am inclined to think that the fault was in the materials used—old candles.

The lunch was a great success. The soup and corn muffins alike were excellent. And the pumpkin pies, as the children would say, "were out of this world." The pies had been baked the day before. I was amused at an aside from Mrs. Wilson, "The childen scrubbed and scrubbed their hands before making the crust. And the crusts of all the pies came out the same color!"

At the close of the meal, I heard one of the girls say, "Now, I suppose we'll wash the dishes!" My heart sank as I looked down that long table at the pile of dishes. But it was not to be.

"No," said Mrs. Weaver, "the cafeteria will take care of the dishes—in the dishwasher." Quickly, the children fell to, stacked the dishes, piled them on the cart, and wheeled them to the cafeteria. In a surprisingly short time the room was in perfect order. Perhaps not doing the dishes would present our critics with evidence that we had "gone soft" in education today. I would not agree. There is a time, as we learn from Ecclesiastes, for all things. I should add to the Preacher's list, "a time to hew to the line, and a time to bend the line." This, I am sure, was a time for bending. The children do dishes every day at home. Besides—there was the school dishwasher.

On the usual school day this would be noon recess time. Today the children were on their own until the campfire activities started. No directions had been given to the children. Nor had there been any formal dismissal. For a moment I wondered how this time would be spent. I did not wonder long. A half dozen were busy at the quilting frame. Any number were knitting. Out-of-doors some were dancing the reels of the morning. In one corner of the school yard a band of Indians threatened an attack on the settlers. It looked as if Pioneer Day was becoming part of the thinking, the feeling, and the acting of the children.

Now for the crowning event of the day—the campfire. The day before, Mr. Brinkley had gone with the children to a neighboring bit of woodland to gather wood for the fire. There was great excitement today in laying that fire, setting a match to it, hearing the first crackle, smelling the woodsy odor, and watching the first flame shoot upward as we gathered on the playground. Some of the children, in the meantime, came in ceremoniously with the covered wagons they had improvised out of their express wagons, boughs, and old sheets.

Soon the fire was burning briskly, and we all gathered around it. Popcorn toasters were brought out, and turns were taken at popping and passing brimming bowls of the hot corn around the circle. And we sang. How we sang! The old songs of long ago: "Home on the Range," "She'll Be Coming 'Round the Mountain," "Wait for the Wagon," "Down in the Valley," "Skip to my Lou," "The Old Brass Wagon," "Oh Susanna."

Mingled among the songs, games were played: Blind Man's Buff, Hop Scotch, Hide and Go Seek, Cross the Brook, Bow, Bow, Belinda.

The day had turned gray toward noon. Now, as the strains of "Oh Susanna" died away, the rain began to fall. We went indoors and "called it a day." It was nearly three—the end of the regular school day. The children gathered their belongings together and, as they were ready, said good-bye to us. Then back they went to the realities of their new homes of the Riverside Community.

II. Before the Day

How did Pioneer Day come about? To begin at the end rather than at the beginning, it was the climax of study and planning begun by a group of teachers in the spring toward the close of the previous school year, and continued with the children in the fall. The study was undertaken as part of The Three-Year Experimental Project on Schools in Changing Neighborhoods aiming at adapting the existing curriculum guides to the needs of children in rapidly changing neighborhoods.

This is the second year in which the North East School has been in the Project, since the school was not established until the Project had been a year under way. North East School is situated in the midst of the Riverside Community. Its 571 pupils are drawn entirely from the community of which it is a vital part.

The pupils are organized in two types of classes: seven "straight" grades, the usual elementary school organization, and eight interage groups. The latter have been established in the effort better to meet individual needs. In these classes, grade lines are eliminated, the children being brought together in what, in the opinion of the teachers, would make good working groups. The children who participated in Pioneer Day are in an interage group. They have been drawn from grades 3, 4 and 5; they range in I.Q. from 65 to 124; and in reading level from grades 2.1 to 7.1.

Pioneer Day was the climax of a study of the Westward Movement, one of the topics designed in the Wilmington Curriculum Guide to develop the theme, *Our American Heritage*. To understand how Pioneer Day came to be it is necessary to trace its development from the first faculty meeting held in the new North East School on September 6, 1960. I was privileged to attend that meeting and subsequent ones (I am a volunteer recorder for the Three-Year Project), and what follows is an attempt in summary form to show the steps in an interesting curriculum process.

The September, 1960 preschool staff meeting was exhilarating. Everything was new—and everybody. Workmen in the halls were still putting the finishing touches on the shiny new building. Parents were thronging the office to enroll new children. The principal was new. The teachers were new to each other as was the custodial staff.

In the midst of all this newness Mrs. Theda Wilson, the principal, presided over the first meeting. Her first emphasis, after preliminary greetings and introductions, was on the community. It is true that she gave facts, but she did much more. She had been busy in the community all through the summer and it had become to her a personality. She spoke of the uprootedness of the people who had left neighborhoods composed generally of people of similar background among whom they felt at home. Now they found themselves among strangers of different races, nationalities, religions, customs. The great need for guidance of families in making difficult adjustments pointed to the close relationship that must exist between home and school. Teachers would need to see the community through the children's eyes and to sense their needs as individuals with unique personalities. On this foundation the creative job of curriculum construction needed to be undertaken.

Mrs. Wilson introduced Dr. Vickery as the representative of The National Conference of Christians and Jews and as a consultant who would help in the work. In this first contact with the faculty, Dr. Vickery gave his major points of emphasis in curriculum development. In brief these were:

1) understanding the children through a study of how they felt toward

themselves, their families, their communities, their country, the world;

2) on the basis of the foregoing, to formulate concepts or generalizations toward which the education of the children should lead, understandings that would serve as guides to behavior;

3) through understanding the needs of children and through clarity of the concepts toward which the work was directed, to plan experiences which would help achieve the goals.

During October and November 1960, Dr. Vickery worked with the faculty on the elaboration of the above points. Many techniques for studying children with emphasis on getting at their real attitudes were developed and tried out by the teachers. They experimented, too, in formulating generalizations and interpreting concepts that were within the children's grasp, that involved people and relationships, that could be put to use, and that were true. Then they began thinking of broad experiences and their related activities through which children could best work toward their goals.

In the meantime Dr. Crosby, as administrative coordinator of the whole, attended meetings and, out of her broad general knowledge of curriculum problems and her specific knowledge of Wilmington, participated in the discussions at crucial points with apt suggestions. In addition, besides handling the mechanics of administration involved in such a project, she supplied in bulletin form quantities of material both clinching the ideas brought out in meetings and supplying additional rich resources.

From January on the faculty engaged in practical application of the theory developed to constructing units of work for their own grades. It was at this time that work really began on planning "The Westward Movement" in Mrs. Coker's interage group. The specialists on the faculty—in art, music, physical and health education—the librarian, and the nurse had wanted to find a way of participating in the Project. After careful thought they decided that they would like to work as a research team on "The Westward Movement." Each specialist searched out the ideas and activities in her particular area of specialization that a teacher of an intermediate group could use in developing such a unit. From then on Mrs. Coker and the specialists worked together hunting out materials, visiting spots for possible field trips, enlisting the interest of the community in lending relics of pioneer days, and reading extensively for the enrichment of their own backgrounds.

The specialists also worked directly with the children. Mrs. Klug ("Mrs. Daniels") in art classes guided the children in dressing pioneer dolls and in producing other pioneer artifacts and arranging them in the display case and on the bulletin board. Mrs. Klug also taught the children how to make looms, to weave on them, and to knit. Mrs. Rittenhouse taught the children the songs of pioneer days. Miss Redding ("Big Sister Sally") in her physical education classes had the children learn the old games and dances and helped them produce the atmosphere of a log-cabin in the multipurpose room. Mrs. LeVigne, the nurse, taught the children the practical ways the pioneers handled illness, the old remedies they used, and the crutches they improvised. She also helped them with the cooking—making the pies, the muffins, the soup. Mrs. Edgell, the librarian, worked from the beginning with both teachers and children in helping them find the books and other materials needed for their study. Coordinating the whole was Mrs. Coker, the classroom teacher. Assisting her was Miss Edith Patterson, the helping teacher. It was Miss Patterson, too, who took the children on the trip to gather wood for the fire.

The children were well under way in their study of The Westward Movement when the idea of Pioneer Day was proposed to them. They adopted it eagerly, and two planning sessions followed in which all participated. The result was a natural movement into Pioneer Day, going on with the activities from the point reached the day before. The lunch and the camp fire alone were special. That is in their final form, because these too—gathering wood, planning the menu, purchasing the materials for lunch, making the pies—had all been in the day's work.

III. After the Day—Reflections

In order to obtain spontaneous reactions to "The Day," Mrs. Wilson asked both the children and the participating teachers to write just how they felt about it.

The responses of the children included both statements as to the activities they liked best on Pioneer Day and generalizations as to their attitudes toward pioneer life. Their statements of specific likes were diversified with no indication of any one activity being more popular than another. Their generalizations, however, were predominantly concerned with human characteristics and relations, and comparisons with the present.

Among the activities, one each gave as the activity liked best: the campfire, songs, lunch, candle making, cooking, butter making, story telling; two each gave preference to dances, school, and knitting. None mentioned quilting, though, as an observer, I should have said from the interest shown that quilting would have held a high place in their choices. Likewise, the rug making was not mentioned.

Included in the generalizations was much of liking and even of nostalgia for pioneer days. Some stated reasons; e.g.:

I would like to live in pioneer days because I think it was wonderful.

I liked their homes and the way they got along together. I liked it in the old days.

I liked the things they did better than today. I liked those days better than today.

I would rather be a pioneer than what we are today. I would go around with my father wherever he went. I would be so smart I'd be able to teach school for them.

I would like to live in pioneer days because I like the adventure and the moving from country to country.

Some characterized specific features of pioneer life contrasting it with ours of today, often to the disfavor of the latter; e.g.:

They got along together; nowadays we don't get along too good.

The pioneers were brave. They were braver than the people nowadays. They were not fighting all the time.

I liked the school because you did not have to bring books home.

In those days they saved a lot of money. They did not throw anything away.

I liked the long dresses that they wore because when it was cold their legs wouldn't get cold.

They had far better table manners than some people have nowadays.

I like the way they kept what little bits they had.

They kept their children dressed well.

I like the way they liked to go to church.

They were brave and bold. Nowadays men aren't so brave.

They had great respect in those days. But now children bark back at their parents.

It is interesting to compare these efforts of the children with the generalizations toward which the teachers in their planning had hoped to lead the children.

What is to be made of this experience?

It is hard to say. First of all, children in general are slow to react verbally about their experiences. This is particularly true with children like these who, in the main, are very limited in their language experiences at home. We will have to wait to know how deeply this experience has and will affect their thinking, feeling, and acting.

Here is what the teachers concerned in the Project thought about it:

Mrs. Coker (the classroom teacher and co-ordinator of the unit): The activities of Pioneer Day were rewarding to me inasmuch as I witnessed the kind of living which comes with complete cooperation within a large group. Though we worked hard our emotions were rather relaxed because, I believe, of a keen sense of inter-dependence in the group.

Mrs. LeVigne (nurse): Pioneer Day may have accomplished several things that we had not planned for. The participants had listened, probed for material, and planned verbally for the day. I think the activities of the day exceeded the participants' expectations.

Mrs. Edgell (librarian): This was an experience for the group that will leave a lasting impression. Learning by doing was very worthwhile. The children spent time reading, and gleaning information on the Pioneer Period from all viewpoints. Then they had the happy experience of putting it into practice.

Mrs. Rittenhouse (music teacher): Living as a pioneer for a day seemed to be the most comprehensive learning activity I have witnessed in the two and a half years I have been teaching. The children involved certainly entered whole-heartedly into all the different facets of the plan and showed that they had been exposed to and absorbed many learning experiences in this unit. Personally it was also an enjoyable day even though it entailed much hard work by all the teachers involved. Perhaps a different class could have a day like this each year.

Miss Patterson (helping teacher): When asked to evaluate Pioneer Day, I wondered what I should say. What skills were learned? What growth evidenced? Who knows? The more I teach the more I realize how little I know about what children learn.

Certainly no book, film, or lecture could have ever given these children the feeling for pioneer life which was evidenced as they helped make soup, sewed on the quilt, did some weaving, tried to make candles, and made butter. They found that life in the early nineteenth century was not all glamour and excitement.

Miss Redding (physical and health education): This was a wonderful opportunity for the special teachers to work with the classroom teacher. Working together gave everyone a feeling of belonging to a group and of playing an important role in it.

Pioneer Day gave some of the parents an insight into the many learning experiences in which the children were involved as they worked on the unit.

I believe the children realized that they could live and work together in a community without fighting. They were able to accept responsibilities. Above all they showed respect for each other.

Mrs. Klug (teacher of art): It seemed to me that Pioneer Day was effective and worthwhile. It is possible for a project like this to become top-heavy, that is, for the preparations to outweigh or not to correlate with the educational values to be derived from it. However, I feel that this was definitely not the case in this instance. I had a chance to observe the class often during their preparations, and due largely to Mrs. Coker's perception and skill, everything they did was meaningful. Even the recipe quantities were worked out by the children. It seemed obvious to me that the class really understood pioneer life and had been well prepared for the event.

It is interesting in the above comments that there seemed to be a feeling that while the undertaking entailed much hard work it should be repeated annually. It is significant, too, that while the project involved much subject matter and much use of reading, writing, and speaking, no claims were made as to any phenomenal growth in knowledge and skills. So often in such projects one gets the feeling that they must be justified on the basis of the amount of academic learning that took place. Further, one often feels a little uncomfortable from the effect given that somehow the activities involved were not completely engaged in because of their own intrinsic worth to the learner but rather for the exercise of academic skills. There was nothing of the sort in this project. The activities were selected because it was believed that they would contribute to deeper appreciation of our American heritage, and through this to the desire to emulate in human relations what was good in pioneer living. If this is accomplished, there can be foundation for the assumption that the children will have increased motivation to learn academically.

What impressed me as an observer on that day was the way children and teachers lived together from 9 a.m. to 3 p.m. in complete sharing in the activities. There was not a single instance in which the teacher gave a command or a reproof to a child. There was no disorder, and this with no adult "watchful eye" on the children. There was complete freedom, and no one took advantage of it. It was natural living.

Nor did the activities end with Pioneer Day. I have learned since that the impetus given on that day has continued in further activity. Their candle making, even though not successful at the first try, has led to making more candles and ceramic candlesticks for Christmas gifts. Two painting projects have also resulted. The children painted pictures of themselves dressed in pioneer clothes and engaged in the activities they would most have enjoyed in pioneer days. Then they painted pictures of themselves dressed in today's clothes paralleling the pioneer activities with those they enjoy today.

Dr. Vickery had been the guiding spirit of the Project since its inception in August 1959. He visited North East on Pioneer Day. He was ill and could not remain for the campfire. But after lunch he lingered a little while and stood with me looking at the way the children during the noon recess were continuing the activities of the morning. I looked at his face, happy in spite of the pain I later learned he was suffering, and heard him softly say, "The thirties are living again."

Dr. Vickery was referring to a chat which we had recently in which we spoke of what I called "The Golden Age of American Education," the 1920's and 30's, a time when childhood came into its own as never before. It was a time when schools were developed in which children learned and lived eagerly, naturally, joyfully; a time when books were written that embodied the spirit of these schools—*New Schools for Old, A Schoolmaster in a Great City, The Play Way, Schools of Tomorrow.* We had talked nostalgically of those days and expressed our grave concern over the trend in education today with its emphasis on standardization, competition, grading, and mechanization. Today I heard in Dr. Vickery's voice the satisfaction, the rejoicing of a lover of people when he sees children living and learning eagerly, naturally, joyfully. How good that Dr. Vickery's Wilmington visits terminated on so high a note!*

Thus far Dr. Snyder's report.

Henry Steele Commager has said, "A child's mind is not a vessel to be filled, but a flame to be kindled." When children and teachers recognize that feelings are facts and when learning in school is rooted in the need to feed the spirit and imagination as well as the mind, the flame is kindled and the mind is freed to comprehend and explore. When children are given the stimulation of developing their potentialities for living in harmony with the finite and infinite worlds, there is hope for a better world which they will create as adults, a world which will make the earth truly the home of man.

---

* Dr. Vickery died shortly afterward in the third year of the Project.

Taking Stock in Mid-Stream

The second year of The Three-Year Experimental Project on Schools in Changing Neighborhoods produced gains far greater than could have been anticipated when the Project was initiated in September 1959. It also revealed areas of need in teacher education for human relations skills, insights, understandings, sensitivities, and knowledge which influenced the direction of the Project in its third year of development.

Charles Franklin Kettering, the Founding President of the Edison Foundation, has written:

> "Nothing was ever built to touch the skies
> unless some man dreamed that it should,
> some believed that it could,
> and some willed that it must."

Participants in the Project had demonstrated the existence of a dream—the dream of creating a kind of living and learning in school with use value for children and their families. Progress in the achievement of more meaningful curricula revealed that the dream may eventually become a reality. The diligence and hard work of the participants to increase their teaching skills and insights prove that the will exists to make the dream come true.

Some of the achievements of the Project schools, some of the problems yet to be met in developing the Project design, and some of the clues for direction in the third year of the Project reported by participants, are included in this chapter.

Assessing the Achievement of Goals

It should be kept in mind that The Three-Year Experimental Project on Schools in Changing Neighborhoods was a pilot project through which we hoped to accomplish three major goals:

1. To determine through action research the possible means for upgrading teaching and learning in a human relations context.
2. To incorporate the results in the Wilmington public elementary school curriculum.
3. To develop a Project design that could serve other communities.

The achievement of these goals required a careful appraisal of where we were, where we had failed, and where we might go in 1961-62, the third year of the Project.

As an important phase of the evaluation of the second year of the Project, participants were asked to respond to a number of questions in order to provide the consultant and Project leaders with an assessment of the areas of strength and needs as the participants saw and felt them. These questions were related to—

a) the use of diagnostic instruments during 1960-61;
b) the kinds of open-ended questions used;
c) the most pressing human relations needs of children identified by their teachers;
d) the scope and spread of experience units developed by teachers;
e) the identification of concepts emphasized in the four major curriculum themes: Home and Family Living, How Groups Function, Neighborhood and Community, Expanding Community (American Heritage);
f) the advantages and values recognized by participants in the Project;
g) the kinds of help and opportunities recommended by participants during the third year of the Project, 1961-62.

In studying the data provided by participants it should be kept in mind that while participants may have developed several units in each class during the second year, only one was filed for analysis. The brief analysis of implications refers only to the units filed. When weaknesses in development seem implicit, it may well be that other units, not available for study, dealt adequately with many learnings.

Use of Diagnostic Instruments by Participants, 1960-61

During the second year of the Project, the participants who contributed to its evaluation (131) were composed of two groups. The first group (38) had spent the first year exclusively in learning the use of diagnostic techniques and instruments. The second group (97) entered the Project as first year participants. They were to experience a combination of learning and using diagnostic instruments and of incorporating their findings in curriculum building. All participants were given a response form asking that they list diagnostic instruments which they felt would aid them in developing an experience unit focused on human relations education. Table 7 reveals the types of diagnostic instruments selected and the extent of their use by participants.

Types and Extent of Diagnostic Instruments   Table 7
Selected and Used by Participants

TYPES SELECTED	EXTENT OF USE				
	Primary Teachers	Inter-mediate Teachers	Teachers of Trainable Retarded	Specialists	Totals
Open-ended questions	68	38	7	4	117
Sociograms	27	20		2	49
Time budgets	17	15	3	1	36
Autobiographies	10	10		1	21
Children's conversations	1	1	7		9
Class discussions	6	2	1		9
Dramatic play	2		3		5
Role playing	4	1			5
Parent conferences	3	1	1		5
Creative writing about family	2	2			4
Home visits	1		3		4
Children's manifest anxiety scale		3			3
Observation of free play			3		3
Interpretation of pictures			3		3
Painting pictures of family activities	2				2
Anecdotal records and observations		2			2
Keeping a diary		1			1
Rules my family expects obeyed	1				1
Constructing a model neighborhood	1				1
Pupil-teacher evaluation		1			1
Walk in neighborhood	1				1
Teacher-child interviews		1			1

The specific diagnostic instruments selected by the participants are significant. Only the first four listed in Table 7 were printed on the response form. All others were culled from suggested instruments entered by participants under the general heading, "Others." It is probable that if all types had been printed on the response form, other respondents would have been reminded of the fact that they had used them, too. It is significant, however, that relatively few participants identified for themselves types of activities and instruments which have diagnostic value.

Of the twenty-two types of diagnostic instruments selected and used by participants, open-ended questions were used most extensively by teachers of all levels and assignments. Sociograms were second, time budgets third, and autobiographies were fourth. With the exception of open-ended questions, there was relatively little use of the wide range of diagnostic instruments available to teachers. This presents a challenge to the leaders of the Project.

Categories and Extent of Use of Open-Ended Questions

Major areas of need for diagnostic efforts by participants included Self, Family, Neighborhood, Other Children (peers), Adults, American heritage, The World, Groups and How They Function.

The concepts children have become clues to their needs in living with themselves and others. Table 8 reveals the categories and extent of use of open-ended questions selected by participants to diagnose children's needs.

It seems that greatest emphasis was placed by participating teachers on securing information relative to children's concepts of self, family, and neighborhood. This emphasis reveals the teachers' concern with discovering needs of children, their families, and their neighborhood environments. There is a marked difference in emphasis between concerns of primary and intermediate teachers regarding family and neighborhood. A plausible explanation is that primary teachers customarily center curriculum experiences in family and neighborhood life, while intermediate teachers customarily center curriculum experiences in studies of the larger community—state, region, nation, world.

Categories and Extent of Use of Open-Ended Questions

Table 8

CATEGORIES	EXTENT OF USE			
	Primary Teachers	Intermediate Teachers	Teachers of Trainable Retarded	Totals
Self	42	49	19	110
Family	80	24	4	108
Neighborhood	61	31		92
Other Children (peers)	18	14	1	33
Adults	12	10		22
American Heritage		7		7
The World		4		4
Groups and How They Function	8	4	1	13

Considering that it is one of the goals of the Project to provide children with *consistent* experiences throughout their school life, it would seem—to the extent that the data in Table 8 are accurate—that the development of intermediate children's deepening concepts of family and community life is not being adequately provided for in the later years of their elementary school life, particularly in view of the fact that relatively little use of other types of diagnostic instruments was revealed (Table 8).

Categories for which least use of diagnostic techniques and instruments was revealed are the American Heritage and World themes. With television available in homes of all economic levels, with automobiles no longer a luxury, with mass media and transportation making it evident that children today live in a rapidly expanding world, it is safe to say that children's horizons are not bounded by the immediate neighborhood. As children live out of school they are incorporating in their beings concepts arising out of their experiences with law and order, government services, social services, morals and values, democratic principles or a prostitution of them, and many other aspects of what the American Heritage is and what it is becoming. Similarly, children are developing concepts of other people and other places in and out of their own country.

Because the roots of concepts are established early in life, and because the intermediate level commonly builds curricula centered in state, regional, national, and world studies, the implications for lack of use of diagnostic instruments and techniques in the categories of the American Heritage and the World themes are serious. Are these studies ignored completely in the primary school? Are these studies built in the intermediate school out of reference to the concepts children already have formed? If these questions are answered affirmatively then there is little reason to doubt the validity of the frequent reports from colleges and universities regarding the abysmal ignorance of the nature and development of their own form of economic and political life revealed by many young people, nor is there any doubt of the failure of education and other social institutions to provide the sustenance of the spirit which was needed by so many young American soldiers who succumbed to "brain-washing" in recent wars. If children's knowledge of the American Heritage and of America's world neighbors is centered in feelings, facts, and information and not in concepts which incorporate facts and knowledge to build generalizations, isolated facts and knowledge will depart in time of stress, and prejudices will prevail. This is the challenge to teachers dedicated to building curricula in human relations education, especially in the later years of the elementary school.

These teachers must be able to assume that their pupils have attained a degree of readiness to learn, which it is the responsibility of the primary grades to instill.

The category, Groups and How They Function, received relatively little emphasis. Concepts in this category could well have been included in those of Self, Family, and Neighborhood. In addition, Sociograms, reported 49 times in Table 7, is group oriented. The use of this type of diagnostic instrument extends the emphasis upon helping children understand and develop skills as members of a group.

The Most Pressing Human Relations Needs of Children Identified by Their Teachers

Categorizing the human relations needs of children as identified by responding teachers is a difficult job. An attempt was made to categorize the teachers' recognition of needs of children in Table 9. Some forty categories of identified needs provide significant information relative to the needs teachers see and the relative importance they attach to them.

Table 9 presents implications of vital concern to those who are engaging in a project centered in human relations education. In the first year of The Three-Year Experimental Project on Schools in Changing Neighborhoods much emphasis was placed upon the needs of children. For the purpose of the study, children's needs as a facet of human relations education were adapted from those identified by Louis Raths: The need to belong; for affection and love; for a minimum of economic security; for recognition and respect; for achievement; for understanding the world around them; for freedom from excessive feelings of guilt; for freedom from excessive feelings of fear.

During the second year of the Project, these needs were incorporated in curriculum planning and became Guideline 1, recommended for building experience units.

To the Project Administrator needs identified by participants reflect—
- a concern for the welfare of children;
- a concern for the social demands of a middle-class society;
- a concern for the improvement of family and community life;
- a concern for the emotional needs of children.

Implied in these concerns is an awareness of an eagerness for helping children achieve the human relations skills, sensitivities, insights, and knowledge which the Project sets as its goals.

Because one problem encountered by participants is that of seeing the relationship between human relations needs and academic achievement, the Project Director examined the identification of needs in Table 9 to spot reflections of this relationship. They are almost totally missing.

The Most Pressing Human Relations Needs of Children   Table 9
As Identified by Their Teachers

NEEDS	NUMBER OF TIMES IDENTIFIED BY				
	Primary Teachers	Inter-mediate Teachers	Teachers of Trainable Retarded	Specialists	Totals
Developing respect for others	25	22	1	2	50
Learning that people must live together harmoniously	26	13	1	3	43
Learning respect for property	19	9		1	29
Satisfying children's need for love and understanding	17	9		2	28
Developing standards for acceptable behavior	15	6	1	4	26
Developing respect for self	10	6	2	2	20
Understanding responsibilities	6	9	3	1	19
Building self-esteem	7	7	1	1	16
Developing feelings of security	9	5		2	16
Learning to share and work together	8	5	1	1	15
Developing broader concepts of community	8	5		1	14
Learning to solve problems in noncombative manner	7	6			13
Developing appreciation of all kinds of work	4	8			12
Developing self-motivation	3	4	1	4	12
Building family responsibility	5	5	1		11
Understanding and accepting other children	5	4	2		11
Understanding privileges and their related responsibilities	5	4	1	1	11
Providing more and varied experiences	2	1	7	1	11
Building moral and social values	6	4			10
Broadening cultural experiences	5	3	1	1	10
Providing better nutrition and rest	4	4	1		9
Raising standards for home living	3	6			9
Learning to make the best of abilities and environment	7	2			9
Feeling wanted in family, school, and neighborhood	1	2	3	2	8
Having better adult supervision	3	3			6
Providing recreational facilities in neighborhood	4		1		5
Understanding that people are alike regardless of race	2	3			5
Understanding that people are interdependent	4	1			5

The Most Pressing Human Relations Needs of Children As Identified by Their Teachers
Table 9 cont'd

NEEDS	NUMBER OF TIMES IDENTIFIED BY				
	Primary Teachers	Inter-mediate Teachers	Teachers of Trainable Retarded	Specialists	Totals
Developing "true" concept of home and family	2	2		1	5
Providing family recreation	3	2			5
Building better communication between parent and child	4	1			5
Learning to spend money more wisely	3	1		1	5
Accepting limitations	2	1		1	4
Understanding personal and family problems	1	3			4
Developing emotional maturity	2	1			3
Learning importance of earning a living vs. welfare hand-out	1	2			3
Understanding authority is needed to protect the weak	1	1		1	3
Identifying potential of children	3				3
Developing facility in verbal communication	2		1		3
Understanding that different behavior patterns are acceptable in different cultures	2				2
Developing pride in neighborhood and surroundings		2			2
Providing varied art activities for home				1	1
Providing success experiences		1			1
Using cultural and recreational resources of Wilmington		1			1
Developing closer relationship between home and school	1				1

One of the major emphases in the teacher education aspect of the Project is the importance of academic skills and knowledges as significant ingredients of developing human relations skills, sensitivities, understandings, and knowledge. It is posited that academic learnings are of increasing importance in a sound human relations education program because of their use value in living; and that, as teachers are increasingly able to root the curriculum in the felt needs of children, motivation for learning increases. The full fruition of goals set by the Project will depend on the extent that these premises are comprehended and acted upon by participants. Implications for renewed efforts and new approaches in teacher education were potently present in planning for the third year of the Project and for projects in other communities.

The Scope and Spread of Experience Units
Developed by Project Participants

Broad curriculum themes of the elementary schools in the Project
were identified as—

a) Home and Family Living;

b) How Groups Function;

c) Neighborhood and Community Studies;

d) Expanding Community Studies (state, region, nation, world).
These became Guideline 3 for teachers developing experience units in
human relations education. It was emphasized that each theme would
permeate the curriculum of the total elementary school, beginning in
kindergarten and continuing through ever increasing levels of maturity
throughout the child's school life.

Table 10 reveals the scope and spread of experience units reported
by participants.

Scope and Spread of Experience Units Developed During the Second Year of the Project				Table 10
Grades	Home and Family Living	How Groups Function	Neighborhood and Community Studies	Expanding Community Studies
K	8			
1	9	1	4	
1-2	2		1	2
2	3		9	
2-3	1	1	3	1
3	4	1	6	3
3-4	3	1	2	2
Primary Unit[1]	7	2	11	3
Primary IPC[2]	3	1	1	
Total Primary Classes	40	7	37	11
4	5	2	1	9
4-5			1	1
5	1			12
5-6	1			3
6	4			15
Intermediate Unit[1]				
Intermediate IPC[2]	1		1	1
Total Intermediate Classes	12	2	3	41
GRAND TOTAL	52	9	40	52

[1] Unit is designated for those participants in a school organized on unit level plan
[2] IPC designates classes for educable mentally retarded

In studying the data in Table 10 it becomes apparent that on the basis of experience units reported, the curriculum theme, How Groups Function, seemed generally neglected in planning learning experiences for children in the Project. Because this theme has a definite role in the other themes, it may well be that provision was made for its development in other experience units. The concepts identified in Table 11 will determine whether or not it was included. Even so, as an identified theme demanding major emphasis, the implication is that it was a neglected area of learning, with all that this means for effective human relations education.

The theme, Home and Family Living, received its greatest emphasis in the primary school, as it had in the past. It is probable that its

Concepts and Their Range of Emphasis in the Elementary Schools   Table 11

Placement and Frequency by Grades

Concepts	Total	K	1	1-2	2	2-3	3	3-4	Pri. Unit	Pri. IPC	4	4-5	5	5-6	6	Int. Unit	Int. IPC
Safety	4		1	1	1							1					
Nutrition	13	3	1				2		1	1	4	1					
Health	7		1	1							1		1	2		1	
Security	4	1		1						1		1					
Sources of Food	6			1			1			1	2	1					
Family	31	4	3	3	4		2	2	5	1	4	1			1		1
Home	28	4	4	2	3	1	1	1	5	3	1		1	1			1
Neighborhood	8		1	1	2		1			2	1						
Heritage	3												1	1	1		
Responsibility	17	1	3				1	2	1		3	1	1	4			
Culture: Other People	7						1				1			1	4		
Family Fun	11	1	2		2		2		3		1						
Clothing	9						1	3	1	1	1		1	1			
Money—how family gets it	5		1				1	1								1	1
Spending money wisely	14				1		2		2		4			2	3		
Moving to improve living conditions	6			1			2						3	1			
Desirable personal traits	4			2	1						1						
Meaning of freedom	2						1								1		
Sharing	3	1					1					1					
Working together (neighborliness)	10		1						4	4	1						
Cooperating: Enriching family living	14		1	1	2	1			5		3	1					
Planning	1										1						
Schools	1							1									

development in even twelve of the classes of intermediate teachers was a step forward in maintaining and continuing this significant area of learning.

The theme, Expanding Community Studies, typically associated with the intermediate level, reflected its major emphasis by participants on that level. The fact that eleven of the classes of primary teachers had some experience in this area may be significant.

The theme, Neighborhood and Community Studies, usually associated with the primary school, continued to be so associated. With the increasing number of intermediate children having meager experiences in neighborhood and city life, it is a cause for concern that so little was reported by intermediate participants. More may have been done, however, for an increasing number of intermediate teachers began units on the expanding community (state, region, nation and world) with a prestudy of the child's community.

The Development of Concepts

Concepts Developed in Theme: Home and Family Living

Concepts emphasized for development by Project participants are reported in Table 11.

The three concepts stressed by teachers of the trainable mentally retarded were:

Nutrition	1 time
Health	1 time
Sharing	1 time

Concepts most frequently emphasized in the Home and Family theme by the group of teachers participating in the Project were:

Family	31 times
Home	28 times
Responsibility	17 times

Implications which arise through a study of the concepts emphasized in the area of Home and Family Living require:

1. An identification of the most needed concepts for effective family living.

2. A questioning of why so little emphasis is placed upon a large number of concepts (23) related to the problems of making a home and creating satisfying family life.

Concepts Developed in Theme, How Groups Function

Concepts emphasized for development by Project participants are reported in Table 12.

Concepts most frequently emphasized in the theme, How Groups Function, were:

Responsibility	33 times
Family Group Work	25 times
Interdependence	21 times

There is an interesting similarity between concepts emphasized most frequently in the theme, Home and Family Living (Table 11) and in those most frequently emphasized in the theme, How Groups Function (Table 12).

"Family" emphasized by twenty-five teachers in relation to "working together" was also emphasized by five teachers in relation to "Family spending" and by four teachers in relation to "family saving" in the theme, How Groups Function (34). In the theme, Home and Family Living, the concept, "family" was emphasized by thirty-one teachers, "home" by twenty-eight and "money" by nineteen.

Concepts and Their Range in Emphasis in the Elementary Schools   Table 12

Placement and Frequency by Grades

Concepts	Total	K	1	1-2	2	2-3	3	3-4	Pri. Unit	Pri. IPC	4	4-5	5	5-6	6	Int. Unit	Int. IPC
Responsibility	33	1	3	3	3	1	2	4	4		3	1	3	1	4		
Courtesy	8		1	1				2	4								
Obedience	2			1								1					
Belonging	7				1				2		1		1		2		
Services for Other Nations	2												1		1		
Pioneers (all areas)	2						1						1				
Family Spending	5		1			1			1		1				1		
Family Saving	4		1						2						1		
Moving (causes-adjusting)	2						1						1				
Respect for Others	11		1		1			1	3				1		3	1	
Safety	2		1		1												
Sharing	9	1	1		1	1	1	1		1	1			1			
Interdependence	21		2	1			1	5	2		4	1			4	1	
Home	5	1				1				1			1		1		
Using Environment	4						1				1				2		
Family Group Work	25	2	4	3		1	1	2	7	1	3		1		1		
City's Services to People	4				2					1		1					
Respect for Authority	6				2				3		1						
Leadership	1									1							
Rules and Laws	2		1							1							
Conservation	5												5				

Similarly, in the theme, How Groups Function, thirty-three teachers emphasized "responsibility," while this same concept was emphasized by seventeen teachers in the theme, Home and Family Living.

With the exception of the three concepts most often emphasized by teachers in the theme, How Groups Function, there is a wide range of concepts (21) with relatively few teachers emphasizing any common one.

Concepts Developed in Theme: Neighborhood and Community Studies

Concepts most frequently emphasized in the theme, Neighborhood and Community Studies, were:

Interdependence of Workers	36 times
Helpfulness and Cooperation	19 times
Keeping an Attractive Neighborhood	15 times

Concepts and Their Range in Emphasis in the Elementary Schools　　　　　Table 13

Placement and Frequency by Grades

Concepts	Total	K	1	1-2	2	2-3	3	3-4	Pri. Unit	Pri. IPC	4	4-5	5	5-6	6	Int. Unit	Int. IPC
Interdependence of Workers	36	6	2	7		4				9	6	1	1		2		
City Safety and Health Services	6		1	1	3	1											
Individual Independence	5					1				1	3						
Helpfulness and Cooperation	19		2		2	2		2		5	2	1	1		1		1
Keeping an Attractive Neighborhood	15		2	1	2	1		1		5	1	1			1		
Safety in the Neighborhood	2			1											1		
Kinds of Work in City	4				2						1			1			
Interdependence of States and Nations	9					2	1					3			3		
Stores as Sources of Supplies and Goods	5	1					1	1	2								
Schools	1						1										
Contributions of Industries	2						1				1						
Transportation	5		2			1	2										
Community Helpers	8		1		3		1		1		2						1
Dependence or Environment	8						1				2		1		3		1
Laws	3												1		2		
Need for Knowledge	8						2					1	1		3	1	
Recreation	5			1			1	1	1		1						
American Heritage	1														1		
Places of Worship	1							1									

The only concept receiving relatively wide emphasis in Table 13, having similar emphasis in Table 12, is that of "interdependence", thirty-six and twenty-one teachers respectively. As in Tables 11 and 12 there is a wide range of concepts (19) with relatively few teachers emphasizing any common one.

Concepts Developed in Theme: Expanding Community Studies

Concepts emphasized for development by Project participants are reported in Table 14.

One concept, the interdependence of people, received relatively wide emphasis by teachers in the theme, Expanding Community Studies (23). This is the major concept receiving wide emphasis in two other themes: How Groups Function, Neighborhood and Community Studies.

Concepts and Their Range in Emphasis in the Elementary Schools Table 14

Placement and Frequency by Grades

Concepts	Total	K	1	1-2	2	2-3	3	3-4	Pri. Unit	Pri. IPC	4	4-5	5	5-6	6	Int. Unit	Int. IPC
Cooperation with Community Agencies	10	2	1	2			1		2		1				1		
Taxes for Government	4		1							1	1	1					
Communicating	5	1	1				2								1		
Interdependence of Nations	2				1										1		
International Relationships	5						1	1							3		
Government	10						1				2	4	3				
American Heritage	7													5	2		
Changes in Living Patterns	2												1			1	
Market	1						1										
Transportation	3	1					1	1									
Interdependence of People	23	2		2			4	2	2		4	1	1	1	3	1	
Safety	2				1				1								
Effect of Environment on Working and Living	7										2			1	2	2	
Contribution of Leaders in all Fields	5										2	1			2		
World Problems	4						1						1		2		
Space Frontiers	2												1	1			
Cooperation	11			2		2		2			1	1	2			1	
Citizenship	2										1	1					
Many Neighborhoods Make a City	6						2	2			1				1		

A relatively wide range of concepts encompassed in the theme, Expanding Community Studies (19), has fewer receiving concerted emphasis by participants than any of the four major curriculum themes.

Advantages and Values Cited by Participants

The advantages and values cited by participants in the Project during the second year may be classified in two categories: those related to teachers (Table 15) and those related to children's living in school (Table 16).

Advantages and Values for Teachers   Table 15

ADVANTAGES AND VALUES MENTIONED	NUMBER OF TIMES CITED BY				
	Primary Teachers	Inter-mediate Teachers	Teachers of Trainable Retarded	Specialists	Totals
Gained deeper insights into social background of children	17	7	4	2	30
Developed greater realization of the needs of children	13	8	2	2	25
Developed closer relationships to children	7	6	2	2	17
Use of question techniques have helped probe children's thoughts	7	8	2		17
Using concept approach helped unify the curriculum	5	7	1	1	14
Developed realization of need for carefully planned use of diagnostic procedures as a basis for curriculum planning	3	3	1	2	9
Developed personal understanding of industries in the area	4	1			5
Developed use of literature to help children develop sensitivity toward people	2	3			5
Developed closer working relationship with co-workers in the Project	2	1		2	5
Developed awareness of need for better housing	3			1	4
Developed deeper understanding of needs of city and other urban areas			2		2
Development of Price Run Council			1		1

All of the advantages and values cited by participants are subjective, personal, and based upon opinions and feelings. Generally, the values cited by teachers in relation to their own insights, relationships, and personal awareness of growth, if actual, should be reflected in more effective teaching and learning for children. In order to weigh the validity of the values claimed, evidence currently not available to the Project Administrator would be essential.

Advantages and Values for Children Table 16
Cited by Teachers in the Project

ADVANTAGES AND VALUES	NUMBER OF TIMES CITED BY				
	Primary Teachers	Inter-mediate Teachers	Teachers of Trainable Retarded	Specialists	Totals
Better appreciation of family and home	8	8			16
Better understanding of responsibility for pleasant day	9	6			15
Greater kindness to and acceptance of people different from themselves	6	6	1		13
Greater awareness of roles of members of family and school staff	8	1		1	10
Better understanding of community and community helpers	8	2			10
Better group work	5	4			9
Greater acceptance of self	4	4	1		9
Better understanding of varying responsibility for families	7	1			8
Greater tolerance of other races and other ways	3	5			8
Greater awareness of relation of personal appearance to feeling of worth	4	2		1	7
Wiser use of money	5	1			6
Greater freedom to express feelings in writing	5	1			6
Greater understanding of skills needed in jobs held by lower middle class	2				2
Better comprehension of current news		1			1
Better care and use of library books				1	1
Better budget of time		1			1

Summary of Principals' Responses
Progress Report, 1960-61

Responses of Project principals to items soliciting information regarding the extent and quality of participation by participants, the values of the study to individual staffs, and other pertinent reactions are included in this report.

Table 17 provides a summary of the principals' responses regarding the extent and quality of staff participation in the Project.

Summary of Principals' Responses Regarding Extent and Quality of Participation in the Project

Table 17

Project Schools*	Number of Participants	Total Staff	Number of Years in the Project		Tendency To Use Diagnostic Instruments		Quality of Effectiveness in Achieving Increased Planning Skills				Quality of Effectiveness in Achieving Development of Experience Units Emphasizing Human Relations				Improvement in Planning	
			1	2	Yes	No	Exceptionally Good	Moderately Good	Fair	Poor	Exceptionally Good	Moderately Good	Fair	Poor	Yes	No
Drew-Pyle	19	25		x	x			x					x		x	
Elbert-Palmer	13	28	x		x			x				x			x	
Gray	39	42		x	x		x					x			x	
Lore	18	41	x			x		x				x			x	
Shortlidge-Washington	17	23		x	x			x				x			x	
Stubbs	9	27	x		x			x				x			x	
Williams	10	44		x	x					x		x			x	
Opportunity	10	10	x		x			x				x			x	
North East	23	23	x		x			x				x			x	
Total	158	263	5	4	8	1	1	7		1		8	1		9	

*12 participating schools considered as 9 Project centers.

Principals' Suggestions Regarding the Planning and Development of Experience Units in the Third Year of the Project, 1961-62

Drew-Pyle Schools

While we talked about generalizations for approximately a year, it seems that full understanding was not reached until the June meeting. I believe another opportunity to write a unit under Dr. Vickery's guidance may produce improved units.

Gray School

1. Within the school, it is desirable that time be set aside for teachers to meet during the planning stage. It would be helpful for teachers to meet in grade or level groups to discuss appropriateness of theme of units, types of diagnostic questions, ways of relating content to individuals or groups; to evaluate progress of unit development and to examine causes of lack of pupil response; and to share ideas in ways of enriching experience and stimulating interest.

2. Teachers who want it, should be given more direct *practical* aid in thinking through possibilities for developing units to meet needs of given classes.

3. Many teachers need help in getting a better understanding of the kinds of open-ended questions that will help children relate to specific units. They need realistic help in devising such questions.

Lore School

Early and frequent contacts among teachers working in the Project. Discussion of a unit actually taught *with the person who developed and taught it* makes for meaningful understanding and clarifies misconceptions.

Shortlidge-Washington Schools

1. We need to motivate learning to support the desire of children to be accepted by peers, to grow more responsible as well as more independent, to explore, and to acquire "good" habits and attitudes.
2. We need to provide proper environment for such growth.
3. We need to use the differences in children to make it possible for each child to grow best in understandings and skills needed in our culture.
4. We need to recognize that the parents want their children to grow along certain lines. (I hesitate to label these values middle class, but the parents are clear in their wishes.)

Stubbs School

1. There must be greater opportunity for teacher-consultant sessions as teachers put into effect through daily planning the units already developed.
2. The principal will need to observe and work with participants more frequently on an individual basis to help teachers realize when the objectives of a given unit have been realized, and to help them evaluate the work.
3. Teachers need more help in studying good sample units objectively.
4. Teachers need more help in using more than one diagnostic technique.

Williams School

1. We need more sessions within the school on the writing of units; to have specific examples of units for study by the group; more discussion on the relationship between the human relations of the members of the group and the teaching which goes on in each class.
2. Because I have not spent as much time on this as was needed, everything has been up in the air, vague and indefinite. We lack the enthusiasm we had last year.

Opportunity School

Our main emphasis will be in this area for our second year in the Project (1961-62). We would like some guidance from the helping teachers.

North East School

1. Start to work on the units early in the year.
2. Show sample units to teachers so that they may see the possibilities.
3. Possibly develop a sample unit together so that teachers can experience the new approach.

Values Identified by Project Principals, 1960-61

Drew-Pyle Schools

1. This year has been unmatched in agency cooperation. The YM and YW, Christina and Peoples Settlements, and the East Side Executive Council have worked very closely with our school to extend wholesome, balanced recreational programs for our children.
2. Our boys have had effective male leadership brought before them. Our girls have been engaged in other than street corner activities.
3. Peoples Settlement and the P.T.A. sponsored a successful concert which will provide deserving boys in our school with camp scholarships.
4. Christina Settlement was instrumental in finding a donor for free lunches during the past winter.
5. The East Side Executive Council met in our school. It made plans for balanced recreational coverage during the summer.
6. Community agencies are no longer planning programs and placing them before us—more and more they are inviting us to participate from the ground floor.
7. More peace and fewer references to poor child behavior have been observed by many this year. The separation of the schools, which permitted more appropriate programming; the reduced enrollment, which may have excluded the real troublemakers; and involvement in the Project, which seemed to increase the sensitivities of teachers to pupils' needs—all contributed to this better living for the teachers, the pupils, and the principal.
8. The Project and the recent bulletins on Social Studies raised the level of Social Studies in our school. Social Studies lends itself better to active than to passive experiences.
9. The temperament and background of our children demand activity and movement.
10. I believe this active social studies emphasis, as well as teachers' sensitivity to children's needs provided the kind of program that brings out the best in children.

Elbert-Palmer Schools

1. Teachers have improved their planning for the needs of pupils in a low-income area.
2. The art of questioning has improved. The teachers question not only for facts but for thinking through problems.
3. I think there is a better relationship between teachers and pupils as teachers have a better understanding of pupils' social problems.

Gray School

1. The Project has made teachers think more of children's needs and how to meet them.
2. The Project has emphasized the importance of long-time planning.
3. Some teachers previously less interested have begun to realize the limitations of narrow content teaching.
4. Teachers are seeking more direct assistance in developing their programs.
5. The Project has given support to the principal in encouraging teachers to develop a program built around a unit of interest with specific goals and purposes.

Lore School

1. The enriching experience of contacts with Dr. Vickery and more frequent visits from Dr. Crosby.
2. A greater awareness of the individual problems of children on the part of *some* teachers. They see children's human relations problems in somewhat clearer perspective.
3. An awareness of the value planning and evaluation have for quality teaching.
4. Contacts with supervisors, consultants, and "master" teachers in sessions where successful units were discussed by *those by whom they were developed.*

Shortlidge-Washington Schools

1. The Project is spontaneous and creative, as actual teaching should be. New ideas are tested in action.
2. We have wider distribution of leadership roles in curriculum planning.
3. Most teachers are following recommended procedures of teacher-pupil planning, setting up problems, choosing ways to work, choosing jobs to do, working, and then evaluating.
4. The individual teacher or the group involved must work out the diverse possibilities and implications of a situation, because answers to problems raised are not in books.
5. Most of the teachers are using open questions regularly. They also use diaries, logs, the unfinished story and so on. We have a growing awareness of the values of such materials.
6. A continuous process of evaluation concerned with evidences of values and indications of needs is necessary to this way of working.
7. Most teachers have emphasized more consistently the importance of people rather than of facts, figures, and quantities.
8. The "feelings are facts" approach indicates needs which challenge the staff. This fosters professional growth particularly in attitudes toward techniques, methods, skills, and ways of working with children.
9. The realization that obedience is for armies; that behavior problems are caused; that some teaching methods cause poor study habits; and other such understandings have reduced the necessity

of such procedures as spelling bees, mass homework assignments, and memorization.

10. Values which teachers reported:
   a) Individual conferences
   b) Help with open-ended questions
   c) Having more ways of gaining information about individual children
   d) Getting viewpoints of co-workers
   e) Exchange of good ideas
   f) Interrelating of ideas
   g) Personalization of curriculum in the child's interest
   h) Making social studies center around the child
   i) Getting a better understanding of the conditions under which children live
   j) Getting a different slant on my unit
   k) Taking an altogether different approach in social studies
   l) Getting help in clarifying concepts
   m) The all-city, many-agency nature of the Project.

11. Of much help to the principal is watching guidance techniques. Samples: Watching Dr. Vickery help other teachers—
   a) analyze purpose for which we ask questions;
   b) work on questions but also share the success of his idea about using games;
   c) work on selecting a story that presents a problem, and use the technique of stopping before the story ends to get out the range of action,
   d) decide on goals, get out a number of possibilities, and help the children to make a choice;
   e) set up the unit such as "It Takes Many Kinds of Work to Keep A State Like Delaware Going" with generalizations, but mainly with activities about people who help us build a new school.

Stubbs School

1. Acceptance of the *unit approach*. All participants freely admit that teaching around an idea is superior to isolated lessons. Lecturing about better ways is not ineffective on those wont to maintain the status quo. Guided participation has brought about acceptance, which is an open door for help in becoming more proficient.
2. The manner in which teachers have worked on grade and level bases, seeking to make human relations teaching more effective, suggests to me that they can be stimulated to do more effective cooperative planning in all learning areas.
3. All participants realize now that they did not know as much about their pupils as they thought. There is greater respect for the use of diagnostic techniques.
4. The bulletins from the director's office, particularly "Some Bases for Curriculum Planning," have been and will continue to be beacon lights as we seek to improve our curriculum.

Williams School

1. The Project has helped new teachers become oriented to school and community.
2. The opportunity for teachers to work together in small groups under Dr. Vickery's guidance has increased the members' appreciation of what is accomplished on different levels. Teachers have become better acquainted with each other and also with more children.
3. Teachers have learned to look below the surface when trying to solve problems.
4. Knowledge and use of diagnostic techniques have become common.
5. As a result of the Project we have made many adjustments in programs.

Opportunity School

1. The Project has stimulated thought and action. After each meeting, and particularly after Dr. Vickery's meetings, it has been difficult to discontinue discussions and the sharing of ideas. Usually they are resumed the next morning.
2. Our perception of causes of children's learning and behavior has improved. We have become more sensitive to the implications of their past experiences and to the values, attitudes, and ideals which they bring from their homes and neighborhoods. When Sammy gets off the bus in the morning and hits one of the younger children we know he has had a difficult family experience that morning and we make a special effort to provide many experiences to build up his feeling of self. There is evidence that the other children sense Sammy's need for this type of attention and that they follow the teacher's pattern of handling the situation.
3. Classroom activities show evidence of planning for individual children at their developmental level. Some children may be learning to zip zippers, others to button buttons, while one or two are working on learning to tie shoestrings.

North East School

1. Our new staff became a close unit. We thought together. We thought in terms of common goals, new techniques, problems to be solved. The year was harmonious because we anticipated problems of adjustment, and everyone tried to see the school and community as our children saw them.
2. We gained new and valuable techniques which enabled us to (a) approach curriculum building in better ways, (b) better understand children's problems as we saw them in relation to their families, (c) become more sympathetic and effective with parents.
3. The Project helped me to know my teachers. I had close contact with them and was able to help some to understand and accept the differences in family roles occasioned by the variable employment and economic picture.
4. All of us gained security in a new situation. Knowing that

competent, professional help in the field of human relations was constantly available, we were encouraged to explore feelings and attitudes.

Principals' Identification of the Most Pressing Human Relations Needs Which the Schools Can Meet Through Instruction and the Total School Program

Drew-Pyle Schools

1. Too many of our children spend their early lives in families, homes, and neighborhoods that are highly disorganized and where too many unwholesome conditions prevail. Very early in life these children are put on their own. Long before entering school, children have learned to live by their wits.

2. Some know a lot and become very aggressive. Others have had their enthusiasm destroyed and fall into a state of complacency.

3. Getting along in a group is our most pressing problem.

4. Accepting suggestions and accepting criticism are our second most pressing problems.

5. Our children are constantly on the defense—protecting their mother's name, their looks, color, poor home conditions, size of their body, inability to grasp quickly. They are easily offended and highly alert to offenses.

6. Our children need, want, and deserve approval, attention, and love. They want recognition and are easily discouraged if they do not receive what they consider a "fair share."

Elbert-Palmer Schools

1. Children who are aggressive and nonconforming in their behavior usually consume an undue proportion of the teachers' time because they disrupt classroom routine. These children desire the limelight, they demand attention from the teacher, and are able to work only a limited period of time without supervision.

2. Patterns of behavior encouraged at home are cause of this aggression. The parents believe sincerely that aggressiveness is essential for group recognition and, therefore, they encourage their children in this type of behavior.

3. A frequent cause of aggressive behavior is that the child does not receive sufficient attention unless he demands it. The parents are preoccupied with their own lives. They may unfavorably compare a relatively unattractive child with other children in the family or reject a child out of their own emotional distress.

4. The classroom teachers have to break down these patterns of behavior, which are encouraged by parents at home.

Gray School

The most pressing needs of our children, as I see them are:

1. To live in a school environment which can in some way counteract the distorted outlook many of them have on education, life in general, and particularly on their own possibilities.

2. To have some purpose to learn.
3. To develop curiosity about the world around them.
4. To overcome their belligerent attitudes.
5. To learn to obey the law, conform to rules, and to have consideration for others.
6. To have faith in others so that they can relax and not be wound up ready to fly off at the least provocation.
7. To have experiences they are deprived of in their homes such as hearing conversations about world, state, or community problems.
8. Most desperately, to share in a multitude of pleasant, beautiful, and informative experiences which will help them to create for themselves a new view of what the world is like.
9. Most pressingly, to believe in their own capabilities, to learn to appreciate others, and to recognize how they fit into a group, a class, a community.
10. To get out of the school into experiences that will enrich their living and understanding.

Lore School

One of the most pressing is only indirectly a need of the children. I see a great need for a better understanding on the part of parents of the school program. This would result in closer cooperation between school and home.

There is a similar need for a more complete comprehension of home and community needs and problems on the part of teachers. Children often seem to be pulled in different directions and toward almost opposite goals and standards by the two institutions society provides for their guidance—the home and the school. Under such circumstances any work to improve the efficiency of the school program in meeting their needs should be accompanied by action to bring greater unity between parents and teachers, home and school.

Shortlidge-Washington Schools

1. In general, our needs are the same as those discovered by some of the research studies. Most valuable to us are—
   a) Havighurst, Robert—*Human Development and Education* (1953), for development tasks;
   b) Gesell, Arnold—*The Child From 5 to 10* (1946), and *Youth, The Years From 10 to 16* (1956), for social emotional development;
   c) Martin and Stendler—*Process of Growing Up In Society* (1953), for social needs;
   d) Redl, Fritz and Wineman, David—*Children Who Hate,* for problem children and how they reveal themselves in group work.
2. Specifically for our schools, we have certain special needs next year. These human relations needs are not based on race, creed, or handicaps of an orthopedic nature. Shortlidge School children will,

for the first time, work with Negroes, visually handicapped, and physically handicapped children. Washington School children will also have a first time with the visually handicapped and physically handicapped children. I expect few problems of human relations in these areas, in regards to desegregation.

3. However, the Washington children as a group are different from the Shortlidge School children as a group. There is, naturally, much overlapping. The Shortlidge children are more cooperative, yet more competitive. They are better able to disagree politely. They work more quietly, fight less, yell less, have better hall manners, but most noticeable to me—they are usually contented and happy, enthusiastic about their work, friendly to adults, and secure in their peer groups. The Washington children have higher peaks of happiness, perhaps I should say they show more gaiety on occasions such as a musical program or a party, but they are more prone to fight, to yell, to be rude, to be defiant, and to complain. At Washington far more complaints come to the office and I see more unpleasant behavior, such as pushing at drinking fountains and loitering on the way to the toilet than at Shortlidge. At Shortlidge the complaints are, "He skipped steps," and "He ran into the street." At Washington the common complaints are, "He hit me," "They are going to beat me up after school," "There's no use telling the teacher," "Somebody stole my bike, lunch, pencil, or other," "He says dirty words," and "He called me names." (Notice that no race problems are involved. Accepted neighborhood patterns are involved, including resentment of authority.)

4. The written work of the children at Shortlidge shows family affection; loyalty to family, friends, and school. The written work at Washington shows far more hostility and trouble. I want to repeat—there is much overlapping. Group membership is necessary to the happiness of the children. The characteristics which cause acceptance vary in the two schools. At Shortlidge the group tends to penalize by "letting alone" the one who is "out" of the group. The teacher has to work for the acceptance of the child who is "out." At Washington the group sometimes tends to make a hero of the one who rebels and to sympathize with the one who complains. Sometimes the teacher has to compete for leadership with the child who will not cooperate. I see the merging of these two groups as the biggest problem we have.

Stubbs School

1. A belief in the dignity of man to the extent that the children recognize the tremendous opportunities available today to all humans

2. A determination to use handicaps and deprivations as a driving force, not an excuse, to be the best citizen possible

3. An understanding of, and an appreciation for the family in our society, and its unique role in this important unit

4. The acceptance of a new set of values affecting the use of time, money, and talents

5. Personal growth in health through attention to diet, rest, grooming, mental attitude, and recreation
6. The development of attitudes and habits affecting girl-boy relationships, respect for authority, and neighborly living

Williams School

1. That school integration is not the solution to all the problems of the Negro race. Integration, in a true sense, and equal opportunity go way beyond school regulations and involve acceptance and respect for differences, the ability to live with these differences, and so on. This and all that it implies would take hours to write up.
2. We must work constantly on helping children and parents to use the opportunities which are available. If they are to improve their conditions it must be done through some effort on their part. At the present much that is done is for them, not by them, and the change is usually a temporary one.
3. To help each individual feel his own value and importance in the world would bring about many changes in human relations.
4. Smaller class size and much individual teaching would do much to increase academic achievement and provide opportunities for each child to be known and for education along the lines which will meet his particular needs.
5. Again, these three needs are ones which I would consider important needs. There are many others which are an important part of the total picture.

Opportunity School

1. Some of the children are over-protected in their families. We need to continue to help them develop independence and to provide many experiences to foster independence.
2. Some of the children come from homes and neighborhoods in which they have a pattern of constant verbal and fist fighting. We hope that if they can develop acceptable social patterns in school they will have a better chance of making a social adjustment outside of school, now and later.
3. We have been working on these two problems and have noted marked progress in school. We need to continue to help both groups become more secure.

North East School

1. To feel secure—Uncertain family and financial situations keep many children upset and suspicious. They need more confidence and faith. In order to have self-respect they need opportunities to show they can contribute something and that they are worth something.
2. To accept differences—The world is changing rapidly and with the breakdown of old prejudices are coming more opportunities for self-improvement and achievement regardless of background.
3. To accept and respect others—Our children usually respect their parents and teachers but not other parents, teachers, or their peers.

They need to know how necessary it is for them to value the contributions and roles of others and to respect them.

4. To respect law and order—Children need to know the reasons for laws and the importance of obeying them, whether they are the written laws of man or the unwritten laws of God.

5. To settle disputes peaceably—Disagreements occur among all groups. People can disagree and not fight. They need to know how to settle disputes.

6. To communicate—Our children need more conversation with adults. They must talk with parents and teachers. Adults must answer their questions, play games with them, read with them.

7. To have values—Knowledge of good manners and simple courtesies make for better feeling among people. Our children must know this. A sense of responsibility and respect for property are essential in good group living.

8. To feel affection or love.

Extending Our Sights Through Action Research

From its inception, the Project has recognized the significant role of evaluation as a built-in feature of the Project design. Implementing the function of evaluation has been a continuing and baffling problem. There have been two reasons for this. One is related to the fact that the Project is a new venture, new in concept and design, in which a design itself had to be created as part of the developmental character of the Project. And the design was achieved as we entered the second year of the Project. The second reason is related to the process of action research.

Why Action Research? Education as a discipline has never fully established its maturity. It has constantly sought to borrow the attributes and functions of other disciplines.

For many years its "supervision" was the "inspection" of industry. Every school supervisor knows that you cannot inspect and grade people as you can apples or bolts nor is this the purpose of educational supervision.

Its "administration" is plagued even today with public attempts to interpret the needs of educational administration in terms of business management. In many localities this results in the imposition of restrictive measures which attempt to define the school administrator's job in terms of length of the school day, length of the school year, vacation periods, and other working conditions which match those of industry and business. Every school administrator knows that you cannot set the limits on a principal's working day or conceive of a Christmas vacation as an unearned luxury. Education is much more than business management.

Its research, in conception and techniques, has traditionally been borrowed from the research of the sciences and social sciences. We have labored for years to make equations between human attributes and the symbols of statistics to equate intangibles and tangibles, and we wonder why—with the vast number of research studies produced in reading, language, human growth and development, teaching skills and methods—these studies mold on library shelves and are not interpreted in practice.

Action research is an attempt to bring flesh to the bones of educational research. The purposes of action research are:

1. To involve people—teachers, administrators, supervisors, other staff members and sometimes children and parents in the exciting adventure of finding out for themselves more effective ways of teaching and learning.

2. To determine the self-perceptions of the needs of the people involved, of adults and children, so that learning has meaning for the learners, whether they be teachers seeking better ways of teaching, children seeking answers to their unasked questions, or administrators seeking more effective leadership skills.

3. To root the development of curricula and total school program in reality—in the reality of the needs of children and their families, in the needs of teachers, and in the needs of American society and its expectations for the good life.

Action research recognizes that much of its content is descriptive and subjective. It has not yet been able to wean itself away from the quantitative context of traditional research, yet it recognizes and seeks ways of working which will make it possible to communicate research data, significant in the descriptive and subjective evidence it discovers, to those who know only the quantitative and objective symbols of traditional research. Until educational researchers, in the context of action research, discover a means of communicating their findings in ways that interpret clearly and command the respect of educators as well as the public, until we grow in skill and in confidence in the validity of our own needs and purposes, until we stop trying to interpret subjective and descriptive evidence in a "foreign language"—that is, the symbols of other disciplines, the products of action research, like the products of traditional educational research, will continue to mold on library shelves.

The Context of Action Research in Education. The 20th Century is characterized by a revolution more potent in its effects upon people today, and upon those who will come after us, than the effects of the political and industrial revolutions of past centuries. Three forces are shaping the current revolution:

1. The determination of men all over the world to achieve for themselves freedom, opportunity, and economic independence;

2. automation, which in ultimately freeing men from drudgery, is denying many of them their established means of livelihood;

3. technology, which while extending man's potential for survival and for intellectual achievement currently beyond his comprehension, is also resulting in economic, political, and social upheaval.

These are the forces which are demanding of the schools a new conception of their role, new responsibilities to society, and new skills in the education of children, youth, and adults. Whether or not schools are to measure up to these demands, the degree to which they are able to foster the "constants" of a great national heritage and the effectiveness with which they will contribute to the shaping of a new heritage for a new people will depend upon the effectiveness of the leadership of school administrators.

One of the accomplishments of the second year of the Project was the development of a design for an evaluation of the Project by the curriculum consultant, Dr. William E. Vickery. This is an achievement comparable in value to the development of the Project Design.

Project Evaluation Design

I. Analysis of children's responses to diagnostic devices (1959-1962)

Purposes:

1. To identify and describe significant social and personal problems as seen by Wilmington children. (Home and family, community, etc.)

2. To trace developments in the same child or class over a three-year period. (Differences and similarities in problems identified, growth in insight, in ability to express ideas and feelings, etc.)

3. To identify and describe experiences common to many children in Project schools which can be used as a basis for curriculum planning, and major gaps in these same children's experiences which teachers must take into account in developing curricula.

4. To determine which diagnostic devices yield the most relevant information and which are relatively unproductive.

5. To identify significant areas of children's experiences not now tapped by the diagnostic devices and to suggest additional techniques that may tap these areas.

6. To determine what needs to be done to ascertain the validity of these diagnostic techniques and to suggest means of doing it.

II. Analysis of the effects of participating in the Project on the cooperating teachers

Purpose: To identify changes (if any) in the teacher's knowledge of and feelings toward the children in his class:

1. Perceptions of cultural differences and his awareness and acceptance of such differences
2. Definition of the teacher's role in classroom management and instruction
3. Concepts of unit planning and the teacher's ability to apply these concepts
4. Ability to use a variety of methods suited to his unit goals (Leading discussions, role playing, literature for human understanding)
5. Ability to use a variety of diagnostic techniques and relate them to his teaching

III. Analysis of the effects of the Project program on children in the classes of cooperating teachers

Purpose: To identify changes (if any) in the pupils'—

1. ability to understand the causes of their own and other people's behavior and to respond in ways that are good for all concerned;
2. ability to behave appropriately in a variety of social situations;
3. ability to use rational, humane, and inclusive standards in choosing associates for work, recreation, and friendship groups;
4. motivation for serious study, not only of human and social problems, but also of other academic subjects;
5. ability to apply rational, objective methods to the solution of problems;
6. mastery of the skills necessary for success in school (reading, written and oral expression, use of numbers and arithmetic processes, etc.);
7. comprehension of concepts, generalizations, and ideas supported by accurate information, human feelings, and the appropriate action-skills;
8. understanding of and allegiance to the values and principles which underpin the evolving American culture.

IV. Possible means of evaluation

A. Analysis of children's responses:
1. Social problems as seen by children
   a. Design classification systems that will reveal the nature of the problems children identify, and the frequency with which each problem is mentioned. (Cf. *Diagnosing Human Relations Needs*)

b. Select for future use those questions which have been most useful during the first two years of the Program; e.g. "What I like and would like changed about my neighborhood," "Best thing that could happen to my family," "Things that make me mad," etc.

c. Tabulate and analyze children's responses. Decide who can do this work best—graduate students who might do this in relation to their class or thesis work? teachers? especially hired research assistants?

2. Tracing the development of a child, selected children, or class over a three-year period (related to III - 1, 3, 6, 7)

a. Identify the children who have been with one or more teachers participating in the Project for three years.

b. Analyze their responses to open questions, time budgets, scores, and cumulative records.

c. Compare their responses with those of a matched control group or with school norms.

3. Experiences and gaps in experience related to curriculum planning

a. Classify the experiences in curriculum areas (home and family, community, etc. as "always," "often," "seldom," or "never" referred to by children in their papers (Cf. I - 1)

b. Compare these experiences with those assumed by the characters in readers, math, and science texts, songs, etc.

c. Identify differences between texts and children's experiences; and experiences the children have had, but which are not mentioned in books.

4. Most productive diagnostic devices

a. Establish criteria for distinguishing between productive and unproductive responses, e.g. personal and social significance of answers, directness of relationship between responses and curriculum themes, apparent freedom and honesty vs. echoing of conventional (teacher's) values, etc.

b. Classify questions on these criteria; check classification with independent judges.

c. Identify reasons for variations in the values of the devices (method of administration, teacher attitude, phrasing of question, etc.).

d. Select questions that seem to yield best results for recommended use in the future.

5. Significant areas of children's experiences not tapped by diagnostic devices used in the Project

a. List children's reported experiences using the data organized in I - 3.

b. Compare the list with reported research such as that by Davis, Havighurst, Warner, Jersild, Prescott, etc.

c. Identify significant areas of experience revealed by research and untapped by the Project's diagnostic devices.

6. Evaluation of diagnostic devices

a. Sampling method: Do independent samples of responses from children of comparable backgrounds reveal similar problems? Can we predict from one sample the responses of children from similar backgrounds?

b. Alternate approach method: Do the responses on children's papers agree with the responses they give in a careful interview? Can we predict from an interview the nature of the children's written responses?

c. Independent observer method: Can an observer identify in playground, classroom, street and home behavior the items reported in children's papers?

B. Effects of participation in the Project on teachers

1. Knowledge of and feelings about children

a. Subjective estimates: personal reports on changes in the teacher's reactions to his pupils; responses on Project evaluation forms

b. Observers' estimates: reports on changes in teachers by the principal, helping teacher and consultant

c. Questionnaire and test measures (not appropriate for Wilmington teachers but perhaps in future project designs) M T A 1 scores, pre- and post-project. Other instruments?

2. Perception and acceptance of cultural differences by teachers

a. Development of a device based on Kluckhohn's concepts. Use this as a pre-test and post-test instrument; as a guide for observation and/or interview.

b. Open-ended questionnaire calling for teachers' subjective estimates of their own changed perceptions

c. Observer's records of teachers' classroom and P.T.A. behavior

d. Consultant's log of changes in what teachers say

3. Role in classroom management and instruction

a. Subjective estimates by the teacher, e.g. reports on use of sociograms

b. Principal's and helping teacher's observations

c. Children's responses to such questions as "What did your class do this year that you learned the most from—enjoyed the most?"

4. Application of concepts of unit planning

a. Comparison of unit plans developed over a three-year period, as judged by a competent curriculum person (or panel of judges)

5. Fitting methods of instruction to teaching purposes

a. Analysis of activities proposed in the unit plan (Cf II - 4)

b. Observations by principal, helping teachers, consultant

c. Teacher's reports of activities attempted and estimates of their effects

6. Ability to use diagnostic techniques

a. Analysis of materials turned in by participating teachers (using such criteria as completeness of material, adequacy of summary, skill in interpretation) over a two- or three-year period

C. Effects of the program on children taught by participating teachers

1. Understanding of causes of behavior and responding in appropriate ways

a. Analysis of children's responses over a two- or three-year period to open questions

b. Teacher logs of class discussions checked by her observations of children's behavior in class, on the playground, and after school

c. Children's pre- and post-responses on a formal "What would you do?" questionnaire

2. Appropriate behavior in a variety of social situations

a. Arrangement of test situations (visit to another school, to a downtown restaurant, etc.) with and without specific training, and before and after planned instruction in the area of coping with new situations and people who are "different." Situations assessed by children, teachers, and participant observers (student teachers?)

b. Children's discussions (or individual open responses) to a problem story, a film, or some other vicarious experience (Cf II - 1)

c. Teachers' subjective assessments of children's growth in this area, checked against the observations of principals, parents, youth workers, and other pupils

3. Choosing associates on a rational, humane, inclusive basis

a. Analysis of sociograms and sociometric interviews by teachers and independent judges

4. Motivation for serious study

a. Children's responses to interest inventories, instruments for measuring aspiration level, and tests of persistence in set tasks

b. Children's responses to open-ended questions such as, "What do you like about school?" or "What don't you like about school?" or "What person your own age do you admire most and why?" administered at the beginning and end of the school year

c. Teachers' logs of changes in children's study habits and patterns

d. Changes in scores on achievement tests (Cf III - 6, 7)

5. Application of problem-solving methods

a. Scores on tests of logical reasoning

b. Test situations (real and vicarious) followed by children's written and/or oral responses checked against teacher's log and observation

c. Observation by teachers, student teachers, and youth workers on children's approaches to out-of-class problem situations

6. Mastery of academic skills

a. Scores on achievement tests

b. Teacher reports on progress

c. Comparison of pupils' products at the opening and close of the school year by independent judges

The project design and the Evaluation design will form a frame of reference and guidelines for planning and action which will be more profitable for other communities than they were for Wilmington because, at Wilmington, we had to feel our way while other communities will have the benefit of our experience.

A New Look at Teaching
Methods and Processes

As the schools prepared to initiate the work of the third year
of The Three-Year Experimental Project on Schools in Changing
Neighborhoods, preliminary plans had been evolved by the curriculum
consultant and the Project Administrator throughout the preceding
summer. The frame of reference for preliminary planning was, first of all,
the Project Design. A second component was the evaluation by
participants in the second year of the Project. And the third component
became the newly constructed Project Evaluation Design.

Because the Project was an exploratory one, among whose major
purposes were those of creating a design for human relations education
and a paralleling design for its evaluation, the third year of the Project
was envisioned as a further opportunity to test the value of both designs.

Problems Demanding Attention

What seemed of greatest significance were the reactions of participants
and the quality of the diagnostic and curriculum materials they had developed during the preceding years of participation.

Among the problems encountered earlier, and which demanded attention during the third year, were the following:

1. The need for participants to comprehend fully the relationship between
(a) diagnostic findings in the human relations needs of children and their
families and (b) an experience unit in curriculum building which would
help children work toward solutions to their problems in living.

2. The need for learning more effective skills in teaching and learning processes, involving the selection and use of many instructional materials, content, and experiences.

3. The need to refine skills in building experience units.

4. The need to more clearly comprehend the relationship between human relations needs and academic needs.

5. The need to develop evaluative techniques and procedures which recognize the subjective and descriptive as well as the objective evidence of growth as measured by standardized tests in subject areas.

Accordingly, a bulletin was prepared by the Project Administrator which sketched the framework of development for the third year. The following is based on this bulletin.

Plans for the Third Year of the Project

The final year of The Three-Year Experimental Project on Schools in Changing Neighborhoods will be a particularly crucial one, for it will bring to a close the formal, exploratory work we have been doing together in our search for more effective processes in fostering children's learning. Equally significant is the function it will serve in making it possible to determine curriculum themes, specific techniques, instruments, resources and human relations goals which we will want to incorporate in future years of teaching and learning. Actually, the completion of the pilot project will serve as a "commencement" in a very important sense. For these reasons it is important to provide an overview of the work ahead in this final year so that all of us may be well-oriented.

Scope of Development

Continued Use of Diagnostic Techniques and Instruments to Discover Children's Perceptions of Needs. Each teacher will use only those diagnostic techniques and instruments which are related to problems of concern to her in developing appropriate curricula. If, for instance, learning to live in groups is an area of concern, a teacher may use the sociogram or other sociometric instruments. If neighborhood and community studies are planned, open-ended questions designed to determine children's recognition of strengths and needs in neighborhoods will probably be selected.

Continued Development of Curriculum Units Focused on Human Relations Needs. Each teacher will prepare one or more experience units to guide her in planning with her group during the year. Several important factors should underlie this planning:

1. The premise, "children learn better when they see a need to learn,"

means that getting at children's felt needs through diagnostic techniques has use value for the teacher.

2. The premise, "a human relations focused curriculum is conducive to the development of human relations skills, sensitivities, knowledge, and appreciation," means that we are concerned with helping children and their families achieve a more satisfying school, family, and neighborhood life. Achievement of the usual academic skills becomes of greater significance than before, for competency in living demands the ability to read; the use of arithmetic, science, and the social sciences; an appreciation for art and music; and the practice of good physical and mental health habits. There is no dichotomy between academic skills and human relations skills. They reinforce one another.

3. There is no requirement to use a special form of planning. A premium is placed upon a variety of ways in learning originally and creatively.

Development of Specific Teaching Methods or Processes. Dr. Vickery will concentrate this year on helping us develop specific methods appropriate to our objectives. These will include—

1. Discussion techniques ("the art of questioning" to foster creative thinking, skill in exchanging ideas, the ability to use facts and information to reach conclusions, the ability to make wise choices, growth in language development)

2. Role playing (to clarify concepts, to develop empathy, to establish rapport, to solve problems)

3. The use of films and other aids for human understanding (to identify with others, to enrich concept building, to increase information and acquire skills)

4. The development of the open-ended story (to think through possible solutions to human problems, to stimulate the coordinating of fact and feeling, to relate to others, to stimulate language development—listening, speaking, reading and writing)

5. The development of "Reading With a Purpose" (to use books to increase children's appreciation of literature focused on human relations, to stimulate strong motivation to read, to stimulate creative thinking and creative approaches to human understanding)

6. Planning for curriculum trips for human understanding (to identify the opportunities for children to experience face-to-face relationships with people in agencies or resources visited, to learn how to deal with acceptance and rejection, to develop skills which demonstrate consideration for people who give time and effort to helping us benefit from a visit, to learn techniques which make people want to help us, to use

field experiences to help us become more academically competent, etc.)

Evaluation. Two types of evaluation are needed, one subjective and descriptive; the other objective.

Evaluation constitutes one of the most critical problems we face. Because this Project is unique, and experimental in the truest sense of the word, established evaluative instruments are lacking. Perhaps we will discover ways of evaluating the subjective and descriptive evidence we obtain in ways which will make a distinct and sorely needed contribution to educational research.

Individual school evaluative efforts make more sense than attempting a project-wide evaluation. This would be in harmony with the individual school approach to participation in the Project.

Early in the year, schools should begin to plan ways in which they will attempt evaluation. Individual teachers, groups of teachers within a school, and the principal may want to attack different aspects. As soon as an idea or tentative plan is ready it should be thoroughly discussed with Dr. Vickery in a consultant session. The following "starters" may suggest paths of exploration, adaptation, or inventiveness which could be developed through all of the resources available.

1. Making a case study of a family having a child in the Project in order to determine how the family provides opportunities at home for using what is learned in school.

2. Organizing a parent group to participate in the use of diagnostic instruments with subsequent group study of findings in relation to similar data obtained from the children; e.g., "What I like and would like changed in my neighborhood." (Comparisons between parents' and children's perceptions should be enlightening to all concerned.)

3. Planning of a study by selected parents to determine carry-over value of things learned in school.

4. Making case studies of one or more children in each of the following categories: one, two, three years of participation by the child in the Project.

5. Studying achievement test scores, available from the regular testing program, comparing achievements of children participating in the Project with those of children not participating in the Project.

6. Collecting evidence of changes in children's behavior which seem to have some relationship to Project experiences.

7. Making a principal's analysis of changes in teaching processes effected by the staff which seem to have been successful.

While it is reasonable to assume that we will have failures, and while it is important to know what has not worked, "success stories" will have real significance, for it is upon these that future developments in shaping curricula and total educational programs will depend. These must be culled so that other teachers in the school and in the system may profit from them.

Organization. The following agenda is suggested for Workshop Week:
1. Principals should discuss with the staff the plans for the third year.
2. Individual problems and needs in each school should be identified as preparation for full discussion during the first consultant session.
3. Resources the staff would like to have available for carrying out its work should be considered.
4. Ways in which opportunities for small group meetings, individual conferences, total school group meetings in a given school should be determined. An exchange among principals who have discovered ways that work may be helpful.
5. A possible plan of evaluation by the participants should be made.
6. Initial tentative experience units may be discussed during the first consultant session. Sample units developed by participants may be borrowed for study.

This plan (encompassed in the first bulletin) was considered by the elementary staffs during Workshop Week in the fall of 1961, and we were off to a good start.

The Consultants at Work

For the third year of the Project, Dr. Vickery planned to continue his service as curriculum consultant, provided by The National Conference of Christians and Jews, on the four days per month allocation established in the second year of the Project. He was to be assisted, as he had been throughout the period of the Project, by Dr. Agnes Snyder, Professor Emeritus, Adelphi College, Long Island, New York, who was contributing her services as a voluntary consultant. Dr. Snyder was to concentrate her help in the North East School, keeping a running record of the consultant sessions and developments in one Project school. In addition, she planned to serve as consultant to the school staff for a language deficiency study to be instituted by North East School.

Master Teacher

The detail of procedures developed in utilizing a consultant is of interest to school staffs.

Records of Dr. Vickery's sessions at North East School are of particular interest, for, in addition to describing the consultant at work, they reveal the identification of language needs which later provided the base for the planning of this special study.

For this reason, the complete record of Dr. Vickery's sessions in North East School, September-November, 1961, follows.

FIRST STAFF MEETING—SEPTEMBER 26, 1961

Dr. Vickery spent the afternoon of September 26, 1961, at North East School in conferences with individual faculty members, in one small group conference with special teachers, and in a general Project meeting.

1:30–1:50 P.M.—MRS. ISAKOFF, KINDERGARTEN

Dr. Vickery asked Mrs. Isakoff if she had made any home visits this year.

Mrs. Isakoff said that she had; that conditions were improving. There was a more settled feeling, more money, more milk being drunk, and clothes were cleaner.

In reply to Dr. Vickery's question as to whether there was more friendliness, Mrs. Isakoff said that there was, but that the ties with the old neighborhoods from which the people had come were still very strong. She said that she would like to formulate questions that would bring more definite reactions.

Dr. Vickery said that he thought the parent-interview schedule (developed in the Project) that showed parents' hopes would help and that he would send her a copy.

Dr. Vickery asked if Mrs. Isakoff kept a record of her interviews. She said that she did.

Dr. Vickery asked if she felt that she was looking at the group as a whole. Mrs. Isakoff felt that she was doing this more than last year.

Dr. Vickery suggested that it might be well to try to get parents to draw pictures of the family to compare with those the children drew.

Mrs. Isakoff referred to the children's telling what they liked about their friends. Dr. Vickery said that what the children said they liked and did not like were clues to their values. He then asked on what particularly Mrs. Isakoff would like to focus this year. Mrs. Isakoff answered that she would like to get the children to communicate more with each other rather than with her.

This led to a discussion of the relation of the children's natural vocabulary to that in readers. Dr. Vickery asked how children's oral communications differed from the vocabulary in first grade books. Could we begin to identify words which best "hitch on" with children's feelings? He suggested a little study of such words trying them out on reading charts. He asked if it was easier for children to connect the written word, "messing," one the children commonly use, than the word "boat" with its oral use.

Mrs. Isakoff was not sure, but said she would be interested in finding out.

Dr. Vickery saw possibilities in a tryout with the use of words with emotional flavor for beginning readers. Mrs. Isakoff suggested that beginning readers might be written from this angle.

1:50–2:10 P.M.—MRS. DOUGLAS, PRIMARY UNIT (GRADES 1–2)

Dr. Vickery summarized with Mrs. Douglas the discussion he had just had with Mrs. Isakoff on the use of emotionally charged words—ones the children used with both pleasant and unpleasant feeling tones—in beginning reading.

Mrs. Douglas commented on the differences between the children's vocabulary and that of their readers. She mentioned, for example, that one reader use "mew" while the children say "meow."

Dr. Vickery said that he would use the children's "meow." He asked Mrs. Douglas how her class was doing.

Mrs. Douglas said that the class had settled down more quickly this year than last year. She attributed it to being more used to both the school and their homes—both new last year.

(At this point, Miss Peaco joined us—we were running overtime.)

Miss Peaco commented that she felt that because the school was not so new this year the children had more stability.

Mrs. Douglas said that she would like to see the primary grades all work together on a common problem.

Dr. Vickery suggested that Mrs. Douglas talk with Mrs. Isakoff about the use of children's own vocabulary, especially "feeling" words, in beginning reading.

Mrs. Douglas said that there were two kindergartens, two first grades, and two first-second grades combined.

Dr. Vickery suggested that the kindergarten teachers might give a list of words used by her children to the first grade teachers in order to articulate the two. He asked what words were used at Hallowe'en. "Ghosts" was agreed to be the most common.

Dr. Vickery asked if "ghosts" would be learned more readily than "cat." He added that the size of the word did not determine the difficulty.

Miss Peaco said that the children learned words from television and that "Rock and Roll" vocabulary was easy for them.

Dr. Vickery said that academic achievements would be stepped up if we connected more with children through words that had meaning for them.

(Mrs. Douglas left at 2:23.)

2:10–2:30 P.M. (SCHEDULED TIME) ACTUALLY BEGAN AT 2:23— MISS PEACO, PRIMARY UNIT (GRADES 3–4)

Dr. Vickery asked Miss Peaco what her emphasis this year was. Miss Peaco said that the emphasis was on homes, the different homes the children have seen, and the work that is done in homes.

Dr. Vickery asked if Miss Peaco was building toward the idea that different people live in different homes for different reasons. He asked if she expected to work on the kinds of houses that help make better neighbors. Does the way the houses are built make for good or poor human relations? Possible distance makes better neighbors. There is a need to see a town as a network of people rather than just persons. It is important to keep looking for significant ideas; e.g., it is important to learn how to live in cities.

2:30–2:50 p.m.—SPECIAL TEACHERS

Physical education	—	Miss Redding
Art	—	Miss Klug
Music	—	Miss Rittenhouse
Nurse	—	Miss LeVigne

The conference was devoted to a discussion of plans for *The Westward Movement* for which resources had been developed last year. It was agreed that Nov. 15 should be given over to presenting the results of the study. The presentation should take the form of living as the pioneers lived. It would include games, songs, dances, preparing meals, eating, etc. However, no definite plans would be made until the children participated in them.

In the meantime, teachers and children would read widely on the subject. Two books suggested were *Giants of the Earth* and *The Choir Invisible*. It was also suggested that comparison be made of the research the children were making with the Westerns on television.

3:30–4:30 P.M.—GENERAL MEETING

Dr. Vickery opened the meeting by stating that while during the coming year the diagnosis of children would continue, the emphasis would be on teaching methods. The meeting today would be devoted to the use of literature for human understanding.

Dr. Vickery had chosen *The Spinster,* by Sylvia Ashton Warner, to use as a demonstration. He said that he had hesitated between choosing a book for children and one for adults. He decided on the latter as probably more effective. He then gave a few highlights of the book—just enough to make it intelligible.

He gave as the setting the school in New Zealand in which most of the children were Maoris. He asked the group what they knew about Maoris. It was brought out that they were proud, fearless Polynesian people, culturally more developed than the Australian bushmen, but close to the Stone Age when the British first settled in New Zealand.

Dr. Vickery then went on to say that the teacher's mother was English and her father Russian, that she had been brought up in England, but apparently left for personal reasons. This was her first year in the New Zealand school. She had what would correspond to a kindergarten in our schools, and had sixty-five children. Dr. Vickery then said that he would read from the book passages that described a day in her school.

The reading pictured a classroom with many activities going on with a teacher whose eyes were on many different things, very warm in her relations with the children, her efforts at teaching frequently interrupted by such personal admonitions as, "Use your handkerchief," "Put your shirt in."

When Dr. Vickery finished reading, he asked: "Would you like to be on a faculty with her?" There was a general laugh that sounded like assent but with realization that it might not be easy.

Dr. Vickery asked, "What would make you want her?" The replies included: "Sense of humor; a child at heart; recognition of her own shortcomings—'the brains I haven't got'; warm feeling."

One of the teachers remarked that the shirt and the handerchief made her feel right at home.

Dr. Vickery asked if there was anything else that made them feel at home with her.

Someone said, "She had the nerve to try things out." Another said, "She had eyes all over the room—her half-finished sentences."

Dr. Vickery then explained the English system of inspection with ratings following. He then asked how the teacher would feel about a low rating.

Someone answered that it wouldn't make any difference because she couldn't possibly be anything but herself.

Dr. Vickery asked them what the teacher's dilemma was. The answer came quickly: "Too many children and she sees the children individually and she couldn't 'get them down.' "

Dr. Vickery asked, "How do you 'get them down'?" The answers: "Get them in groups; get them to interrelate."

Miss Redding said that she had had sixty-five children in gym, but could manage them by grouping.

Dr. Vickery said that the teacher was faced with three choices: Individualize, treat as a mass, compromise. How might she resolve the dilemma?

It was suggested that she get herself organized. But someone objected to this and said she was organized. Someone else said that she had the children at heart but she had no plan.

Dr. Vickery said that the teacher resolved the dilemma, but he would not say how. Instead, he suggested that everybody read the book.

After this, Dr. Vickery directed the discussion to the method he had used by asking, "What was my purpose in reading this book to you?" There was agreement that the purpose was to open up discussion. He asked what generalizations they thought he had in mind. Someone answered: "All teachers have problems."

Dr. Vickery agreed and added that we are in exactly the same dilemma the teacher was in—wanting to meet individual needs but lacking ways of operating.

Then Dr. Vickery asked what was behind his first question, "Would you like her on your faculty?" It was suggested that the question was designed to get the teachers to look at themselves.

Dr. Vickery next briefly commented on the relation of this demonstration with what similarly could be done with children. Knowing children's needs, literature could be used to help them identify their needs.

Mrs. Wilson closed the meeting by saying that Dr. Vickery had demonstrated a method; that he would use other methods; and that, as our unit building progressed, we would use the most appropriate methods for our purposes.

ADMINISTRATIVE PLANNING CONFERENCE—OCTOBER 16, 1961
1:30–3:00 P.M.

Present: Mrs. Wilson, Dr. Vickery, Dr. Snyder, and, briefly toward the end of the conference, Dr. Crosby.

Purpose: To discuss possible follow-up of Dr. Vickery's suggestion at the September meeting that a study be made of the use of children's natural language in experience charts in the beginning reading stages.

Discussion: The discussion was informal, each member throwing out ideas as they occurred in a purely exploratory attempt to determine the value of the idea and possible procedures if adopted.

Agreements:

1. Because of the interest in the idea on the part of the teachers of the primary group reported by Mrs. Wilson, the project should be undertaken.

2. Dr. Snyder would work with the teachers interested. She would meet with them as soon after October 27 as was possible to lay out with them the basic plan.

3. A good design was essential and should be the outcome of the deliberations of the teachers concerned under the guidance of the leadership provided.

4. The preliminary thinking of the present group included the following:

    a. Hypothesis: Children will learn to read more readily if their own natural vocabulary is used, particularly with words charged with feeling.

    b. Main features of the design:

        Stimulating children through all possible devices to use their natural vocabulary

        Collecting the vocabulary

        Developing experience charts using the vocabulary

        Recording the process

        Evaluating results

SECOND STAFF MEETING—OCTOBER 16, 1961
3:30–4:30 P.M.

Dr. Vickery stated the purpose of the meeting as providing a demonstration of the use of pictures in developing good human relations.

First, Dr. Vickery stated that there were many uses to be made of pictures and that it was essential that the particular purpose for which a given picture was used should be very clear. He stated three major purposes as:

    a. Connecting words—symbols—with the realities for which they stand

    b. Stimulating and exploring feelings

    c. Problem solution

The purpose of the demonstration today, Dr. Vickery stated as problem solution. He then asked the group to divide into sub-groups of six. He distributed copies of the same picture to each group. The picture was a courtroom scene. The characters were a man behind an official desk, a woman and a boy standing facing the desk, a man standing nearby whose expression reflected accusation, and a man sitting rather removed from the rest. Dr. Vickery asked that the groups give names to the characters in the picture and then indicate the problem involved. The groups responded:

Group 1: The mother does not like coming into court; she feels the boy has let her down.

Group 2: The boy comes from a poor background; the boy has not been in trouble before; the mother has had to leave her work to come to court; the judge is kindly—has a grandson the same age as the boy; mother was deserted and inclined to vent her unhappiness on the boy; school record not good; interested in sports; the police officer not sympathetic; the boy had taken a ball; the judge will take into consideration the background.

Group 3: The boy has stolen a jacket from a store to keep up with the gang he belongs to; the boy looks ashamed; the storekeeper is angry; mother works hard and is angry.

Group 4: Boy stole a hub cap; mother separated from husband; boy wants to sell hub cap; first offense; judge sympathetic.

Group 5: Mother is a widow. Boy stole article from a family; mother irate; judge inclined to be lenient.

In discussing the reports, Dr. Vickery commented that all were inclined to emphasize the possible leniency of the judge and that none spoke of the boy as "bad." He then went on to indicate questions that might serve as foci in the discussion of pictures with children.

First question: Who are the characters? Identification of personalities is the first step in human relations.

Second question: How is each character involved? This will serve to define the problem and help the children to relate it.

Third question: What factors would the judge take into account (in this particular picture)? This is not simple. The simplest would be emphasizing the factor of wrong-doing and, therefore, needed punishment.

For teachers, it would be important to raise the question as to what they would do about the situation when the boy came back to school. In making a decision, what is good for the child and what is good for the school must both be taken into consideration.

The discussion then moved in the direction of the selection of pictures. The following criteria were suggested:

a. Suitability to the problems children have

b. Relation to the curriculum planning under way

c. Involvement of human relations

d. The solution not too obvious

e. Possibility of alternate courses of action

f. Freedom from stereotypes

At a previous meeting, Dr. Vickery had asked the teachers to bring pictures with them for discussion at the present meeting.

The first picture was a country scene in the fall season. It was agreed that the picture was useful for giving factual information about farm life and that it had the additional value of stimulating warmth of feeling.

The second picture, a storm in the mountains, was definitely a "feeling" picture.

The third, a ball game, was useful in showing how families could have fun together.

The fourth picture, a mother and father with a child coming out of a church, brought considerable discussion as to its suitability at North East School. Some felt it was too far removed from the life of the children at North East. Dr. Vickery, however, brought out the need that children, in addition to using materials familiar to them, had to have some that are in contrast. This picture, for example, would show how different people spend Sundays.

The fifth picture was a "fun" picture—a horseless carriage.

The sixth picture was a story picture. A big frog face was shown, the frog puffed up with pride—ready to burst.

The seventh, eighth, and ninth pictures were story pictures.

The tenth picture was a striking one of a large baby face crying lustily. The question suggested for discussion of the picture was, "What makes a baby cry that way?"

It was agreed that during the coming month teachers would try out with the children pictures for the several purposes discussed at this meeting.

THIRD STAFF MEETING—NOVEMBER 16, 1961
PRIMARY MEETING—9:10–10:00 A.M.

Dr. Vickery distributed the bulletin, "Building Resource Units in Human Relations Education." He asked those assembled to read the introductory paragraph. Then all were asked to read the section, "The Characteristics of Unit Building."

He asked for points teachers wanted underlined or about which they wanted to make comment.

Theda Wilson: "Human relations education is not the edge of the school's program; it is at its very center." Relationship is why we teach. It is not at the fringe.

Claretta Elliott: "Unit teaching makes it possible for children of different abilities to work together toward common goals in the classroom." Dr. Vickery suggested we could provide the activities and stimulus. The greater the range the more likely the child would be interested in exploring ideas. In the long run, each child learns what he selects to learn. Mrs. Elliott felt that each child selects as he sees the relationship of the different activities to the main idea. This would make sharing periods take on new meanings.

Muriel Crosby: Couldn't we talk more about selection? This is another kind of learning experience. When children have this experience each gets something he needs to learn. We can illustrate from our own experience instances when each teacher selected what was most important for her.

There are some things that come naturally. In school we try to replace less acceptable with acceptable behavior. We sometimes make mistakes when we try to stop the behavior instead of providing other kinds on the positive side to get it out of the children's systems.

Dr. Vickery commented that Natalie Cole says that when her children get to the point where they cannot take any more, she turns on the record player and all get up and dance. They know this activity meets with her approval, and it gets things out of their systems.

Claretta Elliott said she felt there were pressures put on teachers. It is difficult to know sometimes how much and what kind of noise is approved by some administrators or supervisors. When a child finishes his work he should have the opportunity to go to the play corner. Here he can become too noisy.

Dr. Crosby reassured her by pointing out that early in life children can learn that the situations determine the kinds of things that are appropriate and what are not. There are some kinds of activities in which reasonable quiet is necessary. Everyone knows you don't build blocks in the library. Children should work out the kinds of activities that don't annoy. They should set these up.

Her second point was that each of us by temperament reacts differently to noise. We can be one way or the other. We assume all feel as we do. Some children are disturbed, and others are not. Some children break out at home because they can take only so much. We must hold on to what is appropriate in each situation. What kinds of activities are appropriate while others are going on? This is a part of pupil-teacher planning.

Helen Taylor noted that when she comes from a music class and finds her children all keyed up and still humming she just continues with music in the class for a while.

Dr. Vickery suggested that the teachers read the rest of the bulletin on relating diagnostic techniques to curriculum planning. Then, between now and December, after reading it over, come together in groups and trade ideas.

INTERMEDIATE MEETING—10:00 - 11:00 A.M.

Dr. Vickery distributed the bulletins and after giving the teachers time to read the first paragraph, asked, "Have you thought of units as a work of art?" He went on to comment that the thing that distinguished the units was the imagination of the teachers. He had started out thinking of units as blocks but had to find something with movement, a human quality. A unit is like unity. It is the whole with the parts interrelated. When he asked if the teachers found any sentences that struck them as being true, three responded immediately.

Azalia Briggs found: "The teacher will never again teach the same unit in the same way, any more than an artist will go on making exact copies of a picture which pleases him." She said she had new ideas and new children. The same thing does not fit different children.

Millicent Ferrell agreed and added that she sees her mistakes, remembers the pitfalls, and tries to avoid them.

Doris Peaco felt that just as an artist can't make the same copies, a teacher loses interest if she does the same thing and so cannot inspire the children.

Dr. Vickery noted that as teachers vary the unit content, they grow themselves in helping children grow.

All were then asked to read "Units in Human Relations Education Deal with Significant Ideas of Lasting Importance" (page 134 in this book), and to comment and ask questions.

Millicent Ferrell had underlined, "It seeks to help children develop for themselves and apply in their daily living a system of ethics based on respect for themselves and a human regard for other people—in short, on the concept of the brotherhood of man."

Arrie Harrison had liked, "Human relations education is not at the edge of the school's program; it is at its very center."

Dr. Vickery asked, "What does it mean to you? How would you do it?"

Arrie Harrison said children don't learn to read for reading. They have a purpose.

Dr. Vickery asked the purpose of writing—To communicate.

Dr. Vickery asked, "How about reading?"—For understanding, information.

Guizelous Molock felt that this puts a direct responsibility on the child.

Dr. Vickery asked how this relates to the sentence, "How about the fourth grade where you teach about Delaware?"

Andrew Lockett, "They develop pride in the state."

Arrie Harrison, "This makes them spread out."

Dr. Vickery commented that it is hard to make a personal relationship between a child and the state. "What are his direct experiences with the state?"

"State parks. They can visit places."

"As fourth graders, they are interested in how it is governed."

"My class is interested in how laws are made. They know the majority rules." (Azalia Briggs)

Dr. Vickery summarized by pointing out that the better children see the use value learning has for now, and the more they see the relationship learning has to the future, the more likely it is to stick.

He then asked for all to read the paragraph "Unit teaching makes it possible for children of different abilities to work together toward common goals in the same classroom." When he asked the question, "Don't we use ability grouping every time we teach?" Dr. Crosby asked if the quality and quantity of learning were not different. The answer is not in the ability grouping.

There are the same problems within the group. Children of high ability are not the same in all things.

Learning is selective for all children. Each of us picked out what meant most as we read. Our interest and problems differ just as do children's so we pick out of the range those that mean the most.

Dr. Vickery closed the session with the same suggestion he made to the primary teachers.

Then he, Dr. Crosby, Dr. Miller, and Theda Wilson went to the multipurpose room to observe "Pioneer Day."

Following the sudden death of Dr. Vickery in November 1961, we were faced with the acute need to plan ways and means to bring the Project to a successful close in June 1962.

The Project Administrator conferred with school staff members, the superintendent, and officials of The National Conference of Christians and Jews, seeking the best solution to the problem of adequate consultant service. For two reasons it seemed wise to become self-sufficient as a school system. The first was the inability of N.C.C.J. to find quickly a replacement for Dr. Vickery. Secondly, the Project Administrator had anticipated the need to prepare staff members to carry on our efforts after the formal closing of the Project in June 1962. During Dr. Vickery's first three consultant sessions earlier in the year, a plan had been developed for the four helping teachers assigned to the Elementary Division as general supervisors to become prepared for providing leadership in human relations education for the future. The plan incorporated orientation by the helping teachers for all staff members entering the school system after June 1962. The helping teachers, Dr. Vickery, and the Project Administrator had met in planning and development sessions for a three-month period, September-November 1961. Upon Dr. Vickery's death, the Project Administrator immediately set in motion training sessions for the helping teachers to assume consultant roles for the remainder of the school year, 1961-62. The plan which was evolved follows:

Consultants in the Making

In late January, a number of all-day sessions with the helping teachers were planned by the Project Administrator prior to resuming consultant work in the schools. It was felt desirable that each helping teacher concentrate on one teaching and learning process in which she felt competent. Each one prepared a special bulletin which was to be developed in consultant sessions and to be left with the participants for additional guidance in using the process. Much assistance in preparation of the bulletins was given each individual by the Project Administrator and the other helping teachers.

The bulletins became an important contribution to the Project resource library under the title "Teaching—Learning Processes in Human Relations Education." In the preface, written by the Project Administrator, the series was introduced as an implementation of the effectiveness of participants in the Project. And it was recommended that participants place their copies in their permanent resource files for future use.

Each bulletin in the series describes an important instrument teachers find helpful in providing experiences for children which will foster the development of human relations skills, information, knowledge, and sensitivities. Specific illustrations, needed resource information, and other related material are included in each bulletin.

At that time, four bulletins had been prepared and distributed by the helping teachers: "Role Playing" by Edith Patterson, "Dramatic Play" by Henrietta Henry, "Construction Activities" by Mildred Patterson, "Curriculum Trips" by Elizabeth Eaton. The latter one is reprinted below as an example of the quality and effectiveness of these bulletins.

"Reading for Human Relations," *The Packet,* Winter 1961-62, (D. C. Heath) is an additional resource in this series.

It is expected that other titles in the series will be added in the near future.

Teaching and Learning Resource Bulletin: Curriculum Trips

EDUCATIONAL VALUES OF CURRICULUM TRIPS

Trips provide one of our most valuable teaching aids. Interest is fostered and understanding developed which will lead to many worthwhile activities.

Before a trip is planned, these questions should be considered: Are the children ready for this trip?

Is this the most efficient and effective way to get needed information and experience?

Will the entire class benefit from this trip?

Is the expenditure of effort, time and money justifiable?

What opportunities are there in this trip for providing experiences with human relations understandings, knowledge, and sensitivities?

Trips can involve: Planning, discussing, investigating, letter writing, interviewing, using the telephone directory, phoning, arranging transportation, figuring schedules and expenses, taking notes, making outlines, observing, recalling, understanding, interpreting, using, sharing and evaluating.

Children can better understand the needs for the acquisition of the basic skills when given an opportunity to use them in an immediate situation such as taking a trip.

A trip, to be a worthwhile experience, must have a definite purpose which is clearly understood by the children and the teacher.

It should clarify, enrich and broaden the area of interest being explored. The children should assist with the planning of the trip and should participate as much as possible in the actual arrangements.

The preparation for the trip and the experiences shared on the journey provide valuable learning situations.

The evaluation of the trip by the boys and girls and the planning for the use and sharing of the experience are other important phases of trip-taking. The evaluation can be a discussion of how their plans succeeded, whether or not their questions were answered, what new interests were discovered, and how worthwhile the trip was. Plans can then be made for recording and sharing the experience. Exhibits of materials, dramatizations, scrapbooks, stories, pictures, and narrative accounts may result.

HUMAN RELATIONS VALUES

Individuals develop sensitivity, appreciation of people, and skill in working with them by face to face contacts. They must be helped to have opportunities to meet many adults and children in different situations. The relationships that children have with fellow pupils, parents, the traffic guard at the corner, the clerk in the store, the driver on the bus, the officer on the street, and public custodians serve as laboratory materials for discussion and interpretation in the classroom. Children need to recognize and to discuss the many differences in people. They need to become aware of their own responsibility for establishing good relations and rapport with the people whom they meet. Children must be helped to realize that what they say, do, and feel usually conditions the responses of others towards them. In like manner, what others say, do, and feel conditions their own responses to these people. Children can be helped to understand how feelings and beliefs determine a person's conduct and that ways of behaving in similar situations differ.

Perplexities which have occurred because one kind of behavior pattern has conflicted with another set of expected behavior patterns can be discussed and interpreted.

Trips offer an excellent opportunity for developing human relations sensitivities and skills through face to face contacts.

CLASS PREPARATION

In addition to adequate planning for the mechanics of the trip and for achieving the educational goals, much of the focus of planning can be on human relations skills. Role playing may be used to sensitize the children to the many ways of meeting various situations likely to be encountered. The consideration of questions similar to the following will highlight human relations values.
—Why is it necessary and also considerate to secure permission to visit a place?
—What information should be sent ahead that would help in making the visit better for everyone? How would this information help?

—In what ways can we be considerate of and be of help to the bus driver, the traffic guard, the guide, the mothers who accompany us?

—How can we show how we feel about the place visited, the exhibits and materials seen?

—How can we make sure that we or another class will be welcome to visit the place again?

The trip itself will furnish adequate situations for further consideration and discussion from a human relations focus.

POSSIBLE SITUATIONS

The situations which follow are examples of the types of experiences which can serve as bases for discussion to help children in their role in developing good human relations and to aid in their understanding of other people's attitudes and reactions.

A Disappointing Trip to the Museum

The trip to the Museum of Natural History had been well planned. The children had read and studied about the birds and animals of South America. They were anxious to view the magnificent specimens in the Museum and to observe the reproductions of their natural habitats. A guide had been requested and a list of questions to be answered had been sent ahead.

It turned out to be one of *those days* at the Museum. Several of the regular guides were out ill. Bus load after bus load of eager children seemed to be arriving continuously, and humanity in all sizes, shapes and colors swarmed everywhere.

The attendants on duty were overwhelmed. Our group was finally sent on its way with an inexperienced substitute guide. She was flustered, insecure, and wanted no questions. The children were rudely herded from one exhibit to another. No questions were answered. The children were told to look and listen.

Bewildered and breathless, they were finally deposited in a small, stuffy auditorium to eat their bag lunches. Some were jolly and well-behaved. Others reacted noisily to the same disappointments.

Per request, the exhibits viewed after lunch were Pennsylvania mammals instead of an illustrated talk on South American animals.

Despite the keen disappointment and the rudeness of certain attendants and the guide, the children conducted themselves remarkably well.

Since the trip took all day, evaluation could not be made until the next morning.

—What human relation learnings could come from this situation?

—In what ways did different groups act in this situation?

—How might they have acted?

—If you had been the emergency guide, what would you have done?

—How do you feel about planning another trip to this same museum?

—What might be a gracious way to help the museum avoid such an experience another time?

The Lost Ticket

The great day had come. After careful planning and a long period of anticipation, the group was ready for the train ride to Chester and back. Each child handed the money the school had provided for his fare to the man at the ticket window. Clutching the precious bit of cardboard entitling them to a ride, the children boarded the train. All went well until the conductor collected the tickets. Joe couldn't find his. Twenty little searchers couldn't find it. Joe's tears were near the surface. The teacher reached in her own purse to pay for Joe's ticket. Jovially the conductor refused her money, saying, "I guess this ride can be on the railroad!"

—What choices did the conductor have concerning the boy with the lost ticket?
—What kind of a man do you think he was?
—How did the group feel about the railroad as a result of this man's choice of action? How might they have felt?
—What new insights did the children get about their teacher?

The Bus That Did Not Come

Everything was in readiness. Well-scrubbed, neatly dressed boys and girls clutching bag lunches, eagerly watched the clock and listened for the announcement, "The bus is here," to come over the intercom. The clock hand jumped ahead minute after minute. A feeling of uneasiness came over the teacher and transferred to the waiting group.

A quick communication from teacher to office to the bus company confirmed fears. A misunderstanding as to dates had occurred. No bus was coming and none was available.

—If you were faced with this kind of problem, how would you handle it?
—How could children be helped to face the necessary adjustments to overcome disappointments?
—What choices of action were open to teacher and pupils?
—How do you think the people at the bus company might have felt about this mistake?
—Have you ever made plans and had something go wrong? Tell us about it.
—When things go wrong after we have carefully planned, how can we make a good situation out of it?

Loss of Goodwill

The manager at the supermarket readily agreed to take Miss M. and her thirty children on a tour of the store and to give them a peep "behind the scenes." The class had seen filmstrips and a movie concerning the many foods in a supermarket and had learned quite a bit concerning its operation. They had read the book, *Let's Go to a Supermarket.*

When the day for the trip came, most of the children were neatly dressed in clean school clothes but some children had put on fussy party clothes and one girl had obtained and copiously used her mother's lipstick. Since the store was only two blocks away, Miss M. hadn't thought it necessary to ask busy mothers to accompany the group.

On the whole, the trip seemed a success. Most of the children politely thanked the manager for the opportunity to tour the market.

But these things had happened:

1. Several children broke out of line and chased over a lawn to get to the front of the line near friends.

2. Bubble gum was chewed and blown and cracked by several while the manager was talking.

3. Several children helped themselves to cookies from a broken box on a shelf.

4. Because there was so much pushing and crowding to get to see the enormous freezer, a stack of packaged vegetables was knocked over.

5. One child contradicted the manager because he explained some processes differently from the presentation in the movie viewed.

6. Several children laughed and made fun of a very fat man who was a stock clerk.

7. Two children returned to school with pockets bulging with gum and candy bars which had been taken from supply bins.

When Mrs. J. requested that her class be allowed to visit the same store, the manager politely refused permission, saying that the district supervisor felt that such visits disrupted store personnel schedules.

—How did behaviors of children differ?
—What kinds of behavior would have made for a better situation?
—How would you have felt if you were the manager? The teacher?
—Why do you suppose the store policy on visiting was changed?
—What plans for restitution could be made for items that had been taken by the children without the manager's knowledge?

Concepts and Generalizations

By using a human relations angle as a focal point for discussing hypothetical or real situations arising from planning and taking a curriculum trip, it is possible to help children better understand some of the following concepts and to arrive at some of the following generalizations.

Concepts:

Consideration	Cooperation	Tact
Responsibility	Appropriateness	Resourcefulness
Politeness	Sympathy	Diplomacy
Empathy	Understanding	Attitudes

Generalizations:

- People's responses to us are often conditioned by our actions.
- People who have jobs to do cannot always stop to talk to us.
- Good planning makes for a more successful trip.
- Emergencies and disappointments must be met with resourcefulness and good spirit.
- People are sometimes rude to us because they themselves are tired, unwell, or upset.
- Rules and regulations are made in the interest of many people.
- They are necessary for pleasant successful group living.
- Unwise actions of a few can deprive many of visiting privileges.
- Differences in people do not indicate either superiority or inferiority.
- The kind of clothing worn is determined by the occasion.

TRIP-TAKING MECHANICS

Permission. It is necessary to have a permission slip signed by a child's parent or guardian before taking him from the school grounds. This is also a requirement for a neighborhood trip on foot.

Transportation. Each school, depending on the size of its pupil population, is allocated a certain number of trips for which the school bus may be used. In addition to the school bus, each school has a small budget for the hiring of commercial buses. Under no circumstances are pupils to be transported in privately owned cars.

Sometimes, a trip need occurs when there is no money in the school budget and the school bus is not available. Discuss this situation with the principal before collecting money from the pupils. The collection of money for any purpose is generally discouraged in our schools.

Follow the procedures recommended by the principal for any trip you take. Discuss your plans with her well in advance of making any arrangements.

POSSIBLE TRIPS

Neighborhood. Many trips can be made within walking distance of school. The neighborhood park, a new house being built or demolished, a ditch being dug, a street or highway under construction, a wind-swept, trash-littered lot—all of these offer possibilities from an educational and human relations aspect.

There are many stores, plants, and industries in different Wilmington neighborhoods. If a teacher sees good experience possibilities in visiting a privately owned place, a personal call will often pave the way and permission may be secured. However, if blanket permission for listing the establishment as a trip possibility is requested, refusal is almost certain.

Therefore, arrangements to visit supermarkets, cleaning plants, bottling plants, food processing establishments, trucking concerns, banks, laundromats, and others, should be made by individual teachers who live in the respective neighborhoods. Here is where a knowledge of good *adult* human relations may come in handy.

Dividing Time

The following report provides an illustration of the effectiveness of teachers in adapting the learnings attained through consultant help in developing a human relations focus in using books wisely. This report, prepared by Madeline Stoops, sixth grade teacher, Palmer School, is a timely one for those who know that "the things of the spirit" really count.

I had been reading aloud to my sixth grade students one of my favorite books—*Rabbit Hill,* by Robert Lawson.

I had read this book in other years to other groups, but this time something real happened. My boys and girls laughed with me at Little Georgie's gay capers. We almost felt we were taking that breath-taking jump with Georgie as he landed, turned seven somersaults, and came up sitting in a clump of soft grass. That was the time he beat Old Hound by jumping clear across Deadman's Brook up Danbury way.

We even joined in his song about:

"New Folks Coming, Oh, My!
New Folks Coming, Oh, My!"

There weren't many words and there weren't many notes, and the notes just went up a little and down a little.

Together we were saddened by Mother Rabbit's inconsolable anguish when Little Georgie mysteriously disappeared after he fell into the rain barrel up at the Big House.

And we laughed off Uncle Analdas' untidy ways and the complete disorder of his burrow since his daughter, Mildred, had married and left home. Then, too, he was full of excuses about not being able to read the letter from his niece, Molly.

We were almost weepy, especially the girls, about poor Mole because he couldn't see. How we all admired the kindness and loyalty of Little Willie, the Fieldmouse, when Mole would say, "Be eyes for me, Little Willie."

In sixth grade manner of speaking we all got a charge out of the conversation between Tim, the gardener, and Louie, the stonemason. This says it briefly:

"These New Folks are queer. Nuts, some might say. Comes of reading books too much. They seem nice and pleasant—but queer. Seems a shame! Readin' rots the mind, so my grandfather used to say."

Together we regarded with wonder the great wisdom and fair play of the Little Animals when they all gathered on the Hill to make plans for the Dividing Night, which was to be held as usual on Midsummer's Eve.

Who told me this?

No one really said it, but it was there. I knew it and my sixth grade boys and girls knew it.

How did we know?

Well, I saw it in Betty's eyes, Elfrieda's smile, Taras' evident reluctance to leave the room for his recorder lesson. It was Grace's look of excitement, Mary's too frequent use of Kleenex, well wadded. It was in Donna's thoughtfulness while she gently fanned me with a folded piece of paper as I read to them on a warm afternoon in July shortly before the close of the term.

I believe the word empathy describes all of this if we think we need to name it.

Is it any wonder, then, that this happened as I finished reading *Rabbit Hill*?

Betty, known in our school for some good leadership qualities but not for scholastic aptitude, got up from her seat saying, "Mrs. Stoops, I just feel like us having a Dividing Day. I just feel like returning these three pennies to Elma. I borrowed them from her a long time ago when I wanted a popsicle."

This was the start of chain reaction!

Cecil left his seat to roll six marbles on Henry's desk. He said, "Bet you thought I'd forgotten all about them, Hen."

Alfrieda said to Betty, "Here's that handkerchief all washed and ironed. Mother keeps asking me if I returned it to you."

Taras said, "Here's that lens from your grandmother's old glasses that you let me use for a microscope that day on the hike, Allen."

Sudden trips to lockers, digging around in desks, boys inspecting their trouser pockets, girls peering into their purses produced many unusual things to return to owners. It was spontaneous, from the heart, and there were plenty of grins, laughs, and looks of surprise.

The Little Animals had their Dividing Night on Midsummer's Eve. We had ours on a warm afternoon in June.

Just to break the spell when they had finished exchanging, returning, and paying off, I said, "Oh yes I, too, want to have Dividing Time."

I pulled out three long strings of candy suckers gay in cellophane paper and a good assortment of flavors. Each child snipped one off with scissors provided and passed the string on to the next one.

Then suddenly Betty said, "There's enough for all—just like in *Rabbit Hill*, Mrs. Stoops."

Those are the words cut in stone that the Little Animals read on the new statue in the New Folks' garden. It was a statue depicting St. Francis Assisi, patron saint of the Little Animals. There was a pool with broad stones, a sort of rim like a shelf and it was set out like a banquet feast every night that summer. All around his feet were the Little Animals in stone and from his hands water dropped, clear, cool water, to the pool in front of him.

The garden flourished. No poison, no traps, no fence, and not a thing in the garden was touched by any of the Little Animals.

The neighbors' gardens didn't fare so well. The gardener couldn't understand it. "Must be beginner's luck!" he said. "Must be," agreed Louie, the stonemason. "Must be that—or something."

chapter

8

Evaluating Progress in Curriculum Building for Human Relations Education

In evaluating the achievements of the school aspect of The Three-Year Experimental Project on Schools in Changing Neighborhoods, it is necessary to remember that the Project was conceived as an exploratory study whose major objectives were the creation of a project design and an evaluation design. The first was accomplished during the first year of the Project and the second during the second year. Because they were achievements out of experience, neither was available at the initiation of the Project as guidance instruments for use by participants. Furthermore, the lack of adequate financial support prevented the addition of staff necessary for carrying out a full-scale evaluation of the total Project. Individual Project schools were asked to select from the Project Evaluation Design some aspect of evaluation of particular interest.

Principals Evaluate the Project's Effectiveness

A comparison of principals' responses at the close of the second year of the Project with those incorporated in Table 18 reveals that:
▪ Holding power had been strong. All Project schools participating in the second year of the Project remained for the third year; all schools (6) entering the first year remained the entire three years. It should not be assumed that the number of participants reported represents exclusively the same individuals. Throughout the three years there was some turnover of staff, with a relatively small number of participants leaving at the end of the first and second years and new participants entering during each of the three years. The total number of teachers affected by the Project was considerably larger than the actual number reported.

- The tendency to use diagnostic instruments to determine the perceptions children have of their own needs had become fairly well established by all participating schools, representing an increase over 1960-61.
- In the second year of the Project, principals had felt that growth in the teachers' achievement of increasingly effective planning skills was exceptional in only one school, moderately effective in eight schools, and poor in one. During the third year there is reflected some gain, with three schools evaluated as exceptional and four as moderate. Loss is reflected in the evaluation of a second school as poor, making a total of two staffs so designated.
- The staff's growth in effectiveness in developing experience units emphasizing human relations was extremely encouraging. There were five schools so designated as compared to none in 1960-61. Two staffs were designated as poor in this aspect.
- Schools with the greatest holding power revealed the greatest growth in effectiveness in both planning and emphasis upon human relations. Genuine interest, commitment to the goal of the Project, quality of staff, and leadership of principals are factors undoubtedly influential in holding power and achievement.

Summary of Principals' Responses Regarding Extent and Quality of Participation in Project   Table 18

Project Schools[1]	Number of Participants	Total Staff	Number Years in Project			Tendency to Use Diagnostic Instruments		Quality of Effectiveness in Achieving Increased Planning Skill				Quality of Effectiveness in Achieving Development of Experience Units in Human Relations			
			1	2	3	Yes	No	Exceptional	Moderate	Fair	Poor	Exceptional	Moderate	Fair	Poor
Drew-Pyle	25	25		x		x			x					x		
Elbert-Palmer	11	32	x			x		x				x			
Gray	39	41		x		x		x				x			
Lore	5	43	x			x					x				x
Shortlidge[2]	14	24		x		x			x			x			
Stubbs	11	30	x			x			x			x			
Williams	5	43		x		x					x				x
Opportunity	10	10	x			x		x				x			
North East	23	25	x			x			x				x		
Total	143	273	5	4		9		3	4		2	5	2		2

[1] 11 participating schools considered as 9 Project Centers.
[2] In 1961-62 the new Shortlidge School combined two old schools, Shortlidge and Washington.

The following reports constitute the answers given by individual Project school principals to the question: "In the total period of participation, what values to the school have been most pronounced?"

Drew-Pyle School

1. Encouraged insightful teaching on the part of the total staff.
2. Afforded all teachers an opportunity to renew their thinking and develop a fresh approach to the social studies program.
3. Assisted teachers in developing skills in teaching for better human relations.
4. Encouraged closer work with agencies serving the people in our district.

Elbert-Palmer Schools

1. Teachers plan for needs of pupils in our community.
2. Teacher-pupil relationships have improved.
3. Teachers' goals are more realistic in terms of child's ability.
4. Teachers are more sympathetic toward pupils' attitudes and ideas. They make an effort to understand causes behind behavior problems and work to solve their problems.

Gray School

1. The emphasis on really knowing how the individual feels and thinks about his life and surroundings. This emphasis, developed through open-ended questions, has sensitized teachers to the needs of children and turned their concern from content to pupil growth.
2. Strengthened the teachers' recognition of the importance of careful planning for a purpose.
3. Helped to unify the approach to teaching throughout the school.
4. Gave teachers a feeling of satisfaction as their units were accepted for bulletins.
5. Increased professionalism.

Lore School

1. Attention was focused on needs of children. Many teachers are more aware of the special needs of "deprived" children, and of the value knowledge about their children's needs has to the teacher.
2. Attention was focused by the faculty as a whole on the importance of attitude in learning. In discussions throughout this year this matter of attitude and its effect on the learning situation has been emphasized. This includes the attitude of the teacher toward the child and the attitude of the child toward the learning situation. I feel that the earlier Project work and contacts with Dr. Vickery alerted us to the importance of this attitude.

Shortlidge School

1. Teachers accept the need for providing a human relations oriented education as shown by choice of units and planning of units.
2. Teachers use more services of others and use them more wisely,

particularly in requests for help from psychologist, social worker, YMCA personnel, helping teachers, and other resource people.

3. Teachers use diagnostic instruments to discover needs and problems.

4. Teachers greatly increased their use of role playing, books about understanding feelings, discussion groups, etc.

Stubbs School

1. Increased use of social worker and school nurse. Since teachers have become more sensitive to human relations, they are more interested in the welfare of their pupils. Therefore, they make better use of the members of the guidance team.

2. More sympathy for the so-called problem child. The so-called problem child is now recognized as a child with many problems. Methods of dealing with him are shifting from punitive to corrective measures.

3. Better relations among pupils. There is more unity and less fighting among homeroom pupils.

4. Better planning among entire staff. Teachers love to share their success stories with others, and this is done rather frequently and informally around the lunch table, in the faculty room, at home, etc. Consequently, some non-participants are trying some of the human relations approaches that they have heard about. The resource units placed in the school library have also contributed to this wider participation.

Williams School

1. The greatest value, in my opinion, was derived from the small group discussions during the first year of the Project. Dr. Vickery's use of group dynamics and his sincere interest in people made this experience a good example of the best in human relations. He did a beautiful job of creating an atmosphere where teachers were at ease in exploring the problems of the community and their own ability or inability to cope with the situation. There was much enthusiasm in experimenting with diagnostic techniques and in sharing the findings.

The individuals in the group grew in their understanding and appreciation of each other; children within the school and the interrelation of the home, school, and community problems.

2. With this fine beginning it was a disappointment to see the loss of interest the second and third years when Dr. Vickery could not give the necessary time to this school.

Opportunity School

1. Teachers have grown in understanding of children's needs. Many new and enriching experiences were planned for the children. There was much evidence of awareness and use of their capabilities.

2. The staff has been encouraged to experiment and wishes to

continue. We no longer talk about limitations of the children but of possibilities. All of us are convinced that no one knows how far our children can go. Their responses are based on experiences which we offer and not on measured intellectual ability.

3. The children are more aware of adults and children in school. In their interpersonal relationships there has been a growth in sharing and empathy for other people's feelings.

4. There has been more individualized instruction and small group work this year. It is difficult to work with some of these children without the help of an aide. We have only made a beginning in this area but have hopes of going further next year.

North East School

1. Focus on language resulted from the use of diagnostic instruments requiring verbalization. We are conducting an experimental study to identify speech patterns and to improve speech and reading. Children will benefit as they gain more freedom of expression and expand their vocabularies. Teachers will gain added skills in helping children to think and speak more clearly and thus receive satisfaction from new experiences and opportunities because they can express themselves more adequately.

2. Staff unity came about as situations and problems were shared and studied. The efforts of a total school endeavor resulted in more immediate and lasting changes than individual or partial efforts could effect. There are fewer fights after school and in the community by children attending North East. All children have been given techniques for resolving differences before situations get beyond control.

3. Increasing sensitivity of teachers to individual differences and problems resulted in a high incidence of accuracy in the early identification of problems and retardation. Over 60 per cent of those children referred for examination as retarded were verified by the psychologist. This early identification will enable us to help them sooner.

4. Curriculum scope and depth were illustrated by the Pioneer Day unit which established a precedent and illustrated curriculum possibilities for children from humble backgrounds. It set a high standard of excellence.

Using wisely the limited consultant service available was a major problem of the Project Administrator. The choice was limiting the number of schools to those which could be adequately serviced, or spreading the service thinly over all schools wishing to participate. The second choice was made. In most schools the choice paid off. The combination of circumstances that resulted in failure for some and success for others must be studied in order to effect wiser administration in the future.

Individual Project Schools Evaluate Themselves

As individual Project evaluations for each participating school were read by the Project Administrator, certain achievements became overwhelmingly apparent. Among the achievements generally cited were the following:

1. The exceptional identification of the participants with their children.

The interest, warmth, and commitment of staff to the children were unmistakable. This represented a radical change for a staff which only three years earlier often complained about children whose deprivation made new demands on their teachers.

2. The deepening insights of the staff who found in their children's behavior an urgent need to help them develop a self-image worthy of self-respect and the respect of others.

3. The tremendous effort of the staff to provide experiences for children which would lift their aspirations.

Typical is Judy's letter which reflects the success of the efforts of one school to instill in its children an awareness of the doors which can open to them if motivation is strong.

> I am so glad you took time out to come to our school and talk to us. I enjoyed your talk very much. When one girl in the front row mentioned teaching and you replied, "forever," I was a little startled. As your talk grew more and more interesting I realized how lucky we are because, as you say, "what is worth having is worth fighting for." I want to become a teacher. Your lecture was a new inspiration to me. I am nine years old. I hope I have a nice character when I am a teacher. Thank you again.

4. The growth in supportive relationships between school staff and the parents in the school.

All parents who love their children seek to protect them. Protection becomes a dominant concern among parents whose children experience a racially desegregated school life for the first time. Mrs. L.'s letter to her child's principal reflects the generally strong relationships found between staff and parents of children in Wilmington's elementary schools:

> After having come to you early last summer with so many questions about your elementary school program, I felt that you might like to know how completely satisfied we are with the training that our little girl, Stephanie, is receiving at George Gray.
> Mrs. Kiziuk is all that we had hoped for in a teacher for Stephanie. Her personality, methods and techniques are helping to shape the attitudes toward work and school that every child must have if interest in school is to continue and the best in him developed. Stephanie loves reading, writing and number work. She sees words and hears sounds in everything. I have also

gathered that she has been disciplined to study without pressure and in quiet. She loves the school, teacher and all classmates; moves off to school excitedly every day; insists on being prepared for all lessons, and brings home school work with enthusiasm. We know that Mrs. Kiziuk deserves much credit for having moved her to perform in this way and we are exceedingly happy about it.

I firmly believe that the impressions, attitudes and habits formed in school in the primary years are lasting, sculpture the child's view of education and life, and temper his performance in all succeeding grades. Moreover, I have seen great numbers of children in Wilmington who have experienced other methods of learning the fundamentals of the elementary grades and who are meeting little or no success in secondary school although they evidence the ability to do much better. There is no place in our competitive society of today for the child who has never been made to work up to the greatest limit of his capacities—certainly not for the Negro child. It was for these reasons that I came to you last year with so much concern.

I do hope that you will go ahead with the plan to let the children remain with the same teacher for three years, so that our Stephanie can have the advantage of two more years with Mrs. Kiziuk.

If we can help our child in any way, or should any problems arise with her behavior or school work, please do not hesitate to let me know. My husband and I will do all that we can to help Stephanie and the school.

5. The conviction of participating staff members that the formal three years of study in the Project was but an experience in getting ready to engage in the continuing task of working toward increasing effectiveness in meeting the needs of children in a changing urban community.

The evaluation of one Project school revealed the accomplishments attained and those yet to be realized. The spirit of this report reflects the deep moral commitment of a school that cares about its children.

Evaluation of Drew-Pyle Schools' Participation in the Project
BRIEF HISTORY OF THE SCHOOL

This history of Drew and Pyle Schools is a short one. It dates back to 1953, at which time the Drew School was opened for Negro elementary children on the east side of Wilmington, and Pyle School was opened for Caucasian children. Despite the youthfulness of these two schools, they have been involved in marked neighborhood changes since 1953.

During the early history of Drew School overcrowdedness was the problem. The Supreme Court decision of 1954 eased this problem for Drew School. Our excess population was transferred to Pyle. Problems of adjustments for Pyle were created and they met them well.

Integration triggered a rapid decline in the white population of the East Side schools. Many parents moved and many children were enrolled in the two parochial schools in the neighborhood, St. Mary's and St. Stanislaus'.

Replacements soon filled the vacant desks of the declining group. First, the Puerto Ricans came. This group was followed by the children of Chrysler automobile workers, transferred from the Detroit plant to the Newark, Delaware plant. The Spanish-Greek (Gypsy) children followed. Last to arrive were the children of families affected by the 1960-61 business recession. The last group returned many old white families to our neighborhood.

Project A's demolition of twenty-two blocks affected our population, but not as much as we had expected. Many families refused relocation away from the East Side. They preferred the conveniences of center city and relocated on the fringe area of the project.

In spite of the fact that most of the Puerto Rican children have moved to the western section of the city, that the death of the Gypsy king has scattered his tribe again, that the Chrysler workers have discovered better housing in other parts of the city, and that employment is returning many white families to the suburbs, our population in terms of numbers remains the same.

Next year, redevelopment will begin in the twenty-two blocks of wasteland surrounding our schools. What this will mean in terms of school enrollment and social and cultural implications for our schools remains to be seen.

PROBLEMS OF CHANGE AFFECTING THE DREW-PYLE
SCHOOLS DURING THE PAST NINE YEARS

Living in a school in a constantly changing neighborhood can have great effects on parents, children and school personnel.

The daily accommodations forced by change tended to blur our focus and to interfere with the continuity of our program. We were not prepared for the many cultural diversifications thrust upon us, and relief was not always immediate. Our strain placed stress upon the children and many trying times were shared.

For example:

■ Our scramble to enroll in Spanish classes to handle the problems incurred by the influx of Spanish speaking children was one such frustration. After a year of Spanish instruction we discovered our formal Spanish was not the Spanish our children were speaking.

■ Most of the immigrants from Detroit had been in accelerated programs. By the time we had set up programs for them, they transferred.

■ Without exception the Spanish-Greek children were in school for the first time. They were bright children and learned rapidly, but they were overly mature and non-reading.

The Three-Year Experimental Project on Schools in Changing Neighborhoods could not have started at a more opportune time.

It was our redeemer. It gave us a focus and provided us with useful teaching techniques and tools for the many changes occurring in our schools.

The strength and popularity of this experience reflect in the growth of teacher participation in the Project during the three years. The Project began with a third of our teachers enrolled. Each year, we attracted more teachers. At the close of the Project, we had the full participation of our teaching staff.

EFFECTS OF THE PROJECT ON THE TEACHER-LEARNING SITUATION

Many good things happened to us during the three years of participation in the Project. These things happened to our teachers, our pupils, our school and our school community. One of the bright spots is that the teaching-learning situation in our school improved.

Following are the areas in which this was noticed:

Focus on Problems Through Children's Eyes. Seeing children's problems through the eyes of children no doubt had the greatest impact on our teachers. For years we have harbored illusions about children; have developed programs around our preconceived notions, and have impugned children who strayed from our path of instruction. Too often we taught children from a middle-class pedestal (even when our childhood did not reflect this background).

While our instruction received polite reception most of the time, some children did rebel. One thing was certain—our instruction was not absorbed by all and the retention of values was not maintained from year to year.

As we freed children's ideas, feelings, and sensitivities, we freed ourselves and our teaching. Our planning improved. Social studies programs became alive. Activities of a meaningful nature increased. Trips were more appropriate. Varied approaches to learning were pursued.

Focus on Neighborhood Problems Through Inter-Agency Cooperation. For years we had thought we knew our community well; we did in some respects. We knew the location of agencies, the general function of the agencies, and the agency heads. We knew little of their work, their programs and their problems. Their leaders knew less about our schools.

The Project encouraged getting together. There were coffee klatches of agency leaders, inter-agency luncheons, meetings with the staffs of some of the agencies, and many agency visits. As a result, two members of our school serve as board members of one agency. Several faculty members do volunteer work at the centers. The YMCA comes into our school to work with our young boys. Peoples Settlement developed a neighborhood service guide for parents in our schools. Christina's clothing center freed us from soliciting clothing for needy families.

In every case of active family membership in one of our East Side community agencies there is a supportive and cooperative family. Agency values are transcending families associated with them. This in turn has immeasurable influence on the child in the classroom as well as in the community.

A Fresh Approach to Unit Building. The use of a fresh approach to unit building has had immeasurable effects on our academic program. Learning seems clearer; learning is lasting. Further, our teachers in the main have caught on to this approach with ease and enjoyment.

The Use of a Variety of Teaching Techniques and Tools. Many of the teaching techniques taught by the helping teachers this year were not new. They had been in moth balls so long that their full value had been overlooked. Reassessment of these techniques, fresh presentations, and a chance to test them under skillful supervision returned these techniques to many class programs.

The successful and converted teachers were those who tried them. From the reactions received it appears that many teachers were successful in their class activities involving creative dramatics, role playing, construction activities and trips.

Cooperative Unit Making Among Teachers and Specialists. Last year, many children in one of our sixth grades reflected serious neglect of health. A preventive and corrective program was developed through the cooperation of the sixth grade teacher, the physical education teacher, and the nurse. Together they produced a very fine health unit for this class.

The music teacher and the librarian worked on a mobile unit for fifth grade teachers. This project dealt with music and literature of the early western pioneer.

The art teacher developed a project based on a third grade social studies theme. This resource unit afforded something of value for all teachers. This unit has been shared by teachers at Gray, Palmer, Washington, Stubbs, and the Drew-Pyle Schools.

Other Curricular Improvements. Other general effects noted by the principal in evaluation of the Project are:

1. The reduced number of instances of teachers lecturing children. Many teachers did not know how to draw children with reading disabilities into intermediate social studies programs.

2. Classroom discussions have increased and reached a high level. This is particularly true in the intermediate grades.

3. Children's writings have a story to tell. They stem from the children's own experiences.

Discovery of Problems. Discoveries made through Project development are:

1. Many of our children are crippled in language. They communicate using only few words. The words, "bothering" and "messing," for instance, can mean many different things.

2. Many children enter our kindergarten and first grade with memory and skill sufficient to handle one idea or one directive. Some of our intermediate grade boys and girls, too, are unable to handle more than one idea, one directive at a time. This indicates a serious failure of the school.

3. We have our share of difficult children. Yet, most of those transferred to Ferris School during the year are not school delinquents. They are after-school delinquents. They fall into the category of slow-reasoning children. They cannot perceive consequences. They cannot seem to resist following the leader. Unsupervised time after school, on weekends, and on holidays is their nemesis. This type of child seems unable to stay out of trouble.

4. We believe that we have many children with slight nervous and mental disorders. The problems are so slight that they take us years to discover. A slight case of palsy was discovered in a child who had been with us six years. We called her nervous and fidgety. She was a bit of a nuisance, but not a serious one.

5. Many types of inconsistent academic behavior have been discovered as we attempted to work closer to the individual. Each door of knowledge that we open reveals our inadequacies. Mr. Reiter, Supervisor of Special Education, has been helpful. He has promised to assist us through one or two faculty meetings next year with identifying clinical problems such as slightly palsied children and the like.

6. In checking social behavior, few children were classed as serious behavior problems. Steady improvement over a three-year period has been the trend. Whether this relates to the Project or the reorganization of Drew and Pyle Schools as primary and intermediate schools or to other factors is unknown.

AN ADVENTURE IN HUMAN RELATIONS CONTINUES

We have many hopes for Project extension next year. We hope to identify the basic experiences of children, see how our pupils stock up against our list of them and find ways of providing the ones they lack in our yearly program.

For example, the music teacher identified a musical selection as a wedding march. Forty-five minutes of questioning by children followed. Not one child in that class had attended a wedding or had seen a real bride.

It is doubtful that we can provide a lifetime of experiences missed by all children, but we are sure that some voids can be picked up in the curricular offerings of a six-year program.

Next year we hope to further our work with parents, community leaders, and representatives. Our big problem here is that of sensitizing persons to the broad needs of our community. Our planning needs go beyond that of tomorrow. We need to plan for today's children's children, for our parents are increasingly younger and many are inexperienced in the ways of the world.

Significant Statements From Project Schools

Space does not permit the inclusion of all evaluations made. Parts of a number of them are quoted, however, for they reflect prevailing conditions, feelings, and facts of significance in planning future steps.

A Question and Some Answers. One school in the Project is especially concerned with social and personal living. In evaluating its progress the staff of Stubbs School asks: "What is today's challenge to our public schools?" They are many. Here are mentioned only a few:

■ Children of varying backgrounds and cultures meeting in our classrooms for educational experiences that are both common and diversified.

■ Pupils with experiences on both ends of the scale far different than those of his teacher.

■ Large numbers of emotionally disturbed children from broken homes or from situations foreign to *home* as we conceive it.

■ Children who thirst for an education, but sometimes wonder whether we want to teach them.

■ Children who hunger for food, clothing, shelter, and for the love of parents.

The Stubbs staff has always done a very commendable job in establishing rapport with pupils, and in helping the disturbed child make a better social adjustment. The following case studies by several Project participants specifically illustrate progress made in the area of social and personal living.

Case A: Pupil A, sixth grader, entered Stubbs for the first time in September. He was described by the sending school as a person who must be watched at all times. His problem was so severe he was under medication at the State Hospital. The receiving record also stated that his mother was not cooperative. At the end of the first marking period, the mother expressed to the teacher her satisfaction with his progress, both emotional and academic. According to the mother, the attending physician doubted the progress stated in the first report, but was convinced after giving the pupil a short quiz in his mother's presence. Following are the scores which this pupil made on the California Achievement Test* in 1961 compared with his performance after one year with the Project teacher:

	Reading			Arithmetic				
	Vocabu-lary	Compre-hension	Total	Reason-ing	Funda-mentals	Total	Grammar	Spelling
1961 (5th)	4.8	6.4	5.4	6.2	5.6	5.8	5.9	5.4
1962 (6th)	7.0	7.5	7.3	6.9	9.1	8.0	6.4	6.2

Note: Data provide grade achievement scores, e.g., the scores for Vocabulary should be interpreted as a grade placement of Grade 4, eight months' achievement, 1961: Grade 7 achievement, 1962. Thus a gain for this child of two years and two months was made in one school year.

Case B: Pupil B was transferred from a parochial school to Stubbs School in September, 1960. Soon after his entrance there were complaints from the parents that children were picking on him, and that it was necessary for his mother to meet him at the close of school each day to protect him. This kind of reception is not typical of the Stubbs pupils, so the Project teacher began to uncover the reasons. The new pupil was inviting the trouble. The principal described this pupil's behavior to the sister of the Catholic sending school and she said it was typical of what he had been doing there. Help was received from the school psychologist and some hard work was done with the parents and their son. Pupil B has been a responsible fourth grader this school term and there has been no report of trouble with his classmates.

Case C: Pupil C was received in our second grade in 1960 by transfer from a southern city. It was obvious that he was from a neglected home. His behavior was typical of an attention seeker and there was very little attention given to cleanliness and other health habits. The teacher and school nurse made reports about the home conditions which warranted the services of a social worker. In September, 1961, this pupil was transferred to the third grade teacher who handled Case B. Although there is much work yet to be done with C, there has been some improvement in personal care. Glasses were provided by the Lions Club. After C broke them, constant work with the mother was needed before she assumed the responsibility of having them repaired.

Case D: Pupil D came to us two years ago from a school in Maryland The accompanying report was frightening. It referred to temper, lack of respect for authority, and vulgar language when angry. We were not long learning that Maryland had sent an authentic report. This boy had such a pleasing personality when he was not in one of those emotional stages everyone was anxious to help him. He was assigned to the same Project teacher for the past two years. Although positive with him when limits needed to be set, no mother could show more love for and interest in this boy than the teacher did. In this case, too, help was received from the nurse, the psychologist, and the social worker. The home is the source of trouble. This child has made remarkable progress and will continue to do so if the home continues to cooperate.

Case E: Pupil E was transferred to Stubbs from another Wilmington school in the middle of the 1960-61 term. His attendance was poor and he had a court record for staying out at night. He was taken from an elderly grandmother for whom he had become too much of a problem and sent to his father who apparently did not want him. These conflicts had made E extremely nervous, shy, and suspicious of adults who wanted to help him. He was assigned to a sympathetic Project teacher, and the social worker kept contact with the home, giving advice that was helpful and making demands when necessary. This youngster's attendance improved before the end of the 1960-61 school term. He repeated his grade but was assigned to another Project teacher. He has been well kept the entire year; shows much less nervous tension; and the one time he became a court case this year, authorities advised me that it was the fault of the father.

These are typical of the many cases that could be reported. I recognize that interest of this nature was demonstrated before the Stubbs staff became active in the Project. It is important, however, to note that there has been a significant change in both skill and attitudes. I do believe that, before our participation, we would have felt that we were helpless to deal with most of the cases described above. Many of us would have felt that these were cases for the Bacon Health Center or Ferris School for Boys. I think that it is a most worthy achievement for us to become effectively aware of the contribution that the school can make to improve understanding and the quality of living through a human relations centered program.

A Census of a School

At the beginning of the third year of the Project, old Shortlidge and Washington Schools were replaced by a single new school. This marked the combination of two schools of middle economic status, only one of which had been recently integrated. The census of the pupil population of the new school provides a significant picture of social and economic forces at work in a middle-income neighborhood.

Census of the Shortlidge School, April 1962

Kindergarten	Grades 1-6	
57	515	children attend Shortlidge.
0	171	previously attended old Shortlidge.
0	165	previously attended Washington School.
1	118	previously attended other Wilmington schools.
0	57	have attended schools in other states.
0	167	belong to Cubs, Brownies, Boy Scouts, Girl Scouts, Boys Club, or church choirs.
0	52	go to the Y after school.
57		play at home after school.
0	60	go to the playground after school.
0	18	attend nursery school or are otherwise taken care of after school.
0	31	go to grandmother's.
0	51	take music lessons.

Kindergarten	Grades 1-6	
0	62	have lessons after school.
2	20	take dancing lessons.
26	297	attend religious services.
10	150	wait for other children to go home.
24	108	are driven to school.
0	65	arrive very early.
47	468	watch TV at night.
0	184	9:30 p.m. is the last TV show seen at night.
1	50	have unemployed parents.
9	110	have parents who work night shifts.
0	5	have parents taking citizenship lessons.
0	72	carry their own keys.
6	89	live in apartments.
51	336	live with both parents.
4	112	live with only one parent.
1	36	live with other relatives.
3	198	have mothers who work.
38	339	expect to attend this school next year.
3	63	expect to move.
16		expect to attend Christ Our King Parochial School.

These data are thought-provoking. Their implications for the social, religious, economic, and educational needs of children are that the advantaged and disadvantaged may be found in middle as well as lower economic groups.

A Principal Assesses Gains and Plans for the Future

Unlike other new schools built in recent years, North East was not a replacement for an outmoded structure. It was built to provide for children in a newly created neighborhood where a public low-cost housing development provides subsidized housing for low-income residents. All of the children of the North East School live in housing units contained in a housing section of a few city blocks in area. The principal reports:

How does one measure progress in an endeavor as challenging as ours? Seldom are environmental factors as controlled as those that shape the lives of our children. This should be good, but these are some of the very factors that make our task unique and almost overwhelming.

Out of this environment we are attempting to discover, encourage, and release latent creative and intellectual powers of children destined to live in a world far more complex and turbulent than that we have known.

One week's apparent progress can sometimes appear to be influenced and even counteracted by the customary lethargy, inertia, or resignation of people who are quite consciously on the bottom rung of the economic and social ladder.

Our task becomes even more challenging when one sees as a goal the identification and education of children with potential who must become the instruments to raise the cultural and attainment levels of a community. This must be done in an environment for higher achievement.

We can measure progress only in degrees and observe carefully anything that might indicate a trend. Last year, our first, we tested theories, and observed, recorded, and tried out a human relations approach to the curriculum since we recognized some basic human needs of our "raw material" and had to understand them in order to reach our children and start where they were.

Now, at the end of our second year, there are some changes which seem to indicate that our methods are effective. It is still too soon for us to be able to say that these changes are trends. Only time will do that. We are viewing them as success stories.

Valerie, a sixth grader, is one success. She and her many serious problems started in her fifth year. At ten years of age she was the oldest of eight children. Small of stature and rather unattractive, she looked and felt that no one in the world liked her. She had been receiving psychiatric help and was taking tranquilizers because she was highly nervous and volatile. She had been her father's constant companion, and had been with him when he was murdered a few years earlier.

Valerie was a fighter. When the teacher did a sociogram with the class at the beginning of the year, Valerie was completely rejected by fourteen children. Two years later, she was rejected by only two. Her group California Achievement scores between January, 1961 and May, 1962 went up 1.7 in total reading, 1.0 in total arithmetic, and 1.3 in total language even though she is on the borderline of normal intelligence.

There are other successes.

In one year some "repeaters" made outstanding gains: Gwendolyn went up 2.0 in total reading, 1.8 in arithmetic, 1.5 in total language. Diana went up 2.4 in total reading to 8.4; 2.3 in total arithmetic to 8.7; and 2.6 in total language to 8.1.

Other standardized test data showed positive changes of more than one year in a one-year period for the present fifth graders, with the greatest change coming in vocabulary where the median difference was +1.7. The group median I.Q. is only 92.

Working with the sixth graders was a unique challenge. More than half of the class (56 per cent) had been in three or more schools. Only 28 per cent had the ability to work up to "grade" according to group standardized test results. This compares with 48 per cent of last year's class. 41 per cent had repeated at least one grade.

In spite of such low level "raw material" this year's sixth grade has achieved more than their last year's counterparts. The greatest gains have been in language. Median spelling scores went up from 5.4 to 6.4, with thirty-two of sixty-three children scoring above grade 6. Grammar, however, is the weakest area. Between the results of the third grade testing and the present sixth grade, a number of children gained three years and more.

All of the changes that are being made are the results of the efforts and dedication of a highly skilled, adaptable staff, whose members share a wonderful spirit of adventure. Through their efforts we have achieved the following:

Major Accomplishments

Organization All classes improved because of the emphasis on the achievement of each individual child. At this time last year there were thirty-two children reading at sixth grade level or better. All were in the sixth grade. This year there are forty-two at this level, many of them in grades 4 and 5.

This year we had eight inter-age groups and eight traditional groups. The interaction of the various ages within the groups is apparently a strong motivating force. In these groups the average and better achievers, though not necessarily the oldest, appear to be moving ahead faster than those in the traditional grades. Standardized-test results bear this out. In addition, considerably more children in these groups are reading above "grade level" than last year.

Project on Changing Neighborhoods Pioneer Day was undoubtedly a high spot in the Project. Its results were far-reaching and well worth the effort. Considerable planning and work were required before and after the day itself. Results were measured in terms of human relations values and academic achievement.

With the staff unified in its emphasis on fostering good human relations these results were evident:
- Decrease in number of fights on all levels.
- Teachers and children thinking and planning in broader terms—in terms of basic concepts and generalizations.

Many teachers, in evaluating the year's work, showed the positive effects of their participation in the Project. A few are quoted here:

I had to find a way to make these youngsters realize that their type of behavior was not accepted by society; that we must treat others as we wish to be treated; and that good citizenship was everyone's responsibility. After much thought (thanks to the Project) I decided to focus on human relations in all units and activities. These youngsters must learn to conform, not out of fear, but through a consciousness that this is the correct thing to do at times.

This has really been a most interesting and rewarding year. I felt that I have developed and grown right along with my children. I felt that as they left me they had learned a number of things that would benefit them for the rest of their lives in their dealings with other human beings. Our children owe a great debt to the late Dr. Vickery, and we teachers do, too.

The fact that my children had a wide range of experiences and varied abilities enabled us to have many meaningful experiences and activities. We did research, gave reports, made a budget, planned how we would spend our money, played roles, and dramatized scenes of family life and family helpers. The room was a living demonstration of how large families can live together in a peaceful, democratic way.

I am concerned about the social security of these boys and girls. Although they are generally cooperative and considerate, the slightest dispute can cause an uproar. There is little control of anger. Feelings are expressed vociferously, attacking one another. Even in sharing sessions there are such expressions as "beat you up," "send for the cops," "go to jail." These children still need much help.

Special Events All of our special personnel—art, music, physical education, library, and nurse—are creative. They supplement and guide the experiences planned and carried on in every classroom. In addition, each uses his special skills and interests to initiate excellent programs. Some were especially good this year.

- Rhythms and Sports Night combined the efforts of art, music, and physical education teachers in showing the community the skills and creative talents of our children and teachers.
- Several assemblies, notably one on Transportation, were meaningful presentations of information gathered by the group.
- Field Day was different and better planned as a result of last year's attempt. Teachers and children planned and participated in the day which culminated in a memorable softball game between the older children and the teachers. The children were obviously and enjoyably magnanimous in even letting the teachers get to the bases. Their affection for the teachers was obvious as they sublimated their desire to win in their effort to give the teachers a chance.

- The art teacher carried on a research project on the effectiveness of various motivations in children's paintings. This was tested on six classes for ten weeks. Resultant paintings were evaluated according to objective criteria developed by Viktor Lowenfeld.

Other Accomplishments Several other desirable changes are taking place:
- Most children are reading at least two levels higher than is normal for them.
- There has been a definite increase in the number of parent visits.
- School pride and school spirit are developing quite openly.
- Assemblies are more meaningful.
- Art work is of better quality with more long-term projects carried on.
- Teachers plan ahead in close coordination with special teachers.
- University of Delaware seniors, who had observed as juniors, requested an opportunity to do their student teaching here next year. Many are interested in working with the culturally deprived later.
- Much more science has been studied.
- Helping-teacher service has been outstanding.
- We were helped a great deal by a full-time music teacher and a home visitor.
- The additional money allocated for basic texts and library books and supplies made a vast difference in teacher outlook and programs.

Our Problems

We are so thankful for our many accomplishments that our problems seem to be minor. They do exist, though, and need to be studied carefully.

1. *Attendance:* After studying last year's enrollment, absence, and tardiness figures we felt that we could improve them by having a home visitor and by attempting to instill in children a sense of time. We succeeded to a certain degree. Attendance improved noticeably in all grades. In no month did it fall below 90 per cent. The kindergarten attendance made the most change for the better. The lowest attendance was still 10 per cent higher than last year.

2. *Language of Children:* As we expected, our children are very weak in language facility. Even when they have been taught the correct forms and can hear and correct mistakes made by others, their own speech is poor and inadequate.

3. *Retarded Readers:* A large number of children have reading difficulties that can only be corrected by intensive individual work.

4. *Classroom Interruptions:* This problem persisted because there was no way to get notices around without using messengers. Now that we

are assured of having an intercom system installed, such immediate notices can be handled with less confusion.

5. *Noon Hour Recess:* Even though our eating atmosphere is good, we are still trying to work out the most desirable solution to supervising the activities of children who have finished their meals.

6. *Use of Library:* In our situation, which demands much work in the area of language, adequate books and library time are requisites if progress is to be consistent and adequate. A part-time librarian is not the answer. Someone should be free or available every day to assist small groups or individual children in selecting books and doing research. With the limited time of our present library teacher such time is scheduled, and she is not always available when she is needed.

Recommendations

1. *Human Relations Approach:* Evidence points out that we must continue to emphasize human relations needs in solving problems. We must remain united in approaching the solution of difficulties and continue to think and plan in terms of major concepts and generalizations.

2. *Special Services:* A full-time library teacher is needed to supplement the efforts of the classroom teachers.

3. *Special Curriculum Emphases:* Arithmetic, especially the newer concepts, should be emphasized more. We need help in learning and mastering these newer ideas. A staff-wide in-service workshop is necessary.

Language study, based on the principles and techniques developed in the Project, is essential. Such a study is being started with our kindergarten and first-grade children now.

The deprived youngster's academic achievement is a frustration for children and teachers. Where it can be expected that youngsters of average intelligence will achieve a year's academic growth in a school year to match the physical age, children of impoverished experience are handicapped academically and seldom achieve more than 6-8 months' growth in subject areas. That North East School is discovering clues for more successful learning is revealed in a comparison of test scores for 55 fifth-graders for a one-year period, 1960-61. These children's group intelligence quotients ranged from 64 to 145. Table 14 contains comparative data revealing that, while the children as a group are below established national norms, they achieved for the first time a full year's growth in all areas of academic learning except in that of arithmetic. Undoubtedly, there are many reasons for this accomplishment—teaching skills and understandings learned through participation in the Project, more effective procedures for grouping children, intense interest and effort by the teachers, greater appreciation of the potential of deprived children, and greater expectations for them. This is a significant achievement, for it proves the academic potential of deprived children provided the proper climate for learning is created.

Objective evidence of academic achievement is usually difficult to secure. The frequency of children transferring from school to school makes it next to impossible to assess the effect of the Project on children's achievement. For example, Williams School, with average daily enrollment of approximately 1100 children, usually has a total of 1500-1600 children in a typical school year. Economically deprived

Comparison of Summaries of Standardized Test Achievement Scores for Fifty-Five Disadvantaged Fifth Graders (Iowa Basic Tests) — Table 19

Test Scores Achieved by Children (Beginning of Fourth Grade)	Range	Median	Above 4th	Below 3rd
Composite	2.1 to 4.6	3.1	1	19
Reading	1.5 to 4.2	2.8	2	25
Vocabulary	1.8 to 4.5	2.6	4	25
Spelling	1.8 to 6.4	2.9	9	24
Language Total	2.5 to 5.7	3.2	7	18
Arithmetic Skills	1.9 to 4.8	3.1	7	23
Arithmetic Concepts	2.6 to 4.4	3.8	9	3
Arithmetic Total	2.6 to 4.6	3.4	7	7
Reference	2.2 to 4.7	3.3	6	12
Work Study	2.4 to 4.6	3.3	3	11

Test Scores Achieved by Children (Beginning of Fifth Grade)	Range	Median	Above 5th	Below 4th	Median Difference 1960-61
Composite	3.0 to 5.7	4.2	6	15	+1.1
Reading	2.5 to 5.5	4.1	4	17	+1.3
Vocabulary	3.0 to 5.8	4.3	3	14	+1.7
Spelling	2.6 to 6.9	4.1	9	25	+1.0
Language Total	2.9 to 7.8	4.2	4	19	+1.0
Arithmetic Skills	2.4 to 5.7	4.3	13	17	+1.2
Arithmetic Concepts	3.1 to 5.8	4.6	17	16	+ .8
Arithmetic Total	2.1 to 5.5	4.4	13	13	+1.0
Reference	3.7 to 5.6	4.5	11	6	+1.2
Work Study	2.4 to 5.7	4.3	6	14	+1.0

children often move five or more times in a school year, with some moving as many as 14 times. North East School's data are significant because they show some success achieved by a group of children that have remained in the same school for a two-year period. Table 19 shows data representing one year of stability in the children's school and home experience.

My Brother's Keeper

From a project geared to the human relations needs of children and their families, and focused on the development of human relations skills, sensitivities, knowledge, and information, evidence points overwhelmingly to the value of diagnostic instruments in helping teachers discover the perceptions the children have regarding themselves, other people, and their physical world.

Learning to Know Children. It has long been a premise in education that to be truly effective the teacher must know her children. While a variety of diagnostic instruments has been used, the favorite of participants in the Project has been the open-ended question. A sampling of children's responses to a number of open-ended questions reveals the wealth of information obtained. Without such information, teachers who commonly do not use diagnostic instruments may well be living with a group of strangers for a year. In addition, it is safe to assume that the curriculum provided for the young strangers may be so unrelated to the problems and concepts they themselves know and recognize that teaching may well be unrelated to the reality of their environment.

Consider the responses of three groups in different Project schools to the question: "What is the best thing that could happen to your family and why?" As the reader studies these responses it should be noted that one school is located in a middle- to high-income neighborhood; two are in very low-income neighborhoods.

> GRADE SIX—SCHOOL III
>
> *Ursula:* The best thing that could happen to my family is to move. I would like to move from the place we are living because of the living conditions. It is very bad. It is also a very slum area.
>
> *Edward:* The best thing for my family is for me to be a good boy. I was real mean but when my daddy got on me I started being a good boy. I'm not a real good boy yet but I soon will be.
>
> *Larry:* I wish that my mother could go to visit her sister and father in Brooklyn, New York for just a week's vacation. When she comes back we can give her a welcome back party.
>
> *Warner:* I would wish for a farmhouse for my family. My mother and father like animals and we can't have any animals in the city. We can have cows on the farm and goats, bulls, and ducks.

Samuel: If we had more money we could get the house over Riverside because the apartment is falling apart. The door is falling down. The ceiling is falling down and when it rains it comes in. We have roaches now but I hope we won't have them if we move over to Riverside.

Joanne: The best thing is to have a brother because I sometimes get lonely and sometimes I don't want to go out and play with my friends. Maybe if I did have a brother I wouldn't be satisfied because I would want a sister.

Lana: The best thing is for us to get money so my grandmother can go to the hospital.

Roger: The best thing is to have a little baby brother because I think it would be nice to have a little baby around.

Sharon: The first thing we need is some money to pay our hospital bills for my mother.

Sarah: The best thing will make my family happy is a new house and some money to pay the hospital bill for my sister baby that is to come and then we will be happy.

Jacob: I would want my family to have an icebox so that every time my mother puts some meat in it would not spoil.

William: It is that we have enough money to pay all the bills off and so we can get the things that we need to have in our home and for my bicycle.

Donnie: That one of our relatives left us his farm after he went away. We could live in peace, way up in the hills. We could grow our food and have a well for water. Our crops could bring us money if we needed any. I would like to have horses, cattle, and sheep on the farm.

Sara: The best thing that can happen to me is when my mother goes to the hospital and has a baby girl and I will be the happiest girl in the world.

Franklin: My family would like to move to another house because when it is cold the owner will not give us much heat to keep us warm. My mother said she was going to move when she finds a good house. That's what would please us the best.

Earl: I wish that we had enough food, money and clothes for every one in our house. Sometimes we run out of food, and money and when we run out of money the bills pile up."

Alan: That I go through a college education. After I get out I would like to have a good job as a doctor.

Edwin: If I had a wish I would wish to bring my mother back. Then we could live in a big house, have two cars, a family car and every day car. When our vacation came we could go to Maryland to visit my aunt.

GRADE SIX—SCHOOL IV

Sandra: The best thing that could happen is that my grandmother be well. "Why" because my mother's nerves or patience aren't as good then.

Peter: I think my family would want my grandfather back. He died about two years ago. And the question why I think you know why.

Barry: For my father to get the job he wants. We need the money and my mother could quit work. It will not hurt his back and it's an easy job, you don't work hard.

David: To have my father come to live with us. So that we wouldn't have to go to New York to see him. And so we could see him every day and not every month.

Raymond: We can get money enough to buy a new home. We need a new home because the one we have now is old and needs fixing up. My mother doesn't like the house because of the steps and it needs fixing. She also wants a powder room. I myself doesn't like the home or the neighborhood.

Sheryl: For us to get rich. You see I have three sisters and one brother. Counting my mother and father there is seven in the family. It takes a lot of money to feed and clothe us. That is why I would like to get rich.

Wayne: My father's back to get better so he can get a better job. But that could *never* happen.

Jimmy: Be happy and be able to help others as much as I can. Because I like to be happy and be able to help others.

Martha: Some people think I'm silly for wanting this but I think I want this more than anything in the world. I would like to have a big brother. All my girl friends have them and want to get rid of them but if they thought about it they really wouldn't. I wouldn't even care if he was grumpy and we had fights just so I had a brother. Another thing I would like is to let my mother be able to walk so we could go more places and do more things.

Kathy: A bigger house so Victor and Michael will have ther own rooms and won't fight, and a playroom in the cellar so Gregg can mess up only that room and mother won't have as much work.

Janet: That we could do things together. It seems like everything we do any more only my sister and I do it. My other sisters don't seem to want to do it or they can't because they have to do something else.

Roger: This isn't really and answer, but this is the problem. My mother works as a school teacher. It has broken up the family and torn it apart. My mother won't quit because we need the money. If my father got a better job, my mother might quit teaching and come home (and clean up the place).

Patty: I think if I could have a father it would solve many problems about the household. For one thing we wouldn't have to live with my grandmother. It would keep her from spending so much on us. If I had a father, my mother might not have to go to work. And she could take care of my little sister instead of having a baby-sitter.

Cynthia: The first one, if my mother didn't have to work so hard. She must work seven days a week as a nurse and when she gets home she is pretty tired and doesn't feel like doing very much work. The second reason, if my sister Rosamond could speak like me or you it would be much easier on all of us. We could understand her better and she could understand us.

Darlene: What I think is my family is a good family but they are not too good. My father he works in the night and he is late getting home. And my mother she works nights too like my father. But tonight my mother gets home in the day.

Richard: I wish my father would come and live with my mother and I. Because my mother and I will be happy.

Brenda: It would be nice if my sister would not fight me. Because she fights me she know I would tell on her. If she does something bad and if my father would not fight my mother.

John: I think my family is happy often but my brother Donald's father ties his hands and whips him. If my brother could live with me and not with his other mother and brother.

Victoria: They mite have a garden. They have a baby. They mite have a car. They mite have new furniture.

Sandra: My family is good. Some time something happens to my family. Some times my father gets in trouble. Something is going to happen to my family.

Jeffrey: I wish we weren't poor and have a little more and I wish I could be happy and not nervis. And I wish my father live with me and my brother and my mother. I wish my brother and me not fighting.

Elbert: Up in my family I can have more brothers than five brothers and we can play together too.

Gail: I hope that my father could make more money. And I hope my Mother could get around the house faster, because she is going to have a baby.

Wilhelmina: My bathroom seat is broke. I want it fix because a lot of water gets on the floor.

Trudy: That my sister, brother, father and mother never fight or shout at each other. Because my parents like friendly people.

Patricia: I think the best thing that could happen to my family is that everyone in my family is to be happy. Spring beauty do not make them happy what can do you know what can make them happy? And I think so because they do not smile.

Raye: That we could get together more. Because we do not get together a lot. My brother my mother and father and my sisters.

Jean: My mother stop getting made at me sometimes. Sometimes she getting made at me for nothing.

Valerie: I think could happen is we might needen some clothing and T.V. and a house and a pretty garden and shoes and things that is needen to our home. We might needen more help. My father is not live with me.

The responses of children to the question, "What do you like or dislike about adults?", are equally revealing: (Children could sign their names or not, as they wished.)

Grade Six—School II

Naomi: When you have something to say to your mother or father and you start to tell them and then they start talking so you stop and listen and when there done talking they always say "now what were you going to say." By that time you have forgotten what you were going to say. And for some reason or other it seems to me whenever you do one little thing wrong they always hit you and yell at you. And then after all they always say "come here I am sorry". After all the hitting and yelling.

Raymond: I don't like when your mother send you to the store so you go up the stairs get your coat on then come down stairs and then the money is gone."

Charlene: I don't like people to call me small and things like that. That is one thing I hate very much and it makes me angry.

Linda: Like if you are planning to go some place you ask them they are going somewhere or I can't go. You have to stay home from school to watch your baby brother or sister. It seems very lonesome at home. But its all right with me some times just long as I go to school the next day.

Alonzo: Grown ups don't do nothing that I don't like.

Donald: When I sit down to eat and when I just open my mouth at the table my father tells me to keep quiet. And then he opens his mouth at the table. But he can talk and I can't talk at the table.

Selma: They holler too much and sit around the house doing nothing. They talk on the telephone too much.

Joann: I like the grown-ups the way they are because if they weren't the way they are now they won't be grown-ups.

Gass who: Grown ups never gave children a chaice to expers there thouts.

My mother makes me mad by making me come to George Gray School. When my mother is not at home and someone else is watching me I ask him may I go to the YMCA and they say no. My mother makes me mad by not letting me go to Pyle school.

Patricia: Talk too much for me.

Linda: When they tell me what not to do and they do it there self.

Geraldine: Why shall I hate grown people, they don't do nothing to hurt me. I love mother very much and I don't hate nobody.

Grade Two—School VI

(Questions asked individually in private interviews)

Betty: All the time when my friend is at my house my mother goes up to the corner.

Juanita: My aunt goes out and leaves my cousin alone. I don't like it.

Minnetha: This big boy he takes kids over to the park and cuts them and tries to take off clothes. He burned a little boy's clothes.

Zelda: They hit on little kids and I don't like it.

John: When they yell and scream it makes me nervous.

Andie: I don't like people who slam doors. I like people who sing in church.

Clara: Those people next door are not nice to us. They never clean up their yard when my father asks as nice as can be. My mother's friend straightens my hair for parties for nothing. She likes me.

Renee: The lady who takes care of us lets us take care of her baby. I really like that baby, too.

Vernon: I like the man who gave me my turtle.

Steven: I don't like people who holler at me for nothin. I like people with soft voices, like my mom.

William: I like grown-ups pretty much all the time.

Robert: I don't like men with knives. Boy they are really mean. I usually like everyone pretty much.

Stephen B.: I don't like mean people—like the man who ran over my dog. I like my father—he is nice and he gives me money.

Pamela: I don't like people that scream and holler at night. They get outside and disturb everyone. I like nice people who smile a lot.

Garry: I don't like nobody. I would like my mother if she were here. (Mother lives in Texas.)

General Analysis: Children in the Project seem to have a good feeling about their community. They listed 133 "likes" divided among 23 items. Their general perception of the community is that of a friendly place providing beauty and recreation facilities for them.

The same children listed 34 dislikes divided among only 10 items. Seven youngsters said there was nothing they *really* disliked.

Incidental to these responses was the revelation of a similar perception about their school and teachers. Though this information was not solicited, twenty-six out of thirty-two papers showed that they see their school as a friendly place where people care about them and where they can learn and have fun.

They also show an interest, a liking, and a fairly good relationship with people.

There seem to be but two curriculum indications here: (1) an interest in nature, and (2) an interest in why the undesirable things in their neighborhood are there.

However, through a discussion of their papers such specific ideas were approached as: 1) "Why do gangs of boys break up our games?" 2) "Why can't people keep their own yards clean?" 3) "I don't mind people playing in my yard, but I don't know why they have to throw things on my steps (pavement yard)." All of these are definite problems that can be and are being used in curriculum planning for this group.

The impression one gets from these papers is that—

1) the children like their community and are "proud of it," to quote one youngster;

2) they feel a friendly relationship with most people in their community;

3) they like their school ("I think the school is wonderful," says Marsha);

4) they dislike noise, strife and dirt (unless they are making it themselves).

As one aspect of study by community agencies who became interested in the children's perception of Project school neighborhoods, a panel of ninth and tenth graders from these neighborhoods, led by a school psychologist and an agency social worker, was held at the close of the first year of the Project. Minutes of this meeting reveal interesting similarities and contrasts to the children's responses. Basically, they are in harmony, however.

The high school children perceived their respective neighborhoods as follows:

> 1. *West 9th and Adams Streets:* Was fairly quiet. Everybody knows everybody. People are friendly but stay to themselves. Freeway has changed neighborhood. Houses are being torn down. Area is noisy now.
> 2. *Twenty-Third and Jessup Streets:* Used to be quiet. Younger people are moving in. Families are now noisier. Price Run Park is nearby. Only change wanted: change in the gasoline buses.
> 3. *West 9th and Washington Streets:* Has quite a few little children in the neighborhood. Sacred Heart Playground is nearby. Change wanted: improve the deteriorating houses around the corner.
> 4. *Eighth and Lombard Streets:* Peoples Settlement is nearby. Neighborhood is run down. Many families moving out, others moving in.
> 5. *Townsend Place:* Friendly neighborhood. Many elderly neighbors and young children. Recreation for young children provided at Palmer School but none for older children.
> 6. *Vandever Avenue:* Area has "gossipers." Neighborhood in good condition. Street lights, etc., good. Price Run nearby.
> 7. *Twenty-Fourth and Carter Streets:* Recreation available in park nearby for children up to age 12. Could stand facilities for other age groups.
> 8. *Twenty-Third Street:* Older people live in area. Park nearby.
> 9. *Twenty-Third and Spruce Streets:* Near Price Run. Mostly older people lived there four or five years ago. Now many younger people live there with children.
> 10. *Near Christina Center:* This group has a "family night" which is successful. Provides good recreation facilities.
> 11. *Near Boys' Club at Seventeenth Street:* Children play in the street. Park and swimming pool are nearby. Boys' Club does much for boys. The houses are good, streets are fair, buses are dirty, noisy and smelly. People are busy. Don't have time to chat.

In general, the students liked their neighborhoods and defended them when they felt the areas were being criticized.

What changes are needed?

Question: *Is there anything that we could do about the people?*
Answer: They aren't that friendly. They don't care very much. The landlords don't care. Many people live in apartments. I guess they can't help it.
Answer: People with large families are the ones who don't seem to care. It lets the whole neighborhood go down.
Question: *What should be done?*
Answer: Go to the Chief of Police if there's trouble. The people need leadership. The people should get together themselves.
Answer: They should get a group together. Find out what's the best way to solve problems. Then work on procedures.
Answer: Neighborhoods used to have leaders—people who were respected.
Answer: One man was helpful, particularly at voting time.
Answer: Ministers and doctors are helpful.
Question: *To whom does your family go for help with problems?*
Answer: People nowadays stay to themselves.
Answer: People work, come home. They don't get involved with their neighbors. They would rather live their own lives.
Answer: My mother says to tell City Council.
Question: *What do you mean by "friendly"?*
Answer: On the street they say, "Hello, how are you?", but they don't invite you in. They keep to themselves unless there is a death—or some trouble like that. Then anybody would help.
Question: *Do you have friends in the neighborhood or are your friends from other areas?*
Answer: Neighborhood boys use the basketball courts but the Boys' Club pulls from everywhere.
Answer: Southbridge has things for kids but I have to go to the East Side.
Answer: The park is for kids.
Answer: Most of my friends come through church.
Answer: My friends are from school.
Answer: My parents' friends are the people they went to school with.
Question: *How is it we have more recreational facilities yet we have higher delinquency rates?*
Answer: Delinquents think it's fun.
Answer: Children like that come from poor families. Maybe their parents are alcoholics.
Answer: We don't have any delinquents in our neighborhood. They come from the other side of the city.
Answer: (From an adult) More delinquents come from the average home than from the deteriorated neighborhood. (He quoted figures.)
Answer: (From an adult) Supervised freedom is the only freedom that is good. Other freedom is license.
Answer: Sometimes the poorer home gives the children more responsibility than the average home does.

Question: *How can the police help more?*

Answer: I know some of the people in Becker's Gang. They are good kids. The ones who cause trouble mainly come from the other side of town, like the Untouchables.

Question: *What has the P.T.A. done to help?*

Answer: The parents meet. We met and discussed a film with Dr. M.

Question: *Do the young people want adult leadership? What kind?*

Answer: Yes. They want one that understands, that is young. At least that is young at heart. One that has lived in the neighborhood.

Question: *How many adults do you know that you really look up to?*

Answer: About half and half.

Notes from the meeting of the adults after the pupils left:

Discussion included:

1. The movement toward the suburbs.

2. The smallness of family units compared with those of previous generations.

3. Increased mobility causing less need of neighborliness.

4. Lack of general responsibility for the neighborhood on the part of those living in it.

5. The attitudes of children who are "picked up" by the police.

6. The help given to neighborhoods by present groups.

7. The importance of family life.

8. The concern of school people with the problems manifested by children.

9. The need that something be done about divorce, common-law marriages, obscene literature, children's absence from church, alcoholism.

10. The importance of working with small groups.

11. The changing suburban neighborhoods.

12. Our moral obligation to do something about conditions in Wilmington.

13. The work of the P.T.A.

Our primary purpose was reviewed as an attempt to discover and develop indigenous leadership in these neighborhoods.

The meeting of May 3 was announced. At that time we shall have the opportunity to work in small groups, to plan what can be done in neighborhoods to get people to do things for themselves, and to try to set up next steps.

Conclusion One: People Have Values

To the Project Administrator, the Project demonstrated conclusively that the use of diagnostic instruments and processes is of extreme value to teachers who would know their children. Diagnostic findings reveal the children's concepts. They provide a realistic base upon which to build concepts, beginning where children are and progressing toward increasingly mature levels. This is one of the primary purposes of education and a sorely neglected one. Great strides have been made by Project teachers in this area.

There has long been an assumption, expressed or not, that lower-income people "have no values." This assumption is often associated with the conflict which sometimes exists between school and home. Because children from deprived homes are more often absent or tardy, because school and library books are more often mistreated in low-income homes, because school drop-outs occur more frequently among deprived, low-income groups their occurrences are often pictured as lacking in interest and appreciation regarding education. Actually, there is no basis for such concepts.

Dirty, ill-kept children are in the minority in Wilmington's schools. Rather, the thousands of clean, neatly dressed children reveal more clearly than words the tremendous efforts of parents, working against overwhelming forces of poverty, to maintain the health and self-respect of their children.

A ten-year-old wrote: "I want to be a plumber when I grow up. But first I must get my schooling. My mother never had any and she says it is the most important thing a boy can have." Could it be that there are "no values," no aspirations, in this poignant expression of a deprived child?

How the Project schools have gone about the business of fostering values is a success story. Let one teacher speak:

My Littlest Angel

One small boy, Carmen, although enthusiastic about our gift project, just couldn't bring in a gift. He said he tried to earn the money, not over fifty cents, without luck. No one needed his services.

He told me quietly and seriously that Mother was having a time finding money for the Christmas gifts for their own family. He knew he wasn't to bother Mother about the money. It was to be earned.

Each day he became more and more concerned and told me quietly at my desk about it. Finally a big idea struck him. He came up to me, with his eyes dancing. He had it solved.

"Mrs. Stoops, could I give my ball point? I haven't had it very long. It's a real good pen and it's got lots of writin' left in it." This was truly an unselfish, thoughtful gesture. I was touched.

I said, "Carmen, this is truly the gift of the Littlest Angel. It's a wonderful idea. It shows your heart is really in the right place." Carmen said, "I don't know what you mean about littlest angel, and of course my heart's in the right place." (Holding his hand securely over where he thought his heart was located.)

Now some explanation was due on my part. Afterwards, I said, "You just reach down in that big paper bag by my desk and pull out something for our Gift Project. I'm all prepared for boys and girls like you who are thoughtful and sincere and are just having trouble getting the money. You may keep your pen. I hope it has lots more good writing in it just for you."

Then I read to my boys and girls the delightful story, *The Littlest Angel.* Many of the children knew and loved the story. Carmen, having been in and out of Palmer School on many occasions, had not heard the story before.

I felt certain that we had one of the "littlest angels" right in our midst that day.

This same teacher, concerned with the fact that her children, who were so often on the receiving end of financial help, should learn to know the satisfaction of giving and doing for others, discussed the subject with her children. Cecil and his classmates distinguished between human values in a mature way:

Cecil: When I was in the fourth grade, I gave a boy a chance to prove himself, because all the other boys picked on him and they knew he couldn't fight. But I could beat them all. So I went and picked a fight and let the boy beat me. Then the next morning I made friends and told him and he wasn't picked on because they thought he could beat them all. The only thing is that this didn't cost me money; it cost me courage.

Donna: On the day before Christmas my mother had to work all that day and my sisters were coming down for Christmas dinner. Mother hadn't finished cleaning the floors and wood work, and she was going to do it when she got home from work at eight o'clock that night. But I did it for her!

I did it because, she would have to do it when she got home from work and then she wouldn't get much sleep.

So I did all the floors and wood work.

Taras: One of the nicest things I did for someone was, when my allowance kept on piling up, I was going to buy a pair of track shoes. So one day I bought them.

Then I heard there was going to be a relay race down in the country where my grandmother lived. So I went up there to pick a boy to race with. At this race they were going to give away a pair of track shoes to whoever won the race in his group.

So, it came time for me and the other boy to race. When we were racing, I just realized that I already had a pair of shoes, so I just slowed down and let the boy win.

I did this because I already had a pair of shoes. What would I do if I had two pairs?

> *Ethel:* The nicest thing I ever did for someone else was when
> I was eight years old.
> My cousin was three, and for her birthday her father said he
> he was going to get her a rocking chair.
> He got hurt on the job he worked on and was not able to buy
> it for her.
> So to make it up to her he sent a letter to my mother and asked
> if she would do something to try to make my cousin happy on
> her birthday. So my mother gave her a birthday party, and I gave
> her a rocking chair that was giveing to me when I was little. She
> seemed to be very pleased with it because that was what she had
> really wanted in the first place.
> Although it was very hard to have it taken away from me I was
> very glad to see her happy.

Values to live by, the values cherished by the Hebraic-Christian tradition expressed in the concept of the brotherhood of man, are not the special asset of an advantaged economic group. They are found among all people, whatever their economic circumstances. And warped values, those that hurt and retard, are found, too, among all groups and individuals. When teachers really know their children, when they identify with them, they realize that generalizations regarding people as an economic class are without foundation. Equally important, Project teachers have learned that they can help youngsters build values which foster sound human relations.

Conclusion Two: Subjective and Descriptive Evidence Is Significant

To the Project Administrator, the subjective and descriptive evidence that the Project was a potent force in fostering human relations skills, sensitivities, knowledge, and information is more powerful than any quantitative, objective evidence could possibly be. It is hoped that the research aspects of the Project will support the conclusions that have been reached. A letter from a small friend, Raymond, reminded the Project Administrator of the dangers of reaching conclusions too early. This youngster was asked by his teacher to write the story of his life.

> I was born in Orange in a teny-tiny little room in Orange
> Memorial Hospital. The year was 1953 and of course that means
> I'm eight years old.
> From then on I was brought up not trying to be a fusaseashes
> hippecritt. Since I have the book 101 Dalmations I seemed to pick
> up the words that Colenol said, "Bladdadash Tibbs." I think I
> might be a person who would make voises when I grow up.
> I think that I might be jumping the gun when it comes to talking
> about my life.

Like Raymond, the Project Administrator may be "jumping the gun," but convictions are deep and commitment is strong.

Conclusion Three: Disadvantaged Children Place Values in People

The focus upon human values found in responses of deprived children led the Project Administrator to conclude that the disadvantaged learn early in life to develop "people-focused" concepts. Neighborhoods are interpreted in terms of people. Money is strong in the consciousness of even the youngest among the disadvantaged, but it is always seen as a means of "going to see Grandma; providing an operation for my father; having enough food for the family."

Among the responses of the economically advantaged children will be found many "people-focused" concepts, but even more that are "things focused." While research treatment of responses had not yet been accomplished, the impressions of the Project Administrator were that the disadvantaged are learning earlier in life what it means to be "my brother's keeper" than are the economically advantaged. This impression, if supported by more conclusive evidence, presents one of the greatest challenges to schools, families, and agencies working with families, for values are formed early in life and the economically advantaged children, as a group, would seem to be disadvantaged in this respect. To the Project Administrator, this aspect of the Project provides evidence to support the conviction that to concentrate efforts toward human relations education for the economically disadvantaged, only, is disastrous. The economically advantaged are equally in need. The Project was unique among major programs in the nation in this respect. It was in the demonstration of the need for all children to grow in the development of human relations skills, sensitivities, knowledge, and information that it has made one of its greatest contributions.

Teacher Education Moves Ahead

In evaluating the progress of the professional growth of participants in the Project, we must again depend largely upon the subjective and descriptive evidence available.

Extent of Participation in the Project. Where participation in an in-service education program is voluntary, as it was in the Project, two of the measures of success are the extent of participation and the holding power. Relatively wide participation in eleven of the fourteen public elementary schools in the city, and the number of teachers who completed the Project, attest to its success.

Improved Holding Power. Of significance to the Project Administrator was the growing trend evident in the school system's ability to retain experienced teachers. Prior to the initiation of the Project in September 1959, increasing difficulty had been experienced in retaining teachers who found the difficulties in teaching in changing schools a burden. Data on turnover of staff were given earlier. Of interest is the fact that at the close of the school year, 1960-61, 39 vacancies in classroom teaching positions were filled. At the close of the third year of the Project, 1961-62, only twenty-one replacements for teachers leaving the system were needed. These vacancies were caused by retirements and all of the usual reasons for leaving the system. Except for a few changes which occurred over the summer, the turnover of staff was down by approximately 50 per cent, the first year since 1951 that such a low rate of loss had been experienced. In addition, the drawing power of the Wilmington schools had improved, with all vacancies filled prior to June 30, 1952, for the ensuing school year. Not for many years had this condition existed. Whether or not the trend will stabilize is questionable, for it was not maintained during 1963-64.

Attitudes Toward Children and Their Families. It is the belief of the Project Administrator that the genuine acceptance of children by the staff of a school is a crucial factor in the quality of teaching and learning that will prevail. Where neighborhood populations change dramatically and quickly, especially where racial desegregation is a factor, staffs have difficulty in accepting children who seem different. This is as true for a Negro teacher having a first experience in teaching white children as it is for a white teacher having a first experience with Negro children. The unknown gives rise to fears and insecurities.

When a predominantly middle-income school changes to a predominantly low-income school, differences in the behavior of children are noted in the initial stages of transition. Different language competencies and usage and the tendency to settle differences through fighting are factors middle-income staffs note first in working with disadvantaged children. Fears that the academic and behavior standards of established schools will suffer are paramount. While there is some factual basis for the fears engendered, most of the fears are rooted in feelings related to the unknown and lack of association with the disadvantaged child and the child of another race.

The Wilmington elementary school staffs had experienced these feelings and fears. Parents, too, had experienced them. Negro parents who wanted to protect their children from possible rejection and prejudice in a bi-racial school were just as fearful as white parents who were concerned about academic standards and social implications.

Some of the Project schools had changed during the first years of desegregation from stable environments to unstable environments. By 1959, at the intiation of the Project, white teachers were beginning to leave the city schools and the recruitment of white teachers was extremely difficult. We were faced with a possible segregation of staff through inability to recruit and hold white teachers as detrimental in its effects as segregation by law. The legal barriers to segregation had been removed, a necessary and essential first step. But the law does not affect feelings of acceptance. Genuine acceptance of others depends upon knowledge, not ignorance; generosity of spirit, not narrowness of soul.

It is in the assessment of the Project in terms of its effect upon attitudes that the Project Administrator takes the greatest satisfaction. Among a vast majority of the staff was found an identification of teachers with their children, a commitment to serve, and a pride in the smallest accomplishment. Going beyond this, however, was a determination not to set preconceived ceilings on the potentialities of deprived children and an almost fierce effort to prove that good education, through enrichment of experience and skill in teaching, can make a difference in the lives of disadvantaged children and in their achievements.

A marked difference in the quality of living in school was consistently noticed by visiting educators and staff members in the schools. During 1961-62, out of a staff of 320, 80 of whom were teachers in their first three probationary years of service, and an additional 35 who were on emergency certificates, there was only one teacher, a beginner, who experienced discipline problems of such severity that there was lack of control in the classroom. And this teacher overcame her problem before the end of the year. In every elementary Project school, there is orderly, comfortable living; there is purpose in children's learning; there is lack of tension produced by unwise exercise of authority. Complaints about children by teachers are no longer heard; nor are the comments *"these* children," "the standards of *our* school are suffering," and other similar expressions of dissatisfaction and insecurity heard in school rest rooms, faculty meetings, or "gab fests." There is a full awareness of the severe needs of many children and a concern for the increasing numbers of children whose emotional health is affected by home and neighborhood environment. But these problems are encompassed in the oft-heard teacher comment, "The school is the best experience in the lives of my children."

With school desegregation now in its tenth year, the quality of parent-teacher relationships is evidenced by an almost total lack of parent complaints of prejudice. During 1961-62, only one instance of prejudicial conduct by a teacher was made and this occurred early in the year in a school having its first experience in desegregation.

If the Project had made no other accomplishment, the pronounced change of attitude of staff toward its children would have justified its development.

Effectiveness of Curriculum Planning. Coupled with change in attitude, there was a remarkable improvement in the quality of teacher planning. At the end of the second year of the Project, the evaluations of the participants and their reactions to learning new ways of planning gave evidence of insecurity. To discipline oneself to plan adequately is a challenge. Planning as a process is a continuing problem to be accepted and mastered by teachers in elementary education. It is much easier and much more comfortable to follow the patterns of textbooks. A number of the Project participants were master teachers and master planners when they entered the Project. For all, however, regardless of level of ability, the new processes of planning required new effort. Teachers responded to new demands in a variety of ways. Some resisted, some explored, some welcomed the opportunity. At the beginning of the third year, teachers were asked to create their own form and structure if desired, adapt the suggested form, or follow it. Personal choice was emphasized. The 1961-62 plans of the participants were studied and it is interesting to note that nearly all reflected a functional use and mastery of the form suggested in the basic curriculum planning bulletin issued at the beginning of the second year of the Project.

A second factor considered by the leadership team prior to the opening of the third year of the Project was the obvious need of teachers for help in comprehending the relationships among achievement in human relations skills, sensitivities, knowledge, information, and academic achievement. Many of the second year plans revealed this need. Human relations needs and concepts were identified, but the content of the plan was centered chiefly in academic learnings, apart from the human relations needs and concepts identified. In the plans of the third year, there was marked improvement in the quality of understanding of this problem and of skill in interpreting understanding. Full fruition of this goal remains a challenge for the future, however.

Discovery. An old Persian proverb tells us that "Speech is the mirror of the speaker." One of the deep convictions developed by Project participants was the need of disadvantaged children to attain competence in their native language. Of all of the effects of deprivation, none is more damaging to personality development and educational progress than inability to communicate feelings, ideas, experiences, hopes, and aspirations. The disadvantaged child is severely crippled by his lack of experience with language. While the natural language of such children is often dynamic, forceful, and descriptive, lack of command of standard English blocks communication, achievement, and, ultimately, economic improvement. In fact, for many deprived children, standard English is a foreign language.

Because of the close relationship between speech used in family life and a child's emotional security, Project participants developed new approaches to language development. Natural speech has a place in the child's life. Standard English is a tool he needs. The research study initiated by North East School, described in the last section of this report, has tremendous potential for developing teaching processes which will point the way to vastly more effective language teaching and learning. It is probable that the results of this study will be among the most significant contributions of The Three-Year Experimental Project on Schools in Changing Neighborhoods.

Section

III

The Community's Role in
Human Relations Education

Section III describes the efforts of participants in The Three-Year Experimental Project on Schools in Changing Neighborhoods to coordinate action among agencies and organizations in the city which are committed to the service of people. Two purposes guided these efforts: the greater involvement of the school staff in the community and the achievement of common goals through coordinated action programs.

chapter

9

Preparing for Cooperative
Community Action

The two basic goals of The Three-Year Experimental Project on
Schools in Changing Neighborhoods, curriculum building and
community action, were recognized from its very inception as parallel
goals of equal significance. The work of the school (curriculum) and the
changes essential in the school community in its broader sense
(community action) had to be interrelated if the schools were to fulfill
their obligations in developing a functional curriculum with "use value"
for the child. A functional curriculum depends not alone upon the school.
The influence of family and community impinge upon the school and
become a force for failure or success of school attempts to provide for
the child a good climate for growth. The schools cannot carry the
responsibility alone, nor can any other single community agency.

Stimulating interest on the part of lay citizens and representatives
of other agencies in the city became an immediate objective. Organizing
for school-community action became a second objective. And initiating
community action during the first year of the Project became the
third objective.

Stimulating Community Interest

In blocking out the chart on "Relationships and Responsibilities of
Participants in The Three-Year Experimental Project on Schools in
Changing Neighborhoods" the involvement of a range of community
agencies was visualized and steps were taken immediately to effect this
involvement. Three prominent lay citizens were invited by the Project
Administrator to become members of the Central Planning Committee.
Together with school staff and the University of Delaware liaison repre-

sentative, these people were present and participated in decision making from the beginning of the Project. They were to help in securing other community participants and to contribute to the development of the curriculum aspects of the study. Community representation every step of the way was to be a valuable source of strength in the Project.

Public Relations

Keeping the community informed is an essential characteristic of a good public school system. Among the efforts made by the Wilmington Public Elementary Schools were the following:

1. A news story carried by the local papers explaining the study and stimulating interest in it was prepared by the Project Administrator and an interested reporter.

2. Subsequent announcements of community developments, in which consultants of prominence worked with participants, were provided the press by the Delaware Regional Office of the National Conference of Christians and Jews. A press report of the first year's progress of the study appeared during the summer, 1960.

3. Project principals discussed the study with local parent-teacher organizations to inform parents of participating schools.

4. The Wilmington Public School System's staff organ, *The Staff Reporter,* which is sent to all staff members and a selected number of community representatives, carried several reports of the Project.

5. A series of almost monthly buffet suppers provided by the Project Administrator brought together a group of approximately thirty people at each gathering, comprising school board members, administrative staff, service staff, community representatives, and consultants. In an informal social setting, guests were able to learn of the Project and become acquainted with each other.

6. At mid-stream of the first year, a program was prepared for the Wilmington Council of P.T.A.'s, an organization comprising principals, parent-teacher leaders, and school staff representatives of all public schools in Wilmington. The consultant described the Project and the progress being made. Thus, representatives of all schools, participating and nonparticipating, elementary and secondary, could be informed and challenged for the future.

7. Some sixty community agency representatives who had expressed an interest in Project developments were sent progress bulletins throughout the year.

Efforts were geared to keeping the total staff, Project participants, parent groups, community agency representatives, the general public, and members of the board of education fully informed. The interest and support resulting from attempts to inform the total community paid dividends and encouraged wider participation of schools in the Project. Schools not officially a part of the Project began to use diagnostic techniques. A number of schools expressed interest in participating in the Project during its second year. And parents raised the question, "Why isn't my school participating in this Project?"

Initiating Community Action

Parallel to the first steps in organizing the curriculum aspects of the study through the diagnosing and analyzing of children's perceptions of their neighborhoods ran plans initiated for organizing community action.

Meetings on Leadership

Because the Project was school oriented, the problems related to organizing for community action became school oriented, too. While at home and reasonably competent in internal school problems, the school staff was inexperienced in community organization problems. Early in the year, discussion had centered on the absence of "leadership" resulting from the moving of recognized, established leaders from the city. From a feeling of hopelessness in identifying new community leaders, the Central Planning Committee had begun to realize that leadership potential among new families existed if it could be identified and developed. The Committee set out to find this potential leadership. Again, the Delaware Regional Director of NCCJ was of inestimable help, securing consultants on leadership for a series of exploratory meetings. One meeting at a time was planned with the next one growing out of the preceding one in terms of needs of the group. The Committee was feeling its way. The following themes emerged:

1. "Changing Patterns of Leadership" (with emphasis on identification and utilization)
2. "Developing Skills and Techniques Needed in Fostering Leadership Potential for Community Action" (with emphasis on practical helps)
3. "Youth's Perceptions of Community Leadership" (with emphasis upon neighborhood strengths and weaknesses recognized by a panel of ninth and tenth graders from the city high schools living in Project school neighborhoods)

The three meetings on leadership, held monthly during the second semester of the school year 1959-60, accomplished two purposes:

1. They provided information and practical approaches to community organization.
2. More important, perhaps, they enabled school staff and local agency leaders to meet one another, to feel at ease in talking together, and to

Relationships and Responsibilities of Participants   Table 20
in the Three-Year Experimental Project on
Schools in Changing Neighborhoods

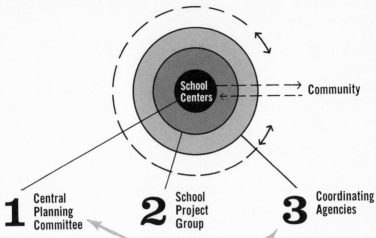

→ Community

1 Central Planning Committee

Chairman:
Project Administrator
Assistant Superintendent of
  Secondary Education
Delaware Regional Director,
  NCCJ
School Consultant, NCCJ
Volunteer Lay School
  Committee
Supervisor, Adult Education
University of Delaware
  Liaison Representative
Principals and Staff
  Representatives
Director of Child Development
  and Guidance
School Psychologist
School Social Worker
Coordinator of Pupil Placement
  and School and Community
  Agencies
Community Agency
  Representatives

Responsibilities
1. To develop framework in
   which Project will operate.
2. To provide guidance and
   direction in the development
   of the Project.
3. To evaluate and report.

2 School Project Group

Chairmen: Principals
School Staff Participants
Members of Project Planning
  Group
Local School-Community
  Agency Representatives

Responsibilities
1. To develop individual school
   projects.
2. To assume leadership in
   effecting curriculum changes
   and coordination of com-
   munity-school action.
3. To evaluate and report.

3 Coordinating Agencies

Community-wide Agency
  Representatives in Project
  Planning Group
Local School-Community
  Agency Representatives and
  School Project Committee
Central Planning Committee

Responsibilities
1. To participate in planning
   and evaluating Projects.
2. To coordinate school-
   community action.
3. To evaluate individual
   school-community Projects
   and report.

spotlight the problems common to all agencies of the community.

More than sixty community agency representatives participated in one or more of the meetings, with approximately thirty attending consistently. The number of school staff members participating ranged from ten to twenty-five per meeting.

The fourth and final meeting of the series was designed to enable Project schools to begin the organization of community action groups on a neighborhood basis. During the meeting, individual schools listed the problems and needs which, in the opinions of participants, were of importance. These lists follow.

George Gray School

1. The following needs exist:
   a. Better parent education and dissemination of information. (Suggested approach: use the services of churches, the coordinator, and local merchants—hairdressers, barbers, storekeepers.)
   b. To enlist people for work on meaningful projects. (Suggested approach: make them feel wanted in the overall organization of our efforts.)
   c. To build a sense of responsibility in parents, especially fathers.
   d. To interest more people in P.T.A.
2. The following problems exist:
   a. Lack of discipline at home
   b. Formation of gangs
   c. Tardiness at school
   d. An unhealthy situation at a corner store
   e. Poor transportation facilities to and from school
   f. Inadequate street lighting

Drew-Pyle School

1. The following needs exist:
   a. The improvement of family life
   b. Counsel for families
2. The following problems exist:
   a. Transient families
   b. Conflict of cultures
   c. How to recognize mental retardation in time
   d. Misuse of welfare assistance
   e. How to teach values to unchurched people detached from other character-building agencies
   f. Block organization

Washington-Shortlidge Schools

The following needs exist:
a. To help children, new to our neighborhood, in making satisfactory peer relationships in clans and on the playground. (Many of these children speak a foreign language or a different dialect; wear different styles of clothing; and sometimes come from an environ-

ment where fighting is the acceptable way of settling an argument.)

b. Better streetlighting, especially at street corners.

c. Knowledge of the children's background with respect to—
1. health problems they may have;
2. aspirations parents may have for their children;
3. children's adjustment to this "better" neighborhood;
4. emotional problems—if any—due to change of environment;
5. size of and relationships within the family;
6. their responsibilities at home—chores, babysitting, homework;
7. recreational habits—movies, T.V. watching, street play, idling at home, hanging out at street corners;
8. family's social life in the community—accepted socially or isolated.

Williams School District

Answers to the following questions must be found:

1. How to provide a play area for the school and neighborhood when the thruway is built?
2. How will the proposed plans for the neighborhood affect the school enrollment? Will it be an industrial development?
3. What provision will be made for the safety of the children during the construction of the thruway?
4. How can the parents of the Williams School become involved in planning a better neighborhood.
5. How can a "Community Feeling" be developed when the population is continually changing?
6. How can the public become aware of the fact that the city schools differ in their problems?

Note: The president of Block Blight, Inc., has been invited to visit Williams School and meet the faculty to discuss the work of Block Blight and the part Williams' staff can play in such a program.

Plans were made for each school-community group to meet again in the local neighborhood before the close of the school year.

As a result of efforts made to initiate community action programs, two tangible results emerged. The first one was that the Price Run Community Council was organized in the George Gray-North East area. The second one was that the participants in the Washington-Shortlidge community group were formulating plans for a house-to-house canvass of needs in that area.

chapter

10

The Community Organizes for Action

During the first and second year of The Three-Year Experimental Project on Schools in Changing Neighborhoods a beginning had been made in achieving the second objective of the Project by stimulating community interest. There remained the difficult job of identifying and developing leadership within the Project neighborhoods, so that the people could be helped to help themselves develop a more satisfying family and community life. How this was begun is the story told in this chapter.

Achievements and Difficulties

During the first year of the Project 1959-60, efforts were geared to—
■ providing opportunities for school, agency, organization, and lay representatives to become acquainted and to establish the kind of rapport leading to sound working relationships;
■ initiating school neighborhood action programs to be developed by professional leadership from schools and agencies as a means of discovering and developing indigenous leadership.

These efforts came to fruition during the second year of the Project. Included among the achievements of cooperative school and agency leadership were:
1. The establishment of Price Run Community Council. A full description of this action is provided in the last section of this chapter.
2. Block Blight, Inc., promised assistance and guidance to home owners desiring to rehabilitate their property in the Williams School neighborhood.

3. A marked acceleration of cooperative effort between the Youth Aid Unit of the Bureau of Police and the schools to *prevent* antisocial behavior of children in a number of neighborhoods.

4. The establishment of an inter-agency council for Drew-Pyle Schools. Of this council, the principal wrote:

> Drew and Pyle Schools have an inter-agency council which meets two or three times a year.
>
> This council is composed of agency representatives who serve our school community. The membership is composed of parents, ministers, P.T.A. leaders, youth service leaders, and school personnel.
>
> Problems dealt with directly concern our small community. It is the philosophy of the group that no one agency is equipped to do all of the jobs needed to be done in our community; that if each agency shares a part of the bigger problem we will be more effective in solving serious problems.
>
> During the past two years this group has assisted the school in many ways. Peoples Settlement cleared an area south of Fourth Street for the establishment of a playground in that area. Christina Community Center provided the school with a free lunch donor and a used clothing outlet. The YMCA and the YWCA established after-school clubs in our building.
>
> Redevelopment officials have kept us alert to the progress of the redevelopment program and the whereabouts of our parents and pupils involved in redevelopment.
>
> This group is interested in working with some of the hard core welfare and court cases that live in our community. Case conferencing has been suggested. We hope to arrange for one case conference before the close of school.
>
> Agency officials have expressed satisfaction with the meetings that have been held. I believe that we have done as much for interagency relationships as for better school-community agency relations.

These and many other outcomes of cooperative school and agency efforts were recognized as primarily school initiated. It was recognized from the beginning of the Project, however, that something more was needed. Just as schools have primary responsibility for the education of children in school, so it was felt the community has primary responsibility for helping children and their families in any needed phase of family and community life. While the schools have a community responsibility for full participation in common community endeavors, other agencies must accept responsibility for coordinating their efforts toward common goals. The responsibility was generally recognized, but the means for implementing it presented problems and hazards originating in the following:

1. Public schools operate within a well-established structure which makes the administration of the school project relatively simple. Community agencies do not have such a structure. Each agency is usually unique, and relatively independent of other agencies. Each agency is responsible to its own distinct administration and board. Establishing a common framework or structure in which agencies could coordinate their actions became one of the gravest problems encountered during 1960-61.

2. Coordinating action programs presented to some participants concern with authority. Did the proposed plan threaten the autonomy of individual agencies?

3. Experience of failure in earlier efforts by others to coordinate action programs of community agencies was a psychological block for some participants.

4. The composition of the membership presented another "unknown" in the experience of the participants. Religious leaders were accustomed to cooperative efforts with other religious leaders; welfare agencies were accustomed to cooperative efforts with other welfare agencies. Organizations generally worked within their own individual structures rather than across the board with other agencies and organizations. Lay people often served on boards of agencies and organizations as volunteer workers or financial contributors, but seldom as equal partners with professionals in coordinating action programs. Added to the vast variety of personnel in the community agency and organization project of the Project were the Bureau of Police, the Youth Aid Unit, a professional sorority, and others, each established to fulfill specific responsibilities. It remained to be seen whether or not a large, disparate membership could eventually function successfully as a group bound together to a common goal by common concerns and common commitments.

5. Some agency officials feared that the main purpose, function, and program of their agency might be endangered if they were to participate in a cooperative effort of another nature. Would there be an attempt made to impose programs upon agencies and organizations? Would a redirection of established programs from outside the organization be imposed?

6. Most difficult of all, where would an administrator be found for the community organization project comparable in function to the administrator of the school project? Lacking funds to employ an administrator and being unable to secure administrative leadership from already overburdened agency staffs, would the "pinch hitting" of the administrator of the Project be adequate for the job?

How these problems and hazards were met provides a fascinating example of group processes at work, processes that deal with—

a) learning ways and means of communicating;
b) establishing mutual confidence;
c) defining a common goal;
d) identifying common problems;
e) seeking mutually acceptable ways of working;
f) gaining new insights and understandings;
g) planning for the development of new skills and new achievements.

That this aspect of the Project got off the ground at all is a tribute to the personal goodwill, professional skill and deep commitment of the members of the group, and to the continuing support and help provided by the National Conference of Christians and Jews through its Directors of Program Development for Schools and Colleges and Program Development for Community Organizations.

The Struggle for a Meeting of Minds

Early in the school year 1960-61, school Project leaders and representatives of agencies and organizations met to review their work of the previous year to report on progress of the various efforts initiated the year before to stimulate school-agency neighborhood programs, and to begin the long process of establishing a community-oriented project similar to that being carried on in the schools.

Out of the meeting developed a plan for agency representatives to establish themselves as an independent but coordinated group in the Project. Agency and organization associations with school personnel were to continue as an important part of the school-oriented aspect of the Project, but these associations, only, were recognized as inadequate if a genuine coordination of the programs of agencies themselves were to bear fruit. Accordingly, the participants authorized the Project Administrator to appoint a Central Planning Committee of Agency Representatives, with liaison representation from the Central Planning Committee of the School Project.

The Project Administrator directed the Planning Committee to:

1. Explore possibilities for coordinated action by (a) identifying possible problems; (b) identifying resources within the agencies to attack these problems; (c) recommending desirable and practical efforts for coordinated action.

2. Define areas of need for consultant services and to determine (a) how they may be used to best advantage; (b) the responsibility of the agencies in implementing consultant services.

3. Establish a pilot program for agencies ready to commit themselves to an action program.

Out of the Central Planning Committee for Agencies and Organizations came recommendations for future action by participants. At this time, the need for consultant service by a professional community organizer, comparable to the function of that of the consultant in the school Project, became apparent. And, again, the National Conference of Christians and Jews came to our aid by providing such service. Dr. Juanita Cogan, School of Social Work, Rutgers University, was made available for four days of consultant service during the second semester, 1960-61.

A report of the work of the Central Planning Committee of Agencies and Organizations was sent to all participants by the Project Administrator. This report identified the lines of direction for next steps.

Objectives of Community Agency Coordination

The first objective of community agency coordination in The Three-Year Experimental Project on Schools in Changing Neighborhoods is to provide help for staff members wishing to work with other agencies in securing help from a specialist and to achieve more effective understanding and know-how in carrying out the responsibilities of leadership in the various agencies. The problems to be dealt with are those of mutual concern to agency people, such as identifying potential indigenous leadership among the people of the community, growing in effectiveness in mutual efforts to help the people of the community, and other problems listed in the minutes. It is felt that if such assistance can be obtained, it can serve only to implement and maintain the uniqueness of individual agency objectives and programs.

NATURE OF CONSULTANT SERVICE

Consultant service will focus upon obtaining information and suggestions for meeting agency problems which individual agencies will adapt to their own purposes and programs as they see fit.

The use of consultant service and the procedures set up for working together will be determined by the participants of the Central Planning Committee of Community Agencies and Organizations. The one-day monthly service available from February through May 1961 *may* be used for work-study sessions by all participants with the consultant in which selected problems may be dealt with; or, the participants may suggest other ways of using consultant service. Obviously, the limited amount of service and the need to get the most possible out of it will condition the procedures that will be used.

ORGANIZATION AND STRUCTURE

The purposes of coordination are to keep lines of communication open, to bring participants together, and to obtain help on problems common to agency people.

Participation of agency representatives is entirely voluntary, with agencies assuming no financial obligations and no commitments to redirect their programs. To my way of thinking, the last thing we need is another agency and the most unfortunate thing that could happen would be any attempt to impose conformity upon the various agencies. It is my suggestion that we avoid formal organization and structure and that we merely see this experience as an opportunity to come together informally to gain what we can from it. No agency representative will be responsible to anyone except his own director or board. As Project Administrator, my sole function is to tie together the various activities of the Project, both in its school and agency aspects. The participants themselves and the Central Planning Committee will determine action to be taken.

NEXT STEPS

The Central Planning Committee of Community Agencies and Organizations has recommended that we seek the consultant service offered tentatively by NCCJ, and that I act as coordinator until such time as professional coordination is desired and possible. The following steps are proposed:

1. That each agency and organization consider whether it is desirable to participate for the remainder of the year in sessions to be planned with the consultant, in order to deal with problems of agency leadership selected by the Planning Committee. One or more staff members of participating agencies may enroll for consultant sessions, but attendance for the full one-day work sessions should be consistent.

2. That agencies and organizations electing to participate fill out the attached form and mail to me no later than January 15.

3. That the present Central Planning Committee appointed to make recommendations for action to the total group, having accomplished its assignment as reported in the attached minutes, consider its work completed.

4. That from the agencies and organizations participating in the proposed action plan, a new Central Planning Committee *be elected* by the participants for guiding and directing the work of the next four months. It seems to me important that the Central Planning Committee be constituted of agency and organization representatives who are participating in the action program and for this reason I suggest the election of a new Central Planning Committee.

The report was accepted and participants in the Community Organization Project agreed to hold four work-study sessions with the consultant—one monthly from February through May. Plans and developments occurring during the consultant sessions follow.

Work-Study Session No. 1. It was agreed that the day would be "open-ended" within the following framework:

1. Obtain from the consultant her beliefs and experiences regarding the possibilities inherent in coordinated action by agencies and organizations in a community. Such a statement will enable us to become better acquainted with the consultant and help us determine whether or not we are communicating with each other.

2. Discuss and thrash out with the consultant some of the problems with which we have been dealing.

3. Consider the two basic issues about which we are primarily concerned:

a. Ways in which professional leadership might develop understanding of the forces at work in the city (political, economic, cultural, etc.) which agency staffs must recognize in serving people and carrying out programs

b. Ways in which agencies and organizations, through coordinated efforts, may become instruments for social change.

4. How we proceed from this general session will be determined by the group.

The first session with the consultant was geared to seven objectives earlier identified by the participants:

1. Establishing a framework for cooperative effort

2. Developing acceptance of, and putting into action, new approaches to parent-teacher work

3. Establishing lines of communication with the people of a community

4. Developing concepts of leadership suitable to the needs of today

5. Finding potential leadership in a community

6. Developing insight into problems of neighborhood people by the leadership group

7. Learning how to deal with specific problems of special-interest groups such as political, religious, educational, and civic organizations

At the close of the session, two problems for studying the second work-study session were agreed upon:

1. Ways in which professional leadership might develop understanding of the forces at work in the city (political, economic, cultural, etc.)— forces which agency staffs must recognize in serving people and carrying out programs.

2. Ways in which agencies, through coordinated efforts, may become instruments for social change.

Work-Study Sessions Nos. 2 and 3. A continuation of the problem of finding a common meeting ground for action became the most outstanding characteristic of the struggle begun a year before. As group meetings progressed we attempted to obtain from each participant priorities of problems of concern to individual agencies and organizations. A sampling of these problems provides interesting study.

Boy Scouts of America, Del-Mar-Va Council

There exists an intergroup situation which leads to misunderstanding as to motivation and purpose of various groups.

We need an action program to further intergroup relations,

such as Brotherhood Promotion, Know Your Neighbor, and Racial Tolerance.

Delaware Congress of Parents and Teachers

We need to find out what *new* program(s) each agency can establish without assistance from other agencies and then determine which programs can be combined with those of other agencies for the most efficient use of facilities, time, and funds.

Kingswood Community Center, Inc.

We need to identify and develop indigenous volunteer leadership in the community.

National Association for the Advancement of Colored People

In the field of housing, we need to help all citizens, particularly minorities, to acquire the quality of homes and neighborhoods they desire and can afford.

Peoples Settlement Association

It seems that the group did not know enough about the overall community, the many overall problems facing the community and the goals that could be established to meet community needs. As it is now, one leader sees only housing and the political structure; others see their own agency operations in a given area, etc. A social welfare conference with citizen participation and good speakers would bring to light what the concerns ought to be.

Phi Delta Kappa National Sorority
Rho Chapter

We need to develop leadership in communities that will organize and devote its efforts to the prevention of panic and of the decadence of good sound communities brought about by undesirable elements.

Young Men's Christian Association of
Wilmington and New Castle County

We need to develop ways of working with both the youth and the adults in the changing areas of the city.

The types of program that we have traditionally provided do not meet the interest (and needs) of these persons. On the other hand, we do not seem to have the "contact" to get feelings and expressions of interest.

This might involve developing leadership, or programs beneficial to their development as contributing citizens in the community.

Young Women's Christian Association
of Wilmington, Delaware

We need to make it possible for any person to rent or purchase a home in any area of the city, according to *his ability to pay*. The organization of neighborhood councils is merely an attempt to bring pressure for better living conditions and will fail unless there is willingness at the upper level of official or unofficial authority.

If the agencies could work together to lay the groundwork to make natural living conditions function, a climate of calmness would prevail. There are many sections of the United States where both races live and attend school together, and have done so for several years, without incident.

St. Patrick's Roman Catholic Church

Justice in the area of housing is perhaps the number one national problem. Racial discrimination, the unconcern of landlords, and the neglect of tenants are specific areas of this problem.

Youth Aid Division
—Department of Public Safety

Select one area where there is a density of various minority groups. Then give priority to:

1. Parent-education
2. Educational facilities adapted to the needs and interests of the children to be served
3. Make available to the persons in this area the full facilities of a child-guidance clinic on a full-time basis.

Zion Lutheran Church Neighborhood House

What are the needs of the people in the areas we serve?

I don't mean the needs as *we* see them, but the needs as they— the members of the areas—reveal them to us. Anyone can walk down certain streets and remark that the housing is bad. Anyone can enter some of these houses and see how these people must live. Anyone can read the newspapers and discover the "run-down" areas are highest in crime and delinquency. We suspect that the Negro desires fair treatment all down the line in schools, housing, stores, restaurants, hotels, movie houses, etc. But until we know the needs of these people as *they* see them—in their respective areas—I doubt whether any help inflicted upon them will do much good.

A subcommittee was appointed to summarize the problem priorities and to make recommendations for action.

Summary and Recommendation for Action

A study of the individual statements of problem priorities submitted by participants resulted in the following categories identified by the subcommittee. Agencies expressing concern are listed after each problem.

Categories of Problems Reflecting Emphasis on Process
1. Developing leadership and programs (*YMCA; Kingswood Community Center; Peoples Settlement; Mary Todd Gambrill Neighborhood House; Peninsula Conference Projects*)
2. Helping the professional leader identify the real needs of people served by the agency (*Zion Lutheran Church; Girls' Club of Wilmington*)
3. Developing cooperative procedure among agencies (*Wilmington Housing Authority; Delaware Congress of Parents and Teachers;*

Social Action Committee of First Unitarian Church; Welfare Council)
4. Improving Inter-Group Relations *(Boy Scouts of America—Del-Mar-Va Council)*
   Categories of Problems Reflecting Emphasis on Direct Action
5. Selecting a neighborhood or area inhabited by various minority groups for an action program, emphasizing parent education, expansion of educational facilities, and the establishment of a child guidance clinic. *(Youth Aid Division, Wilmington Bureau of Police)*
6. Housing with emphases on: upgrading of property, elimination of restricted properties, human values entailed in making a house a home, etc. *(YWCA; St. Patrick's Church; Rho Chapter; The National Sorority of Phi Delta Kappa; NAACP)*

Premises Upon Which Recommendations Are Made. Since the inception of the Project the following purposes have given direction to the incorporation of community agency representatives as participants:
1. The need to upgrade professional leadership so that it is better able to discover and develop indigenous leadership among the people served by the agencies.
2. The need to coordinate the work of the agencies so that through their programs the agencies serving the people of a neighborhood are more effective as an integrative rather than a disintegrative force.
3. The need to foster voluntary rather than structured, formal action, which provides for freedom of choice, freedom of direction, and the incorporation of help received within our group in ways which best meet the needs of individual agencies.

As we have worked together and as the priority of problems statements reflect, there have been two major demands among the members of the group:
1. That we secure help in meeting the problems of professional leadership in becoming—informed; better able to identify the felt needs of people; more skilled in communication; more able to develop programs that meet the needs of the people; more skilled in getting people to work together; more able to bring to bear available resources in the solution of problems.
2. That we develop an *action program* centered in a mutually agreed upon problem of concern to our community.

Courses of Action. It seems to the subcommittee that we have two choices for direction:
1. We can concentrate upon the problems of leadership alone, which has the hazard of a theoretical approach.
2. We can become more effective leaders by meeting the needs of professional leadership, as described above, through making a concerted effort to deal with the problem of housing, in all of its ramifications. This is the action problem most frequently cited as a priority by members of the group. Learnings coming out of the

effort to deal with the problem of housing are applicable in dealing with any community problem. This second choice offers the opportunity to meet the two major demands of the group.

Recommendations. It is recommended that:

1. The group coordinate its efforts in attacking the problem of housing on a neighborhood basis with a decentralization of group effort.

2. The work-study session of March 28, 1961 be centered on a consideration of ways and means professional leaders may use to foster action on this problem by the people they serve.

3. The participants organize to coordinate their efforts in the four individual centers listed below which are committed to serve all the people in the neighborhoods in which they are located: Kingswood Community Center, Peoples Settlement, Mary Todd Gambrill Neighborhood House, Hilltop Association.

4. In order to deal with the action problem of housing, participants associated with each of these centers take the responsibility for incorporating other participants in the group who represent wider geographical boundaries such as Youth Aid Division, Boy Scouts, Girls' Club, YMCA, and YWCA.

5. The participants determine ways in which help may be given in seeking solutions to the action problem, Housing, through their own programs. For example:

a) Block Blight, Inc., is obviously concerned with upgrading property.

b) Girls' Club is concerned with helping girls become homemakers.

c) The schools, through their curricula, are deeply involved in upgrading family life through the kinds of experiences and learnings they provide. For older children, for example, child care is an area which should receive more emphasis in the curriculum for older children to whom baby-sitting is a common experience.

d) All agencies are concerned with inculcating human values which do not tolerate the injustices reflected in restrictions on housing based upon race or religion.

Conclusions. The subcommittee feels that in making the above recommendations we have an opportunity to begin to plan concerted action on solving a problem of great concern to four neighborhoods.

In attacking the problem, we have the opportunity to upgrade our professional leadership skills through the remaining work-study sessions with the consultant.

In concentrating on four centers represented in the group of participants we have the opportunity for cooperative action in what might be considered pilot projects for other centers in the city.

Following consideration of the subcommittee report, participants reacted individually and these responses were summarized by the Project Administrator for further consideration by the group as follows:

Summary of Responses on Problem Priorities

NUMBER OF RESPONSES RELATED TO ACCEPTANCE OF
SUBCOMMITTEE RECOMMENDATIONS

Number of participants accepting recommendations of subcommittee	15
Number of agencies represented by accepting participants	13
Number of participants rejecting recommendations	2
Number of agencies modifying recommendations [1]	1
Number of participants modifying recommendations [1]	1

MODIFICATIONS SUGGESTED

1. Broaden "Housing" to "Family Living," stressing quality of living, family disorganization, economic problems, vocational guidance, etc.	2
2. Share information obtained by schools	1
3. Provide emphasis on cooperating procedures	2
4. Provide greater emphasis on developing indigenous leadership	2
5. Limit to one vital problem; e.g., Housing	1
6. Use any modification necessary to unite the group for action	1

SUGGESTIONS FOR PARTICIPANTS FOR SECOND CONSULTANT SESSION

1. Give opportunity for each agency representative to speak on problems he faces	1
2. Structure meeting	1
3. Provide oral report by subcommittee	1
4. Secure help from Dr. Cogan on roles of various agencies in working on Housing	1
5. Provide case material from one of the neighborhood agencies as a focus for discussion led by panel. Group and Dr. Cogan concentrate on refinement of methods, etc.	2
6. Consider possibilities of establishing Community Relations Council	1
7. Help group to persevere patiently	1
8. Look at many problems related to housing problems, e.g. family disorganization, economic conditions, vocational guidance, etc.	1
9. Select an area for a field project; appoint a committee to plan	1

SOME IMPLICATIONS INHERENT IN THE RESPONSES

1. The promptness with which you responded, the care and thought that are evident in the quality of your suggested modifications and suggestions on procedures for the second consultant session indicate that we are getting closer to teamwork than we may realize.

---

[1] These participants suggest modifications which enlarge on the recommendations, rather than rejecting them.

2. Implicit in many of the modifications and suggestions is a recognition of the need to broaden the problem of *Housing* to, perhaps, that of *Upgrading Family Life,* or something similar, in which the many problems centered in home and family living may be dealt with. I like this approach for it opens up the way for wide participation in keeping with the goals and objectives of varied agency programs.

3. There is evidence that many participants want action in dealing with a specific problem and that it is recognized that the skills of leadership may be refined and broadened through the action approach. This approach should certainly reconcile what appears to be a sharp cleavage in the group between those who want to work on processes and those who want to deal with a specific action problem.

4. There seems to be acceptance of the wisdom of developing a pilot project or projects in one or more neighborhood centers. We have four agencies represented in the group which have distinct neighborhood boundaries and are committed to serving all the people of a specific neighborhood, regardless of race, religion or other selective factors. These four were spotted in the subcommittee report. If such a project (or projects) develops the judgment of the center concerned must necessarily be the deciding factor.

Some participants have received indications that other agencies would like to join us. I suggest that invitations be withheld until after the second session, when we will decide whether we will continue or not. Until we can get ourselves straightened out on goals and course of action, additional participants, with their need for orientation, might unnecessarily delay matters.

Good preparation for each work-study session and the skill of the consultant made it possible to achieve an agreement on the "task," or goal, acceptable to all participants by the third work-study session.

The task follows:

We, the Community Agency and Organization Participants in The Three-Year Experimental Project on Schools in Changing Neighborhoods, address ourselves to the task of improving the quality of relationships among people
In order to:
Affect the direction of community change.

In order to clarify the interpretation of the chart by John Davis, of the YMCA, the following suggestions are made by him:

"A. That the group of persons that has been meeting be divided into two major groupings. One section to consist of the social agencies that are involved in the Project; this group would include churches that operate social agency type programs and the specific social agencies. The other section includes groups that are interested but do not operate programs per se; this grouping would include P.T.A.'s, A.A.U.W., and similar type organizations.

Organizational Structure for a Project Design   Table 21
for Meeting the Human Relations Needs of Children
and Their Families Through Community Action

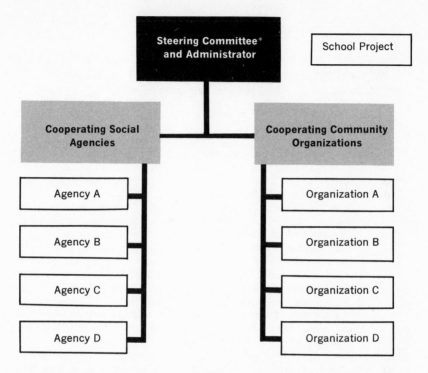

*Steering Committee composed of selected representatives from Cooperating Agencies and Organizations.

"B. That a steering committee be named from the two groups mentioned in A to coordinate their actions.

"These groups would then take on separate, but coordinated functions each equally important. The separate groups would identify areas of concern and recommend to the Steering Committee which would then select the specific problem(s) for concentration and area(s) involved. The separate groups would then approach the problem from their most effective means; the first section through group programs, training, and their usual means of operation to approach the problem, also utilizing new approaches developed through consultation with Dr. Cogan. The second group would then approach the problem through most effective means such as talks, serving as trainers, developing pressure groups for political action, and other means developed through consultation.

"The basic organization that we now have would remain necessary. It will require an administrator, the consultant, and liaison with the school phase and both portions of the community aspect of the Project."

THE PROGRAM

The programs of the various agencies which offer particular opportunities for achieving the task were discussed for illustrative purposes.

Work-Study Session No. 4. By the close of the third work-study session, the struggle for a meeting of minds seemed to have been won.

In planning for the final session, we accepted three jobs:

1. A consideration of an analysis of one city area to determine the nature of the area with emphasis on—
   a) the kind of relations among the people living in the area;
   b) identifying the resources which may be drawn upon to improve these relations.

The area is defined as: Lancaster Avenue to Eighth Street; Shipley Street to Jackson Street.

Captain Hollahan of the Youth Aid Division, will present a picture of forces at work in this area; others of the committee associated with it will participate.

Prior to the meeting, arrangements will be made to provide a police-guided tour of the area for all who have signed up for the tour. You will be notified of the date and time later. Tours will probably be held the week of June 12.

2. Participants will make action plans.

We agreed that each participant would analyze specifically a plan for carrying out "The Task." In other words—"What will you program for?"

These plans will be used by the committee to analyze the role the total committee or members of it will play in helping individual agencies.

3. A nominating committee report:

John Davis was elected chairman of a steering committee whose members are to be selected by him. This committee will draw up a slate of candidates for membership on the Steering Committee. It will also prepare, for consideration by the group, a suggested identification of responsibilities of the Steering Committee.

The session proceeded very much as planned. The analysis of the human relations needs of people living in the neighborhood given by Captain Hollahan led the group to a consideration of the means we might bring to bear on the problem of helping people help themselves. The seriousness of the problem may be seen from the impressions of the Project Administrator as she toured the area with other participants.

Neighborhood

This is an area which I know fairly well. My office is on the eastern fringe and I travel a good bit through the area as I visit schools. On this tour some of my earlier impressions were reinforced and I took a new look at some neighbors and how they live. Impressions that stay with me are the following:

- The vast number of store front churches. These are the churches our children refer to when they describe "getting happy on Friday night," emotional orgies frightening to youngsters. My thought as I passed these churches, "Do they help or exploit our horribly deprived people?"
- The vast number of liquor stores. The liquor stores generally stood out as well-kept property in the midst of decay. The only paint I saw being applied on this tour was on a liquor store already in trim shape.
- The array of beer halls through whose secluded fronts could be seen patrons at the bar.
- The dilapidated dwellings, multi-family homes, flats over first floor businesses, windows and doors open to provide a bit of air in steaming heat, screenless windows for the most part. The sidewalks, of course, the only desirable living room for sweltering families.
- The lack of privacy—a privacy provided too often by cheap plastic draperies—a privacy thwarted by draperies knotted to admit the air.
- The rare plot of grass in a small front yard and the rotting fences of other plots long since bare.
- The quick and touching snatches of beauty—a pink rambler, a window box with petunias spritely and colorful, a pot of artificial flowers in the window, marks of a home where somebody still cares.
- The children playing on narrow sidewalks—cool, almost naked, and clean.
- The diapered babies, plump and bare, healthy in the midst of squalor—and the effort of those who nurture them.
- The only rickety baby, standing on bowed legs in a doorway.
- The nakedness of people on city streets—a beauty in the young bodies of children, but ugliness in bodies bent to living.
- People living together, colored and white, neighborliness apparent in chattering groups.
- The loungers on the "labor market"—sidewalks by the railroad tracks—"a club" for those with the meager hope of a day's work.
- The shrill quiet of the pool halls as players recognized the sergeant riding by.
- The genial greeting, "Hi, sheriff," as an old man saw our guide.
- The bookie and numbers fronts—and the helplessness of those who know they exist but are hampered by laws which protect the guilty in order to protect the innocent.
- The prostitution of the democratic principle when those who must make democracy work complacently blame the other fellow—the landlord who exploits, the code enforcement machinery that doesn't work.

■ The fashionable churches of bygone days, some still living in the past with congregations, loyal and true, trooping in from the suburbs each Sabbath, others becoming citadels of hope for new congregations.

■ The remembrance of a touring school administrator who long ago heard and pondered Elizabeth Barrett Browning's lines,

"The poet hath the child's sight in his breast
And sees all new, What oftenest he has viewed
He views with the first glory"

and the urgent need for adults who see with sight of poet and child, and comprehend what the city tells them.

The close of the final work-study session, 1960-61, during which the school Project principals participated, resembled very much the close of the first year of the Project. As in the preceding year, the final session found agency and organization participants clustered around the principals of the Project schools to work out action proposals for school neighborhoods.

From their efforts to organize participants into a truly functional, voluntary action group also came agreement for the establishment of a Steering Committee to take over the functions of the Project Administrator and the election of members of the Steering Committee.

The functions of the Steering Committee as defined below were defined and accepted.

Responsibilities of Steering Committee: The Task. The project of meeting the human relations needs of children and their families through community action shall be the primary concern of this Steering Committee. This can best be achieved through their counsel and coordinative efforts:

1. To support the agencies, organizations and indigenous leadership through personal relationships and marshalling of resources available in the community for achieving the goal of a solution to a problem of concern to people.
2. To assist the agencies and organizations in selecting the specific problem and approach to action which can be initiated, identifying the role of each group in the action program.
3. To coordinate functions and services of Agency and Organization Committees.

   a. To assist these committees in developing techniques for, and skills in, identifying the felt needs of people in the neighborhood.

   b. To assist these committees in developing techniques and skills for stimulating people in a neighborhood to become aware of possibilities for meeting their felt needs.

c. To assist these committees in identifying potential indigenous leadership among the people of a community.

4. To evaluate the effectiveness of the effort of the Steering Committee and to encourage each of the agencies and organizations to evaluate their effectiveness and approach to the problem or concern identified for action.

5. To serve as a liaison between the agency and organization aspect of the Project and the school aspect of the Project.

After almost two years of agonizing effort, victory in the battle for a better city through the coordination of the programs of agencies and organizations seemed possible of attainment. The work had only begun. In a very important sense, the final session of the second year marked a "commencement." An unknown author has written:

"The past rides on the crest of the present as it moves into the future."

Participants know that the past gives us roots for the future. We know that the past has the power to help us direct and affect the changes that are constantly occurring in the lives of people, and that the future can be strengthened by the past rather than victimized by it if we have the energy, skill, and courage to bend and shape it to our will.

It Can Be Done

One of the most notable achievements of cooperative action by school and agency personnel occurred in the establishment of Price Run Council. A description of the development of plans for the Council and its initiation, prepared by Mrs. Clara Klug, art teacher in North East School follows. The northeast section of the city represents the school districts of George Gray School and North East School.

The Formation of a Community Council

The Price Run Community Council is an organization of individuals and representatives of groups in northeast Wilmington whose purpose is to make their community a better, safer place in which to live. This report will trace, with as much accuracy as possible, the sources of the ideas that led to the formation of the council and will outline the progress from its inception to the present time (June 1961). This is very much a "live data paper" since the first meeting, at which the idea of organizing a community council in this neighborhood was expressed, took place on May 3, 1960. I have no doubt, however, that the idea was present long before that time in the minds of many educators and social workers concerned with this area. Before discussing the formation of Price Run Council, however, it is necessary to tell a little about the community concerned.

Community Background

The community included in the Price Run Community Council encompasses all the territory north of the Brandywine River and east of Market Street within the city limits of Wilmington. The area is bisected by North East Boulevard, a busy, four-lane highway flanked by industries, junk yards, used car lots, and eating places. This seems to be a psychological as well as a physical barrier to the inhabitants, as I shall point out later. There is a large park with swimming pool in the area, and, in 1953, there were twenty-seven industries, mostly clustered along Vandever Avenue at the south and North East Boulevard and the railroad to the east. The railroad is the eastern boundary of the housing area. Beyond it at the south is a large unused swamp called Cherry Island Marsh, and to the north between the railroad and the Delaware River is a cluster of heavy industries.

Three of the four government-subsidized, low-cost housing projects in Wilmington are in this area: Eastlake and Eastlake Extension, each with two hundred units, and Riverside, with four hundred units. The latter two are on the east side of the North East Boulevard in an area which formerly was marshland. To the east of these developments are the railroad, industries, and the Delaware River. Most of the rest of the dwellings in the area were originally one-family row houses. However, there is a tendency for landlords and owners to make multifamily dwellings of these, and many property owners are worried about this change. The social worker at Kingswood Community Center said that in 1946, when he first knew this area, it was primarily an Italian neighborhood. Now, however, he estimates that in the section between the Brandywine and Twenty-eighth Street, at least, the area is seventy to eighty per cent Negro. This is probably due to the fact that the housing projects are integrated, and, of course, there is tremendous pressure for housing for Negroes since, in Wilmington, the availability of housing for them is so limited.

The economic level of the majority of the families is low since there is a ceiling on wages above which a family is not eligible for government housing. In a survey made in the Eastlake Extension area, it was discovered that seventy per cent of the families are without permanent fathers. That is, there is no male breadwinner in the family. In a surprising number of the families, men come, stay for a while, and then leave.

There are two schools in this community: George Gray School, an old school with a population of more than a thousand children, and North East School, new this year, with a population of five hundred.

North East is located, as its name indicates, on the east side of North East Boulevard in the Eastlake Extension housing district. George Gray is on the west side of the boulevard in the southern part of the area. Eighty per cent of the pupils at North East are Negro, while about seventy per cent of those at George Gray are Negro.

Two social agencies are located in this district. The Fletcher Brown Boys Club, a Red Feather agency affiliated with the National Boys Clubs of America, has a membership of five hundred boys and provides recreational and educational activities for about one hundred fifty to two hundred a day. Boys admitted are between the ages of seven and twenty-one, and in addition there is a mothers' club which meets monthly. However, only white boys are allowed in the Boys Club, and this engenders a great deal of ill will in the neighborhood. When I asked the director what the proportion of whites and Negroes is in the area, he said he wasn't sure, but a survey had been made and was to be presented to the Board of Directors next week, after which they would decide whether or not to integrate the club. [2]

The Kingswood Community Center, also a Red Feather agency, has recreational and educational programs for all ages and both sexes, regardless of race or color. There is an all-day nursery school for three- and four-year-old children of working mothers. Some five-year olds come in for half days after school. There is a men's club, a P.T.A., and many other activities for children and adults. The social worker said, when I asked whether volunteers from other groups in Wilmington came in to help, that he believed in training leadership within the community. It is a slower process, he said, but more beneficial to the people at Kingswood. There is also a Kingswood Neighborhood Council which tries to do on a small scale what the Price Run Council will do for the whole community.

Other recreational possibilities are the Walnut Street Y.M.C.A. and Peoples Settlement, both south of the Brandywine. George Gray School is open for supervised recreation two nights a week to both elementary and high school youngsters, at different times.

I could find out very little about the churches in the area. There are five. Two ministers are active in the Price Run Council.

Origins of the Community Council Idea. The Price Run Community Council was formed as a result of the community aspect part of the Project sponsored by the Wilmington Public Schools and the National Conference of Christians and Jews. The Project is now in its second

---

2 Policy on integrated membership was achieved in the spring, 1961.

year. Twelve of fifteen elementary schools are participating, with from one-third to the entire faculty of each school as participants. The work is carried on with the help of a consultant from the National Conference of Christians and Jews, Dr. William Vickery, who spends four days a month in Wilmington. Dr. Muriel Crosby, Dr. Agnes Snyder, and the helping teachers act as consultants for the participants when Dr. Vickery is not in Wilmington.

The first year was spent in diagnosing the human relations needs of children in the schools. Such a diagnosis is impossible without considering the family background and neighborhoods of the children and ultimately the communities in which they live. As this became apparent there was increasing participation in problem solving with community agents. The following quotation is from a year-end report of the Project made by Dr. Mary C. Dennison, principal of George Gray School. (It is the section on participation with community agents.)

1. Mr. Dudley Finch and Miss Edna Buffington, of the Housing Authority, have worked with us in sending us information of new families with elementary school age children. Mr. Finch came to the school and brought members of his staff to discuss problems of mutual concern in helping new tenants orient themselves to the school.

2. Mr. James Tyler has eliminated the kindergarten program for five-year olds once carried on by Kingswood Community Center after an invitation to Gray School. During his visit he saw the kindergarten equipment and program. Children of working mothers in half-day program at Gray are still provided an activity program at Kingswood for half-day. Mr. Tyler planned an orientation meeting for all new residents in the Riverside area. He invited the principals of Gray and North East Schools.

3. Nurses from the State Board of Health have arranged interviews at the school to clarify situations. They came to give us information and to get information about needy children in the district.

4. Following an attack by a gang of boys on two or three other boys at Twenty-second and Locust Streets, a conference was called by the Welfare Council at the Boys Club to see what action would be taken in such matters. Vandalism had also occurred at the Club. Those present included representatives of the Welfare Council, Peoples Settlement, Kingswood, Boys Club, Youth Aid, the Gray School principal, and several others.

5. We maintain a very fine relationship with the social worker at the Delaware Hospital who is in frequent contact with the school to make possible better use of clinical services to our children.

Preliminary Meetings

Because of contacts in many of the participating schools such as those just quoted, a School-Community Action Planning Meeting was set up for May 3, 1960. At this meeting the group was broken up into sections according to the geographical area of their interest.

In the George Gray School sectional group, there were nineteen people, five representing the school faculty, five the P.T.A., and, in addition, there were the principal of North East School (not yet opened), director of Kingswood Community Center, pastor of Ebenezer Church in the community, a representative from the Wilmington Housing Authority, the main office of which is in this area, a Board of Education social worker, and representatives from the NAACP, Family Court, Department of Public Welfare, and the Youth Aid Division of the Bureau of Police.

The following problems were identified for action:

1. Need for better parent education and dissemination of information through—use of churches; use of a coordinator; use of hairdressers, barbers, storekeepers.

2. Need to work on projects that are meaningful to residents in the area. They need recognition and to feel a relationship with the organization.

3. The need to build a sense of responsibility, especially in the men.

4. Need to reach and encourage more parents to work in the P.T.A.

5. Disciplining children by parents is an ever-present problem to be solved. Too many gangs form at night.

6. Need for better behavior.

7. Fighting, especially on the way to and from school, is a problem.

8. Other problems are: lateness in school, the situation at the corner store hang-out, poor transportation facilities, inadequate lighting.

It was decided that a council of leaders from the community, representatives from various agencies and from the schools, and key parents meet regularly to discuss ways to solve these problems. The next meeting was set for May 24, at George Gray School.

Twenty-four people attended the meeting on May 24. There were representatives from the schools and George Gray School P.T.A., the Kingswood Community Center and its P.T.A., Wilmington Housing Authority, two churches and the Wilmington Council of Churches, the Boys Club of Wilmington, the Delaware Hospital and the State Board of Health. Some time was spent discussing further the problems of the area, but most of the time was used for organization. A steering committee was chosen and a president and a secretary named. The group chose a name for the council, The Price Run Community Council.

The steering committee met twice during the summer. It discovered that there was a small organization, the Price Run Community Association, comprising a section about five by ten or twelve blocks, whose members were concerned with the problems of homeowners in this area. Representatives from this association were invited to the community council. The committee stated the aim of the organization: "to improve the community, promote leadership, locate the needs and problems in this area and work them out or solve them." It was recommended that all officers, if possible, be residents of the area. Organization plans and by-laws were drawn up to present to the council.

On September 22, 1960, the entire council met at George Gray School. It considered the by-laws and statement of purposes prepared by the steering committee. It was decided that it was time to publicize the council and to hold an open organizational meeting. So far there had been no publicity about the council because, "It was deemed wise to postpone all publicity until the fall when an all-out effort would be made to engage the interest of one representative from each block, if possible. The Council committee wants all new members to feel they are in at the beginning.

Meetings of Price Run Community Council

Very careful preparations were made for the first open meeting which was held on November 3, at the North East School. It was an excellently planned meeting, attended by about 75 people, the majority of whom were residents of the area. There were short talks by four people who had been active in forming the council. Dr. Muriel Crosby spoke about the problems of changing neighborhoods in Wilmington. Everyone wants better things for his children than he had for himself, she said, and in order to change things for the better in any neighborhood, the people themselves must want to change. She pointed out that social workers and teachers can only help, the residents themselves must do the changing. James Tyler, social worker at Kingswood Community Center and chairman of the meeting, told of the work of the steering committee. Their purpose, he said, was to bring together both individuals and representatives of groups to solve community problems. He said that the objectives of a community council as the steering committee saw them were as follows:

1. To recognize and solve problems in the area.
2. To improve the community.
3. To coordinate the work of groups and individuals.
4. To encourage participation of individuals in neighborhood activities.

He also spoke of the hope of the committee that block organizations could be formed to facilitate community improvement. The next speaker was Wagner Jackson, assistant director of the Wilmington Housing Authority, who spoke about the community problems from the point of view of housing. He had the following specific suggestions to offer to help keep homes from becoming substandard:

1. Talk to your neighbors and see how they feel about the block and the neighborhood.
2. Get together with people who feel as you do. Make a list of evidence of housing deterioration.
3. Decide what improvements you can make yourself, and make them.
4. List the conditions for which agencies can help; contact the agencies and make your wishes known.
5. Organize a community council which can put pressure on the City Councilman from this ward.

He further stated that he believed leadership for the council must come from neighborhood residents. Mrs. Mary Paynter, a housewife, who is secretary of the George Gray School P.T.A., spoke from the point of view of a special interest in children and youth of the area. She said she felt that more constructive leisure time activities were needed for the young people. She was convinced that parents could help their children become more interested in community affairs by being volunteer workers and leaders in various groups in the area.

The meeting was then broken up into five small discussion groups, each with a leader, and participants were encouraged to discuss what was wrong with the community and what a community council could do to improve it. Some of the points mentioned were:

1. There is not enough protection in the way of traffic lights, guidelines, and crossing guards for children going to and from school.
2. There is too much litter in the streets. Trash is not collected often enough and people do not take pride in the appearance of their neighborhoods.
3. There are too many children roaming the streets at night. The curfew should be enforced.
4. There should be a recreation center like Kingswood on the west side of North East Boulevard because parents do not want their children to cross such a busy highway.
5. The Boys Club should be open to *all* boys.
6. Too many houses in the district are being made into multiple family dwellings. The housing code is not being enforced.
7. There is not enough public transportation in the area.

It was decided by the group to meet again in three weeks to discuss these problems and to start organizing a Community Council.

At the second open meeting of the Price Run Community Council, November 21, at the George Gray School, the Rev. William R. Grace, of the Hilltop Neighborhood Association, explained a citizens' organization, how it works and what it can do. It had been his experience, he said, that a group cannot get active in a program of community betterment if it is not willing to get into politics. Areas of concern which had been identified at the first meeting were discussed further in five small groups at this meeting. They were:

1. Zoning and code enforcement
2. Recreation
3. Home maintenance and upkeep
4. Bus transportation
5. Highway crossings

Tentative by-laws were presented and candidates for officers of the council were named.

On December 5, the final organizational meeting of the Price Run Community Council was held at the Riverside Community Building. Samuel Albert, Councilman-elect of the ninth ward, spoke to the group about how he felt the Council could use political and governmental services. He spelled out exactly what must be done to get traffic lights at certain corners, what can be done if neighborhood property runs down, and so forth. The proposed by-laws for the organization were then discussed, some changes were made, and they were adopted. As finally stated, the purposes and objectives as set forth in the bylaws are:

> The purpose of the Council is to bring together representatives of community organizations and individuals of the area who will work cooperatively toward making the community a better place in which to live. In accomplishing this purpose the Council would:
> 1. Identify problems and work to eliminate them.
> 2. Plan and carry out programs to improve the community.
> 3. Coordinate the work of organizations and individuals.
> 4. Encourage participation of all individuals in the neighborhood.
>
> Specifically the Council would:
> 1. Work to improve the physical aspects of the community through City Departments on such items as streets and lights and other public services, and through emphasis on individual responsibility, including home maintenance.
> 2. Work to awaken interest in individual advancement through educational and vocational programs.
> 3. Stimulate establishment of and participation in constructive recreational leisure time programs in the community.

4. Develop better moral, spiritual, and cultural standards by promoting appropriate activities.

5. Encourage formation of block clubs with similar aims and objectives.

Five officers were elected: president, vice-president, treasurer, and recording and corresponding secretaries. There were about 40 persons at this and the November 21 meeting.

The most recent meeting of the Price Run Community Council was held January 12, 1961, at George Gray School. The newly elected president, Raymond T. Evans, presided. Just 26 people were present. Seven of them were school and agency people and the rest were residents of the area. The guest speaker was Mr. Sweeney, Executive Secretary of the Department of Health in Wilmington, who spoke about housing and code enforcement. He outlined the work of his department in inspecting housing and enforcing code violations. He spoke of the difficulties faced because of under-staffing of the department and of the difficulties of locating the owners of some substandard housing. During the question period there was a rather sharp interchange between some of the members of the Council and Mr. Sweeney. Some of the questioners obviously felt that the Board of Health should do a better job at enforcing code violations, and Mr. Sweeney defended the Board vigorously. The chairman stepped in at this point and very wisely, I thought, indicated the common interests of the two groups and how they could help each other. At this meeting, dues were collected to help defray postage and mimeographing expense. The dues are one dollar for individuals and five dollars for organizations per year. Two standing committee chairmen were appointed as an outgrowth of the discussion, a chairman for housing and one for publicity.

What will be the future of the Price Run Community Council? It is impossible to say now, of course. It seems to me that these next few months will be the critical time in its existence. After much careful planning and groundwork, leadership is in the hands of residents of the area, as it should be. The chairman is experienced; he is also president of the Kingswood Men's Club. Will the citizens be interested and active enough to make their council a success? It is hard to say. Certainly, the issues which have been raised so far are of immediate concern to the area residents. Does the drop in attendance augur failure for the Council? It is too soon to tell how significant that is. As I indicated before, North East Boulevard is both a psychological and a physical barrier difficult to cross. When meetings are held on the east side of the Boulevard, many people in Riverside and Eastlake Extension will attend who would not cross the barrier to go to meetings on the other side. As Dr.

Crosby said in her talk at the first meeting, other people can help, but only the people who live in it can really change the community.

This report of the initiation of a community council, written at the time of its initiation, would not be complete without a report of the answers to the questions above, given by the Price Run Community Council through its actions during the first year of its existence. It has flourished exceedingly well. Its major emphasis has been upon the prevention of the passing of a new housing code by City Council—a housing code which would have opened the door for the conversion of single-family to multiple-family dwellings, usually the first step in creeping blight.

Further evidence of the success of the Price Run Community Council is seen in the efforts of citizens in other sections of the city to establish similar councils in which officers of the Price Run Community Council are being asked to serve as consultants.

That "it can be done", as evidenced by the citizens in northeast Wilmington, is a powerful psychological force in lifting the morale of a city struggling to overcome the problems of change.

Moving Closer Toward School-Community Cooperation

At the close of the second year of The Three-Year Experimental Project on Schools in Changing Neighborhoods principals were asked to report on progress made in establishing cooperative action programs. Illustrations are quoted from the reports of each principal.

Drew-Pyle Schools

1. This year we were able to bring the YW and YMCA closer to the children of our school. Both groups sponsored clubs in our school. The YW provided volunteer leadership, the YM paid leadership. This year we had the lowest incidence of budding juvenile delinquency among our third-grade boys in many years. In fact, this has been true of all our boys and girls.
2. Peoples Settlement and Drew-Pyle School P.T.A. sponsored a joint venture that will assist in sponsoring boys in our area for summer camps.
3. This group also sponsored the Fellowship Choir in a choral concert that attracted folks from all over the city.

Elbert-Palmer Schools

1. We are in need of a branch library in the Palmer-Elbert community. I am hoping to interest the parents in working for a branch of the Wilmington Library. Teachers and parents have discussed this possibility.
2. There is very little recreation in the Palmer-Elbert area. I have

talked with teachers and parents to arouse interest in some form of recreation for the year 1961-62.

Gray School

1. The Price Run Community Council, made up of the citizens in the school district, has functioned as a strong unit in its effort to maintain the quality of living in the community. The need to contact City Council on zoning brought out strong leadership.
2. The increase in the number of Negro leaders has been considerable. They have been of great assistance as the change occurred in the community.
3. The participation of several ministers and church members in the Council and their new interest in the affairs of the total community in the district have been good.

Lore School

1. A meeting of three community leaders has resulted in scheduling of what may become a new community association to serve this area of southwest Wilmington.
2. P.T.A. plans indicate greater interracial cooperation and participation. Plans for next year's programs and activities portend closer attention to school and community needs.

Shortlidge-Washington Schools

1. Mr. Turner of the YMCA is our best single resource. Many of our children belong to the Y and he works with the school.
2. We have a growing number of organizations such as Cubs, Brownies, and Scouts. P.T.A. is active, supporting, helpful. Neighbors near new school are interested, have expressed pleasure at thoughtfulness of workers, etc., but are especially pleased with the use of grass instead of seed supplied for lawns.
3. We are beginning to organize some swimming groups.
4. A community group on rehabilitation of property is active, but the school is not involved.

Stubbs School

1. The widening of Tenth Street and the increasing number of blocks where flower boxes are being placed in the windows have improved our community. This is the result of many active forces in the community, of which the school is one, who encourage people to have pride in their surroundings.
2. There is increased evidence that the city board of health is enforcing the health code, thereby decreasing the pressure on parents to pay luxury-apartment prices for slum privileges. The P.T.A. has conducted many meetings on these problems and gladly welcomes the opportunity to call to the attention of officials any malpractices it discovers.
3. Action to curb juvenile delinquency. The P.T.A. met with officials of the Board of Park Commissioners, the Youth Aid, and the Detective Bureau to present some of their grievances and

to seek direction to correct faults. There was good rapport, and action committees were formed.

Williams School

1. Most of our activity has been confined to P.T.A. and various parent groups.

Opportunity School (for trainable retarded children)

1. Since our children come from all areas of the city and some county communities we do not have a school community.
2. The intellectual and socio-economic status of the parents is quite heterogeneous. The P.T.A. has worked diligently in attempting to get all of the parents active in the group.
3. Our problem is one of closer school-parent cooperation rather than school-community cooperation.

North East School

1. School Visitation Night. In the fall we invited the parents to come to see us. They came in large numbers. In return, we plan a community visitation night for next year when teachers will visit parents in the homes.
2. P.T.A. Activities. Parents and teachers worked together to promote a school fair, the proceeds of which are to go toward our summer program.
3. Price Run Council. Parents and teachers belong to this.
4. Pre-School Registrations. Our mothers take care of this.
5. School Lunch Week. Parents responded very well and asked if we could plan another.

Increasing community interest in the schools was apparent. The groundwork for cooperative action in school neighborhoods was being laid.

chapter

11

The Community in Action

Community participants in The Three-Year Experimental Project on Schools in Changing Neighborhoods have looked upon their efforts as the building of a cooperative action program which will foster the renascence of a city.

The creeping urban deterioration of the twentieth century may well be likened, in its effects upon human beings, to the darkness of the Middle Ages prior to the Renaissance. Modern man experiences the same terror in his struggles for a bit of security to maintain life in an economy, which demands increasing skills and is subject to the continuing traumatic changes in the lives of people. Just as the Renaissance brought a golden age, so the future, with its promise of the release of human potentialities, holds unlimited hope. But for those in transition between despair and hope life can be overwhelming.

The commitment of professional community leaders has been one of helping people help themselves, and to make it possible for the families of the community to find inner resources, moral values, and awareness of their own potentialities for creating a good life. By influencing the direction of change, they enable people to become the masters of their own destiny rather than the victims of change.

A picture of changes occurring in Project school neighborhoods at the close of the second year of study is provided in chapter 2. These changes were significant, reflecting rapid change for some school neighborhoods and hopeful signs of prevention of deterioration in one.

The Shoulder to the Wheel

At the close of the second year of the Project, plans had been developed by community participants to coordinate their efforts in working toward a common goal through their own unique programs. A steering committee had been elected to act as a coordinating group for all participants.

The uniqueness of this effort in the community-oriented aspect of the Project had been evidenced in the following ways:

1. The voluntary nature of the participants. Informality and the avoidance of unnecessary structure emphasized the need for freedom to participate or not.
2. The avoidance of creating another organization with the hazard of form without spirit or meaning.
3. The maintenance of integrity toward the programs for which agencies and organizations had been created.
4. The emphasis upon mutual help, support, and understanding.
5. The need to share in each other's successes and problems.

During the third year, 1961–62, the steering committee met approximately four times at luncheon meetings, chiefly to plan the direction of general meetings. Meetings of the total group were planned to inform participants of progress made by agencies and organizations, secure resources for those requesting help, and maintain interest.

Four general meetings of the total group of participants were held during the year. Progress reports were made by individuals and reports on studies being carried on by other organizations were made. Major emphases were upon being informed and keeping lines of communication open. In attempting to avoid the hazards of rigidity in structure, it seemed to the Project Administrator at mid-year that we were running the risk of an informality which would weaken the group. After consultation with the chairman and representative members of the steering committee, it was agreed that a bulletin from the Project Administrator would be helpful. Accordingly, the following bulletin was prepared: It was productive in its response.

Progress and Plans

Our two years of very close association in the Project make me very conscious of a void this year in spite of continued and close personal and professional contacts with many participants and agencies.

Some of the outstanding community developments occurring this year are of interest to participants in pursuing our common goal:

1. The AAUW carried out a three-session conference for representatives of women's organizations in Wilmington and New Castle County. These

were designed primarily to inform, to arouse a feeling of responsibility shared by city and suburbs, and to interest women in the possibilities for service. Approximately sixty-five women participated. A number of our colleagues from various agencies were program participants. The tremendous interest of participants reflects the success of this venture.

2. The Price Run Community Council continues to be a force for good whose influence is felt throughout the city. Most notable of its efforts has been the fight for an adequate housing code. Price Run Community Council officers have been frequent consultants to other groups organizing community councils.

3. North East School, the Wilmington Board of Education, and Kingswood Community Center are cooperating in offering an evening course in reading for parents who have never learned. The teacher who is conducting this course reports great enthusiasm and real progress. The principal reports that one of her youngsters who had problems is straightening out as she and her mother, a student in the reading course, study together each evening.

Will those of you who are making progress toward achieving the goal we set for ourselves last June drop me a line on the progress you are making? This would be very much appreciated. I will see that the good word is passed along.

School Progress

You all know of the great loss the schools suffered in the death of Dr. Vickery. Our staff has rallied around and a fine job is being done to assure success of the Project.

Both local and national officers of NCCJ are giving us magnificent support.

Within the next month the second annual report of the Project will be out and you will receive a copy. The printing of this report has been made possible through an anonymous contribution to the NCCJ, Delaware Region. It means much to me that a layman in the city thinks enough of this Project to provide financial support.

When you receive the report, you will want to study it carefully because it contains much of value to agencies and organizations as well as to the schools.

Planning Ahead

In preparation for the third annual report, will you begin to keep a sampling of any materials that reflect developments in your agency or organization, so that they may be attached to your official report? Information and forms for this report will be sent to you in late spring.

As I work with many of you in the various activities with which we are concerned, I am constantly impressed with the fact that in addition to the tangible results of our work, the most significant achievement we have made is the establishment of warm and supporting personal and professional relationships which will stay with us and grow long after the "tangibles" have disappeared. This is an achievement to be prized and nurtured.

When our community group gets together next time, I hope we will have a full turnout and a bang-up reunion.

One of the responses to the bulletin of particular value is quoted.

The YMCA of Wilmington and New Castle County and Its Role in the Three-Year Experimental Project on Leadership in Changing Neighborhoods

Many programs and activities have been initiated in the community since the inception of the Three-Year Experimental Project on Leadership in Changing Neighborhoods. It is impossible to identify precisely those programs and activities which have started as a result of the Project from those which might have started through the normal concern for the community. In my estimation, this identification is not important—it is only important that the programs and activities have started, and the effect they have in developing the leadership within the changing neighborhoods of our community. Therefore, the programs which are identified in this paper as being sponsored by the YMCA are by no means all the result of the Experimental Project, for some were started well in advance of the Project. However, others are a result of the Project or, perhaps even more important, are a result of the relationships among persons that were established as a part of the Project.

FOR YOUTH

Through the cooperative effort of the elementary schools in Wilmington, programs have been started with the youth in several schools which are quite valuable and have made new opportunities available to these youngsters. A consultive relationship has been established in the Shortlidge and Highlands schools where the principals and youth work secretary of the Central Branch work together with young boys who would benefit from the YMCA program experience.

At the Shortlidge School, the boys are invited to the YMCA one evening a month for a gym and swim program. The principal and youth work secretary working together have provided memberships for several of the boys who then participate regularly in the program of physical education and swimming at the YMCA. Also, some of these boys have formed a Gra-Y Club which meets each Friday evening. This is a small group under the supervision of an adult leader whose activities are designed to meet the needs of the members at their own developmental level.

The same type of program has been initiated at Highlands School but has not reached the stage yet where a definite friendship group has been formed into a club.

Through the cooperation of the principal and faculty of the Drew, Pyle, and Stubbs schools and the leadership of the youth secretary at the Walnut Street Branch, Gra-Y clubs for boys have been established at these schools. These small friendship groups meet at the school one afternoon a week, and then on Saturday morning participate in physical and swimming programs at the Walnut Street YMCA. Through small club groupings, the youngsters learn the essentials of cooperative planning, leadership development, democratic action, and participate in programs where they have an opportunity to share with and understand others.

For Teen-Age Youth

Through the cooperative efforts of the youth worker at Trinity Episcopal Church and the youth secretary at the Central Branch, a small club of junior high school age neighborhood boys has been established and meets weekly in the YMCA. This program is a combination of club and recreational activities. Even with their brief history they have already accepted a project of selling mints, the proceeds of which will help to provide similar programs in underdeveloped countries. Also in cooperation with the West Presbyterian Church, facilities have been made available for a co-ed teen-age group to use the swimming pool at the Walnut Street Branch on a monthly basis as a part of the church's teen-age program for the youth in that neighborhood.

In cooperation with the Peoples Settlement Association, information has been made available to the Hi-Y and Tri-Hi Y clubs throughout New Castle County for the weekend work camps sponsored by Peoples Settlement. Some of the teen-age youth of these clubs have participated and had a very fine experience in this program.

For Unemployed Youth

The Walnut Street Branch YMCA has become increasingly concerned over the youth 16 to 22 years of age who have dropped out of school and are unable to find employment. In seeing a way to help these youths, a program has been developed enabling them to participate three mornings a week in recreational activities at the Walnut Street Y. This is seen as the first step in a long-range program. The primary objective is to encourage this group to participate in the recreational programs of the Y and to establish a relationship with the staff. The ultimate objectives would be that after a relationship has been established, additional programs can be initiated which would make possible counselling with these young men as to their interests, their needs, and steps to be taken to help them meet their needs and become useful active citizens of the community.

FOR ADULTS

About five years ago, the Industrial Services program of the Walnut Street Branch YMCA was established. The primary purpose of this program was to help well-qualified Negroes in getting employment in keeping with their interests and qualifications. The program was designed—

1. to consult with employers in a program which encourages the hiring of the best person for a particular job without regard to race;

2. to interpret to the Negro community, the youth in particular, the talents, skills, qualifications needed for business and industrial jobs;

3. to help applicants measure their qualifications against the requirements for employment in the field of interest, and then make a referral of the individual as openings occur for which they are qualified, or help the individual get additional training as needed.

The Industrial Services Committee is composed of business and educational leaders within the community who have done an outstanding job in carrying out the purposes of this program. Many persons have found employment through the services of this group. It is not an employment agency. Placement emphasis is centered on job opportunities which generally have not been available to qualified Negroes, and on Negroes now working in jobs that do not make full use of their skills.

The work of the Industrial Services Committee has opened the door for qualified Negroes to hold jobs as stenographers, technicians, scientists, professional nurses, accountants and bookkeepers, department store sales clerks and buyers, driver-salesmen, and similar previously all-white occupations.

As we moved toward the close of the third year of the Project, the Project Administrator sent a request for a progress report to each community participant. The purposes of this report were twofold:
1. To determine the extent of action engaged in by participants.
2. To consider suggestions for continuing efforts following the formal closing of the Project.

A Report of Progress

During the four-day work sessions with Dr. Juanita Cogan last spring (1960-61), we agreed upon a "task" or objective which we would work to achieve within the context of our various programs and commitments. The "task" is as follows:

"We, the Community Agency and Organization Participants in The Three-Year Experimental Project on Schools in Changing Neighborhoods, address ourselves to the task of improving the quality of relationships among people
In order to:
Affect the direction of community change."

The minutes of the work sessions reveal that we spent some time examining the programs represented by participants, identifying problems for cooperative action in the Project school neighborhoods, and planning for future implementation of our "task."

HEARTENING SIGNS

Students of the Wilmington scene find much encouragement in the multitude of signs of positive action in the community. Where less than three years ago we had only two neighborhood councils, we now have twelve. Price Run Community Council has been a trail blazer and is demonstrating what can be accomplished by citizens who care. Churches of many denominations are moving way out front in stimulating the people to action. New citizen groups are springing into being and some older ones are getting a second lease on life. Regardless of the initiating source, an examination of membership reveals that usually a number of participants in the community aspect of the Project are deeply involved in the work of the citizens' groups.

A REPORT OF FUTURE PLANS FOR THE SCHOOLS

As you know, the formal aspects of the Project terminate at the end of the present school year. This study has prepared the staff for the big job ahead, which is just beginning. Incorporated in the future work of the schools in carrying out the "task" will be a continued use of the skills we have learned in identifying the human relations needs of our children and their families and the skills we have learned in providing curricula which will help children find use value in what they learn. New emphasis will be placed upon discovering ways of helping children become motivated to learn, and plans must be developed by the school staffs to be more effective in working with parents.

All new teachers entering the system will have as part of their formal orientation direct teaching of the skills of diagnosing children's needs and the skills of building a human relations focused curriculum. We need your help.

A REPORT OF YOUR PROGRESS

The community aspect of the Project has had profound influence in the schools. Working relationships between schools and others in the community who are committed to serving people, and, in the serving, making it more possible for people to help themselves, have reached a new level of quality.

There is increasing support of each other's efforts in carrying out specific programs.

Advice and suggestions are increasingly sought by participants as a means of implementing action programs.

The Wheel Turns

Responses to the request for progress reports were received from eighteen agencies and organizations. These reports were organized to facilitate study of all responses received. Their study provided a base for evaluation of the community-action program.

To the Project Administrator, the most significant achievement was not the tangible evidence of progress reported, but the intangible accomplishments in human relations. The first and second annual reports of the Project were replete with the difficulties encountered in welding together a group of widely divergent members whose major common characteristics were the commitment to a dream and the service to others. These are the bonds that held us together. That our association had cemented these bonds and fostered achievements undreamed of earlier is demonstrated in some of the observations made by participants:

> "Our Community Center programs have been strong in the past, but I am aware of a new quality in them that is attributed to the association I have had in this group."
>
> "As a new director of a long established agency, I followed leads I obtained in this group. I surveyed needs in our inner city center and found that we were duplicating services of other agencies in our neighborhood. I found that our second center, located in south Wilmington, is the only agency in the area. We are concentrating all of our efforts next year in the south Wilmington area. We are enlarging our facilities and planning with the principal and staff of the neighborhood schools. We have secured help from the women in the neighborhood who will clean and polish; the men are building shelving and making other improvements. We expect to establish a youth study center and other service facilities. Only through work with this group could I have gained the insight needed and the help to bring to fruition a major new program of service."

And from a young priest, who will leave for military service, came the observation:

> "I have always needed confidence; I still need it, but I have grown in confidence through my association with participants in the community group."

When people experience the power to help others and in so doing enrich themselves, feelings become facts and the ability of "faith to move mountains" becomes demonstrable.

During its final meeting of the year, it became obvious that the community group of the Project had no thought of terminating its work at the close of the formal aspects of the Project. Plans were developed providing for four workshop-type sessions for all participants during the school year 1962–63. During the summer, members agreed to continue working with neighborhood needs as the major focus for action during the ensuing year. Representatives from one area of the city had already defined their focus as family life. Others were concerned with discovering ways of helping families on a busy street in the inner city which was to be widened. This development, which consisted of removing four feet of sidewalk on each side of the street, would result in the loss of a major part of an outdoor "living room" for many inner-city families. In a densely packed neighborhood with hundreds of small children with no open space to play, the street widening program presented not only a safety hazard but a genuine social hazard to family life in the inner city.

The Pebble in the Pool

At the close of the formal period of the study in June 1962, the Project was only one of a number of forces at work in the city. Since 1959, the arousing of people to action had accelerated. An increasing number of organizations, institutions, and lay groups were moving into positive action on their own initiative. All seemed motivated by the same purpose which had directed the participants in the Project. There was much communication with Project participants among the groups. Each participant in the Project held membership in many other groups, which had been undoubtedly a positive force in shaping action of many non-associated groups. There was a rising tide of determination among all economic groups in the city's population to create a new city, built upon a proud heritage and which people can inhabit with comfort and satisfaction.

Foremost among current developments was the creation of a city-wide network of neighborhood councils, some initiated as Project efforts, many as the result of efforts of clergymen and others. Regardless of the primary source of initiation, Project participants were usually active in the planning and initiating groups. In 1959, at the initiation of the Project, only two well-established, active neighborhood councils were in existence, the Hilltop Association and the Eastside Neighborhood Council. By June, 1962, ten additional neighborhood councils had been organized and they had become federated in the Wilmington Federation of Neighborhood Councils. Outstanding among these councils was the Price Run Community Council, a direct outgrowth of action by participants at the close of the first year of the Project. This Council's work in preventing the passage of an undesirable housing code was a crowning success. It demonstrated that potential indigenous leadership could be discovered and developed.

Information on the development of the neighborhood council movement had been supplied by the Welfare Council of Delaware, an organization which, through its research and service, was sparking efforts of tremendous value to the city. At this writing the roster of community agencies and organizations contains no less than forty-nine names!

Those who have dropped a pebble into a pool of still, clear water and watched the ever-widening circles of ripples spreading over the surface until the perimeter is reached will find a similarity between the pebble and The Three-Year Experimental Project on Schools in Changing Neighborhoods. In a very important sense, the Project has been a pebble dropped into the pool of the city. Its influence has touched the lives of many people. Because the focus has been upon human relations, the relations of individuals to other individuals and to human institutions, there is little doubt that its influence will continue in many overt and subtle ways. To the Project Administrator, the permanent values of the Project are found in:

1. The firm and substantial extent and quality of personal and professional relationships found among professional leaders of community agencies and organizations.

2. The contributions of lay groups to professional programs.

3. The willingness of many to seek help and the eagerness of many to respond generously.

4. The recognition of responsibility of those who have for those who need.

5. The arousing of the suburbs to a feeling of responsibility to the city.

6. The acceptance of the fact that all children are our children.

These are the evidences of achievement that cannot be "measured by line and rule, but only by the heart and the imagination."

When, as happened in the Project, a Unitarian suburban women's club organizes a live summer theater program for disadvantaged Catholic, Protestant, and Jewish children of the city, followed by an outdoor supper in a lovely suburban home; when transportation is provided by the Catholic parochial school bus—artificial barriers break down and human beings move a little closer to brotherhood. Herein lies the hope for the city.

A Course to Steer By

*Section IV presents the practical problems
encountered in the administration of The Three-
Year Experimental Project on Schools in
Changing Neighborhoods. Unlike most projects
centered in the solution of problems related
to schools in changing neighborhoods, the
Wilmington Project received no foundation
aid nor special financial assistance from the
Board of Education. Communities faced with
increasing costs of education and with the
problem of developing effective programs
with limited funds must find the ways and
means necessary to do the job.*

*Included, also, are follow-up developments
occurring since the completion of the formal
study. An important aspect of the evaluation of
the Project is the extent to which gains are
reinforced in the years ahead.*

Trials and Tribulations

Administering a project in human relations education has its own satisfactions and its own burdens. An analysis of each by the Project Administrator may be helpful to those initiating a similar adventure in human relations.

New and Deeper Concepts

First among the satisfactions is opportunity for personal and professional growth of the administrator. To know one has grown in understanding opens up vistas of potential that challenge the individual to further growth.

1. The Project Administrator has learned never to refer to a neighborhood or to a home as a "slum." She has learned to know, too, many parents who, in spite of the degradation of poverty, provide a family climate of love and warmth. To provide a decent home for a child in circumstances almost overwhelming is an achievement of pride and satisfaction. To hear one's home and neighborhood described as a slum hurts the spirit.

2. The Project Administrator has learned that to ascribe "rootlessness" to people on the move is evidence of an assumption without reality. Roots are within people. People on the move are seeking a place to put their roots down. Just as the plant purchased at the greenhouse thrives in a garden which nourishes it and protects it, so people are seeking an environment that can give them a chance to grow and thrive. Undoubtedly, there are individuals whose experience in life has withered and crushed the roots of hope and achievement, but they are not to be confused with groups of people of any economic level, stereotyped by ignorance as "rootless."

3. The Project Administrator has obtained evidence which supports a long held conviction that children—all children—have a right to become established as human beings, capable of loving and being loved, because the adults in their world assume the responsibility for controlling environmental conditions which will foster their growth and development as individuals worthy of respect. Preparing children to meet the vicissitudes of life by harshness, in whatever form, merely cripples them. Already, at an early age, many children have been overwhelmed by the crushing burden of their lives. Of all people, teachers have the obligation of creating conditions in school which are warm and supporting; of demonstrating through their own relations with each other and with children the power of love of one's fellow man. In the Project Administrator's yard is a gnarled and twisted ivy plant. In times past it has put out roots and vines which have covered the house. The old plant has had many hazards to face. Its vines have been cut back to the soil; each winter month fuel delivery inundates it with oil so that it appears to wither and die. But each summer, it revives and flourishes. In years past, someone gave it the chance to become rooted so firmly that it seems impregnable. Young, new plants cannot take the strain and stresses of such treatment. So it is with the children. The community that builds into its children the inner resources and strength to meet life and not be overwhelmed by it, is building a future for itself that cannot be purchased in any other way.

4. The Project Administrator has discovered what may be one of the most important clues to the education of disadvantaged children we have yet uncovered. One of the blocks to adequate self-direction by disadvantaged people seems to be the inability to understand the relationship between cause and effect. Social service personnel constantly run into the seeming inability of low-income families to plan the use of resources wisely. Food money is not budgeted and the receipt of the relief check or weekly pay envelope often means full stomachs for a few days thereafter and empty stomachs prior to receipt of the next check.

School personnel disclosed an interesting situation in which parents of sixth-grade children, promoted to junior high school, had generally failed to attend a preceding spring meeting arranged by the junior high principal to help orient them to problems which might arise when their children entered a new school. The elementary principal explained that her parents seldom anticipated problems; that promotion meant all was well. She suggested that if such a meeting were called in the fall, after problems had arisen, the parents would turn out en masse.

The Project Administrator recalled an important finding in children's responses to diagnostic questions. Evidence pointed to the fact that generally children of deprived neighborhoods disliked most the adult who "yells at you." Middle-income children disliked the same thing, but they always went further and added a reason for the adult's yelling, e.g. "because he likes a nice lawn." Much earlier in life, the middle-income child is seeing the relationship between cause and effect. Unless people are able to anticipate possible results related to choices of action, they are unable to make wise choices. Being able to make choices based upon the possible most desirable results is essentially being able to think ahead and plan. Disadvantaged children and their parents have revealed the same need. The challenge to curriculum planners is that of building into the curriculum experiences which enable children to discover the value of defining alternatives, anticipating possible outcomes, and making a deliberate choice. It is the opinion of the Project Administrator that if disadvantaged children have such experiences they will grow to adulthood with more control over their lives than their parents now possess.

5. And, finally, the Project Administrator has learned the power of dedication. Had there not been so many people in school and community who possessed faith, commitment, and determination, the success of the Project would not have materialized.

Problems of Administration

It is to be expected that numerous problems may be anticipated in administering a project in human relations education. It is undoubtedly true that problems will arise which could not be anticipated. The second annual report, delineated the problems of administering the Project. Most of these were centered in financing the Project and in building staff and public support for it.

The most serious problem, and one not usually found by other major national programs in progress in urban areas, has been one of securing adequate financial support. Unlike other programs, the Project has had no foundation grant for its support, nor has the school system provided additional support beyond the regular resources available to the public elementary schools.

The National Conference of Christians and Jews, the sponsoring organization, has provided funds for some services through its national and regional offices. But this organization is itself dependent upon grants to carry out its activities.

Lack of adequate funds has prevented the securing of staff for the research aspect of the study. Necessary enrichment experiences for children, which the Higher Horizons Program of New York City has demonstrated to be so essential to disadvantaged children, have been extremely limited.

The work load on the Project Administrator and Project school principals has been exceedingly heavy, for no released time from regular duties was made available.

The usual routine of printing necessary progress reports became a major effort of the Project Administrator in her search to find someone in the community able and willing to invest in people.

In preparing a financial report of the Project, the Project Administrator concluded with the following statement:

> While any estimate of the cost of the Project must include an estimate of the financial value of the services of consultant, administrator and others, all of these services were incorporated in their regular assignments.
>
> Actual financial costs of the Project other than services have been extremely small and are due to additional secretarial service, publication of the annual reports, and related office supplies and postage. This sum has amounted to $15,992.[1] Probably never before in education has so much been accomplished at so low a cost. The fact that it has been accomplished should not lead others to assume that the education of disadvantaged children is inexpensive. It is doubtful that many individuals could or would be willing to carry the back-breaking load assumed by those committed to this Project.
>
> The satisfaction of achievement offsets the burdens of administering the Project.
>
> We have demonstrated that much can be achieved without money, by utilizing available resources in more productive ways.
>
> We have built into the staff, through emphasis on teacher education, a battery of skills and understandings which will not dissipate when the Project is closed.
>
> We have rallied the community to cooperative action which has been productive for each participant, and has brought the quality of public relations enjoyed by the schools to a level unprecedented in this community.
>
> The threats of power-structure blocks and political animosities have not materialized.
>
> We have a new morale, engendered by accomplishments, which gives us confidence in continuing our efforts, for we know that only a beginning has been made.

To the Project Administrator the experience of steering this adventure in human relations might well be called by Irving Stone's magnificent title, *The Agony and the Ecstasy,* for there has truly been much of both in her experience.

Long ago, Thomas Paine wrote: "He who would make his own liberty secure must guard even his enemy from oppression; for if he violates this duty, he establishes a precedent that will reach to himself." Participants

---

[1] Including contributions for follow-up purposes 1962-63.

in the Project might well paraphrase Paine's statement: "He who would make his own life secure must also make his neighbor's life secure; for if he violates this duty, he has set a precedent that will reach to himself."

Deficits and Assets in the Administration of the Wilmington Project

At the close of the second year of The Three-Year Experimental Project on Schools in Changing Neighborhoods, the full impact of the problems related to its administration was felt. The "hindsight" of the Project Administrator may well serve a useful function as "foresight" for future project administrators. Hazards and blocks are cited with partial solutions.

Time for Orientation and Preparation. Because of urgency, the presentation of the proposed project by the Delaware Regional Director, The National Conference of Christians and Jews, and the initiation of the Project were almost simultaneous. Necessary orientation in which the following problem areas might well have been anticipated and planned for was omitted.
1. The careful defining of responsibilities for the school project and the community project between The National Conference of Christians and Jews and the schools.
2. An understanding of the scope of the school project by the Administrator, the school leaders, and the participants.
3. The need for a broad school project design which would help participants to understand the relationship between what they were doing and where they were headed in the Project, and to incorporate evaluation procedures from the beginning.
4. The need to study and estimate staff and financial needs to carry out the Project in relation to secretarial service, research staff, preparation of needed instruments.
5. The need to study and define the role of the University in the Project (in research; in teacher education).

Securing Necessary Support for the Project. Each school system will have its own peculiar conditions affecting support of a project. However, factors which will greatly affect the success of any project include:
1. The need to secure the support of the central administration and the principals. Wilmington has been fortunate in this respect for we have had exceptionally strong and active support from the superintendent, and generally strong support from participating principals. The fact that principals entered the Project voluntarily was an important factor in the success of the Project.

2. The need for strong and supporting working relationships between the Project Administrator and the local director of the sponsoring organization. Because of a change in the local directorship of The National Conference of Christians and Jews during the second year, the Project Administrator was somewhat handicapped, a handicap which the national office of The National Conference of Christians and Jews helped to mitigate.
3. The need to secure Board of Education support and the support of the local community. The Project has been fortunate, indeed, in securing both. Board of Education members have generally participated rather fully through attendance at evening meetings for school personnel, community leaders, and consultants. Lay citizens have participated on the Central Planning Committee of the school aspect of the Project and in community agency meetings. There has been great demand for reports of the Project by civic, religious, and service organizations.

Securing Adequate Administration of the Project. Many of the preceding problems and developments relate to:
1. The need for full-time administration of the Project by the Project Administrator. No time from the regular job of assistant superintendent in charge of elementary education was allowed. Much of the work has been accomplished as a means of carrying regular responsibilities for in-service education, curriculum development, and administration of the Elementary Division.
2. The need for full-time secretarial service for the Project. During the first year, no secretarial service was provided. One week of secretarial service for preparation of the progress report was provided by the local director of The National Conference of Christians and Jews. Halftime secretarial service was provided by the national office of NCCJ beginning October 1, 1961, the second year of the Project, and extending through the first follow-up year.
3. The need for a coordinator of the community Project, a job taken on by the Project Administrator during the first two years of the Project for lack of other help.
4. The need for staff to prepare the numerous bulletins needed in developing the curriculum aspects of the Project. Needed bulletins had to be prepared by the Project Administrator, with some assistance from the helping teachers.
5. The need to consider carefully the hazards of volunteer supplementary consultant service. Many of our hopes to expand the amount of time for adequate consultant service were centered in volunteer services, in both school and community projects. The hazards of consultant volunteer service are many and were experienced during the Project. We were fortu-

nate to have excellent volunteer service from Dr. Agnes Snyder throughout the study.

Clearer Sailing

All was not gloomy, however. Although many problems remained un-
solved, much was achieved in solving others. Dr. Vickery was unceasing
in his efforts to help meet many problems which arose. In fact, the
teamwork between the administrator and the consultant may be identified
as the most important single factor in assuring success of the Project.
Other important success factors were:

1. The interest and support of the national office of The National Conference of Christians and Jews, which provided strong consultant service
for the school-aspects of the Project; strong, but limited, consultant service for the community-aspect of the Project; half-time secretarial help
during the second and third years of the Project.

2. The interest and support of the school staff as shown by an increase
from 6 to 12 participating schools in the second year and an increase
from 65 to 165 participating teachers in the second year.

3. The interest and support of the community reflected in the amazing
support among lay groups and organizations; tangible contributions which
were made to the schools; the number of meetings of organizations and
citizens requesting information on the Project.

5. The support of the Board and members of the Delaware Region, NCCJ,
who appointed liaison officers to the Project during the second year; met
with the consultant and administrator to discuss progress; made an attempt to secure foundation funds; contributed the printing of the first
progress report as a public service and were involved in securing aid to
print the second and third progress reports.

In summary, what has been accomplished without an operating budget
is nothing short of amazing. When the gains are balanced against those
things impossible of accomplishment without a budget, the credit side
of the ledger certainly outweighs the debit side. The price is great, however, to those who assume additional responsibilities. Only time will tell
whether or not the cost will have been justified.

Facts and Figures

Communities, boards of education, and school administrators must
rightly be concerned about the costs entailed in a project such as the
Project. School systems usually budget funds for instructional purposes,
for the in-service education of the staff, and for school-community relations. Each department of a school system, whose functions include the
areas mentioned, legitimately contributes to the financial support of such

a project. This means not a duplication of funds but certainly an increase in budget requirements, for education is not cheap in a city in the process of rapid change.

During the three years of formal study, the actual cash expenditure for the Wilmington Project was extremely small.

Budget, 1959-62

*Contributed by the Delaware Region, The National
Conference of Christians and Jews:*

Postage and Office Supplies	$ 473
Consultant for Community Agencies	25
Typing of First Annual Progress Report	120
Printing of 3 Annual Progress Reports	7,500
Total	$8,118

The annual progress reports were printed through the efforts of the Board members of the Delaware Region, NCCJ. Lay citizens of the community contributed the necessary funds, two in the name of the Delaware Region, NCCJ, and one in the name of The Cathedral Church of St. John, of the Episcopal Diocese of Delaware.

Contributed by The National Conference of Christians and Jews:

Postage and Office Supplies	$ 425
Half-time Secretarial Service for the Project Administrator (Beginning October 1960 and continuing through the first follow-up year to August 1963)	5,581
Typing of Second and Third Annual Reports and the Final Report of the Study	1,093
Total	$7,099

Actual cash contributions for the support of the Wilmington Project totaled $15,217.

A more realistic estimate of the cost of administering the Project is revealed in an estimated budget in which services provided by the Wilmington schools and the sponsoring organization are equated with the cost of such services. The following budget is an estimated one, but reveals actual costs more realistically than the one revealing cash contributions only.

Estimated Project Costs, 1959-62, and Estimated
Follow-up Costs, 1962-64

Contributed by the Delaware Region, NCCJ

1959-60

Postage and Office Supplies	$ 184.15	
Typing of Annual Report	120.00	
Consultant for Community Agencies (approx.)	25.00	$ 329.15

1960-61

Postage and Office Supplies	$ 290.45	
Printing of First Annual Report	1,500.00	$ 1,790.45

1961-62

Postage and Office Supplies	$ 275.00	
Printing of Second Annual Report	2,500.00	$ 2,775.00

1962-63

Printing of Third Annual Report	$3,500.00	$ 3,500.00

Total for Three-Year Period and Follow-up
Year 1962-63 $ 8,394.60

Contributed by The National Conference of Christians and Jews

1959-60

Consultant Service by Dr. Vickery (two days per month—10 months, plus approximately one day per month of preparation)	$1,650.00	
Travel Expenses of Consultant (estimated at approximately $40 per day)	800.00	
Consultant for Community Agencies Project, NCCJ—plus expenses (approximate)	75.00	$ 2,525.00

1960-61

Consultant Service by Dr. Vickery (four days per month—10 months, plus one day per month of preparation)	$2,750.00
Travel Expenses of Consultant	1,600.00
Half-time Secretarial Service for Project Administrator (actual)	1,504.83

Preparation of Manuscript for Second Annual Report	225.00	
Consultant for Community Agencies Project, NCCJ (four days including expenses)	500.00	
Consultant Service, Program Director, Community Relations, NCCJ (two days, including expenses, approximate)	190.00	$ 6,769.83

1961-62

Consultant Service by Dr. Vickery (September through November— four days per month of preparation)	$ 605.00	
Travel Expenses of Consultant	480.00	
Half-time Secretarial Service for Project Administrator (Allocation—$2500)	1,952.50	
Preparation of Manuscript for Third Annual Report	300.00	
Postage and Supplies	250.00	$ 3,587.50

1962-63

Postage and Office Supplies	$ 175.00	
Half-time Secretarial Service for Project Administrator	1,913.00	$ 2,088.00

1963-64

Preparation of Manuscript for Final Report of Study (approximate)	$ 568.00	$ 568.00
Total for Three-Year Period and Follow-up Year		$15,538.33

Contributed by the Wilmington Public Schools

1959-60

Project Administrator's Services (approximate) (Estimated on basis of ⅓ total work load)	$5,000.00	
Half-time Secretarial Service	2,500.00	
School Truck Mailing Service to Schools (approx.)	200.00	$ 7,700.00

1960-61

Project Administrator's Services (approximate)	$5,000.00	
One-fourth Secretarial Service to Supplement half-time NCCJ Secretary	1,250.00	
School Truck Mailing Service to Schools	200.00	
Contribution of Fees Earned by Speeches by Project Administrator (To Delaware Region, NCCJ—$50; to NCCJ Account with Board of Education for postage—$150.00)	200.00	$ 6,650.00

1961-62

Project Administrator's Services (approximate) (Increased by need to act as consultant to Project because of Dr. Vickery's death)	$7,500.00	
One-fourth Secretarial Service to Supplement half-time NCCJ Secretary	1,250.00	
School Truck for Mailing Service to Schools	200.00	$ 8,950.00
Total for Three-Year Period (No estimate of services is included for follow-up years.)		$23,300.00

Summary of Financial Contributions 1959-62, and Follow-up Years, 1962-64 (including estimates for cost of services)

Delaware Region, NCCJ	$ 8,394.60
The National Conference of Christians and Jews	15,538.33
Wilmington Public Schools	23,300.00
Grand Total (1959-64)	$47,232.93

In the light of the financial resources provided other school systems securing grants from foundations, frequently accompanied by special matching funds from school boards, the actual financial support of the Project has been infinitesimal ($15,992); and the estimated budget, including services of regular employees of the Wilmington Public Schools and the sponsoring organizations, relatively small ($47,232.93).

While we have achieved unusual returns from our small investment, lack of money blocked a number of developments needed in the Project.

Unachieved and Achieved Goals

Five areas of development in the Project suffered in varying degrees from lack of funds:

1. *Curriculum,* particularly in terms of additional specialized staff such as social workers and remedial teachers.

2. *In-Service Education,* through lack of an adequate amount of consultant service.

3. *Research,* through lack of research staff to (a) fully capitalize on the analysis of children's responses to diagnostic questions, (b) analyze curriculum units prepared by teachers to reveal areas of strength and weakness in planning, and (c) complete a technically sound evaluation of achievement.

4. *University Affiliation and Coordination,* through lack of staff for the local university to gear pre-service and in-service education of teachers and administrators to a human relations-focused professional education.

5. *Community Coordination,* through lack of funds to employ a community organizer to provide overall leadership, direction, and consultant service to participating agencies and organizations.

With the resources available, achievement toward Project goals was remarkably good in the areas of curriculum, in-service education, and community coordination.

In research and local university affiliation we were not so fortunate. With the exception of efforts of individual Project schools to evaluate progress continuously, objective evaluation of the total Project suffered. Subjective evaluation has been more productive, for in the field of human relations, growth in attitudes, values, and relationships, statistical treatment is next to impossible.

A second area, practically untouched, has been a major weakness of the Project, namely, the inability of the participants to involve the local university in a coordinated program of pre-service and in-service education of teachers and administrators. It is the Project Administrator's judgment that a human relations-focused education is a necessity for all candidates for professional certification. In-service education then is enabled to build upon the foundation provided in teacher-education institutions. Attempts were made, unsuccessfully, to initiate this action.

Lack of funds, obviously, has had its disadvantages. However, the need to meet problems with little additional financing of the schools in changing neighborhoods has resulted in satisfying results:

1. We have built into our staff attitudes, understandings, and teaching processes which will stay with us long after the Project becomes a part of the past.

2. We have developed warm and supporting relationships between school and community which have created a climate of helpfulness and have prevented many potentially disastrous events in a tension-ridden city.

3. We have learned that the power of dedication cannot be purchased and that when it is present, there is little that cannot be accomplished.

As we move into the future, an effort that has won so much respect and support from the community may expect to win reinforcement financially for those unfulfilled goals of the Project which represent for all of us "promises to keep."

Building the Future

Far too many projects in education blaze for a brief period, but when the peak of "newness" fades there is little evidence of lasting value. Changing cities and the needs of disadvantaged children will be with us for many years to come. The formal study of The Three-Year Experimental Project on Schools in Changing Neighborhoods was but a beginning of the long struggle ahead.

In the Schools

The first year, 1962-63, following the formal completion of the Project, was a significant one, for it demonstrated the determination of the staff to bring to fruition its commitment to the people of the city. Responsibility for establishing gains made and skills learned had been accepted by the principals of the schools and the helping teachers.

The Problems of Staff Turnover

The loss of twenty-five of the participants over a four-year period, 1960-64, and their replacement by teachers lacking the experience provided in the Project, posed a real problem to the city's schools. The efforts of the helping teachers assured continuing in-service education in human relations through a series of orientation meetings required of all new staff members during their first three years on the job. During these meetings newcomers learned diagnostic techniques and the use of diagnostic instruments. They were helped to use their findings in building experience units in human relations education. This effort was supplemented by the guidance of the principal in each school.

Unless this effort is continued in future years, in a relatively short time turnover of staff will eliminate a majority of the original participants and the expenditure of the energy and effort of many people will be lost.

Principals assumed responsibility for working with their total staffs in human relations education. Ten of the eleven Project school principals filed progress reports. Of these principals, nine reported continued use of diagnostic procedures to identify the human relations needs of children.

Continuation of the development of planning skills was reported as being carried out exceptionally well in five schools and moderately well in five other schools.

Continuation of emphasis upon the development of experience units was reported as proceeding exceptionally well by two schools, moderately well by seven schools, and only fairly well by one school.

These reports show that, in the judgment of the principals, the teachers are using new skills and understandings to advantage.

A Look Ahead

Acute needs of a city in the process of change demand that school personnel continue to "move mountains" so that children are able to grow toward maturity, competent, self-directing, and sensitive to the need to deal cooperatively with the problems of living. Families, too, must have the help of agencies and individuals if they are to become able to help themselves in creating a good life.

The schools have been fortunate, indeed, to have so many on the staff committed to the people they serve. Only through widespread support, genuine interest, and cooperative effort of so many people in the community have the schools been able to plot the course they have taken. Continuance of these efforts is the challenge of the years ahead. Particularly encouraging is the effort made in schools which were not official participants during the three years of formal study.

In the Community

Unlike the participants in the school aspect of the Project, those in the community aspect remained together for a fourth year of formal work during 1962-63. At the close of the year, the Project Administrator sent the following bulletin to community participants with a sampling of activity reports received from some of the agencies:

> For four years we have worked together with tremendous benefits to the elementary schools of Wilmington. Much progress has been made in developing teamwork in Project school neighborhoods with resultant benefit to children and their families.
>
> The formal aspect of the Project in the schools terminated in June, 1962. Each school is continuing its efforts individually to

root the gains made, with George Gray School and North East School notable examples of excellent follow-up activities in enrichment and language development. Outstanding parent-school efforts are being made in Stubbs, Drew, and Pyle Schools. Follow-up activities of all schools during 1962-63 have been reported in a final bulletin, and I believe you will find these reports heartening.

The progress reports of a number of agencies for the school year 1962-63 present a similar, heartening picture.

As Project Administrator, I feel that the community aspect of The Three-Year Experimental Project on Schools in Changing Neighborhoods has served its purpose. We have learned to know and respect each other. We are knowledgeable about many agency programs being carried out with increasing effectiveness. We have excellent working relationships.

I feel that, as needs arise, cooperative effort should continue on a school-neighborhood basis rather than on a city-wide basis.

I hope that you will be willing to meet once each year with the elementary-school administrators to hear of developments occurring in the city schools and to help us map directions for the future. Each one of you is a valued member of the school family. Your help and guidance will be needed as we attempt to make education a vital force for good in our city. I extend my thanks and deep appreciation for your generous support of an effort that has been truly "an adventure in human relations."

Sampling of Progress Reports, Community Participants, 1962-63

Girls Club of Wilmington, Delaware

Approximate number of people served:
1,100 children
  250 youth
   75 adults
(Families are not included in our program, but are invited to open houses, special events, dramatic performances, etc.)

Implementing the Task through previously established programs:
1. The Woman's Club more than doubled its membership in the fall of 1962. Many new activities were enjoyed this winter, including a class in millinery, Christmas crafts, Christmas decorations, dramatics, and modern dance. In addition, sewing, bridge, and ceramics classes were available. Outside speakers covered the use of color in the home, and flower arrangement.

The Woman's Club also participated for the first time in the "Table Topic Tea" and more of the women visited the show than in previous years.

Last spring the mothers made a trip to Washington. One to New York is scheduled for May 1.
2. Mrs. Henry M. Canby, President of our Board of Directors, visited many neighborhood and nearby county schools to inform the principals of our program.

School faculties were extended an invitation to a tea on April 24. Approximately thirty school personnel attended. Following the tea a tour of the building was conducted.

3. Homemaking activities continue to be stressed, and have had a beneficial influence upon the members.

The National Girls Club of America, Inc. each year offers member clubs an opportunity to compete in National Awards.

This year, three members of the Wilmington Club won three of the five awards offered:

- The Reader's Digest Career Key Award—Our entry won in Region IV and was awarded $500.
- The Young Homemaker of the Year Award—Our entry won, and received $300.
- The Girl of the Year Award (new)—Our entry won, and was awarded $500.

Our three winners plan on spending the money to further their educations.

The girls, selected to partake in the competition, have been active in all phases of the club program.

4. Girls Club members who did not rejoin in the fall of 1962 were contacted by a newsletter, and in midwinter a second letter was sent to the parents. It was reported that the majority of these girls were having transportation problems or heavy school schedules.

5. Our three Volunteer Groups continue to be an important part of our program. They consist of—

Junior Leaders	girls 11-12 years of age
Leaders-in-Training	girls 13-14 years of age
Senior Leaders	girls 15-18 years of age

Over 3,000 hours of volunteer services will be contributed this year to the club by these three groups.

6. Many of our programs have been open to nonmembers, as several times during the winter activities are open to members and their guests.

New programs initiated to implement the Task:

1. A new extension program was initiated in January 1963 to meet the needs of girls in other areas of our community. One meeting is being held every Monday and Wednesday afternoon from 3:00 to 5:00 P.M. at the George Gray School. Another meeting is being held every Tuesday and Thursday at the Mary C. I. Williams School. From its beginning the extension program has proved highly successful with a remarkably steady attendance.

One hundred girls' applications were accepted at the George Gray School from 4th, 5th, and 6th year pupils. Forty-five others applied whom we were unable to accept because of lack of personnel. At the Mary C. I. Williams School the program was opened to 5th and 6th graders only. One hundred girls joined.

The program will be conducted for a twenty-seven-week period.

Sewing, cooking, drama, good grooming, and dancing are offered. In addition there have been special events.

2. A new set of slides covering activities at the club has been developed, and so far these slides have been shown at several school and service club meetings this year. Two more showings have been scheduled for late April and early May.

Many families are unaware that the Girls Club exists, and much work is needed to better acquaint the community with our services.

3. A new program, "A Homemaking Show," has been planned for mothers and daughters. This will be held in conjunction with the celebration of National Girls Week, May 6-11.

The evening's entertainment will consist of a "fashion show" (all clothes modeled will have been made by girls in the sewing classes), a "tempting table settings" contest, a clothes line art exhibit, and a craft exhibit.

It is felt that more emphasis should be placed on the home-making arts, and on giving the girls more opportunities to show their work.

4. In 1962 a new summer club-house program with special appeal to girls eleven years of age and older was offered. We plan to continue this program.

Field trips to New York, Washington, and Philadelphia, paid for by the participants themselves, were popular features of this program. Trips to local or nearby points of interest, with the Girls Club board members furnishing the transportation, were made possible. Longwood, New Castle and the County Fair at Harrington were also visited.

Agency cooperation with other agencies and organizations:

1. Girls Club members stuffed thousands of envelopes for the Tuberculosis Association in the early fall of 1962.

2. Posters are made yearly for the Flower Market Fair.

3. The Girls Club entered the Table Topic Tea which is a benefit fund raising activity for the Wilmington Symphony.

4. Participated in the United Community Fund Recognition dinner, with a short skit, following the 1963 campaign.

5. Entered the C.Y.O. "Youth on the Go." The Girls Club had a booth and displayed craft, art, and sewing articles. Also distributed literature regarding Girls Club.

6. A circle from Grace Methodist Church asked to meet here recently. Following their program, slides of the activities of the Club were shown and a tour of the building taken.

7. Cosponsored a City Wide Doll Show with the Epsilon Chapter of Beta Sigma Phi.

Programs and activities to be continued:

1. The Board of Directors has included in the 1963-64 budget a request from the United Community Fund for funds to continue the two extension programs, for the year of 1964.

2. The Board is also requesting additional funds in order to employ additional, part-time staff which would enable more girls to join the Girls Club extension program.

3. The Board of Directors will continue to develop its public relations program in an effort to better acquaint the community with the Girls Club.

4. The activity program at the Club will continue with changes being made to meet the needs and interests of its membership.

New programs and activities considered for initiation:

1. A committee will be appointed this year to formulate long-range plans for future expansion of the Girls Club.

2. A training program for volunteers will be inaugurated in the fall of 1963 for adults and our teen-age membership.

3. A study hall with adequate supervision is also planned.

4. A day time program for young married women and girls who have left school is also being considered.

(One of our young staff workers recently gave a short talk and her concluding remark ·was: "There is work to be done, character to be built, and happiness to be shared."

Neighborhood House—Peninsula Conference Project

Approximate number of people served:

169 children
207 youth
 43 adults
264 families

Implementing the Task through previously established programs:

1. Continuing cooperation with the schools.

2. Constant attention to the human relations needs of all age groups: physical needs of clothing, food, and medical care; friendships with parents and families; behavior problems.

3. Continued program for all age groups.

New programs initiated to implement the Task:

1. Sewing classes for women, teen-agers, 5th- and 6th-grade girls. (These activities also include knitting and crocheting.)

2. Family night one night a month with programs of interest, such as
    a. slides taken since moving into our new location;
    b. a playlet "Scattered Showers," with a discussion on discipline and punishment entered into in a heartening way by those in attendance;
    c. a special film "King of Kings" preceding Easter week;
    d. a social night—get-acquainted program.

3. A night for adult men to come in and play games such as pool, table tennis, checkers, chess, etc.

4. A new emphasis on calling at the homes of our families.

Agency cooperation with other agencies and organizations:

1. We were represented at—
    a. all Welfare Council meetings;
    b. Prisoner's Aid Annual Meeting;
    c. Peoples Settlement Annual Meeting; most of the "Experimental Project on Schools in Changing Neighborhoods" meetings;

d. YWCA annual meeting and luncheon;
e. "Agency Executive" meeting—under welfare program.
2. We cooperated with—
a. public schools in P.T.A.;
b. South Wilmington Community Council;
c. Federation of Community Councils.
3. We organized a "Charm Course" in cooperation with the Walnut Street YWCA.

Programs and activities to be continued:
1. Continuation of our visitation program (most enthusiasm shown by workers and those visited.)
2. Continued cooperation with YWCA
3. Greater extent of cooperation between the public schools, P.T.A., and community interest groups
4. Enlarged program for adults

New programs and activities considered for initiation:
At the present time I am not able to say. During the week of April 28th we will be meeting with a representative from our New York office and a personnel member from Nashville to study and evaluate our present program and see where we need more stress, what to emphasize in our program, and how best to go about it. Staff and volunteer help will be considered as to best use of time.

Peoples Settlement

Approximate number of people served:
14,860 children and youth
8,810 adults

Implementing the Task through previously established programs:
1. We work through—
5 clubs for children under 12 years old;
1 Junior High Boys Club;
1 Junior High Girls Club;
1 Senior High Boys Club;
1 Senior High Girls Club;
1 Golden Age Club (men and women 62 and over);
1 Preschool group;
1 Women's group (Hobby Day);
1 Fellowship Choir;
1 Weekend Work Camp;
1 Basketball team—senior boys;
1 Flower box project to plant flowers in boxes each year in co-operation with the Garden Clubs of Wilmington;
1 Fall Conference with agency representatives and community people on some phase of agency work;
1 Summer Day Camp;
1 Boy Scout Troop;
1 Girl Scout Troop;

Work projects for neighborhood teen-agers;
Friday special cultural program for youth (music, movies, dancing, puppet shows, etc.);
1 Garden Club—Eastside Garden Club;
1 Basketball team.
2. We make available professional staff to Eastside Neighborhood Council.
3. We accept applications for surplus foods. Distribute surplus foods in cooperation with State Hospital once per month to about 900 families.
4. The "task" selected is the goal of social work. In all of the activities, the objectives are to build relationships and to effect change in individuals and in the community.
5. Materials on relationships, human development, and community change are used in training and supervising leaders in the respective club groups.

New programs initiated to implement the Task:
1. Hobby Day for Women and Pre-School Children program: Children 3 and 4 years old participate in a program under the supervision of a trained teacher assisted by another trained person. The purpose of this activity is to provide wholesome group experiences for the children. (A school principal advised such activity to help prepare children for school.)
2. Hobby Day for Mothers: Held each Wednesday from 1 to 3 P.M. Most mothers like to remain while the children have their own program. The women engage in a variety of activities including cooking with the help of a nutrition teacher, sewing, making hats, discussion, and reading. The mothers have planned trips during evening and weekends.
3. Day Camp in the Country: Sixty children had their first experience in day camp in the country Woodlawn Estates for six weeks. On Parents Day the children expressed their enjoyment and outdoor learnings in skits, discussions, and exhibits.
4. Worked with League of Women Voters in its housing program. Assisted the League in continuing its interest in Poplar A.
5. Cooperated with Health Department, Greater Wilmington Development Council, and Housing Authority in Community Development and Neighborhood Conservation.
6. Coordinated efforts in agency planning through Eastside Conference of Executives.
7. Arranged ball games through W.A.B.C. League.
8. Sponsored young people for training in getting and holding a job. Secured jobs for youth with the Employment Service Council of Churches.
9. Arranged to use Walnut Street YMCA facilities, swimming pool, etc.

Agency cooperation with other agencies and organizations:
Peoples Settlement cooperated with the schools in the area and with the sixteen agencies of the Federation; e.g.,—

1. Young people from Howard High School distribute surplus foods to nearly 900 families each month. We accepted children for day camp referred to us by the school.
2. The Eastside Neighborhood Council cooperates with other councils through the Federation in working on community improvement. Cooperated with Conference on zoning, housing, and code enforcement in getting a new city housing code.
3. Stored clothing for United Church Women to be used by migrant workers. Occasionally a package of used clothing is given to the Settlement for families in the neighborhood. The guidance counselor at Bancroft Junior High School referred to us some families who needed clothing.

Programs and activities to be continued:
1. All the activities listed above are to be continued.
2. Work program for teen-agers in the neighborhood during the summer and weekend camping.
3. Study hall for elementary grades, junior and senior high school under the supervision of former teachers.
4. A play period Saturday mornings for pre-school children.
5. Tutoring service for persons who want to learn to read and write, or advance in their education.
6. Expanding program to help high school drop-outs get and keep a job.

Welfare Council of Delaware

Approximate number of people served:
We do not have direct services, but work mainly through other organizations and agencies. We work with well over one hundred groups of this kind, but we do not have attendance figures per se. Our work is often with one representative of a group who, in turn, brings the information back to members of his group.

Implementing the Task through previously established programs:
1. Continuing to make available to individuals, agencies, institutions, organizations and other groups basic census data, knowledge of which is fundamental to their program planning.
2. Continuing and deepening our relationships with physical planners, governmental and nongovernmental, at city, state, county, and regional levels. The major purpose of this program is to share our knowledge of the social needs of people. We have been concerned especially with urban redevelopment, housing, inner-city and metropolitan area problems and with the provision of adequate land for recreation and conservation.
3. Strengthening our community organization services. These are available to assist in the solutions of community problems such as medical care for persons receiving old-age assistance, illegitimacy, juvenile delinquency and problems of the provision of services, either by one or groups of social agencies.
4. Working closely with groups such as the East Side Conference of Agency Executives and the Recreation and Group Work Section of

the Conference of Agency Executives to encourage and strengthen relationships among social agency executives.

5. We should like to state, as we did in the 1961-62 report, that because of the nature of the services of the Welfare Council of Delaware, it is difficult to distinguish between "previously established" and "new" programs.

6. Our basic services: study and research, planning, coordination, helping to set and maintain high standards of service, information, and education—all in relation to social welfare—are of a continuing nature.

7. Our programs have as one of their goals the improvement of relationships among social welfare agencies and between them and the total community. In the last analysis, this is a matter of improving the relationships among people.

New programs initiated to implement the Task:

Usually our programs, in themselves, are not new, though special projects or materials often are. It would not be correct to state that the following were initiated solely as a means of implementing the Task, although they do help to improve the quality of relationships among groups and to affect the direction of community change.

1. We made available "The Socio-Economic Status of Nonwhites in Delaware, 1950 and 1960" on a limited basis to assist especially those groups concerned with integration, civil rights, employment of minority groups, etc.

2. We made special demographic materials available to the Council of Churches of Wilmington and New Castle County in connection with its inner city parish program. Met with interested groups and individuals to help interpret this material.

3. We made a number of studies and reports relating to community problems and services. Among these are:

Recommendations of the Committee on the State of Delaware's Responsibility in the Field of Recreation

A Community Service Plan for the Aged in Northern Delaware

Report of the East Side Study Committee

A Group Care Service for Older Children in Delaware

4. We worked with the State Department of Public Welfare in its Pilot Project in the Rehabilitation of Dependent Families of Delaware.

Agency cooperation with other agencies and organizations:

A major and continuing purpose of the Welfare Council of Delaware is cooperation with agencies and organizations. It is extremely difficult to say which of these contacts is specifically aimed at implementing the Task. However, the following seem to be most closely related:

1. Furnishing and/or interpreting demographic materials to a wide variety of social agency, church, school, and other community groups such as the police and physical planning bodies.

2. Working with inter-agency, study, and special project committees.

Here Welfare Council representatives have their best opportunity to help groups understand each other's functions.

3. Providing data, consultation, and other services to individuals, social agencies, and other groups interested in community social welfare problems.

New programs and activities considered for initiation:

1. The Welfare Council of Delaware will begin work on the second phase of its "Community Profile." The demographic profile, though it must be kept-up-to-date, is well on the way to being completed. The next step will be a social profile, aimed at inventorying community social problems, their incidence and location and community services, their kind and extent. The Council's Research Department will be enlarged.

2. Working much more intensively with the City of Wilmington and community groups interested in the community urban renewal program.

3. Working more intensively on community health services problems.

Wilmington Housing Authority

Approximate number of people served:

1773 families

Implementing the Task through previously established programs:

1. We continue to give assistance to and to cooperate with the Price Run Community Council in matters affecting the neighborhood in which three of our public housing projects are located. Examples: elimination of traffic hazards; provision of better street lighting and signs; elimination of illegal activities; combating juvenile delinquency.

2. We continue to cooperate with the school "visiting teacher" respecting the provision of information necessary for her work with parents and guardians of students living in our projects.

3. We continue to publish in school-related activities Authority tenant bulletins.

4. We continue cooperation with neighborhood schools on specific problems, as requested.

5. We continue to cooperate with the Department of Public Safety regarding the elimination of illegal activities in the neighborhoods.

6. We continue to cooperate with numerous public and private agencies and individuals in providing decent, standard low-rent housing for those in need of housing.

7. We give personal assistance in the organization of several new neighborhood associations and councils, and to city-wide federation of such organizations and councils.

New programs initiated to implement the Task:

A social worker was added to the Staff of the Wilmington Housing Authority in the capacity of Tenant and Community Relations

Worker. She works directly with the tenants with the purpose of upgrading the occupants of the low-rent housing projects. It is her primary job to work with problem families by assisting with their budgeting; offering suggestions and solutions to their areas of difficulty by checking with the various social agencies engaged in the case; referring them when necessary to the agency best equipped to handle the particular problem.

The social worker has thus far received help for tenants in financial difficulty from the Twenty-Five Neediest Families Fund, has arranged to procure furniture for others in need through the Salvation Army, and has secured food from her church's supply of surplus food for distribution among Project families. In addition to periodic visits to established Project residents, she visits with newly arrived families with a firm resolve to help in any way possible.

Agency cooperation with other agencies and organizations:
The agency cooperated with—
1. the Price Run Community Council in matters affecting the neighborhood such as eliminating traffic hazards, provision of better street lighting, and working together to devise ways and means of combating juvenile delinquency;
2. the Board of Education by working closely with the schools in the neighborhood of our projects, furnishing information needed on specific problems and regarding the students living in our projects;
3. the Department of Public Safety regarding the elimination of illegal activities in our neighborhoods;
4. With other public and private agencies too numerous to mention.

Programs and activities to be continued:
All that seem necessary or desirable.

New programs and activities considered for initiation:
No specific programs or activities are currently being considered. Such programs will be developed as the opportunity or need arises.

Rho Chapter—The National Sorority of Phi Delta Kappa

Approximate number of people served:
75 children
76 youth
225 adults
75 families

Implementing the Task through previously established programs:
1. Operating a Service Center. Rho chapter is interested in being of service by helping people help themselves. Plans have been made to operate a "Service Center" in the community fringing on the redevelopment area.

In teams of eight, members of the sorority made a house-to-house survey in order to find out some of the needs and anxieties of the people. Open-ended questions were asked, such as "What do you like about your neighborhood?" "What changes would you like to see made?" Many liked the neighborhood because the people were friendly. Many felt the effect of demolition. Many were afraid to walk in the streets. Some needed help with using surplus foods to best advantage.

2. As a follow-up of the survey, Rho Chapter co-sponsored a workshop with Drew-Pyle and Stubbs Schools P.T.A.'s held on Thursday, March 21, 1963 at Drew School. This was the first activity of our "Service Center."

New programs initiated to implement the Task:
1. A one-day, Chapter sponsored, youth conference was held at St. Matthews Church. Leadership training was emphasized.
2. Rho Chapter presented a human relations program. The theme was "Wilmington Moves Forward." A panel discussed "Job Opportunities." A question and answer period followed.
3. Operating the Service Center described above.

Agency cooperation with other agencies and organizations:
The agency cooperated with—
1. the Eastside Community Council;
2. Peoples Settlement (Rho chapter became a member of the Association. Several members met regularly with the executive committee of Peoples Settlement and supported the community program that the Settlement initiated);
3. Drew-Pyle and Stubbs School P.T.A.'s in planning and presenting a workshop session. The following areas were emphasized:
   a. planning meals using surplus commodities;
   b. budgeting—stretching the family dollar while making the home comfortable and attractive;
   c. improving family relationship (a film);
4. the Recreation Committee at Delaware State Hospital by giving and supervising a Christmas party and a June party for the patients in one of the buildings;
5. the Recreation Committee at Gov. Bacon Health Center by giving and supervising a birthday party for the boys and girls in one of the buildings;
6. the Chapter also gave standardized tests for scholarship awards.

Programs and activities to be continued:
Rho Chapter will continue—
1. the Service Center;
2. our service at Gov. Bacon Health Center;
3. our service at The Delaware State Hospital:
4. standardized tests for scholarship awards.

New programs and activities considered for initiation:
Other activities for the "Service Center," probably panels or forums. (The workshop was very well received.)

Suggestions and comments regarding continued cooperative action:
1. Continue meetings of Community Group on Changing Neighborhoods.

2. Continue well-planned meetings of the larger group. Probably one where organizations might report on new action taken; two similar to the ones held this year.

Presbyterian Church of Our Savior

Approximate number of people served:
100 children
100 youth
300 adults
200 families

Implementing the Task through previously established programs:

1. Study Hall Program: Monday and Thursday evenings 7:30-9:00 with tutors from suburban churches, to aid Junior High and Senior High students through individual counseling and through use of our church library of 2000 books which includes many textbooks on different subjects.

2. Stewardship Co-op: An effort on the part of the church to secure full- or part-time employment primarily for drop-outs, but in many instances also for high school students, thus providing them with income and help in building a definite sense of responsibility and self-respect, while providing them with an opportunity for automatic stewardship on the basis of hours worked.

3. Music Program: Our Music Director is operating four separate choirs in our church program: Primary (grades 1-3), Junior (grades 4-6), Teen-age (junior high and senior high), and Adult. This program includes piano and voice lessons for all ages and organ lessons for adults. The rates are nominal so as to keep costs at a level that all can afford.

4. Sports Program: This program includes softball, basketball, volley ball, putt-putt golf, and touch football. It provides many opportunities for fellowship, learning the meaning of good sportsmanship, and working together with others as a team. It is open to all our youth and adults in the community.

5. Summer Program: An extensive ten-week program for all ages from primary age to adult. It includes mass participation and small group emphasis, directed by a special summer staff brought in for this purpose.

6. Vacation Church School: A ten-day period of worship and Bible study for groups from primary age to adult. It is led by church members and summer staff.

7. Spiritual Retreats: Periods of from one to three days spent by individuals in study and quiet retreat designed for spiritual nourishment and understanding.

8. Choir Retreats: Periods of two days when the teen-age and adult choirs usually go to another church where the time is spent in singing special hymns, part-practicing (soprano, alto, tenor, bass, etc.), worship, and recreation.

9. Work Caravans: Periods of from three to five days when communicants-in-training and communicant members travel to various

churches in other parts of the country to learn how the church witnesses in various types of communities and situations; and to perform some work project *with* groups from the churches involved, such as painting, furniture repair, and various other jobs. Time is also provided for visiting and sight-seeing, particularly of a cultural nature.

New programs initiated to implement the Task:
1. Music Program: This program as described above was begun in Sept. 1962.
2. College Bulletins and Catalogs: One entire section of our study hall library was set up for college bulletins, catalogs, and brochures, in an effort to keep the aspect of a college education before our young people at all times and to encourage them to think along these lines.
3. Vacation Choir School: A period of ten days toward the end of the summer, similar to the Vacation Church School, except that the emphasis is on music and choir work for all ages.

Agency cooperation with other agencies and organizations:
The church cooperated with—
1. the Presbytery of New Castle;
2. the Council of Churches through Youth Employment Service;
3. the Department of Public Welfare by aiding in furnishing information where possible, and food where necessary;
4. the Wilmington Housing Authority by participating in inspection tours;
5. the Kingswood Community Center through program cooperation and coordination;
6. the Price Run Community Council by participating in community projects;
7. the Ninth Ward Protestant Parish Council by attempting to coordinate programs;
8. the Prisoner's Aid Society by counseling released prisoners;
9. the Wilmington Police Department by attempting to aid in teen-age gang control;
10. the Family Court by counseling for families in need;
11. the Municipal Court by counseling for persons involved in court cases;
12. the Welfare Council of Delaware by participating in Christmas Basket Program;
13. the Traveler's Aid Society by directing and aiding transients to proper agency;
14. the Vocational Rehabilitation by working with handicapped individuals in counseling and direction;
15. the Opportunity Center by obtaining our own printing from this agency to aid the handicapped.

Programs and activities to be continued:
Study hall program, music program, sports program, summer program, vacation church school, vacation choir school, caravans, retreats, worship services, Sunday church schools.

New programs and activities considered for initiation:
Boy Scouts of America, Girl Scouts, scholarship fund for prospective college students in need, more adult programming, Women's Association (in process of organization at present), men's council, adult education.

St. Matthew's Community Center

Approximate number of people served:
62 children
136 youth
47 adults
121 families

Implementing the Task through previously established programs:
1. Discussion Groups—inviting speakers to address our young people.
2. Conferences with parents and children for discussion of personal problems.
3. Active participation in league sports—basketball and bowling—to meet and compete with various denominational groups in New Castle County to further goodwill, sportsmanship, and fellowship.
4. Referrals to proper service agencies and potential employers.

New programs initiated to implement the Task:
1. Children's Choir: One which will not only assist in our church, but will eventually also perform throughout the community.
2. Boy Scout Troop: Will serve the community in many ways through their volunteer services.
3. Teen-age Club Groups: Formed to discuss topics of the day to further the participants' character development, and to enable them to discern both sides of any situation. These groups discussed domestic as well as world problems.

Agency cooperation with other agencies and organizations:
The Center cooperated with the
1. Family Court and the Youth Services Commission—conferences on individuals known to all of us.
2. Through the Conference of Eastside Agencies (Peoples Settlement, Christina Community Center, Walnut YMCA, Walnut YWCA, Wilmington Public Schools, Board of Park Commissioners, St. Michael's Nursery, Central Baptist Church), we try to prevent the overlapping of programs; to offer suggestions as a group to each other so that we might fill any gaps in programs which exist in our locale; and to sponsor specific activities, youth conferences, work camp, housing discussions.

Programs and activities to be continued:
Personal counseling, group discussions, children's choir, intra-agency sponsorship of programs, family counseling, referrals to proper service agency.

New programs and activities to be continued:
1. At the present time St. Matthew's, through its Board of Direc-

tors, is making a survey of the needs in our immediate community to determine the program for the coming year. It is our hope after this survey to make available a program which will meet the needs of our community without duplicating services now offered. We are now contacting the other agencies in our vicinity so that we might locate a gap in services if one exists.

2. Tentatively, we anticipate a program directed to teen-agers and young adults with the emphasis on job procurement, working with school drop-outs, and other activities which we hope will make them better adults and enable them to adjust to our changing community.

YMCA of Wilmington and New Castle County, Delaware

Implementing the Task through previously established programs:

The small, purposeful Gra-Y club program for boys in grades four through six was continued at the Drew, Pyle, Stubbs, Elbert, Dunleith, and North East schools. This program provides an opportunity for the members to develop inter-personal relations and provides an outlet for physical energies.

New programs initiated to implement the Task:

1. Y-Indian Guides: A group was started in both the Highlands and Shortlidge schools. The purpose of this program is to foster companionship between fathers and their 6-8 year old sons.

2. Gra-Y club programs were started in Highlands, Lore, Shortlidge, and Williams schools for boys in grades 4-6.

3. A summer Day Camp was conducted in Rockford Park for boys and girls of the city. Both boys and girls between the ages of six and eleven participated.

Agency cooperation with other agencies and organizations:

1. The YMCA cooperated with the Wilmington Public Schools in the use of school buildings and in the employment of school personnel for the supervision and instruction of the Gra-Y Physical Fitness Program.

2. The YMCA supplied the overall supervision of the program, manuals for club work, and texts for the Physical Fitness curriculum.

3. One-day camp was conducted in cooperation with the Kingswood Community Center. The YMCA and Kingswood worked together in planning the program, enrolling campers, training and supervision of staff and financing the program.

Programs and activities to be continued:

1. Subject to the continued cooperation of the schools, the Gra-Y, Y-Indian Guide programs will be continued in eight schools where they are now being conducted.

2. The Day Camping program at Rockford Park will also be continued.

New programs and activities considered for initiation:

1. The YMCA would establish the Gra-Y program in Cedar Hill

and Harlan schools if these schools so desire, and financial support and leadership are available.

2. The YMCA would also consider some type of program for boys in the first, second, and third grades.

Suggestions and comments regarding continued cooperative action:
1. Continued meetings of COMING (Community Group on Changing Neighborhoods).
2. Quarterly meetings of four subgroups representing the four geographical areas of the city—north, south, east, and west.

Current School-Community Action Programs

The school year 1963-64 marked the fifth year (the second Project follow-up year) of staff effort to improve human relations education. A sampling of experiences planned for fall workshop in each school, representing the launching of the in-service education program for the year, reveals the continued efforts of the staff to build sound working relations with the community agencies.

Several staffs visited one or more agencies or invited agency representatives to confer with the staffs in their schools during the first week of September.

Mrs. Kathryn Y. Hazeur, Drew-Pyle schools principal, describes the work of her staff during fall workshop:

> "Boys" is the name of one project being carried on in Drew and Pyle schools this year. It was conceived during the time that we were reorganizing our schools on a unit level basis.
>
> While this reorganization was in progress, girls were easily distributed among the classes for unit level purposes. They fell neatly into all categories of achievement, cooperation, and aspiration. Boys, on the other hand, fell towards the bottom of the scale. A disproportionate number were identified as underachievers with poor motivation or behavior problems.
>
> Now that the picture was clear, we could not ignore it. Something had to be done for our boys. It would be sinful in the face of the many opportunities available to these boys for us to do nothing about getting them ready for the good life ahead.
>
> We had no pat answers for this problem. We started with the fall workshop. Two and one-half days were spent exploring and sensitizing teachers to the problem. Resource specialists from the community dealing with boys were called in. A court probation officer told us about the boys who came in conflict with the law. The physical education supervisor for our schools told us about the apron-string-type boys. The school social worker told us about the boys from fatherless homes. The school psychologist spoke about the underachieving boys. A group worker from the YMCA talked about the regular guys.

We had a local psychologist in private practice explore with us some of the problems we face with boys. He upset our "tidiness-dress-up" ideas. He felt that clothing and dressing-up were not natural interests of boys between the ages of nine and thirteen. He felt the boys would naturally fall into patterns of neatness near the close of the junior high school.

He felt that too many teachers pressed for a mold, a typical child. He felt that a good way to change a child's behavior was to let him feel and know that there was support and concern for him as an individual. He also felt that teachers should be aware of a child's need to let off steam or hostility.

Following are implications that developed from the two days' sessions:

1. We decided to show our concern for the feelings of our boys by giving them honor and leadership positions in the classroom and the school (such as room messengers and office helpers).

2. We planned to acquaint the boys with men who are assuming a constructive role in our community. We thought we would go beyond our usual reference list of doctors, dentists, and lawyers. This time we would seek storekeepers, barbers, and firemen.

3. We planned to invite the boy leaders from the junior high school to come over and help orientate our boys for the next step.

4. We decided to take a close look at our reading program to see if the boys were having ample time for readiness or if we were killing them off with impossible and laborious reading tasks.

To date, our program has gotten off to a fine start. The director of a settlement house, formerly a probation officer, and another male staff member come to us two hours a week to counsel with twenty-four boys in groups of six. The editor of the *Defender* newspaper is searching for the time to help. We are lining up other local persons to come and help. We have quite a job ahead of us, but we feel that this is not an impossible task.

The Community at Work in the Schools

Bringing the community into the schools is as important as taking the schools into the community. The world of childhood is one world. Community resources being utilized by the elementary schools of the city reveal the extent of continued effort to firmly root the gains achieved in the Project.

A sampling of cooperative effort reported by the principals is revealing.

George Gray School

Brandywine Methodist Church is cooperating with the schools to assist where financial needs exist.

The Girls' Club of Wilmington is providing a very fine after-school program on Mondays and Wednesdays for the girls of Gray School.

The Trinity Methodist Church has just opened an evening study hall for pupils in the neighborhood of the church.

The *Park Commission of Wilmington* sponsors the Evening Recreation Program which draws three hundred participants. They meet twice a week, on Tuesdays and Thursdays, from 6:30 to 9:00 P.M.

North East School

The *Hanover Women's Association* provided several volunteer teacher aides and contributed clothing, magazines, phonograph records, a picture for the library, $18.50 for lunch money, toys, smocks for art classes, books, games, and five tickets to the National Ballet presented at the Play House on November 9, 1963.

The *First Unitarian Church* contributed magazines, smocks for art classes, three volunteer teacher aides.

The *YWCA,* Walnut Street Branch provided adult evening classes meeting on Monday evenings, 7:30 - 9 P.M., a Y-Teen Club, staffed by a Y-Teen Director and a volunteer school sponsor (after school).

The *YMCA* organized the Gra-Y, staffed by the Boys' Work Secretary and the school sponsors (after school).

North East School P.T.A. provided leadership for the Boy Scouts of America Troop 961.

Lore School

A number of agencies are contributing specifically through services to the children of Lore School.

West End Neighborhood House—Probably the most recent manifestation of this cooperative effort was our faculty meeting of Monday, November 11. Under the leadership of a group of teachers who recognized the need for an increased understanding of the services available to their boys and girls, members of the staff of the West End Neighborhood House were invited to address the Lore School faculty. They presented a complete outline of the available services and invited our suggestions as to how these services might be improved and better adapted to the needs of the children as we see them. The response was most favorable and there were a great many questions asked by teachers. Special interest was expressed in the new study room which the Neighborhood House provided. It is equipped with reference books and will be available to children between 5:30 and 7:00 P.M. each weekday evening. Some teachers felt that the hours were less than ideal but it was the consensus that they were the only ones that could be worked out considering the limitations under which the Neighborhood House functions. There was also some very helpful discussion of the matter of homework in public elementary schools in the city.

YMCA and YWCA—Another agency which is working closely with the Lore School as well as other schools in our community is the YMCA. There is much evidence of entire interaction and complete cooperation in the efforts of this agency and its sister agency, the YWCA, in the programs which they are providing. We have a Gra-Y for the 5th- and 6th-grade boys which meets two afternoons a week from 3:15 to 4:15 P.M. in our gymnasium. A member of our staff who inaugurated this excellent program last year is again in charge of it this year.

The Y-Lassies will again be conducting a similar program for girls one day a week. This is to begin shortly.

Junior League of Wilmington—During the 1962-63 school year, we had the valuable and unstinting assistance of two entirely dependable reading aides from the Junior League of Wilmington. Although this program could not possibly fill the need for a trained reading teacher, it was of great value to a number of youngsters. This year, the Junior League has sent us five volunteers. We have had a preliminary meeting and some of these ladies are already working with groups of children. We are placing major emphasis in this program on intermediate-grade children. Many of these are victims of the oversized classes in which they have been placed since entering school. Their teachers on each grade level have been prevented from giving the individual attention essential in reading instruction. It is hoped that these fine, conscientious Junior Leaguers will be able to give many of these children the boost they need to prevent their becoming the school drop-outs of a few years hence.

Other Agencies—In addition to the above-mentioned programs, there is an open line of communication between the school and all social agencies of the community and a variety of activities results from the spirit of cooperation. The Boy Scout and Girl Scout organizations are in frequent contact with the teachers and the principal, and troops and packs meet regularly in the school or nearby.

Several churches in this area maintain study halls and/or recreational programs, the sponsors of which often contact teachers for consultation and vice versa.

The Lore School principal is a member of and in regular contact with the two community councils serving this section of the city. There is much cause for gratitude in this area of school-community cooperation although still "we have miles to go before we sleep."

Highlands and Cedar Hill Schools

YMCA—At Cedar Hill School, the YMCA is initiating an after-school recreational program two days a week. A Y staff member is in charge and is working with boys in grades 4, 5, and 6. At Highlands, the same agency is offering a similar program two days a week for the same age group.

YWCA—The YWCA is offering an after-school program for girls of the upper grades at Highlands once a week. Cedar Hill children are using both the Boys Club and the Girls Club extensively; in fact, Cedar Hill is their best customer!

We appreciate the many, many services rendered by these fine agencies.

Opportunity School (for Trainable Mentally Retarded Children)

Bryan Dance Studio—The head of the Bryan Dance Studio and eight assistants, all of whom are certified Red Cross swimming instructors, volunteer their services for a half day each Friday morning to teach the children swimming at the YWCA.

Lay women—render the following service: One gives us a whole day a week in which she teaches music to all the children in small groups. One is a volunteer in the school every day, all day. She takes the younger children to the bathroom. Another gives us two hours a week to help with the class which has the wheel-chair children. A sophomore at the University of Delaware is giving us two hours a week of volunteer help in one of the class-rooms.

Drew-Pyle Schools

Peoples Settlement—The Director and Group Worker of Peoples Settlement work two hours a week in our school giving personal counseling to boys. The Director works with boys who are reasonably well motivated but need to reach higher aspiration levels. The Group Worker works with boys who do not have a male adult living in the home.

The Wilmington Garden Club—sponsors: (a) Conservation Project relating to the farm; (b) Beautification Project with individual progress Class pupils and the Student Council.

YMCA—The Boys' Group Secretary at the YMCA meets once a month with a group of boys from each grade level (beginning with the third grade). He also meets with each group of boys the remaining three weeks in club activities at the Y. This program begins at the close of school. The Secretary has had a tremendous influence on many of our boys. His character-building program is well defined and fits into our school program. From time to time he drops in, eats lunch with the boys, and talks with their teacher.

Shortlidge School

YMCA—Our gym teacher (volunteer) has a Gra-Y program on Tuesday afternoons, 3 P.M. to 3:45 P.M., and Wednesday afternoons 3 P.M. to 4:30 P.M. for fourth, fifth, and sixth grades in our school gymnasium.

Unitarian Church—Six member of the Unitarian Church Service Committee are working as teacher aides this year.

One of the important accomplishments of the Project has been the opening of school doors. When the community goes into the schools, problems are shared and individuals "identify" with the children of the city.

Section

V

Follow-Up Projects of Significance

*Among the many follow-up projects of The
Three-Year Experimental Project on Schools in
Changing Neighborhoods being developed in
the elementary schools, two of unusual
significance are reported in Section V.*

*"A Stitch in Time" describes the first effort
of a preventive nature which has occurred
in Wilmington. The Highlands School, one of
three elementary schools which did not
participate during the period of formal study,
took a long, hard look at its neighborhood
and decided during 1963-64 to keep it the
desirable place it was.*

*"The Language Development of Disadvantaged
Children," a study by North East School, may
well make a significant contribution to
education. Begun in 1961-62 to meet an
acute need of children blocked in potential
academic and human achievement because
of serious language handicaps resulting from
deprivation, a first year progress report,
1962-63, has been prepared by the consultant,
Dr. Agnes Snyder, and is included in
this section.*

331

chapter
14

A Stitch in Time

Unless change occurring in a neighborhood is sudden and dramatic, residents seldom become aware of the beginnings of change. Yet every neighborhood inevitably changes over a period of years. Creeping blight is harder to detect than is a sudden danger to a pleasant, comfortable neighborhood. Such potential dangers as a change in zoning ordinances which might permit commercial establishments in residential neighborhoods for the first time, or the conversion of single-family to multi-family homes are so obvious that residents are immediately aroused to action. The little pockets of blight, tucked away in unseen corners of a pleasant, wholesome neighborhood, are usually unknown to most of the residents. But it is the little pocket that is the potential spreader of the blight germ through an otherwise desirable neighborhood.

Prevention is easier than cure. It is prevention that is the motivation of the principal of Highlands School in initiating school-community action. Dr. Agnes Snyder, consultant to the Project, has recorded the initial efforts of a school community determined to maintain its fine quality of living.

Developments continuing during 1963-64 indicate that this report is but the opening chapter in what will be a truly memorable saga of a fine community determined to stay that way.

Highlands School Community Looks to the Future

My occasional visits to the Highlands School during the past three years always left me with the feeling of a good life for children being lived in that school. There is something about the broad hallway as you enter that "looks happy." There is an effect of roominess, of quiet cheer. A lot of it comes from the colorful paintings on the walls done by the children, different on every one of my visits. There are more of them in the principal's office.

> As you well know, many changes have taken place in the city of Wilmington in the last decade. It is a well-known fact that even the most stable neighborhoods can be expected to change in a ten-year period. Highlands School is completing its first decade.
>
> During the current school year, the Highlands family has been studying changes in our school district. Exciting possibilities are opening up which, if met by cooperative action, will help us keep the Highlands district the desirable place in which to live that it now is.

Of course, I accepted the invitation. That a school is part of its environment and, to be effective, must be part and parcel of its problems and resources is axiomatic in my education philosophy. Besides, I had become deeply involved in the Project. I had sat in on many meetings in which the schools and the social agencies sought common ground in re-enforcing each other in their efforts to overcome the blight that had fallen on so many communities—deterioration of housing, delinquency, and all the other ills accompanying rapid changes in the population of urban centers.

But this had a different ring. It was sounded in the phrase " . . . help us keep the Highlands district the desirable place in which to live that it now is." Here were perceptiveness, foresight, appreciation of the present, sensitivity to the total panorama of inevitable change, and dangers to be averted. "A stitch in time?" I asked myself.

Now for the luncheon. Being the first to arrive, I sat near the back of the room as inconspicuously as I could. Presently, Miss deHan came in and welcomed me. I watched the children setting the table and noted the care with which they arranged flowers here and there, carefully choosing this arrangement for one place and that for another.

The guests began to arrive. It was an impressive assembly of community-minded leaders:

The Assistant Suprintendent in Charge of Elementary Education, Wilmington Public Schools

The Director of the Youth Aid, Wilmington Bureau of Police

The Director of the Wilmington Housing Authority

A Staff Associate of the Welfare Council

Highlands School Parent-Teacher Association Officers

The Captain of the Wilmington Bureau of Police

The City Planner, Wilmington Committee on Zoning and Planning

A Lay Resident of the Neighborhood

The Director, Delaware Region, The National Conference of Christians and Jews

A State Senator, Resident of the Neighborhood

The Superintendent of the Wilmington Public Schools

A Priest from St. Ann's Roman Catholic Church

The Gra-Y Development Leader, Young Men's Christian Association

The Director of Personnel, Joseph Bancroft Company

The Pastor of the Westminster Presbyterian Church

Here we were, a group representing home, school, church, social agency, industry, government, housing, law enforcement. I was appreciative of being part of this group. I reflected that if we learn how to bring the talent represented in such a group as this into constructive action, the effects will be felt on a larger scale than just in the community on which attention is centered.

Luncheon was served. I was amused at the way, without formality, we "fell to" on the delicious luncheon the cafeteria staff had prepared. After luncheon, Miss deHan welcomed the group and introduced those present.

Miss deHan referred to the Project, administered by Dr. Crosby for four years. While the Project was formally closed June, 1962, at the end of the three years, it is continuing in a number of neighborhoods, Miss deHan said. She went on to indicate that while the Highlands neighborhood was not one undergoing the dramatic changes that characterized many others, there were new indications that the stability of even this neighborhood was being shaken.

Two Signs of Change

The signs of change referred to by Miss deHan were found in two major areas: (1) the condemnation of a row of houses in the 1700 block of Union Street, and (2) the sale of some and the demolition of other homes in the Rockford-Kentmere areas. Because Miss deHan was sensitive to the effects such changes would have on the children of Highlands School, she was having a study made of the two situations and a record kept of their development.

Miss deHan briefly sketched the historical background of the community and gave a vivid picture of it as it had been during the period of the old Bancroft Mills. The Bancrofts had created a typical English mill village with houses provided and kept up by the management and with many welfare features for the workers. Now with the transfer of the mills to the Indian Head Company, a more modern regime was under way. In particular, research has been expanded, and this requires more buildings. To meet this need, some of the housing now occupied by the mill workers needed to be demolished.

Miss deHan spoke of the fine cooperative relations between the Mills and the school both under the Bancroft and the Indian Head management. She expressed her belief that all with a stake in maintaining a good, enjoyable neighborhood would work together to that end. She said that she had called this meeting to pool the thinking of those living or working in the Highlands area with that of those who could view the local problem in a broader setting.

The Children Speak

She then spoke of the importance of involving children in community concerns and spoke of the special study made by the fourth grade in connection with the study of Delaware as part of the school curriculum. She introduced three members of the fourth grade who presented the following reports.

> Good afternoon, friends. As a fourth-grade pupil in Highlands School, I'm very happy you came to our school to hear of what's going on in our neighborhood.
> My name is Barbara D., and I thought I'd tell what we're studying in class about our school area. One of the sections we've been interested in is Rockford; another is Kentmere. These are two communities very close to Highlands, and many of the children who live there attend our school. Both Rockford and Kentmere are close to Bancroft Mills where textiles are dyed and treated. There are four streets there: Riddle Avenue, St. Helena's Road, Rockford Road, Ivy Road.
> Most of the people who live there work at Bancroft's. Some of their fathers did too, and even their grandfathers. They like living there because it is close to their work.
> Rockford and Kentmere are very historic parts of Wilmington. We've studied about what they were like long ago, and we thought you might like to hear a little about the history of these two communities. Janet G. will tell you about how they used to be.

Barbara nodded to Janet and sat down, while Janet proceeded:

> When the textile mills started along the Brandywine River back in the 1800's the workers lived close to them. One of the oldest mills was Riddle's. Later on it became part of Bancroft Mills.
> The Bancroft family came to Wilmington from England and

lived on the Bancroft Estate all around the mills. They built homes for the workers in the late 1800's; they started a kindergarten which is still operating. There was a store where groceries and household supplies were sold.

One of the most important buildings in Kentmere was the chapel. Services were held there, and other kinds of affairs, too. It was like a community hall. It was a place where the Company used to have its big Christmas party for all the mill families. Patriotic services were also observed in Riddle Chapel. This was a real gathering place for all the people in Kentmere and Rockford.

On one of our walks there this spring, our class saw where it used to be. It had been cleared away just a few months ago, since it hadn't been used for years.

The Bancroft family always took an interest in the workers and let them live in the Mills' houses at low rent. The Company kept up the houses well, and looked after the people. They had such a complete little neighborhood that they had many of their needs taken care of right in Rockford. There was even a school there— old No. 27.

As time went on, in the 1900's, the workers still lived in the houses, but changes took place. The school and the grocery store closed. The people could go in their cars to other places.

Now Rockford and Kentmere are changing again.

Virginia C. will tell you what is happening now.

Virginia responded:

Today, lots of things are happening in these two areas. Because the Bancroft Company, now owned by Indian Head Mills, is doing a lot of research and experimenting, they have to build research buildings. One of these has already been built. It is the Ban-Lon Center.

In Rockford, the houses on Ivy Road are still the same as they were, but on Rockford Road they are being closed. That's where the new experimental station will be.

We saw land in Kentmere being leveled off and cleared. Some say an apartment house is to be built there, but we are not certain about this.

I suppose when we're grown up, Rockford and Kentmere will look very different. All kinds of scientific work will be going on around the mill. More things like Ban-Lon, Everfast, Ever-Glaze, and Mini-Care will be worked out.

It has been interesting to see the changes taking place so close to school. We like to study about these things, and we hope our story has told you something of these changes near Highlands.

A Picture Report

The reports of the children were followed by slides taken of the neighborhood. Miss deHan made occasional clarifying comments. I saw Highlands School in relation to the neighboring Delaware Art Center and Sienna Hall, a Catholic boys' home. Some of the mill buildings, old and new, began to take on meaning—the retail mill store, the Ban-Lon Research Center, the old water tank. Beautiful scenic views appeared, including the creek and the wooded hillsides. I saw streets—Ivy Road, St. Helen's Road, and others—some industrial and some residential; historic buildings—the Chapel, the Bancroft homes—suggested a past in which many a human story lay buried.

After the pictures we talked over what we had seen and heard. I was glad when the Superintendent commented on the clarity of the children's reports and the poise with which they were given. It was good, too, to hear him say that if changes are imminent, *now* is the time that the right steps be taken.

Miss deHan commented on the pleasant relations that the school had held both in the past with the Bancroft management and now with the Indian Head Company. She mentioned the history of the mill, which Mr. McIntyre, President of the Company, had contributed to the study the school was making. She then called on Mr. Whiteside, Personnel Director, to give his thoughts on the changes taking place.

Bancroft Mills Explains Plans

The Personnel Director of the Bancroft Mills reenforced the Superintendent's remarks on the children's reports, especially mentioning their fidelity to facts. He said that the school would not lose through the housing changes since many of the houses would now be sold to the residents. Some demolition was necessary, he said, because of the need for space for more research buildings. He said that research had always been carried on at the Bancroft Mills and that Indian Head was simply experimenting further in dyeing and glazing in the interest of finding better processes. With reference to Riddle Chapel, he said that for many years the main function it had served was as a place for the annual Christmas party, but with the present 1700 employees it was no longer adequate for even this. In the meantime its age had brought need for so many repairs that it did not seem worthwhile to make the necessary expenditures and so it had been razed. Mr. Whiteside closed by saying that nothing definite had been decided about the demolition, except in the case of a group of houses on Rockford Road adjacent to the present research center.

Miss deHan then stated the two-fold purpose of the present meeting: To give information and to consider whether or not a neighborhood council might be formed to help preserve the significant features of this impressive neighborhood. She asked for discussion.

The Assistant Superintendent in Charge of Elementary Education spoke of the contrast between the Highlands community and so many of the city areas in that it did not present the truly formidable problems so many did. She mentioned the rich natural and cultural resources of the community. Brandywine Park, for example, she said, was the best in the city for children to enjoy. She spoke of the beautiful setting of Kentmere and how hard it was for people to move out of it. But, she said, changes were in the wind. Offices were moving into Delaware Avenue nearby. She closed by saying that we must keep these good Mills families and not let things happen to them.

Recommendations for Action and Next Steps

The discussion then became general and centered around housing problems. There was a general feeling that unfit buildings on Union Street should be demolished but that as far as possible good housing in the Mills area should be preserved. One participant asked, "What next?" The Assistant Superintendent suggested that a survey being made by the Welfare Council be studied as soon as it would be completed, and that on the basis of this, the group might wish to come together again in the fall to do some further planning.

Here was a school that was interwoven in all aspects of its community. The luncheon, bringing together representatives of all the forces acting upon the life of people of a community, was a meaningful beginning of a future deeply rooted in the ideals and the aspirations of the past and present.

Quotations from a letter from the principal of Highlands School reveal that follow-up steps in "A Stitch in Time" are being taken.

> At our P.T.A. Executive Committee meeting on October 8, some rather exciting things happened. First of all, the members decided to encourage, promote, and participate fully in our Highlands community study. The theme for our year will be *The Highlands Community: Yesterday, Today, Tomorrow*.
>
> As a group we shall start by having our November meeting devoted to a presentation by the City Planner, the Director of the Board of Health, and the Personnel Director of Bancroft Company on the current situation both city-wide and in the immediate Highlands neighborhood.
>
> From that opening drive, we hope for study groups. One will write a history of our area and collect significant mementos of the past. One member has pictures from a Bancroft Company magazine published in her grandfather's time. Another group will concentrate on restoration activities in Rockford and Kentmere. A third will study ways of preventing deterioration, awakening community consciousness, and studying zoning and other matters of immediate concern.

We hope to see these small groups in action from November to March when we will bring together our efforts and report to the general P.T.A.

It was suggested that retired employees, elderly residents of the neighborhood, and concerned lay people be invited to join in our undertaking.

The Language Development of
Disadvantaged Children

During The Three-Year Experimental Project on Schools in Changing Neighborhoods the staff of the North East School became increasingly concerned with the language handicaps of its children. One of the significant findings of the Project was the identification of handicaps resulting from the inability of economically deprived youngsters to grow in command of their native language—a handicap resulting from deprivation and lack of experience. The staff became convinced that without greater competence in the English language, children of deprivation would forever remain on the lowest rung of the economic ladder. North East School decided to do something about this.

During the last year of formal study in the Project, which closed in June 1962, the staff of North East School developed a project design for its subsequent language study. Dr. Agnes Snyder was appointed consultant to the staff whose work would be developed under the leadership of its principal.

The first progress report, prepared by Dr. Snyder, follows. Readers of the report will be interested in the setting of the language study, for Dr. Snyder has interwoven her story with the total life of the school.

Emphasis on Language

Background: An Adventure in Human Relations

In the spring of 1962 the Wilmington Three-Year Experimental Project On Schools In Changing Neighborhoods was drawing to its official close. Schools participating in the project were concerned that the continuity of those fruitful years should not be broken. Understandings, processes, techniques, and materials developed cooperatively were there for further building.

What should be the next steps? As each school proceeded according to its specific needs within the framework of general principles and processes as developed in the Project, future activities would necessarily vary among the schools. At North East School there was no question in the minds of all that the greatest academic handicap under which the children in this school labored was their inadequacy in language both spoken and written.

Planned as part of the Riverside low-income housing development in north east Wilmington off Governor Printz Boulevard, the school opened its doors for the first time in September 1960 just after the first residents had moved into their new homes. Everything was new—school, homes, and community. The 505 children were all new to each other; so were most of the 15 members of the faculty. The school was integrated with 20 per cent of the children white and 80 per cent Negro.

The physical surroundings in the homes were good. All that modern construction could supply in the way of basic comforts and sanitation was there. But very few of the homes had much of cultural stimulation—books, interests, conversation—to raise the intellectual sights of the children. Their horizons were limited by the paucity of their environment, and their language was correspondingly inept.

To add to the problem, there were the children who had come from the Deep South. Many of them used a vernacular full of strange phrases and words puzzling to Delaware ears. This, with their beautiful soft voices and slurred words, often made them in the beginning unintelligible.

North East School was not in existence at the beginning of The Three-Year Experimental Project On Schools In Changing Neighborhoods in the fall of 1959, but had entered into it vigorously in the second year of the Project. Now, in the spring of 1962, the faculty saw the improvement of language as an imperative means for improving human relations. Faulty communication, it was realized, is the basis of much misunderstanding between individuals and groups, even among nations. Improving the language of the children of North East School was viewed as a contribution to improving their ability to get along with others and, small as it might seem, a contribution thereby to the total sum of human understanding.

There was, moreover, a very practical side to the problem. Unless the children gained command of English, there was little chance for academic success in any field. They would not be able to meet high school standards, and their chances for higher education were practically nil. And where would they be vocationally? With automation making unemployment one of the major problems today, and with the acquisition of skills so dependent on the use of language, it is incumbent on the elementary school to provide the foundation on which so much depends. So reasoned the staff of the North East School as it started planning next steps.

Planning Begins

The growing feeling of the faculty began taking form at a staff meeting on February 19, 1962. Dr. Crosby, Mrs. Wilson, and I had had a conference previously. We started this meeting by throwing up a few ideas for discussion. We emphasized what seemed to us basic in effective language teaching:

1. That improvement in language has its beginning in the strong desire of children to speak or write, and that this exists only when they have something to speak or write about.
2. That language cannot be taught as a thing apart, but must be linked with vital experiences.
3. That formal language drill is necessary, but comes after and not before the child has abundant experience in expressing himself freely.
4. That different occasions require different kinds of language ranging from the very informal to the formal, and that children should be taught to realize that appropriateness is important.

Out of the discussion that followed, certain agreements were reached. Basically, the teaching techniques which Dr. Vickery had started with the faculty and which the helping teachers were to continue were to be used throughout. The techniques involved the selection of a situation problematic in character and closely related to the lives of the children; the discussion or acting out, as seemed appropriate, of possible solutions; the formulation by the children of relevant generalizations.

Dr. Vickery had demonstrated the above technique in the use of pictures and in storytelling. The helping teachers during the rest of the year would demonstrate its use in other situations. All teachers would try out these different techniques gradually as the helping teachers demonstrated them and provided explanatory materials. For this purpose a resource bulletin was written by the helping teachers on each of the above techniques.

It was assumed that these techniques, requiring thinking at every step, would help in the improvement of language. Teaching straight thinking makes for clarity of language. Back of good thinking is the attempt to solve problems. Moving from the immediate problem to a generalization and eventually to a principle is the culmination of thinking. Language and thinking are inseparably related and interdependent.

Besides the emphasis on thinking it was agreed that every possible effort should be made to enlarge the experiences of the children through events at the school and through trips beyond the school borders. Experience is the basis of thinking and language.

All of this was general; the total school was involved. But it was also decided that some informal experimentation was in order so that records might be made of children's reactions and thus supply data for more specific study of the techniques involved.

Accordingly it was planned to study intensively the responses of six children in each of the following classes to one or more of the given techniques:

The teachers met with Dr. Crosby and me on March 15 to plan more specifically. The teachers mentioned some of the things that they had found effective in language study. They all felt the need to preserve children's spontaneity in the beginning even at the expense of good taste. Mrs. Jackson illustrated by telling how a child one day reacted to the game "I have a riddle." Mrs. Jackson sang to the children:

"I have a riddle, I have a riddle. Who says 'Quiet, please'?" whereupon a child replied:

"I know your riddle, I know your riddle. The teacher says 'Shut up'."

The teachers spoke of the effectiveness of placing a new picture on the bulletin board each morning and having children talk about it; of story telling; of role playing. Also, the importance of the casual and incidental situation in evoking children's language was indicated.

The meeting culminated in the following agreements:

1. The study should include language reactions of children a) to incidental situations; b) in planned situations.

2. Each teacher should write a little sketch of all that she knew about each of the six participants with emphasis on their characteristic language patterns.

3. Each teacher should record language used in incidental situations, being careful in every case to include—

full name of child;

full name of teacher;

the date and time of day;

the situation that brought forth the language; and

the actual language used.

4. Each teacher should use a picture for the first planned situation, but the pictures would not be uniform. Instead, they would be selected on the basis of the teacher's knowledge of the children's needs, problems, interests. The picture should be close to the children's own lives.

5. Agnes Snyder would record just what happened in each of the planned situations.

6. The group of four teachers would meet frequently to discuss progress.

7. A schedule would be made for both the meetings and the planned situations. It was decided to get the work under way Tuesday, March 20.

Experimental Tryout

Two of the planned situations were tried with each of the four experimental classes, one set in March and the other in April. My detailed notes are on file. The following gives just the highlights.

In the March tryouts different pictures were used. The picture used by Mrs. Jackson with her kindergarten group showed a boy kissing a girl, both splattered with mud, and a wheelbarrow of mud nearby. Mrs. Isakoff with her kindergarten group used a picture of a moving-day scene showing a girl seated near a packed barrel while a moving van stood outside. Mrs. Douglas with her interage group showed a picture with several boys repairing a scooter while one boy served them with cookies. Mrs. Elliott with the first grade had a picture of a family looking at a house, an automobile nearby, and a man on a ladder looking into the chimney.

In each case, the teacher and I sat with the little group in one part of the room while the rest of the children, unsupervised, worked at their tables. The arrangement was not good, for, although these North East children are unusually self-directing and cooperative, their normal activities created enough noise to make it very difficult to conduct discussions with the experimental groups. Even more of a handicap was the fact that I was not used to the children's voices and found it almost impossible to understand them. My responsibility was the recording of the discussion, and I found this a most difficult task indeed. Added to the foregoing I became so interested in the substance of the children's comments that I often lost track of their speech forms. However, by checking my notes afterwards with the teachers' recall of the discussions—the teachers understood the children much better than I did—I managed to make a fair record of what had been said.

Probably the most positive result of the first round of tryouts was the evidence of the efficacy of well-chosen pictures related to the children's daily lives in stimulating the free use of language. These conversations, in their spontaneity, were very revealing of the content of these children's minds, the imagery that occupies them, the raw material of their thinking, and hence of the language with which one must begin to build. Frequently there were expressions of warmth in family relations, especially toward babies and grandparents and much mentioning of family visiting. Punishment was taken as a matter of course and "beltings" were accepted as inevitable and without rancor. Bugs and roaches were just part of life and gave no undue concern. The same is true of "cops" and fights. Food and clothes loomed large as the desirable things in life. Standards of health, cleanliness, and behavior have obviously been given much attention in school because the children referred to them frequently in terms of "ought to" and gave them at least verbal acceptance. I carried away an impression of children who take the good with the bad in life, not unduly worried about unfavorable conditions, and, on the whole, getting a lot of enjoyment out of mere living.

Although much was derived from this tryout in the way of deeper understanding of the children's thinking and feeling, not much was gained as to the knowledge of their speech forms. Certainly it was obvious that trying to work with one group apart in a classroom with all the other children in the room on their own was just too difficult. Recording long-hand, likewise, could not be sufficiently accurate to supply basic data for the analysis of children's language. It was, therefore, decided to have the next series of tryouts made with small groups off to themselves in separate rooms and to have the discussions tape-recorded.

In the April tryouts it was agreed that each teacher should choose for discussion the situation she felt most suitable for her children at the time. The tryouts took place in the week before Easter and the children's minds were set on the coming holiday. The teachers went along with the children's immediate interest in guiding the discussions. Mrs. Isakoff led off with talking about the letter the children wished to write to accompany the Easter basket they were making for Mrs. Wilson. From this she moved to another picture discussion, showing a picture of a woman about to leave a room in which a boy was standing and a baby was in bed. Mrs. Jackson's children started talking about dyeing eggs in school and then led off into dyeing eggs at home and all kinds of home activities. Mrs. Elliott tried role playing, the children enacting a number of scenes involving salespeople and customers, most of the purchases centering around Easter. Mrs. Douglas used the story of Cinderella as an introduction to making wishes.

Toward the close of the activities, the teacher with each of the four groups led the children into wishes—for themselves, for members of the family, for teachers, for the school.

I took no notes, but depended on the tape recorder. Later the teachers and I listened to the recordings and tried to analyze what we heard. I was unable at the time to type or have typed transcripts from the recordings. At best I managed a summary of each. Mr. Russell, a speech teacher in the Wilmington Public Schools, cooperated by listening in on one of the recordings for the purpose of analyzing them from the standpoint of speech. He said that, in general, the weaknesses were the common ones of omission of endings, the *d* sound for *th,* and running words together. We noted, too, the frequent use of such expressions as *acting up, pair of clothes, beaned* (hit on the head), *not older yet, got it offen him.* But, again, as in the first series of tryouts, we were not successful in pinpointing language needs.

On the other hand, this series was rich in its revelation of the things these children really cared about, their genuine concerns. As in the first series, food and clothing, the necessities of life, were in the forefront. Again, grandparents and visiting figured largely. There was the same acceptance of the good with the bad, of punishment, and the same feeling of warmth in family relations. It seems highly significant that, as different as were the takeoffs in all of the discussions, invariably sooner or later these common elements of day-by-day living came to the fore.

As I listened to the recordings—four times in all—I became increasingly interested in the nature of the concepts these children had and the generalizations they formed. The following are a few samples:

Kindergarten: "bunny rabbits . . . new clothes . . . Easter baskets . . . dyeing eggs . . . Easter bunny coming to tell it's spring."

First grade: "a man dressed up in an Easter suit plays he's a bunny . . . Jesus hangs on a cross . . . baby born in Bethlehem . . . first holiday . . ."

Kindergarten: preacher—"buries people," teacher—"gives things to children."

Interage primary: wishing—"you take a wishbone out of a turkey and wish for something . . . you want something very bad . . . something you wish you had or wish to be but you never have it . . .;" college—"you go to play football."

The fact that most of the concepts were given in terms of use or action is indicative of the elementary character of these children's thinking. Similarly, the very limited meaning these concepts have—Easter and college for example—is evidence of the need for abundance of experience if formal education is to have any meaning for them.

The following illustrate the stage of ability to generalize the children had reached:

Kindergarten: "you heat milk bottles by putting them on the stove . . . when you dye eggs you put water on the stove to boil, put vinegar and dye in it . . . something bad happens when you 'act up.' "

First grade: "glad when Easter comes—the trees bloom, bugs are on the trees and it's spring and everything is happy . . . some people must die so other people can live."

Interage primary: "if you're younger you can do anything you want . . . big boys in college are bad, on the team they're real bad."

The generalizations about Easter and spring are probably echoes of immediate classroom experiences. The moralistic ones reflect what may be an all-too-ready willingness to verbalize in terms of the standards of behavior held up to them by adults. Funerals are frequent among these families and all the relatives, young and old, attend. Conversation at these may account for the sage generalization on death.

In the first year of the Project much attention had been paid to techniques for diagnosing children's attitudes toward self and others. In these tryouts I was glad to see the teachers use one of these, asking children to tell what they wish for. The following is illustrative:

For self

Kindergarten: "an Easter basket with candy . . . to be a teacher because I like to bring things . . . to kids like toys . . . airplane to fly in, to own an airplane . . . to be a preacher, to take people to the grave . . . when they're seventy . . . bicycle . . . a present, big box with a skirt and two blouses in it . . . two skirts . . ."

First grade: "to be a princess so I could tell people what to do, to boss people around . . . to be a doctor to keep people from getting sick . . . to know everybody in the whole world . . ."

Interage primary: "to be a princess . . . to have many mothers so I'd get more things . . . to have happy times . . . to do everything mother asks me . . . to be seventeen and go to dances . . . to be nine like my brother, to carry things from store . . . to be nine to play baseball but not on a team, they hit too hard . . . to go to college . . . that baby sister was older . . . to be a teacher . . ."

For Mother:

Kindergarten: "an Easter basket . . . a ballet dress . . . a typewriter . . . to move to a new house . . . diamond ring . . . necklace . . . pair of shoes . . . new clothes . . ."

For the family:

First grade: "wish my family was rich . . . money to buy more food, snacks, trading stamps, clothes, suits, chair covers . . ."

Interage primary: "that uncle would get out of the warehouse soon . . .

that cousin with broken arm would get out of hospital . . . that the family would play together . . ."

For Mrs. Wilson (principal):
Kindergarten: "an Easter basket . . . a new dress . . . a new top (table) cloth . . . skirt . . . earrings . . . pink Easter hat . . . new clothes . . . slip . . . blue glasses . . ."

For the school:
Kindergarten: "a new rug for the kindergarten floor . . . to paint the walls—'they're dirty near the door' . . . a trash can . . . the room cleaned up . . . a beauty parlor . . . the bunny to come . . ."

For me (Agnes Snyder):
Kindergarten: "a new dress . . . flowers . . . black glasses—'they'd look better on you' . . . a pair of clothes . . . skirt . . . blouse . . . black hat . . . pocketbook with money in it (Child commented: 'I like dollars better than anything') . . ."
Interage primary: "that you were real young . . . that you wasn't old . . . that you would live longer . . ."
Miscellaneous: "that no people would ever die, so people would live until 170 or 106"—First grade "thirty pieces of silver for the church."

As the above listing indicates, the teachers were not uniform in asking children to express their wishes. Hence, there is no opportunity to compare age groups in their different wishes for self, mother, family, etc. If this sampling can be regarded at all as evidence of the level of aspiration of these children, their wishes are all bound up with the realities of their lives. There is the same concern with food and clothing—even for Mrs. Wilson and me—but with the additional element of luxury items such as necklaces and diamond rings; the same verbalization of moral standards instilled by adults—"To do everything mother asks me," for example; and the same preoccupation with death.

What had we learned in this second tryout? Not much more than in the first that would give us a basis for the improvement of the children's language. But again, as in the first, everything pointed to the needs for widening the horizons of the children through vital experiences and for teaching them little by little the art of clear thinking. We had reinforced, too, our belief in the goodwill of the children, their trust in adults, their eagerness to please, their friendliness, and the warmth of their emotions. These were our building blocks forming the foundation on which we could structure a language program.

In the meantime many informal conferences were held among the teachers participating in the experimental tryouts, and in June two more formal conferences were held after I had submitted my report on the work of the year. At the first of these Mrs. Wilson was present with us and at the second both Mrs. Wilson and Dr. Crosby were there.

At the first conference the teachers told of some of the things they had found effective in evoking spontaneous language from the children, and thus something of their feelings and attitudes. Mrs. Elliott, for example, said that she had asked the children which room in their house they liked best. She had received the following answers:

"The bedroom—you can lock yourself in."

"The kitchen—you can help mother."

"The dining room—everybody's there."

To the question "What do you not like?" a reply had been "When my two small sisters go into my bedroom."

Mrs. Jackson said that she had continued her practice of putting a different picture on the bulletin board. She always chose pictures close to the children's own problems and interests, and had found that it almost always stimulated children to talk freely about themselves.

Mrs. Douglas said that she had received interesting answers to the question "What is the happiest moment you remember?" One boy answered "When I went to Gaylords (an outlet store) with my mother and could try on shoes." He explained that before this his mother had bought his shoes without him trying them on.

References were made by each of the teachers present (Mrs. Isakoff was unable to attend) to the way children were noting each other's language and making corrections. Mrs. Douglas gave as an example the comment of one of her boys while pointing to a classmate: "That boy used bad English. He said 'no got.' "

The teachers mentioned characteristic expressions of the children such as:

"It (fog) was so thick that I couldn't see the school"

"It was a froggy day"

"Me wants to paint"

There was agreement that while the children should be corrected in their language forms, this should never be done in a way that would destroy the free expression of their ideas.

The teachers were eager to continue the emphasis on language but felt that the time had come for wider participation in the school. On the basis of this year's experience they made the following proposals:

1. Include *all* the children in the classes of the four participating teachers in this year's tryout.

2. Continue the same grouping of children (those in this year's tryout) in successive grades until they have completed Grade 3. Where the

teacher does not remain with the same group for the successive year she should continue in the study with a new group each year until the first group has completed the third grade.

3. Let the four participating teachers continue in the study with new children each year until the first group completes the third grade. This means a four-year study.

4. Pretest all children in the four classes of this year's study and those who will begin in these classes in September 1962.

a. Use whatever good standard language tests are available

b. Let participating teachers devise tests to appraise the children's concepts and generalizations—e.g. If you had one wish what would it be? What is Easter, Christmas, etc? What do you mean when you say "mess with," "bean you" (typical of the children's language); Draw something that tells how you feel when something "horrible" happens.

5. Repeat tests each year during the period of study.

6. Procedures should emphasize:

a. Broadening and enriching experiences in and out of the classroom.

b. The continued use of the devices for understanding children developed in The Three-Year Experimental Project on Schools in Changing Neighborhoods.

c. The continued use of techniques for curriculum development and for teaching developed in the Project.

d. The development of thinking through problem solutions, and the building of concepts and generalizations.

e. Techniques for improving speech as the need indicates.

f. The incorporation of the children's natural language in the development of reading materials growing out of the children's experiences.

A New School Year Begins: 1962-63

For the third time in the history of the North East School the faculty met for its opening meeting. In the morning all had attended the general meeting of the entire faculty of the Wilmington Public School System. There they had shared with others the knowledge, the wisdom, and the spirit of two esteemed leaders in education in two outstanding addresses: "Education in 1980" by Superintendent Ward I. Miller and "Crossroads in Education" by Assistant Superintendent Muriel Crosby.

As others would be doing in their schools, the staff of North East, with the rich background of the morning as a springboard, would now in the afternoon look ahead in planning the year specifically for North East. The planning was broad at this first meeting, but there were a number of items that had bearing on the future of the work in language. One matter of regret was the announcement of the resignation of one of the participants in the experimental tryouts in the spring, Mrs. Elliott, because of change of residence to another city.

A more pleasurable report was that made by Mrs. Douglas of her summer experience in the workshop conducted by the National Conference of Christians and Jews at Rutgers University. Mrs. Douglas delighted the group with her very human account of the many incidents of personal interest that had marked the summer. She said that, because of her experience at North East, she found herself familiar with many procedures and ideas new to most of the group. However, she said that she had learned much in the techniques of presenting alternatives and focusing on problems in guiding children's thinking.

An answering note was struck in all of us who had had difficulty in understanding some of the children's language by an experience Mrs. Wilson had had while in Santo Domingo during the summer. Mrs. Wilson said that the difference in language among the three main population groups—Spanish, West Indian, and English—is a real source of cleavage among them. The West Indians are deeply religious and so avidly read the Bible that their daily language takes on a Biblical character. To illustrate Mrs. Wilson told of an incident in which a cook had been asked to take a meat grinder apart. There was complete bewilderment in response. So the person making the request proceeded to demonstrate. Immediately light broke. "Oh," the cook said, "you mean to render it asunder." Mrs. Wilson said, "Our problem is to reach children through being familiar with their natural language, letting them use it freely, but then leading them into the more acceptable forms of speech." She then raised a provocative question, "Does progress in language come in sudden spurts or is it gradual? Is there a period in a child's life when he directs himself in changing his language pattern, or does change come in imperceptible stages?"

Mrs. Klug, art specialist, told of a disappointment she had had when, after a very enjoyable trip to an art exhibit, the children gave so poor an account of it in writing. Dr. Crosby volunteered that much talking should precede writing and suggested that the teacher jot down bits of the children's conversation and later read them back to the children as a stimulus to their writing.

I reported on the results of last year's tryouts and the suggestions made by the participants. Agreement was reached, and many suggestions were made by the teachers for inclusion in the program: vocabulary lists, study of synonyms, role playing, and the other techniques used in the past.

There were no children present in school on the day of the above meeting. They came the next day. But, as only morning classes were held that first week, the teachers spent the afternoons planning individually and in groups for the year and in making visits to the children's homes.

The cooperation of the parents had been requested for these home visits and Mrs. Wilson, with the teachers, had prepared the following list of questions as indicative of what we hoped to learn from the visits:

- What do you think are some of the problems of our community?
- What do you like about our school?
- What are some of the things you like about our community?
- How do you think the school could better serve the community?
- What do you think our community needs?
- What would you want the school to do?
- What would you like to see changed in our community?
- What do you think parents and teachers can do together?

These were not to be used formally, questionnaire-fashion, but as something to fall back on when conversation lagged.

Now it was Friday afternoon, September 7th. The first week of the school year was over, and the faculty assembled to pool what the members had learned from the home visits. The discussion was informal. In no way did the eight guiding questions mar its spontaneity.

Apparently there was no difficulty in having the parents talk about *community problems.* The safety of the children on the street seemed to be the major concern. The cars drove too fast. The danger, it was acknowledged, was aggravated by the behavior of the children. When drivers tooted their horns the children yelled back. In general, the children played too roughly. When rebuked the older children resorted to retaliatory acts such as cutting the clothes lines of those who had taken them to task. When new families moved into the community children of the old residents fought them. One parent said she did not feel free to talk with her neighbors if their children had been fighting. Another said that there were gangs, she was afraid of them, her son had been beaten.

Lack of playgrounds within the housing project was mentioned by some. When Kingswood was suggested some said that there was fighting there. Kingswood is a community center and, in the original planning of the housing project, efforts had been made not to duplicate the facilities of Kingswood and North East School.

Difficulty in shopping was a problem frequently mentioned. The nearest shopping mart was too far to walk with heavy bundles to carry. There was a bus, but the fare was twenty-five cents each way. Parents with children going to the P. S. DuPont Junior High School—to which most of the North East children went after they completed sixth grade—complained of transportation difficulties.

The *attitude toward North East School* was generally good. Several said that the school was "wonderful." One parent, about to move, expressed herself as being sorry because she hated to see the children leave North East. Parents, while obviously pleased with the school, showed the same language difficulties the children experience in attempting to be specific.

The same was true when the parents tried to tell *what they liked about the community*. There was great disparity between those who were community-minded and those who were scarcely aware of the community. Among the latter were a brother and sister who had lived in the community since its beginning, who said they loved their home, hoped they might stay in it, but had no interest in the community. A young couple said they were perfectly happy in their home, but did not even know the name of their next-door neighbor. Those who were community-minded were inarticulate as to why.

There were intelligent questions and suggestions as to *school-community relations*. One parent was puzzled as to whether her child was in the third or fourth grade. It was explained to her that her child was in an interage group and just what that meant. A parent whose son was entering the first grade that year wanted him in an interage group. She, too, was given an appropriate explanation.

Among the constructive suggestions made was the recommendation that the teachers of P. S. DuPont Junior High School and those of North East get together and plan parents' meetings on different nights so that parents with children in both schools could attend both meetings. A father whose youngest son was now 35 and who told Mrs. Wilson how well he had brought him up responded agreeably to Mrs. Wilson's invitation to attend the North East parent meetings and share his experiences with others.

A parent who had twins in the first grade wanted to know why the school had separated them by placing them in different classes. This was explained. Explanation was given, too, to the parent who wanted more homework and more phonics for the children. This same parent stressed her belief in the virtue of cleanliness—yards, houses, bodies, minds!

Some interest was shown in adult education. One mother asked that the school have basketball teams that she might join in the evenings. A Puerto Rican mother with numerous children running about said that her husband had gone to North East at night and learned to speak English. She, too, wanted to go and learn to speak English.

The two *community needs* that seemed uppermost were better transportation and more police protection. Some spoke of the need for greater cleanliness of some of the yards and houses. The teachers commented on the great differences seen in cleanliness. Often two houses next to each other represented the greatest extremes in this respect. Some of the parents spoke regretfully of others who took little home responsibility for the children, leaving everything to the school, especially training in manners. In commenting on this, one mother said that after working nine years she had now quit because she knew it had been a mistake to leave her children unattended. The teachers noted the number of grandparents taking care of their working daughters' children. One old grandfather was babysitting with six children. He said that he had fought in World War I. There was a visiting grandmother who was pleased with all she would be able to tell when she returned home to South Carolina.

What did the visits accomplish? The most important values were not immediately obvious. They will show in the deepened understanding of the background of the children and, through this, in the greater ability of the teachers to identify with their children's problems. What had been general was now specific in terms of furniture, neatness, cleanliness, disorder, tones of voice, speech, likes, dislikes, goodwill, hostilities, hopes, regrets—the colors, sounds, and smells that make images that cannot be erased from memory.

"Things before words" is as essential a maxim for the education of teachers as it is for children. The teacher must know the life the children live. These home visits merely open the doors to understanding of the daily life of the children we teach. We should share it wherever we can. Then will our teaching become effective for there will be the kinship between teacher and learner that bridges the gaps that inevitably exist. The teaching of language, more than any other subject, requires this. We are to understand the language of the children, of tongue and of heart, if we would have them understand ours.

An Overview of a School Year—1962-63

Home, school, and community. There must be no walls between them if the school is to accomplish its educational purposes. This conviction has given direction to the Project. It accounts for the two-fold organization of the Project from the beginning—with a school group on the one hand and a community agency group including parents on the other, both held together by a central planning committee. North East as a member-school typified the resulting activities.

The home visits paid by all the teachers at the beginning of the year was only a sendoff for the close relations between the homes and North East School. One rarely entered the office of the school without seeing a parent who had come for a conference with a teacher or principal, usually not because of a child's misbehavior, but for counsel on some home or community problem. There were parent-teacher meetings regularly—not on the same night as those of P. S. DuPont High School! Many besides the Puerto Rican mother came to the adult classes "to learn to speak," to cook, to sew, or just for fun. A regular schedule was set up whereby parents were invited to have lunch with the different classes in the course of the year.

The police department was represented in the community organization group of the Project, and such problems as the parents of North East had brought up were discussed in the specifics that make action more probable. Similarly, the regular meetings of school people with representatives of other agencies brought about personal relationships resulting in closer cooperation. In North East there was increasing cooperation between the school and Kingswood, the recreation center about which one of the parents expressed concern over the discipline. A Gra-Y Club was established for the older boys jointly sponsored by Mr. Molock of the North East faculty and Mr. Poe of the YMCA, with weekly meetings, and a monthly "Men's Day" when the club members dressed "in their best" and had lunch together with their sponsors.

Cordial relations were established with junior and senior high schools. It was felt most important that the children of North East should know something of the life that lay ahead of them if they continued education beyond the sixth grade. Relationships with P. S. DuPont High School, which North East children would attend after completing sixth grade, were of greatest importance. Here in particular, home, school, and community met on common ground. The sixth grade children were given a day off to visit P. S. DuPont, to sit in classes, to talk with the pupils and teachers, and to hear from the principal what life in the junior high school was like. Two joint faculty meetings were held during the year, one at North East and the other at P. S. DuPont, to help in the articulation of the two. The principal of DuPont, John A. Stanavage, spoke to the parents of North East at one of their meetings in order that they might understand what the junior high could give the children and how to make the most of the opportunity. He and a panel of his students spoke to the fifth and sixth grades at North East.

Other activities included a musical performance given by the North East children at Springer Junior High School, and a return visit by the Springer youngsters to give their rendition of *The Barber of Seville* for the North East children. The Wilmington High School brought *The*

Wizard of Oz one Saturday morning to North East. Some of the children heard the Wilmington Children's Orchestra give a concert in the Salesanium High School. The Junior League brought the children an exciting puppet show. The women of Hanover Presbyterian Church became interested in the school and contributed in a number of ways—a gift of aprons and toys, for example—to the pleasure of the children.

The faculty contributed largely in bringing the outer world to the children. Mrs. Rittenhouse, music specialist, accompanied two friends—violinists Dr. Slovin and Dr. Kay—in a recital of chamber music for the children. She went with the North East Glee Club to participate in the choral concert around the huge Christmas tree in the Wilmington Rodney Square, and to sing at a public meeting at the Kingswood Housing Authority Building.

Through Mrs. Klug, art specialist, the children had another puppet treat when The Story Book Puppeteers put on a performance at the school. She also took them on several trips—to the Parks Studio, the Zion Lutheran Church, the William N. Cann Studios, the Wilmington Art Center, and Clemente's Bus Stop.

Miss Redden, physical education specialist, brought the children awareness of the national physical fitness program. The annual spring play and game evening brought the community together for an evening of sports in which the children exhibited their skills and their enjoyment of play.

Mrs. LeVigne, as she performed her nursing duties, lost no opportunity for instruction in health habits. Often she went into the classrooms when her individual conferences with the children indicated need for general instruction in some aspect of health. This she reinforced with instruction to parents with the use of films and other visual aids at parents' meetings and in office conferences.

Mrs. Edgell and her successor Mrs. Gill, part-time librarians, did much to extend the children's horizons through the world of books. Attractive displays, story hours, instruction in library usage—all served to give the children familiarity and often love of books. Through close cooperation with classroom teachers, the librarians were a source of reference and materials for the units of work undertaken in class.

Visitors were frequent, so frequent that children became accustomed to them and generally went on with their work heedless of the presence of strangers. Students from colleges, teachers from Delaware and out of state, came individually and in groups. There were three visits that were outstanding and on which the teachers capitalized for their value to the children. One was the visit of Mrs. Ruth Tooze, author and storyteller, out of which grew the North East Storytellers Club; another was the visit of Dr. Miel's graduate class in supervision from Teachers College, Columbia University; the third brought the Far East to the children in the person of Mrs. Lakshmi Navaratnam from Malaya.

The classroom teachers carefully related trips to the curriculum units being studied. These included the University of Delaware farm, the Philadelphia Airport, the Hagley Museum, Huber's bakery, the Dover Museum, the Wilmington Post Office, the 30th Street Station in Philadelphia, Western Union, and the Diamond State Telephone Company. In addition, whenever anything in the immediate neighborhood served as a resource to clarify studies under way, it was used; e.g. when Mrs. Douglas' class studied magnets, she took them to a nearby junkyard to see a huge magnet lift parts of old automobiles.

An interesting experience the children enjoyed was their use of the public address system. Here was a means of formal communication, part of today's world with wide application. Here, too, was direct instruction in the use of carefully prepared formal language.

As the year progressed and the knowledge of the children and their environment deepened, we felt increasing confidence in the soundness of the assumptions on which we had launched our language emphasis for the year. Above all else, these children desperately needed experiences. They needed them for their intellectual and spiritual awakening, as a means of expressing themselves orally when raw emotion could all too readily find an outlet in the use of fists, for the enjoyment of beauty, for the opening of new worlds, and as a foundation for practically all other learnings.

As to specific language instruction, there was much. The concentration was on just two things: vocabulary building and the free flow of feeling and thought in speech. It was hoped in the beginning that much attention would be paid also to definite teaching of logical thinking. While there was such teaching, it was soon found that not as much headway could be made in this year as had been hoped. Too much was needed with respect to having something interesting to talk about and to finding the words needed for it.

The attention the teachers were paying to vocabulary building was evident in every room. On all the walls were charts with word lists needed in talking or writing on whatever topics were under consideration at the time; e.g. weather, farming, industry, nature study, transportation. The special teachers supplemented this general vocabulary by building up the terminology unique in their fields: music, art, health, physical education.

The children found writing most laborious. Here the charts on the wall to which the children could refer for spelling were a help. Writing was not neglected, for it was realized that oral and written language reinforce each other, and the two must be developed simultaneously, but it would take a long time before fluency in the children's written language would be at all comparable to that of their oral speech. A high degree of sensitivity will be needed to know how and when the mechanical side of language can best be taught. But taught eventually it must be. Hopefully the basic elements will be mastered by most of the children by the time they complete the sixth grade. But it cannot be hurried.

Against this general background of the school year, a few of the experiences have been selected for more detailed analysis in the following pages: Mrs. Tooze's storytelling and the Storytellers' Club; some of the visits to the school; the puppeteers; the use of the public address system; and a few of the activities in their relation to the total program.

Mrs. Tooze and the Storytellers

Mrs. Tooze's Storytelling. In December Mrs. Ruth Tooze with her mobile library of 800 children's books spent two weeks in Wilmington displaying the books and telling stories to the children in the elementary schools. She spent December 5 at North East School. In the morning Mrs. Tooze met with children in different age groups. She had recently spent two years in Cambodia and had written a book on the country for children. In each group she told the children of her experiences in Cambodia adapting her selection to the age of the children and showing them the many native artifacts produced from local resources. Following the talk on Cambodia she told stories to the children—"Moby Dick" (subsequently pronounced "Moka Dick" by the children) to the older children and folk stories to the younger ones.

Mrs. Tooze told her stories dramatically, making them live for the children through tone of voice, facial expression, gesture, and diction. The children literally sat on the edges of their chairs, never took their eyes off Mrs. Tooze, and often burst into peals of delighted laughter.

The next morning Mrs. Wilson asked each teacher to send two children who had heard the stories to her and me to talk over the experience. We went into the soundproof room and used the tape recorder. Later I transcribed the recording on the typewriter. The verbatim report is on file. A few excerpts must suffice here, chosen because they illustrate both the children's interests and their characteristic language forms. Mrs. Wilson guided the discussion with a few questions. Some of these follow, along with samples of the children's responses.

Q. *What are some of the things you liked about Mrs. Tooze?*
A. I liked when she told us how to make music, how to play that thing, how to make the drums and guitars and stuff.

A. I liked the part about Cambodia and how they made the bells and things.

A. I liked the story when she was talking about Moka Dick. I was chewing gum and I got so interested in the story that I swallowed it.

A. I liked when all the animals got up on the donkey's back.

A. I liked the part when she said she was riding an elephant.

Q. *Some of you said you liked the way Mrs. Tooze told stories. Why?*

A. When she was telling about the man that was four fathoms high, every time she got to the man who was four fathoms high she would look up like that (child stood and stretched his arms).

A. I like when she said big, round, crispy doughnuts.

A. I like the part when she said "And there she blows—who o o o" (child gave a good imitation of a blowing sound).

A. I liked when she said "Hee-haw" (again a child gave a good imitation and laughed).

A. I like when the man said he would catch Moky Dick and she said "I'll just spit in his eye" (general laughter).

A. I remember when she was telling us how big the tiger was she kept on going farther out and kept on changing her face.

Q. *What made Mrs. Tooze's storytelling different from yours?*

A. She writes books and she knows how to say the words.

Q. *What could you do to tell stories the way Mrs. Tooze does?*

A. You can act like the persons in the story.

A. If you're afraid you can make like you're not as brave, try to overcome your fright.

A. Speak right out.

A. If you're carrying water you can act like it's heavy.

A. You can make like strain when you're holding up.

A. By talking out loud so people can hear you.

A. Make your story sound interesting.

A. She knew all the story she was going to tell so she wouldn't have to wonder what words she was going to say next.

A. She said she wrote real books. She wrote library books.

A. She had to know the story. She couldn't just make it up. Then she wouldn't always tell it the same way and the children would know it wasn't true.

The discussion moved back and forth between recall of incidents and the children's comments on what they liked about the way Mrs. Tooze told her stories. Many facets of Cambodian life were discussed—school, weather, recreation, clothes, food, religion. At one point Mrs. Wilson asked if they would like to live in Cambodia. The following is an excerpt of the conversation.

Q. *Does anyone want a ticket to Cambodia?*

A. I wouldn't mind.

A. I'd like the bananas.

A. You'd go swimming instead of going to school in the afternoon. You'd go without paying. You have to pay over here.

A. I'd like to ride the elephant.

A. If I went to Cambodia I think I could learn them some things and they could learn me some things, how to make their tools and balls.

Q. *What would you teach them?*

A. I'd teach them about arithmetic and reading and what kind of money we have.

Then came a discussion as to whether they would want a one-way or a round-trip ticket if they went to Cambodia. Those who wanted a round-trip ticket had this to say:

"I wouldn't want a one-way ticket because there mightn't be any way of getting back."

"I'd like to have a round-trip ticket so you can see different places."

"I want to come back here because in Cambodia you have to walk to school and here you can ride buses and just walk across the street."

"I'd rather have a round-trip ticket because you can go fishing."

"I would like a round-trip ticket because I'm not used to the people in Cambodia and I'm used to the people here."

"I want a round-trip ticket because their sun comes up at six and goes down at six and I wouldn't want to get up that early in the morning."

"I want to come back because we wear a lot of clothes."

"The only thing I want to come back for is my mother."

Those who wanted a one-way ticket said:

"A one-way ticket. When you want to go some place you have to buy gas and an elephant don't drink gas."

"I'd take my whole family with me. Stay there the rest of my life, take the things I need with me like a car and clothes."

When faced with leaving home for good, nearly all of them wanted the assurance of a round-trip ticket which would bring them back home.

Toward the end there was considerable interest in Mrs. Tooze herself. They wanted to know where she was born. This grew out of their idea that she had an accent and thought she might be a foreigner. Mrs. Wilson told them that others might well think that we have accents, and gave them a little explanation about regional differences in speech. Several times they made some reference to Mrs. Tooze as an author. They did not call her that but with something of awe they would comment on her writing books. Two comments in particular seem to indicate the birth of new conceptions:

"When I asked her how long it took her to write a book, I didn't know it took her the whole two years that she was there to write a book."

"It's because when Mrs. Tooze writes a story it takes her so long because she has to be sure everything sounds right. If something don't sound right people won't like her books and won't read them; and read other books, and her books will get all dusty."

The conversation lasted for well over an hour, and there was never a moment when the attention lagged. Instead, the enjoyment of talking about Mrs. Tooze and her stories was as great as during the original listening to her. There was nothing of the usual classroom atmosphere. They were just a group of children sharing with appreciative adults an experience that meant much to them. There was truly a free flow of expression. If they couldn't find the correct word, "thing" would do or "stuff," and everybody understood. There were no corrections to inhibit spontaneity. Children and adults were re-living an experience together. There is no better condition for learning.

Of course, like all children, these youngsters found their keenest enjoyment in incidents full of action—those that were unusual and yet with elements of the familiar; those that were grotesque like a camel on an elephant's back; or those that were just amusing. There was, too, the human ambivalence of the desire for adventure, of going to far-off places with the tug of home usually winning. As in most of our other experiences, here again we saw the strong hold that money, food, and clothing have on these children who are faced constantly with the practical needs of life.

As to language, I said that my report was verbatim. This is true as far as the actual words are concerned. But it does not give accurately the sounds, the rhythm, the cadence characteristic of these children's speech. I wish that I knew how to render these, but often I had to play back a sentence or a phrase as many as four times in order just to get the words. The more I listen to these children the more I wish that we might have a fine speech specialist who could make their speech more intelligible but without loss of its charm.

At one point when the children's enthusiasm over the way Mrs. Tooze told stories—her gestures, the way "she made her face look," how "her voice would sound big and then whisper,"—was at its peak, I heard myself say, "Would you like to tell stories the way Mrs. Tooze does?" "Yes! Yes!" came a chorus of voices. Mrs. Wilson was quick to pick it up. "You can" she said, "but it will mean hard work." "We'll work!" "Well," said Mrs. Wilson, "you know we have club hour once a week on Thursday. How would you like to be one of the clubs—a storytellers club?"

Of course they would—and so the North East Storytellers Club was born on December 6, 1962.

The Storytellers Club. The Club met for the first time on the next day, Friday, December 7. The children could not wait a whole week until the regular Thursday club meeting day. There were fourteen children present, the group that had met the day before. I regretted not being able to be there on that first important day to see if there was a carry-over of enthusiasm. Judging from Mrs. Wilson's notes, there evidently was.

Two children volunteered to tell stories on that first day. Mrs. Wilson reminded the children that since they wanted to learn to tell stories they would all listen with the question in mind, "How could the story-teller improve?"

In response to Mrs. Wilson's request for suggestions for the club, the children proposed that—

a. they work in two groups, younger and older;

b. they have a play about Christmas—one person telling the story and the others acting it out in the background;

c. they have a president and vice-president;

d. as people tell stories they suggest ways to make it more interesting.

Somehow only the last suggestion was ever carried out. Though all grades were represented—from first through sixth with the greater number from the third and fourth grades—no grouping was mentioned again until, toward the middle of the semester when other children asked to join the club, someone suggested that there be two divisions, one for the original members and one for the new. However, the new members soon proved their ability, and the group remained as one until the end of the year.

Shayne, one of the volunteers of the day, told the story, *The Three Little Pigs*. Here were the comments:

"Keep hands down because they bother people."

"Think of the story right along instead of stopping all the time."

"Talk to the whole group instead of one person."

"Slow down and think so that you don't have to stop and correct yourself."

Then almost all the children wanted to see if they could tell the story better. A number did, and there really was improvement. Now came a surprise. Someone suggested that they might go around to the different classes and tell their stories. Of course they wanted to do it at once. Here Mrs. Wilson admonished them that some practice was needed first. She also mentioned that teachers would need to be asked if they wanted this, and if so, to say when it would be convenient. The children accepted the advice with their usual grace and planned for the next meeting. Since Christmas was near, they decided they would tell Christmas stories. Lamar, Emmanuel, and Lorraine agreed to be ready with stories they would find and prepare.

The pattern set at this first meeting continued weekly throughout the year. Criticism gradually became keener. There were frequent references to "what Mrs. Tooze would have done" under this or that circumstance. How could they put more action into the telling? They had difficulty at first in synchronizing the action with the words. They would say, for example, that "he knocked on the door" and *then* knock; or "the giant tramped, tramped" and then a pause, followed by the tramping. When this happened, someone would say "Mrs. Tooze did it when she said it."

The matter of voice pitch was of concern all through the year. Many of the children found it difficult to adjust their voices to an audience situation but talked in their usual conversational manner. "Make yourself heard" was a frequent caution. "You talked too fast" or "You talked too slow" was likewise frequently heard, and the children became quite "tough" on those who punctuated their narratives with "er's."

One of the real problems we encountered was one that is basic in all efforts at expression. We were, after all, in a school setting, and children very readily learn to give the kind of school response they think is expected of them. How were we to help children feel the story, identify with the emotions of the characters, really be them? I recall one successful effort Mrs. Wilson made. The children were working on the story, *The Three Billy Goats Gruff.* Mrs. Wilson asked the children to tell what they thought the troll looked like. They described him variously as short, ugly, long-nosed, wobbly. Several of the children acted out their ideas of the troll. Then there was practice to differentiate among the three Billy Goats. The children showed differences in speaking in three voices ranging from very small to very loud. After all manner of attempts at characterization the child who had first told the story retold it with much better results.

In the beginning these very gracious children were somewhat reluctant to criticize each other. I recall, in particular, an incident illustrative of this. Lorraine had told a story haltingly and monotonously. When she finished Mrs. Wilson asked the children what they thought of the way Lorraine had told the story. Right around the circle, one after another said that he had liked the story. All but Willie who stood boldly against the tide and said, "I don't know what she said." This released the rest. Wanda chimed in with "I didn't get the meaning." Shayne said that Lorraine should have used more expression. Wanda asked Lorraine

"Did you get the meaning?" Unabashed, Lorraine replied "No." Christine advised Lorraine to read it over again.

The desire of the children to tell the stories they had prepared to the different classes in the school had been gratified. The teachers had co-operated by arranging definite dates with the storytellers and by filling out a form Mrs. Wilson had supplied on which the reactions of the children to the storyteller were indicated. These comments became a very real stimulus toward improvement. In general there were more favorable than unfavorable comments and the storytellers became very popular, particularly with the younger children.

Some of the teachers gave both their and the children's reactions. Here are some of the things teachers said:

"Rapt attention! the children asked that Willie come back again and tell more stories."

"Christine was a great success! The children gave her rapt attention. After she finished, the children clapped spontaneously."

"Children were interested and showed disappointment when it ended sooner than they expected."

"The children enjoyed the story, *The Little Man in the Red Coat*. They especially liked the gestures Harrison made as he told about the forty-foot nose. The children wanted to know if the story was in the library."

Such suggestions as the following were also made:

"After telling the story she should discuss it with the class or have them ask questions about it."

"Display pictures of the characters in the story."

"I feel that the storyteller must remember the age of the group."

"Linda should choose a shorter story, talk more slowly and make it clear what the story is about before she plunges into it."

"I would suggest that Lorraine create more interest before telling the story, discuss words that might be new to the class. She talks too fast and she should speak more clearly."

"A little slower."

"Harrison usually selects fairy tales to read. I would like to see him read adventure stories and others in addition to the fairy stories."

Following are quotes from the children's reactions:

"I liked the motions he made."

"He spoke loud and clear and the way he said it you could see pictures."

"He did not use *and* and *um* while he was thinking about what happened next."

"Woodie's story was too short. It sounded like a rhyme to me."

"Willie moved his feet like a goat."

"He was a scary troll."

"He told us good stories."

The children in the club were interested in such comments as the above, and took them very seriously. I noticed an awareness on the part of the children of their audience's responses. They knew when they had failed to hold the attention of their group and were quite objective in trying to get at the cause.

One of the comments of the teachers—that the children tell something other than fairy tales sometimes—echoed a concern that had gradually been growing on us. Nothing we could do seemed to move the children off the fairy-tale and folk-tale level. Our librarians, first Mrs. Edgell and then Mrs. Gill, had drawn the attention of the children to other types of stories and had, along with Mrs. Wilson, told other types. But to the very end of the year they were still on the same level.

Our records show the following, many of them told over and over:

The Three Little Pigs	The Three Bears
The Night Before Christmas	Three Billy Goats Gruff
The Little Red Hen	Jack and the Bean Stalk
Hansel and Gretel	Stone Soup
Pears and Apples	Golden Pears
Little Red Riding Hood	Shoes for a King
Peter and the Wolf	Dapple Grimm
Golden Goose	The Man in the Red Coat

There were two that were different. Linda undertook to tell in detail a whole book she had read, *Dot for Short*. The children simply said, "Too long." The other came from Donna who, although she joined the club late in the year, was immediately at home and volunteered to tell a story at her first meeting. Obviously she made it up as she went along, one incident leading into another, never pausing, just free, imaginative flow, utterly regardless of time. Later she told an original story most effectively, *Shoes for a King*.

Another bit of originality was shown by Wanda. She announced that she had a story to tell called "Goldy Worm." Whereupon she gave her adaptation of the story of *Goldilocks and the Three Bears*. Instead of Goldilocks we had Goldy Worm and instead of the three bears there were three apples. She followed the plot of the original story faithfully but with a great deal of ingenuity substituted appropriate settings for the worm and the apples. The children were delighted. At meeting after meeting they called on Wanda to "tell it again."

Much as the children reveled in the fanciful, there were usually touches of realism in their versions of the old tales. The most pronounced example of this was in their different tellings of Andersen's story, *The Princess and the Pea*. Apparently the children could not see how the princess could possibly feel just one pea beneath twenty mattresses, so Christine made it twenty peas and the rest who told the story kept the twenty. Willie wanted to know how the princess managed to climb all the way up on the twenty mattresses. This was solved by having two men throw her up. But how did they get the twenty mattresses piled up in the first place? The king piled as many as he could, then the queen stood on his shoulders and piled up some more, and the prince stood on her shoulders and piled up the rest. But how did the princess ever get down? Many solutions were suggested, but the final one accepted had her tie two ends of the sheet to the corners of the mattress, tie knots in the sheet and let herself down with it. The climax was reached with the disposal of the peas. Andersen had his single pea placed in a museum where one may still see it. But the children had different ideas. Moreover they had twenty peas. One would make a necklace of them; another a pot of pea soup; and one would flush them down the toilet!

Why this absorption in these old fanciful tales? Some of these children were in the fifth or sixth grade, but their relish of them was as strong as that of the younger children. Is it because these children had not grown up with these stories as we are inclined to think all American children do? Were they in many cases new stories to them? Or are they lingering in this realm because it gives them the comfort of the known and, with their limited environment are they late in venturing into the new? And why this mixture of fancy with the realities of their daily lives? It would seem that they go just so far into the unknown and then quickly retreat to what they know is real. This is a mere surmise. But, even if we cannot be clear as to the whole explanation of their behavior, we now know these children in a way that will make us able to teach them and learn with them as we could not have done without this shared experience.

We know, too, that they have grown in self-confidence, in their feeling that they have developed something that gives pleasure to others. They have become aware of their shortcomings in communication and have acquired a healthy, self-critical attitude. They have learned, too, to criticize the performance of others constructively and objectively; and they know that this skill they are developing is appreciated by others.

These are no small learnings. They have become assimilated into the total personality structure. What shall we strive toward next year when the club meets again? Not all the children will be back, for a few have gone on to junior high school. Some, too, may have moved away, for there is much moving about in this community. Some may have lost interest. There will be new faces, too, if the interest engendered in the school as a whole last year is an indication. We will see what happens on the first club meeting in the new school year.

Puppeteers

In early spring, the Story Book Puppeteers presented *The Talking Hen;* a fanciful story written by the producers.

There were no children in the room when I arrived to see *The Talking Hen* except for a few older boys setting up the room with chairs for the expected audience. But soon the children came in walking in that same free, relaxed, orderly fashion characteristic of the North East children. They were seven- and eight-year olds. I sat down toward the side front where I could see the play and the children at the same time.

The stage had been set up. It was a simple boxlike affair, tall in proportion to width and depth. There was no ornamentation to distract attention from the play, just a covering of dark cloth except for the opening. But there was focus in the bright red curtain brilliantly lighted from two side sconces. In this spot lay the lure of the magic to come.

When all the children were seated, Mrs. Klug (art teacher) came to the front of the room and said to the children, briefly and simply: "We are going to have a special treat today, a puppet show. I am not going to tell you anything about it. The puppets will do that." Again, focus. Mrs. Klug sat down. The lights went out. The room was dark, all except for the brightly lighted stage as the red curtains parted. The show was on!

The story was entitled, *The Talking Hen.* A father had died leaving his fortune to two of his sons. To the youngest son, Johnny-Joe, he had left only a hen. But the hen could talk. The hen advised Johnny-Joe to sell her. He was unsuccessful in his efforts until a witch offered to buy her. Johnny-Joe sold her, but was immediately regretful and wanted to get back the hen. The ghost of the father appeared and showed him how this could be done. First, he whistled for the fox. But the witch overcame the fox. The same fate met the dragon, the next to be called. But the black cat came by showing how Johnny-Joe could trick the witch into giving him the magic words for getting the hen back. The boy carried out the cat's directions, transformed the witch into smoke and the hen into a beautiful princess. Johnny-Joe and the princess loved each other and lived happily ever after.

The story was well portrayed. The action was direct, the language simple, the characters few and gradually presented. The action was good and the dialogue clear and interestingly spoken.

The children were immediately attentive as Johnny-Joe and Biddy-Hen appeared. They watched, absorbed in the laments of Johnny-Joe and the affectionate caresses of Biddy-Hen. When the curtains closed after Biddy-Hen told Johnny-Joe to sell her, the children immediately applauded. It was a restrained applause, and their silence seemed to indicate thinking about what this strange scene meant.

In the second scene, the witch came on and the sale was made with the curtains drawn while Johnny-Joe wept over the loss of Biddy-Hen. Again there was applause. This time it was louder than after the first scene. Now, there was quiet talking, fingers pointing to the stage and other indications that the talk was about the play. The first laughter came when the witch said to Biddy-Hen as she carried her off: "Come with me, you bunch of stuffed feather!"

The third scene was longer than the preceding ones and packed with action. The ghost of the father appeared, and efforts were made to have the fox and the alligator get rid of the witch. There was strenuous fighting between the witch and the fox and the witch and the alligator. The action was intense, and was accented by strong words and screaming. Of course, the children laughed excitedly and jumped up and down. Another laugh occurred when the witch threatened to turn the alligator into a lollipop, although there was no similar response when the witch threatened to turn the fox into a sandwich. The applause at the end of this scene was very loud.

The fourth scene was full of suspense as the cat showed the way to get Biddy-Hen back. It was mysterious, too, as the smoke began to rise and the eerie words, "Abra cadabra, dicky-doo" sent the witch up in smoke and transformed Biddy-Hen into the most beautiful princess in the world. The curtains closed, and the children happily applauded.

The puppeteers came forward, showed the puppets, talked naturally with the children, let them examine the puppets as the children repeated parts of the dialogue.

A little later another performance of the same play was given. This time the children were older. Mrs. Brown's fourth grade and Mr. Molock's individual progress class. The reaction was very different. There was complete attention but no audible response during the first two scenes. The first laugh came in the third scene when the witch threatened to turn the alligator into a lollipop. Then, too, there was a laugh when Biddy-Hen came in with the green cap and the alligator said, "We eat our hens raw."

When the puppeteers came out to talk with the children and show the puppets, the children were positive in insisting that they were not afraid of the ghost. They went behind the scenes and wanted to know how everything worked. They were interested in the mechanics of the performance, particularly in how the smoke was made. The younger children had not indicated this kind of interest at all.

Since the children had viewed the puppet show in two groups we decided to have the discussion similarly in two groups. This gave us the opportunity to compare the reactions of different age groups. There were eleven children in the older group ranging in age from nine to twelve. There were eight children in the younger group, two of whom were seven years old and the rest eight. The discussions were held on the same day with only lunch intervening after the performances. Mrs. Wilson and I were both present for the discussion with the older group. Mrs. Wilson started the discussion with the younger group but had to leave almost immediately and asked that I carry on.

Mrs. Wilson had not seen the puppet shows and therefore started [as she had in the discussion of *Smoke for a Strawberry Dragon*] by telling the children that she had not seen the play and would like them to tell her what it was about. Both groups started in a fragmentary way with no regard for sequence.

> THE OLDER GROUP:
> "The witch stole the chicken and she sold it for three golden bags."
> "She said—she went—they went at the circus and they saw you know a piece of witch."
> "Um—the goose turned into a—um—the bird turned into a princess."
> "The boy wanted the crocodile and the fox to eat the witch."
> "And the witch said that she was gonna turn the alligator and the fox under spell."
> "The father came."
> "The father died."

> THE YOUNGER GROUP:
> "I liked the wolf."
> "There was a story, there was a story of a boy and a hen when the father died he sold the hen for five bags of gold and then he started that a witch—so the witch . . ."

The children of the older group continued to throw out bits of information about the play until I said, "I am afraid Mrs. Wilson is not getting a very clear idea of what happened. Suppose we begin at the very beginning. One of you start until I raise my hand and then another go on from there." The children seemed eager to comply. The following quotes are the responses of the first three children. Others went on to the end in much the same style as those who began.

> "It begin by the chicken and the hen and the boy—um—had the hen—um—when his father died—um—and the father wanted the

boy to sell the hen because it was a talking hen. Some of the boy's brothers were left money. Others were left big plantations and the boy was all alone and had nothing but the talking chickens."

"He went to the circus to sell the chicken and he got three bags of gold and went back home and started crying. When the chicken said I know a good idea. You can go and try to sell me. Then, you can get yourself some money and have yourself a happy ending. Then, he went to the circus and then he said I'm tired of everybody laughing at me because I'm trying to sell you. Then the chicken said, 'Wait for the old woman with the patch on her eye.' "

"After he started crying, after he saw the chicken because the chicken because he wanted him because he was a talking chicken and he didn't want nothing happening to it."

I started almost immediately with the younger group to have the story told in sequence. At first there was no regard for sequence but after some effort on my part the following was produced (the first little girl would probably have gone on to the end though the other children were all clamoring for a chance to take part):

"When his father died there was none but him and the hen so he was buried. He said, 'How can I get some money?' and the hen told him sell me for five bags of gold. He went to the circus and everybody laughed at him and said it's not worth five bags of gold so a witch came and he she said, 'I'll give you five bags of gold for that hen.' So she gave him five bags of gold and she gave him the hen so he wanted the hen back and the father came and he was a ghost and he came back to earth and said, 'Why did you sell that hen?' He said, 'What did you do with that hen?' So she said he said, 'How can I get the hen back? I want the hen. How can I get the hen back?' She said he said, 'Whistle. There's a wolf a fox hiding behind some tree.' "

"It was an alligator and the fox. The witch and the alligator was fighting and the witch throwed the alligator down. And the alligator got torn down and and the witch was gonna cook the hen."

"And then the father said, 'I have another friend, the alligator.' So he whistled for the alligator and the alligator came and he said that he couldn't do much so he tried a little bit and the witch throwed him down and she started laughing."

"And then the cat came up the wicked black cat came up and the black cat said, 'I hate the old witch. I'd do anything to get away from her. She make me eat the garbage and drink sour milk' and then he said, 'I'd give anything to get away from that witch.' So he said the witch put a wicked spell on the red hen the talking hen and then he said and he called the witch and the witch came and started laughing and she said, 'Who called me?' and then and then the boy said, 'I did' and . . . ."

The rest continued in much the same vein. Their eagerness to be called on continued to the end.

In both groups there was marked difference in language among the children. The same tendency to repeat phrases, to confuse pronouns, to use a noun and then follow it with a pronoun, *was* for *were* and *throwed* for *threw* was evident in both groups. On the whole I should say that the interest was higher and facility greater in the younger group.

We asked both groups which parts of the play they thought were funny. The older children replied:

> "When the father came out of the grave he said, 'Wooh, I'm the ghost.' "
> "I think the part was funny when he kissed the princess and he came out and said they'd be happy together."
> "I think it was funny when the witch said she'd turn the wolf into a lollipop."
> "When the alligator said, 'R a a a h'."
> "It was funny when the alligator almost bit off her head."

The younger group's responses were less mature consisting mainly of merely mentioning a character rather than an action:

> "The—ah—fox."
> "The witch and the alligator was fightin."
> "The cat."
> "The witch and the fox."
> "The witch the witch and the smoke."
> "Johnny Joe threw the money down."
> "When Johnny Joe was kissing the hen."
> "The witch and the wolf."
> "Johnny Joe was kissing the princess."

A similar difference was shown between the two groups in response to the question, "What parts did you think were sad?"

> THE OLDER GROUP:
> "When the boy sold the chicken for the five bags of gold and he started crying."
> "When the father came out of the grave and then he began talking to his son and then he started crying."
> "When he came out of the grave and the boy was happy that he came back to life."
> "When he saw the chicken he began to cry. That chicken meant a lot to him."

> THE YOUNGER GROUP:
> "The wolf and the crocodile."
> "I thought the witch was cooking the hen."
> "The cat and the witch."
> "When the witch said she was going to eat the hen for dinner."

"The ghost."

"When the witch said she was going to eat the hen for dinner."

"When the cat said the witch make him eat garbage and drink sour milk."

"When the little boy's father came home."

"He was sad because the witch was gonna eat the hen and he didn't have no way to get her back."

The tape recording of these conversations made me realize how well-founded was the concern of the teachers over the language needs of the children. Only a very few were able to carry a narrative forward for more than a sentence or two. I keep thinking of the contrast this is to the straightforward way the children in the Storytellers Club master stories in great detail. Of course, the circumstances are entirely different. As shown earlier, the stories told in the club are old favorites they tell over and over again; the material of the puppet shows was entirely new, and they were trying to reproduce it after one exposure. This points up the necessity for the use of much familiar material in the improvement of language, and of repetition of desirable language forms.

I am sure that my efforts to secure sequence at this particular time were ill-advised. The children had seen the puppet show. Only lunch intervened between the show and talking with Mrs. Wilson and me about it. Here they had been in a fanciful world of talking hens, witches, princesses, alligators, foxes. A lot of new sensory stimuli, magic, struggle —were all in their consciousness unassimilated. Of course they blurted out what first came to mind. They knew that the story had a happy ending—they lived happily ever after—and the order of events leading to the climax did not matter. I should have been satisfied.

When should we have children discuss an experience? Like everything else, it all depends. Generally speaking, however, I believe the children should have a chance to talk it over among themselves, with the teacher an appreciative and observant listener, noting leads that she will follow at opportune times. This is a difficult art to master, the art of sensitive watchfulness and listening, the art of selecting the matters of genuine concern to be followed up later from the momentary, fleeting, superficial interests of children. It means note-taking as part of the teacher's skill, for without notes there is little hope of continuity in teaching. Again, it is the supreme art of knowing "when."

Daily Announcements

Each day from October 16th to the end of the school year, a child made announcements to the school at large of the events of the day and of any other information that it was desirable for teachers, children, and parents to have. Reading the prepared statements made by the children for this responsibility gives quite a picture of the life of North East School.

The announcers were rotated among the classes, one child serving each day for a week. The information given came from the office, from the teacher, and from the children. The class worked together in the composition of the announcements. A form was provided with a set opening statement and closing, much as on television and radio. The child's name and teacher's name were included on the form. A typical sample follows:

> May I have your attention, please? May I have your attention, please?
>
> Good morning. This is Andrea . . . , your student announcer for the week from Miss Peaco's room, presenting the school news and special notices for the day.
>
> Today is the first day of Brotherhood Week. This is a special week when everyone tries very hard to get to know a different person or group. This is a week when there should be very few fights because *everyone* is trying to be friendly. Can we make this a good week?
>
> Today at 2:00 P.M. the principal of P. S. duPont High School is coming to our school with some of his students. They will talk to the fifth and sixth graders.
>
> Congratulations to the chorus members who sang at the Riverside Community Building yesterday. Your singing was fine, and your behavior was excellent during the long program.
>
> Note: Chorus members who did not meet their responsibilities yesterday are to bring notes from home explaining their absence. These notes should be brought to Mrs. Wilson this afternoon or tomorrow morning.
>
> Teachers will meet in the library after school for a short meeting.
>
> Today we welcome a new boy from George Gray school who is in Mrs. Brown's room. His name is Wayne.
>
> That is all. Thank you.

Mrs. Wilson asked the teacher to fill out a form regarding each child's announcements, giving the following information:

What was the name, age, and grade of the child selected?
How was the selection made? (By teacher, class, voluntary, etc.?)
How did class react to child's presentation?
Was there any follow-up? (By you, class, family, child?)

> A few sample responses follow:
>
> *Dorenda . . . , age 9, grade 3*—Dorenda was among four nominated and voted upon by the class. She received the highest number of votes.
>
> The entire class thought Dorenda's presentation the very first morning was good. They said her voice sounded clear, but it was suggested by a few children that she slow down just a little. On her

final day it was still the opinion of the group that she spoke too rapidly.

As part of our language arts work we decided to allow a few boys and girls each day to make believe they were student announcers until they all had a turn. We were to listen for clear enunciation, and proper pronunciation, and good delivery—not too fast and not too slow.

John . . . , age 9, grade 3—I selected him because I thought it might help him to make a self-evaluation.

The children were surprised at his ability and were also happy that he represented the room as well as he did.

The class gave constructive criticism following each day's announcement, and we practiced the correct pronunciation of words he had mispronounced.

Robert . . . , age 10, 5th grade—The children recited a poem they had memorized. The one who recited best was selected by the class. The boy selected did not want to announce because he felt he could not do a good job.

The class applauded Robert when he returned to the classroom, although he was extremely nervous. The class told him he had done well and would do even better the following day. They encouraged him, and during the announcement they visibly suffered when he stumbled on a word. They groaned, wrung hands, etc.

At the parent-teacher conference Mrs. . . . , Robert's mother, told the teacher that the week of announcing was the best thing for Robert. She said he took the job very seriously and practiced the announcement with her each evening. She said that it had given him a great deal of confidence—which he needed. Robert has been asked to give many reports since then. The teacher has found him better able to handle himself orally. The class is quite anxious for our turn to announce again.

Nancy . . . , age 8, grade 3—Nancy volunteered to be our student announcer.

Tuesday, we couldn't understand all of the words. Her voice was shaky. Wednesday, many of her words were not too clear. Thursday, she didn't read smoothly. Her words were not clearly spoken, her voice was still shaky. Mispronounced several words. Friday, Nancy's voice was clearer. She did improve. This was her best day.

Nancy has a very soft voice. This was an incentive to speak louder. We discussed the importance of being heard and of being understood.

As the reports of the teachers indicate, methods varied in the handling of the announcing activity. But from the reports and from interviews with the teachers, it is fair to assume that this was one of the best means used to develop both desire to improve language and an objective critical faculty toward their own usage of language.

Relationships

It would be difficult to trace all the relationships between language study and the other aspects of the curriculum. Over the years the Wilmington Public Schools have engaged in continuous curriculum building grade by grade, area by area. The findings are published in handbooks— the latest one for the kindergarten in 1963—and resource bulletins. These give a common basis for all the elementary schools of Wilmington. All that has been discussed here has been in the nature of the enrichment material and the specific approaches made at North East School.

Unit planning stressed by schools participating in The Three-Year Experimental Project on Schools in Changing Neighborhoods was grounded firmly in the content of the social studies, natural sciences, language arts, arithmetic, music, and art outlined as guides for all Wilmington schools. While the units generally emphasized one field of study more than others, which was inevitable since they were based on problems, activities, and the developments of concepts and generalizations, related fields needed to be utilized. Hence at North East, where unit planning predominated during the past year, subject lines often disappeared as children realized what varied information was needed for the solution of a problem. And, most important, the need for language was always there.

Trips. A few of the trips mentioned earlier in this report, are offered as illustrative of the ways in which language functioned in the development of units.

Mrs. Taylor included a trip to the Wilmington Post Office in her unit on *Communication,* with her inter-age class (grades 1 and 2). The big trip had been preceded by smaller ones in the immediate neighborhood. The children noted the mailboxes with their lists of the time that mail is picked up. According to their reading ability they either looked at pictures or read books about the mail, talked about what they were learning, and prepared questions they wanted to ask when they reached the Post Office. But they forgot the prepared questions in their interest in what they saw. One entirely unexpected question that came from a child while at the Post Office had to do with why so many men are needed there. Mrs. Taylor found that no child in her class had anyone in his family connected with the postal service.

After returning from the trip the children wrote letters, some, of course, by dictating them. Mrs. Harris wrote to the children, the children to her, and the children to each other as well as to the Wilmington Postmaster. They put their letters into envelopes and stamped them with their own self-made stamps.

Finally they conceived the idea of arranging their classroom furniture to correspond with the streets they lived on. A sign was made for the name of each street and placed on a corner desk, and each desk had a house number. Cardboard mailboxes were made and placed on the desks, and a postman was appointed to deliver the daily mail. In the course of the development of the unit the children learned 38 words, among them *deposit, United States, signature, invite.*

Mrs. Douglas took her children in an inter-age group, grades 1 to 3, on a visit to the University of Delaware farm in connection with her unit on *Family Life.* The children said that they wanted to see how baby animals lived with their mothers and fathers and how the caretaker's family lived on the farm.

I happened into the classroom on the day after the trip and listened to the discussion. Mrs. Douglas asked the children what they saw first. Answers came from all over the room, "The farmer's house." Mrs. Douglas then asked the children how the farmer's house differed from theirs. Answers: The farmer's house was made of wood and theirs of brick; the farm house was pointed and theirs was flat. This led to a discussion of the electric fence they had seen. The children realized that it was meant to keep the cows in, and Mrs. Douglas led them to see the need for this and how it worked—that the cow's nose was the first part of her body to touch the fence and, because the cow's nose was wet, she received a shock. A very interesting discussion followed on the change from the large bales of hay to small pellets for easier handling.

The children were apparently quite excited over seeing the caretaker's children come home from school and go into a house so different from those in the housing development where they lived. They enjoyed seeing the many different animals and seeing a cow milked. But when Mrs. Douglas asked them if they would like to live on a farm, many of them did not want to because "it was too dark at night;" while one little girl was most vigorous in her objection to the farm because "it stinks."

Mrs. Douglas said that she makes much use of large vocabulary charts to familiarize the children with the spelling of new words. There was one in evidence giving the farm vocabulary with which they were becoming familiar.

Mr. Molock teaches the upper individual progress class composed of sixteen children ranging in age from nine to thirteen, and from grades one to four in academic achievement. He said that one of the most stimulating experiences of the year was the visit he made with his class to the Diamond State Telephone Company located quite close to the school. When he found that only three of the sixteen children had telephones in their homes, he helped the children to make a telephone set. They learned how to dial, to make person-to-person calls, and to differentiate ways of making social, business, and emergency calls. Like others, Mr. Molock found that the questions raised in preparing for the trip gave way to better ones when the children were face to face with conditions in the new situation. Mr. Molock said that he certainly was surprised when one of the shyest girls wanted to know how the money came back to you on a dial phone.

Mrs. Harrison's 4th and 5th grade group took three trips in connection with their study of Delaware: The Hagley Museum and the Art Center in Wilmington, and downstate to Dover. Mrs. Harrison does not believe in having the children prepare questions beforehand. She prefers that the children be immersed in a unit before taking a trip, and then seeing what they can see. I was present at one of their discussions on the Hagley Museum. I found them recounting their experience in an informal way, exchanging comments with each other.

During their study they had become interested in the flour and the powder mills. This apparently held over for they compared with each other the details of what they had seen in the two mills. But on the spot, they asked the following questions:

Where did the children play when the duPonts lived at Hagley?

What did Mr. duPont shoot with the gun hanging over his desk?

Do the geese on the Brandywine stay there all year with their families?

What was the mill race?

Out of this discussion of the mill race grew an interest in the word *race*. Used in this way the word was new to the children. Mrs. Harrison had them list all the different definitions of the word *race* that they knew. They covered them all. Later in the year I found charts of homonyms, synonyms, and antonyms on the wall. A fine interest in words pursued throughout the year grew out of the trip.

There is much to be learned about taking trips. How much preparation in advance? How much discussion and, above all, *when,* after the trip is taken. I like to think of trips as resources to be used by children when something that they have read makes them want to see its reality, or when they hope to find an answer to a question which books do not give. Then, when home conditions permit, close bonds between home and school can be formed by involving parents in responsibility for accompanying children on trips assigned as homework.

Letter writing is, of course, a language-accompaniment to trips. The problem here is to keep the letters from becoming mere formalities, something to do because it is expected of you. It is most important to teach children the courtesies of life, but how can we do it making sure that there is genuine feeling behind the words? I found a refreshing bit in the letter of a child who had gone on a trip on which two parents had accompanied the group. After thanking the host, she added: "I am so glad the two parents behaved so well on the trip."

Special Fields. In the fall of 1961 Mrs. Coker's 4th and 5th grades had worked out a unit on *The Westward Movement* which culminated in Pioneer Day. In the course of the study, Miss Redden in physical education, Mrs. Rittenhouse in music, Mrs. Klug in art, Mrs. LeVigne in nursing, and Mrs. Edgell, librarian, had all contributed through their special skills to make pioneer life in the West very real to the children. This experience stimulated the special teachers to participate wholeheartedly in cooperating with the classroom teachers in the effort to improve language.

Each in his own field helped bring broadening experiences to the children and each, too, made a special effort to acquaint the children with their specialized vocabulary. Since the experiences have been mentioned earlier, only the work in vocabulary building will be discussed here. Abundant use was made of charts and of having the children use words new to them whenever the occasion warranted.

Miss Redden emphasized the words used daily such as *shower, sprinkle, spray,* and *locker.* She also emphasized words connected with exercise: *flex, flexion, relief, exit, entrance.* In connection with the last Miss Redden remarked that while the children were familiar with the word *exit* through seeing it frequently on signs, *entrance* was new to them. (Mr. Molock had made the same observation.)

Miss Redden noted the disparity between the children's written and oral English. Although they were quite fluent when speaking, writing was an almost impossible task. For that reason she had the children write, using the vocabulary they were learning. She said they were surprised when she, a physical education teacher, asked them to bring pencils to class. She gave occasional vocabulary tests leaving the charts with the vocabulary on the wall because she realized how frustrated the children would be over the spelling.

Mrs. Rittenhouse proceeded in music much as Miss Redden had in physical education. She said that this year, more than in the past, instead of casual mention of musical terms she emphasized their meaning. She, too, used charts and gave occasional quizzes. She made a chart of musical instruments, and the children learned to distinguish and name them. I was present at a very interesting demonstration of this at which the musicians explained the different instruments and their sound and place in the orchestra.

Mrs. Klug related the many experiences in art she brought to the children both within and without the school; in language through discussion of the experiences and writing about them. At times she cooperates with the classroom teachers by having the children illustrate the poems and stories they write. An interesting experience in vocabulary building grew out of the study of textures and the moods created by their colors. The children learned to feel the difference between warm and cool colors and to find adjectives that describe the different ways textures feel.

Mrs. LeVigne went directly to the classrooms to give health instruction when feasible, but the major part of her work was done in the health offices with small groups or individuals in connection with their health needs. Mrs. LeVigne, like the others, made much use of vocabulary charts. In particular she tried to give children the correct vocabulary for bodily functions. This she found most important because often children could not tell her what was wrong with them because they simply lacked the needed words.

Mrs. Edgell and later Mrs. Gill did much to help the Story Tellers Club improve. They introduced the children to new books and magazines but, as Mrs. Gill said at the end of the year, much needs to be done to encourage children to enter new fields of reading. They like to keep to the familiar. Valuable help was given the classroom teachers by the librarians in helping them locate materials for their units.

Looking back over the year, it is the relatedness of all its parts that make for the happiness of all—children, staff, and parents.

Choral Speaking. Choral speaking became very popular among children and teachers at North East. The start was made at a faculty meeting, January 14, and all during the spring term one could hear children intoning poetry they had learned. It came about through the suggestion of Mrs. Wilson that Mrs. Ferrell, teacher of grades four and five, but formerly a specialist in speech, should share her knowledge and interest with the rest. So this particular faculty meeting was given over to Mrs. Ferrell.

Copies of a six-page monograph (on file at North East) on Choral Speaking, which Mrs. Ferrell had prepared, were distributed to us. In simple clear-cut language this gave us the aim and fundamental principles of choral speaking. I liked, in particular, the way the aim was stated:

"To enjoy the speaking of poems together and to say them so that others may also enjoy them."

After discussing the aims and principles with us, Mrs. Ferrell swung us into action. We started choral speaking with the poems included in the monograph.

How well selected they were: *Mud* with its "squishy, squashiness;" *the squirrel*—"whisky, frisky, hippity hop;" *the haunted house* that fairly "made the blood run c-o-o-o-ld;" *The Frog That Went A Courtin'* "with sword and pistol by his side;" and, finally, Mrs. Tooze's *America* with "its families, its voices, its dreams."

We read each of these, first in unison and then in parts. The parts were taken by the "boys" and "girls," but since there was only one man among us we divided into "the dark or heavy voices" and "the light and airy ones." Then, too, some lines were done by soloists. First, we did each poem without the tape recorder and then with the recorder. Of course we were interested just like the children, in hearing how we sounded. Every time, without exception, that I used the tape recorder with the children, they eagerly asked at the end, "May we hear it?"

Mrs. Ferrell probably placed the greatest emphasis on choral speaking this year, but the influence of her children's efforts spread rapidly through the school. I was interested in Mrs. Ferrell's observation that her children liked poetry in dialect, particularly that of Paul Dunbar and James Whitcomb Riley. She mentioned Riley's *Raggedy Anne* and Dunbar's *Lullaby* as favorites.

Riessner in *The Culturally Deprived Child* brings out many characteristics of the language of deprived children which we at North East experience daily in working with the language needs of our children: that they understand more than they give out; that they are more articulate in spontaneous speech, in unstructured situations, in action, in fantasy. All of this has been a matter of observation by the teachers of North East.

Choral speaking in its unique combination of impression and expression seems admirably adapted to meet just the situation Riessner describes, and the teachers have found it so. First, the children are exposed to the beauty of the poet's words. By living with a poem until little by little more of its meaning, more of its relation to self become evident, there is a natural impulse to want to share it. An outlet is found in chanting the poem at different voice levels akin to the performance of an orchestra.

I was interested in a comment made by Mrs. Bond, teacher of a first grade: "We used choral speaking a great deal. The four poems learned correlated with our work. The first two were about snow, the others were about plants, flowers, and the sun." Mrs. Bond had, through the year, literally brought the outside world of nature into her classroom. There were always growing plants, all manner of seeds sprouting, flowers and leaves in the room. With choral speaking I can well imagine the additional meaning to all this that poetry gave to the children.

Weaving poetry into social studies, the sciences, and all other fields takes children beyond the factual, to viewing events and things with the interpretation of the poet in giving meaning to life. Sharing this in choral speaking serves to enhance the experience.

Evaluation and a Look Ahead

Teaching, evaluating, planning—the three are inseparable. I found this so very true in writing this report. As I looked back over the activities of the year, my mind inevitably moved toward appraising, toward the future, to the gaps that needed to be filled, to spots that could be improved. While the three processes are continuous and inseparable, there is also a time when we must pause and more definitely evaluate and plan. This is one of those times, at best a preliminary to the work the teachers will do when they return in the fall. Each teacher at the close of the school year in June—on his own—did the same thing. So we will begin with what they said, of necessity being limited here to excerpts and confining these to those that have to do with the language study.

> *Mrs. Bond, grade one:* The language arts program was one of the highlights of the year. . . . Our science and social studies classes particularly were planned so that each child had opportunity to express himself.
>
> *Mrs. Grant, grades two and three:* In language arts we stressed talking. We also worked on creative writing where we could. At the outset it was a rather difficult job to get the children to speak voluntarily. . . . By June, I could truthfully say that everyone could join in some type of discussion group. I was particularly delighted because of a little girl whose tests indicated that she was a candidate for the individual progress class. She finally 'spoke up' during the last week of school. . . . She was extremely shy and even hesitated to speak when spoken to directly. During the last week of May she volunteered to lead devotions and participated in a play by speaking a few lines.
>
> *Mrs. Price, grade two:* (began teaching this year after eleven years away from it) I was appalled that most of my second graders couldn't even write their names, couldn't relate experiences intelligibly, and lacked self-direction and self-discipline.
>
> *Mrs. Briggs, grades five and six:* In social studies we tried something new. We *debated* the question of whether Canada should accept nuclear weapons from the United States. . . . This required a lot of research by both teams as well as by those not on a team. . . . Less aggressive pupils even had a chance to speak for or against. This gave them a chance to overcome some of their shyness and timidity. . . . I feel that this experience was more than just an activity in social studies. It gave them also experience in the field of language arts, such as organization of materials, selecting only that material pertinent to the question, and writing it for presentation.

New words and phrases were learned such as *affirmative, negative, pros, cons, colleague, opponent,* as well as a new concept of *argument.*

Mrs. Cobb, individual progress class, primary: During the year each child learned to express himself a little more clearly. He had many opportunities to hear himself on my tape recorder. The children discarded *dis, dat, dese,* and *dose* for *this, that, these,* and *those.* Also, they learned to pronounce *with* correctly, thereby discarding *wif.* This was a happy experience—not an embarrassing one.

Mrs. Dawson, grade one: This unit (one on seeds) was highlighted by our class being in charge of the seed sale at school. The children enjoyed speaking over the intercom for a week to tell the other classes about seeds. For each of six days a different child gave hints for planting seeds and reminded children to bring their money for the purchase of seeds. All the children had a chance to audition for the presentation and the other children made the selections. It was a good experience.

Mrs. Douglas, Inter-age group, grades one, two and three: The language project carried out throughout our school has been helpful in enriching, increasing and improving our language. We have reminded ourselves that there are many ways to say the same thing. We have put forth much effort to learn colorful words and to use them orally and in creative writing. . . . The enunciation and pronunciation showed improvement as we did a lot of work with choral speaking this year.

Mrs. Gibbs, grade three: Spelling seemed to have much more meaning to the children when it was taken from basic words that they needed consistently in their writing. A very few of the children were ready to write at the beginning of the year; therefore we decided (or I should say, I decided) that we would talk. Talking about realistic things seemed to be a hardship so we started making up stories about anything. The children became more interested and thus gained more self-confidence. Some of the results were almost unbelievable! In some cases, the most bashful people in the class became the most talkative.

Mrs. Harrison, grades four and five: The language effort of the school was part of all activities. Provisions were made for discussions, debates, story telling and poetry both original and standard, choral speaking, diaries, acting, autobiographies, nonsense verse, and stories from pictures.

Mrs. Isakoff, kindergarten: The children had many opportunities to express their feelings and imagination through story telling, describing pictures, and group discussions. I feel that they made major strides in vocabulary growth and in ease of expression. They enjoyed acting out stories. They are particularly at ease in role playing. Here you can clearly see the problems of behavior they have witnessed in their homes and duplicate in the classroom. They also played school a great deal and imitated the manner in which I held a book and read.

Mrs. Jackson, kindergarten: Our major emphasis was the language study this year. Very few children could express themselves adequately or fluently at the beginning of the school year. They spoke saying just a word or two or a phrase at most. Every possible opportunity was used to develop better speech patterns: listening to and retelling stories, rhymes, poetry, finger plays, records and singing, and telling stories about pictures. . . . Most children are now expressing themselves in complete thoughts and a few tell *lengthy* stories.

Miss Peaco, grades three and four: Science terms have aided in broadening our vocabulary. . . . Cursive writing, punctuating sentences, spelling, writing paragraphs, letter writing, and choral speaking have been part of our language program. . . .

Mrs. Taylor, grades one and two: Our groups in reading were constantly changing. . . . The children learned to use many new words in expressing their ideas orally and in writing. For example: One child said, "You want us to be *responsible* for our behavior, don't you?" Another one asked, "When we are talking together, are we *communicating?*" . . . Activities in library, gym, music, and art were rich and meaningful. New words introduced in these areas were reinforced in the classroom. Many of these words became part of the children's vocabulary.

Mrs. Walker, grade six: For the first time I used the tape recorder in my language program. We recorded and read poems together. The children enjoyed this. The most significant thing realized was teaching the children the importance of correct pronunciation, clarity in speaking, and inflection. . . . Some of the children are handicapped in expressing themselves because they do not have enough descriptive words at their disposal. The children were sometimes asked to describe music to which they were listening, the pictures they were seeing, or the feel of something they were touching. We feel that this approach helped somewhat in satisfying their want of more descriptive words . . .

Of course the above is purely subjective. But looking on as I had the opportunity to do—my major responsibility was that of a recorder and, to some extent, that of a participant in discussions and faculty meetings —I was impressed with the degree to which they reflected my observations. It was most gratifying, too, to note the way in which the human element was so much in the fore, for example, in the pleasure taken in the progress of the shy child. The strategic role of language as a means of bettering the lot both of the individual and the whole of humanity was ever in mind. Of course it was good to see how the processes decided upon were used—the effort at encouraging the free flow of oral language, talking before writing, experience, and vocabulary building.

We have little to offer at the moment in the way of scientific evaluation of the progress made. In her annual report, Mrs. Wilson submitted the following data in the field of language based on the California Achievement Test given to the same pupils in a period of one and one-third years:

The most striking thing in the table is the very wide range in language ability among the children in January 1962, and the fact that this range was not appreciably narrowed one year and four months later in May 1963. In only one case, spelling, was the median gain equivalent to the year and four months that had elapsed between tests. It is gratifying to note that vocabulary, on which attention had been focused, made next to the highest gain; and spelling, with the special effort made for its improvement by the use of charts giving the words used in the class activities, made the highest gain.

A different form of the same test was given to the same group, in which some few changes had occurred because of the moving of students. The results show what a tremendous task lies ahead in the effort to improve the language ability of these children. This is true because so many are so far below the expected grade achievement, and because of their wide range in ability. Meeting individual differences under such circumstances is indeed a challenging task. I want to know who the children are that are well above the norms for their grades. Are they being sufficiently challenged?

The fact that the median gain was lowest in language mechanics is not cause for concern at present. Attention to correct form was intentionally subordinated to the encouragement of articulateness. But it most certainly is a matter of concern in long-view planning. I made note of characteristic incorrect speech patterns both as I observed in the classroom and as I typed from the tapes. I do not claim accuracy nor completeness in these because in spite of myself I found myself writing the correct form rather than attempting to reproduce the children's words. This is merely indicative:

no got	me wants to paint
you can make like	things like I need
he don't	gonna (going to)
much different	they wasn't
I seen	you wasn't
don't want no	live peaceful
have yourself some money	ghostes
throwed	didn' have no

There were many variations to the above depending on the context, but the examples given probably suffice to show the type of errors made.

Then there is a problem of enunciation noted by Mrs. Cobb in her recording of the children's speech: *dis, dat, dese,* and *dose.* Omission of the g-ending in words such as eating was so common that for all I know I am probably omitting it myself by now.

Structural difficulties, too, are numerous. The ones I was most sensitive to were:

- Connecting innumerable phrases with *and*.
- Mixing the gender of pronouns, using *he, she* and *it* indiscriminately.
- Using a pronoun to reenforce a noun—*the boy he went*.

It might be interesting if each teacher compiled a list of the speech patterns he thinks need correcting most. All might agree on a master list of the correct forms and put up a united front for their mastery. Do you remember the old 100 spelling demons we were supposed to teach? Charts like the vocabulary ones used so effectively this year might be tried.

But all this is dealing with symptoms and not with the disease. The real problem is that of causing children to want to break the language patterns that since birth have become built into their total personality structure and which are the accepted patterns of their family and neighborhood. Until the *want* is there, these obliging children might well learn the forms they know will please us—school language—and revert to the vernacular when they are out of our presence. The forces against us are very strong. Family allegiance and peer allegiance both operate. If we would change the language of these children we must so do it that the change will not make them too "different." This means that we must keep them from being snobs as they learn a better way of speaking than that of their parents or neighbors.

We can take our cue from two of the most successful activities in language that we had during the past year: the daily announcements and the Story Tellers' Club. Here the children had audience situations with approbation and criticism from their peers. They *wanted* to speak clearly, they *wanted* approval. We must continue these and find similar audience situations as motivation.

But, again, we need to go deeper than this. It is not only that the children need to try to improve their language; it is rather a matter of raising their total level of aspiration. Bringing in young accomplished people, such as the boy from P. S. duPont who played the saxophone for the children this year, is helpful in showing what young people can do. Taking them to hear the Wilmington Young People's orchestra is another. Living examples of what is possible often provide a powerful stimulus to ambition of a high order. Indeed, the whole effort at North East to expand the horizons of the children is a step in the right direction.

Literature has raised the sights of many a child beyond anything offered by his physical environment. The lives of heroes of the past and present, of those who have found happiness in an absorbing interest or service—told in history, biography, fiction, poetry—have given the inspiration that has made many a human being go forward to achieve his potential. This brings me to one of my puzzlements of this year—the absorption of our children in fairy tales and folk lore, particularly the way the Story Tellers' Club remained on this level through the year. How will we help the children to do more diversified reading? Certainly we are not ruling out the fanciful, but we also want them to know the beauty and the challenge of the real world.

As I look back over the years in which I have had the privilege of being connected with the Project and look forward to the future, I am consumed with the desire that we build that future on what has been. I sometimes think that education is a "fickle dame" so ready to discard the old and take on the new, so wasteful and yet at the same time so loath to discard the traditional rut. I am thinking, in particular, of all that fine resource material that has developed over the past four years. I do so want us to read it, to reread it in the light of our growing experience, and to produce more to meet our new needs.

It is hard for me to think of weaknesses in the past year. I am too filled with enthusiasm over its achievements. And I have not told the half of it. There is so much more than I have been able to recount here, long though this report is. But I really should find some flaws or this might not be taken seriously. So—I quote from Mrs. Wilson who said to me: "Next year we need tightening." You know, I believe that if we just take these words of Mrs. Wilson as a springboard or a text and explore them for all we can get out of them, we will together locate our weaknesses and plan intelligently for the year ahead.

Epilogue

Chapters 13-15 reported follow-up efforts through September 1963-64 in schools and community to establish goals and relationships gained during the formal period of The Three-Year Experimental Project on Schools in Changing Neighborhoods. Developments occurring during the two follow-up years, 1962-64, and plans for 1964-65 reveal that human relations education is firmly established in the public elementary schools of Wilmington. A "morale booster" to the staff is the fact that during each follow-up year of the study, the Wilmington Board of Education has contributed modest funds to the schools for support of several individual projects. Some of the major achievements of 1963-64 which are continuing during 1964-65 follow:

1. The Highlands Community Council has become a reality. Two hundred residents of the community met weekly during 1963-64 to organize and operate as the sixteenth neighborhood council of the city. Its "success stories" include the winning of a battle to improve public transportation in the neighborhood and the prevention of a zoning change which would have permitted the establishment of light industry in the area. One of the most tangible success stories is the involvement of older elementary children in the adult council and in the problems of the community.

2. The Language Study of the North East School continues to search for a breakthrough in the language blocks revealed by disadvantaged children. Findings to date support the research of Loban[1] and others

---

[1] Loban, Walter. *The Language of Elementary School Children,* Research Report, No. 1, The National Council of Teachers of English, Champaign, Ill.

regarding the significance of oral language power in building reading competence. This study will become a separate report upon its completion in 1968.

3. All elementary schools are emphasizing provision for experiences which raise the aspiration level of the children and result in greater academic competence.

Community agencies, organizations, and lay people continue their efforts to assist the schools and coordinate their programs.

1. Two branches of the Girls Club are established in schools located in deprived areas.

2. All schools, except one that has a large percentage of Jewish children, have after-school Gra-Y Clubs (YMCA) for older, elementary-age boys.

3. Three schools have an after-school Pre-Teen Club (YWCA) for older elementary-age girls.

4. Approximately forty suburban women serve the elementary schools as volunteer aides, a minimum of two half-days per week per aide. Working on a one-to-one relationship with children, the aides provide the individual attention many deprived children need. In addition, these women, whose sphere of influence is great, become supporters of the schools and are among the best public relations agents the schools have.

5. Close personal and professional relationships between agencies and the schools serve as preventives in crisis-producing situations affecting the schools.

6. Social welfare services provided by churches, organizations, agencies, and individuals continue to multiply.

Citations received by the Wilmington Public Schools are a deeply appreciated recognition of the efforts of the staff. These include the following:

The National Sorority of Phi Delta Kappa, 1962

> WHEREAS, Dr. Muriel Crosby through her outstanding leadership in the field of Human Relations; through her educational publications and writings in human relations relative to: "The Wilmington Three-Year Experimental Project on Schools in Changing Neighborhoods" did incite enthusiasm, study, and action in the City of Wilmington, Delaware
>
> Be it *Resolved,* That we, the National Sorority of Phi Delta Kappa at its Eastern Regional Conference held at Roanoke, Virginia, April 28, 1962 at the Lucy Addison High School go on record as commending her for leading the way in helping to develop the fullest potential of every child.

The Committee of 39, 1963

Quoted from the *Staff Reporter,* Wilmington Public Schools, Vol. 15, No. 8, April 1963:

1963 GOOD GOVERNMENT CITATION TO
WILMINGTON PUBLIC SCHOOLS

The Committee of 39's good government citation for 1963 was presented to the Wilmington public school system for its achievement in the field of human relations at the seventh annual "salute to good government" dinner meeting late in March. The award was presented by Everett Wilson, president of the Committee of 39. Reading the citation, Wilson said that in a period of emotional stress and public furor the public schools in Wilmington were integrated with a minimum of incident, in steps taken "only after the most careful preparation."

The process, he said, "stands as an example of public officials and public servants acting in a responsible manner in an area of great import and significance in our day."

He also called attention to the three-year study on changing neighborhoods, termed "an adventure in human relations," which has received national attention. The citation, quoted here, mentions the leadership of Dr. Ward I. Miller, retiring this year as superintendent of schools, and the dedication of Dr. Muriel Crosby, director of the study and assistant superintendent for elementary education. Dr. Miller received the award on behalf of the school system.

The Committee of 39 is a non-partisan organization working for better government. Here is the text of the citation as it is recorded in the history of the city of Wilmington:

For the quiet, but significant record of achievement it is making and has made over a period of years, we cite the Wilmington Public School System, particularly in the field of human relations.

In a period of emotional stress and public furor not only in the State of Delaware, but in other parts of the country, the public schools of Wilmington were integrated with a minimum of incident. This was accomplished in two steps: In 1954, grades 1 through 6 were integrated; the following year, grades 7 through 12 were included to complete the change-over to an integrated school system. These steps were taken only after the most careful preparation. The administrative staff of the Wilmington Public Schools met and consulted with teachers and parents of both races for some time previous to this action. The result was an acceptance of integration by the individuals most directly affected, and by the community at large. The process by which the transition took place, the fact that the task was undertaken and put into motion before the Supreme Court decision was announced, and that it was accomplished so successfully, stands as an example of public officials and public servants acting in a responsible manner in an area of great import and significance in our day.

Further, the school system has recently completed a three-year study, "An Adventure in Human Relations." Jointly sponsored by the Board of Education and the Delaware Region of the National Conference of Christians and Jews, the study was made to develop for the entire community an action program to meet the needs of changing neighborhoods in Wilmington. It involved the elementary school system in an effort to design the necessary educational programs that will assist in raising achievements and aspirations of children who are culturally deprived, and enlisted the assistance and support of community agencies and organizations in an over-all community action program. The study has received national attention and recognition as a means of meeting the increasingly complex problems of urban centers through a combined school-community approach.

In citing the Wilmington Public School System for its record of accomplishments in human relations, we recognize the administrative leadership of Dr. Ward I. Miller, whose term of office as Superintendent of Schools has spanned a time of accelerated social and economic change. The City of Wilmington has been most fortunate in having had as head of its school system a man who is so dedicated to the interests of children, and so steadfast in his determination to provide them with a good education. He has earned the respect and admiration of his staff and of the whole community. His goals have been high, his achievements in the face of many difficulties have been noteworthy.

We recognize too the dedication of Dr. Muriel Crosby, director of the study on changing neighborhoods, "An Adventure in Human Relations." Her enthusiasm and her deep conviction have been deciding factors in giving the study meaning and purpose and insuring that the findings of the study have taken on form and substance.

We present this good government citation to all the members of the Wilmington Public School System. As a public agency, you have made a notable contribution to the public welfare and general well-being of our community and our State. We now present this citation to Ward I. Miller, Superintendent of the Wilmington Public Schools, in tribute to the outstanding service the school system has performed in dealing with a crucial contemporary problem, human relations.

The National Education Association, 1964

WILMINGTON, DEL., SCHOOLS CITED AS "PACEMAKERS" BY NEA PRESIDENT

Seattle, June 27—The Wilmington, Del., public schools were cited today for "attempting to stop blight before it gets started."

The citation was made by the president of the National Education Association, which is opening its 102nd annual convention here tomorrow. The convention runs through Friday.

Robert H. Wyatt, NEA president, citing the Wilmington schools as a "Pacemaker: 1964" praised them as "leaders in a new area of educational concern—halting social blight through education."

Wilmington has attempted this, he said, through a program "designed to ease the burdens of schools—and the children they serve—in changing neighborhoods."

And in Wilmington, he said, change has been everywhere. Residential areas change fast. Once-populous neighborhoods are deserted and once-empty neighborhoods grow explosively. Middle-class residents flee to the suburbs and abandon the city to slums.

The changes, he said, "brought problems in understanding between old residents and new, between teachers and the new kind of students they were getting. With a wide variation in income, cultural backgrounds, and even language, communications were difficult. "Sometimes," he said, "the teachers literally could not understand what their students were talking about."

With the help of the National Conference of Christians and Jews, a three-year experimental project was set up to teach the teachers about their students. Questionnaires were the first thing. Each teacher sent one home. The information she received helped her to better understand the environment and home problems of each child in her class. Later she visited the homes of her students and talked to the adults there.

Once she understood what kind of background the child came from, she could more easily fit her teaching to the needs of each child.

But the schools did more than this. When the Project began, there was local neighborhood leadership in only two areas. But where only two areas had neighborhood councils five years ago, now sixteen neighborhoods have them. And in eight of these areas, Wilmington educators played a major part in helping develop the necessary leadership.

The changes in the schools have not been dramatic. There have been no new courses instituted as a result of the Project. But, for many children, the whole focus of the curriculum has been shifted to more exactly meet their needs.

The Wilmington teachers have found, Wyatt said, "that what produces a response in a middle-class child from a secure home may produce nothing at all with children who have been deprived of security since birth. And this," he said, "is where the curriculum shift has occurred—in using new appeals to interest new types of students."

"I wish I could say," Wyatt declared, "that Wilmington has become a city in which everything is gleaming and bright, where people understand one another, where problems of schools in changing neighborhoods are no longer present. But that's not true yet in Wilmington, or anywhere else, for that matter. But in Wilmington, at least, they're trying . . . and succeeding."

While recognition of the work of the elementary staff of the Wilmington Public Schools is satisfying, we take our directions for the future from Walt Whitman, who wrote many years ago:

> . . . it is provided in the essence of things that from any fruition of success, no matter what, shall come forth something to make a greater struggle necessary.

A complete development of a design for a human relations focused curriculum will be found in *Curriculum Development for Elementary Schools in a Changing Society,* Muriel Crosby, D. C. Heath, Boston, 1964, which is, in an important sense, a companion volume for *An Adventure in Human Relations.*

All royalties from the report, *An Adventure in Human Relations,* are assigned to those who have made it possible:
The Public Elementary Schools of the City of Wilmington, Delaware
The National Conference of Christians and Jews
The Delaware Region, The National Conference of Christians and Jews

Index

Activity, 125-26
Academic learning, 121
  needs, 189
  growth in, 222; 226-32
American Association of University
  Women, xii
A Stitch in Time, 331-39
Attitudes, change in, 232-48
American Council on Education, 96

Boy Scouts, xii
Bradford, William, 20

Commager, Henry Steele, 153
Committee of 39, 389
Common learnings, 122
Community
  action, 34-43; 252-55; 285-94
    planning for, 259-84
  changes in, 6-7; 16-20; 45-52;
    71-87; 270-72
  consultant services, 260-84

  coordination, 259-84
  councils, 273-82; 293-94; 387
  leadership, 252-55; 272-84
  organization, 38-43; 253-55; 256-59
    design for, 269
  stimulating interest in, 250-52
Concepts
  categories of, 126-27
  development of, 121-24
  evaluation of, 163-68
  planning for, 127-29
Consultant service
  evaluation of, 213-15; 301-302
  methods, 192-210
Curriculum Development for Elemen-
  tary Schools in a Changing
  Society (Crosby), 122; 392
Curriculum development for human
  relations education
  bases for planning, 121-29
  concept development, 122-24
  design for, 121-53

design for evaluation, 182-87
evaluation of, 155-61
methods, 190-210
Staff meetings, 192-210
Standardized tests
achievement tests, 93-94; 222; 226-32
group intelligence tests, 10; 92-93
Stone, Irving, 299

Taba, Hilda, 100
Teacher education, xii
effects of diagnostic learning, 118-20
evaluation of, 155-79; 211-39
extent of participation, 244-45
materials for, 202-10
methods used, 190-210
Teaching processes, 11-14; 190-210
Time budgets, 99; 101; 107-11; 119
The Agony and the Ecstasy (Stone), 299
The Language Development of Elementary School Children (Loban), 388
The Lonely Crowd (Riesman), 82
Three Year Experimental Project on Schools in Changing Neighborhoods
administration of, 296-308
awards, 388-92
basic assumptions, 34-35
budget for, 298-307
cooperative community action, 249-55; 256-84; 285-94; 309-30
design for curriculum planning, 121-53
diagnostic aspect, 96-118
evaluation design, 182-87
evaluation of cooperative action, 285-94

evaluation of curriculum development, 162-68
evaluation of diagnostic aspect, 155-61
evaluation of in-service education, 168-79
follow-up programs, 331-39
goals, 34; 36-43
initiation, 22-23
methods used, 188-210
of progress, 211-48
overview, xi-xiii
plan of action, 35-43
procedures, 23
project design, 38-43
relationship of diagnosis to curriculum development, 98-120
standardized tests, 10; 222; 226-232
United States Supreme Court
decision on desegregation of the public schools, 1; 3-6
Values
conflict between, 19
design for evaluation, 182-87
development of, 9-10
in-service teacher education, 211-39
of diagnostic instruments and their use, 232-48
of project in-service education, 165-79
Vickery, William E., 148
consultant service, 192-202
on building resource units, 130-53
on diagnosis of human relations needs, 96-117
on project evaluation design, 182-87
Welfare Council, xii
Whitman, Walt, xii, 392
Wilmington Board of Public Education, 18